LAWS OF CHANCE

A BOOK IN THE SERIES

Radical Perspectives: A *Radical History Review* book series

SERIES EDITORS: Daniel J. Walkowitz, New York University
Barbara Weinstein, New York University

LAWS OF CHANCE

Brazil's Clandestine Lottery and the
Making of Urban Public Life

AMY CHAZKEL

Duke University Press

Durham and London 2011

© 2011 Duke University Press

All rights reserved

Printed in the United States of America on acid-free paper ∞

Designed by Heather Hensley

Typeset in Arno Pro by Keystone Typesetting, Inc.

Library of Congress Cataloging-in-Publication Data appear
on the last printed page of this book.

Duke University Press gratefully acknowledges the support of the
Research Foundation of Queens College of the City University of New
York, which provided funds toward the production of this book.

For my parents,
JANE DEBORAH HOCHMAN and
MICHAEL FREDRIC CHAZKEL

CONTENTS

ILLUSTRATIONS

TABLES

ABOUT THE SERIES

History, as radical historians have long observed, cannot be severed from authorial subjectivity, indeed, from politics. Political concerns animate the questions we ask, the subjects on which we write. For over thirty years the *Radical History Review* has led in nurturing and advancing such engaged historical research. Radical Perspectives seeks to further the journal's mission: any author wishing to be in this series makes a self-conscious decision to associate her or his work with a radical perspective. To be sure, many of us are currently struggling with what it means to be a radical historian in the early twenty-first century, and this series is intended to provide some signposts for what we would judge to be radical history. It will offer innovative ways of telling stories from multiple perspectives; comparative, transnational, and global histories that transcend conventional boundaries of region and nation; works that elaborate on the implications of the postcolonial move to "provincialize Europe"; studies of the public in and of the past, including those that consider the commodification of the past; histories that explore the intersection of identities such as gender, race, class, and sexuality with an eye to their political implications and complications. Above all, this book series seeks to create an important intellectual space and discursive community to explore the very issue of what constitutes radical history. Within this context, some of the books published in the series may privilege alternative and oppositional political cultures, but all will be concerned with the way power is constituted, contested, used, and abused.

In *Laws of Chance*, Amy Chazkel follows the fascinating trajectory of a notorious Brazilian institution, the illicit lottery known as the *jogo do bicho*, or animal game, from its creation in the 1890s through much of the twentieth century. She acquaints the reader with a shifting (and sometimes shifty) cast of characters ranging from well-heeled financiers and skeptical jurists to small-time ticket sellers, street peddlers, lottery players, policemen on the take, and old men playing dominoes in a public square. Dating from the first decade following the end of slavery and the founding of the republic, this lottery, Chazkel shows, became an integral feature of life in Rio de Janeiro during a period of massive urban renewal programs and the expansion of petty trade, as well as a constitutive element of urban policing. The key question, according to Chazkel, is not so much whether illegal activities were taking place, but why and how this popular gambling pastime became criminalized. The result was not the massive arrest or imprisonment of ticket sellers and purchasers, but rather a "gray area" that allowed the police considerable latitude in restricting the use of public space. Central to Chazkel's argument is her rethinking of what many historians see as the central flaw in Latin American legal culture: the "gap" between formal legal codes and policing practices, a concept which rests on the expectation of a direct correspondence between the letter of the law and its enforcement. Instead Chazkel argues that this "gap" is precisely the space in which a range of authority figures could enjoy a certain degree of flexibility or wield arbitrary power. In this vein, it is significant that the crackdown on the jogo do bicho in 1917 had the effect, not of erasing this "gap," but of inciting even deeper cynicism about Rio's police force. It is the final irony of this intriguing historical study that the illicit jogo do bicho ends up being regarded, in the popular milieu, as the most reliable and credible institution in everyday life.

ACKNOWLEDGMENTS

This book has trotted along at my heels for more years than I care to admit. Anyone who has accompanied me in my life over this time has had to deal with its presence and the yapping pack of deadlines, worries, and tasks that always accompanied it. I wish to thank my friends and family for their forbearance and support through this whole process.

Tracing this book to its beginning, I owe my profoundest debt of gratitude to Gilbert M. Joseph and Stuart B. Schwartz and also to Jean-Christophe Agnew and Barbara Weinstein. I thank them for their brilliant advice on my scholarship over the years, their warmth and kindness, and for the time they invested in me. I owe a sizeable intellectual and personal debt to many on the Yale faculty, especially Emilia Viotti da Costa, John Demos, Michael Denning, Dolores Hayden, Patricia Pessar, and Lídia Santos. In recent years, my CUNY colleagues have provided me with an intellectually interesting and nurturing environment. Dean Elizabeth Hendrey and Frank Warren, the most thoughtful and supportive department chair a person could ever hope for, deserve special mention.

Participants in the Boston Area Latin American History Workshop at the Rockefeller Center for Latin American Studies, the Law and Society Graduate Student Workshop, and the Laboratório de História e Antropologia at the Universidade Federal do Rio de Janeiro / Instituto de Filosofia e Ciencias Sociais, the Yale Graduate School Interdisciplinary Colloquium on Urban History, the CUNY Center for the

Humanities, the New York City Latin American History Workshop, and the Columbia University Brazil Faculty Seminar offered me valuable input as this project developed.

I have had the great fortune of being a member of several writing groups. Each contributed something indispensable and unique at a particular stage in the writing process. Michael Cohen, Jay Garcia, Victoria Langland, Mark Overmyer-Velazquez, and Fiona Vernal provided motivation, substantive suggestions, and precious friendship as this project took shape. For their brilliant input at subsequent stages, I would like to thank the members of the "Little Summit," Seth Fein, Joanne Freeman, Chris Hill, and Pablo Piccato; and Sarah Covington, Sujatha Fernandes, David Kazanjian, and Josie Saldaña of the most recent collective.

I owe my most enthusiastic thanks for solidarity, friendship, and intellectual support to José Celso de Castro Alves, Desmond Arias, Bert Barickman, Jeremy Baskes, Peter Beattie, Dain Borges, Denise Ileana Bossy, Marcos Luiz Bretas, Andréa Casa Nova Maia, John Chasteen, Sarah Chinn, John Collins, Ray Craib, Roberto DaMatta, Jerry Dávila, Brodwyn Fischer, Moira Fradinger, Zephyr Frank, Denise Frossard, Peter Fry, Olívia Maria Gomes da Cunha, Paul Gootenberg, James N. Green, Mônica Grin, Marc Hertzman, Gilberto Hochman, Tom Holloway, Jeffrey Lesser, Zeca Ligieiro, Rick Lopez, Joseph Luzzi, Bryan McCann, Felipe Magalhães, William Martins, Lígia Mefano, Nara Milanich, Zachary Morgan, Isadora Moura Mota, Álvaro Nascimento, Ángel Oquendo, Julia Ott, Marco Antonio Pamplona, Ben Penglase, Kristin Phillips-Court, Luciana Pinheiro, Leigh Raiford, Gautham Rao, Chico Romão, Micol Seigel, Satadru Sen, Thomas Skidmore, Carlos Eugênio Líbano Soares, Aoibheann Sweeney, Gail Triner, George Trumbull, Daniel Levinson Wilk, Daryle Williams, Erica Windler, Joel Wolfe, and James Woodard. While I regret that word count limitations force me to stick you all so telegraphically on a list, as I type out the letters of your name I picture a conversation over coffee, a long walk along the *calçadão*, or tough love expressed in red ink in the margins of a chapter draft. I hope that you each read between the lines your precious individual contributions to this book.

The staffs of libraries and archives in the United States and Brazil guided me through the challenges of the research process. In the United States, I would like to thank César Rodríguez at Yale as well as the staffs of the Oliveira Lima and University of Florida at Gainesville libraries. The New York Public Library gave me a serene working space in the Allen Study.

Individuals too numerous to list assisted me in my research in Brazil, including the amazing staff of the Arquivo Nacional, especially Sátiro Nunes; Beatriz Kushnir and the rest of the staff at the Arquivo Geral da Cidade do Rio de Janeiro; Maria Angélica Varella and Carla Ramos at the Setor de Periódicos in the Biblioteca Nacional; Paulo Knauss, Johenir Jannotti Viega, Lícia Medeiros, and all those at the Arquivo Público do Estado do Rio de Janeiro who always welcomed me so warmly; the librarians at the Casa de Rui Barbosa who introduced me to their rich collection of juridical texts and *folhetins*; and Pedro Tórtima at the Instituto de História e Geografia Brasileira for bringing to my attention some key sources.

My research would not have been possible without support from the Yale University Graduate School, grants from the University of Florida at Gainesville Latin American Studies Travel Grant, Yale Council on International and Area Studies, Yale Department of History Mellon Research Grant, Alfred J. Beveridge Fellowship, John F. Enders Grant, John Perry Miller Award for Research, and the Yale Latin American Studies Mellon Fund, and fellowship stints at the Gilder Lehrman Center for the Study of Slavery, Resistance, and Abolition, the CUNY Center for the Humanities, and the David Rockefeller Center for Latin American Studies. The PSC CUNY funded my final forays into the archive.

En route to becoming a book, a version of chapter 1 appeared in the *Journal of Latin American Studies* (volume 39, August 2007).

Valerie Millholland, Miriam Angress, Gisela Fosado, Mark Mastromarino, and many others at Duke University Press shepherded this book through the publication process, and the anonymous readers vastly improved it with their many insightful suggestions. Thanks for believing in this project and patiently teaching this novice author about the process of producing a book—and, in the unforgettable words of one of my readers quoting the famous equestrian sculptor, of whittling away "everything that doesn't look like a horse."

Last but certainly not least I would like to acknowledge my wonderful parents, to whom I dedicate this book, as well as Jack; and Ala, my critic, editor, mentor, best friend, and partner in crime. Of all my interlocutors, though, I thank Aya the most. She bore the brunt of the time I put into finishing this book. Pound for pound, she's the one with the most eloquence and good sense. With her, I won the lottery.

A NOTE ON BRAZILIAN CURRENCY AND ORTHOGRAPHY

The basic currency unit in use in Brazil throughout the period on which this book focuses was the *milreis*, which Brazil adopted in 1846. One milreis, written as 1$000, was the equivalent of one thousand *reis* (the plural of *real*), an older monetary unit that had diminished radically in value by the mid-nineteenth century. One thousand milreis equals one *conto*. In 1942, the *cruzeiro* replaced the milreis and the conto. Dollar equivalents cited in this book are based on an annual average of the month-end closing quotations. Sources of historical exchange rate and cost of living data are cited in the endnotes.

The Brazilian Portuguese language had not yet been orthographically standardized in the late nineteenth century and early twentieth. For all proper names of persons I used the spelling that most frequently appeared in the contemporaneous documentation. I spelled all proper names of places according to present-day conventions. All other words are spelled according to today's standard. Documents from the late nineteenth century and early twentieth variously call the animal lottery that is the subject of this book the jogo dos bichos, the jogo do bicho, and the jogo de bicho. I use today's standard name, jogo do bicho, except in some direct quotations.

MAP 1 Brazil: Major Cities and Political Boundaries, ca. 1900.

INTRODUCTION

On July 25, 1907, two police soldiers banged on the door of the home of Carlos Figueiredo, a forty-four-year-old gilder, in a working-class neighborhood of Rio de Janeiro. Figueiredo's wife answered the door, and the two men entered without her consent and proceeded to rifle through his possessions. The police finally found the evidence they sought stuffed behind the statues of saints on Figueiredo's household altar: seventy-eight torn slips of paper with handwritten columns of numbers on them.[1] Most Brazilians today would readily identify the bits of paper the police found over a century ago as tickets for the clandestine lottery called the *jogo do bicho* (the animal game). Long disassociated from the zoo in Rio de Janeiro that gave it its name, the jogo do bicho still exists throughout Brazil. All that is required to play is a few cents, the ability to walk to the street corner, a bit of luck, and a willingness to risk arrest. Ticket buyers wager small amounts of money in the hope of multiplying their investment twentyfold or more. Today, as they did a century ago, jogo do bicho dealers consistently honor their pledge to pay any player who selected the winning number.

This book owes its existence to the paper trail that this and thousands of other stories left behind in over a century of the persistence—and illegality—of the jogo do bicho. The jogo do bicho first spread through Rio de Janeiro, then the nation's capital, as a diffuse practice of questionable legality in the 1890s. It soon became a prominent feature of the city's

FIGURE 1 "The zebra won in the jogo do bicho, and I ended up in jail," pamphlet by Franklin Maxado (ca. 1980).

cultural landscape, then a nationwide practice, and, in the twentieth century, a fully blown organized crime network. Elite magazines referred to the jogo do bicho with a wink and a smile. Residents of Rio and eventually all of Brazil wrote songs and theatrical pieces about it and played it routinely and, one suspects, unrepentantly for the past 115 years. This story, as quintessentially local as it is, suggests a larger process that shaped the hemisphere's modern cities at the dawn of the twentieth century. The ambivalent and contested criminalization of popular practices like the jogo do bicho generated a legal, cultural, and social dynamic that lies at the center of urban public life in Latin America and elsewhere.

The jogo do bicho resembles innumerable gambling practices that emerged throughout the Americas and Europe with remarkable simultaneity: the numbers game in the United States, side-betting on horse races in England, and La Bolita in the Caribbean, to name a few.[2] Outside the Atlantic world, too, history supplies vignettes that illustrate both the ubiquity of games of chance and their perennial illegality. People in late nineteenth-century China, for example, were known to bet on the results of the civil service exam.[3]

Societies in all places and epochs have come under the thrall of practices based on venturing one's worldly possessions for the possibility of winning money or other prizes. Why people gamble is more the stuff of myth, folklore, and human psychology than of historical analysis. Games of chance have a metaphysical dimension, too: the divining function of gambling points to a universe of hidden causalities and stands as a metaphor of the knowability or unknowability of the future and the causes that bring it about. Some observers argue that the modernizing, Western world has tended to engage in games of chance whose logic parallels that of capitalism or, others say, that pronounce poignant critiques of the ideologies capitalism implies.[4] The abiding attraction of risk and chance in Western society has been accompanied by moral trepidation and a sense of mystery and danger. In Brazil and elsewhere in the Western world, gambling has both parodied and epitomized the ideas and practices of modern society by trading on the volatility of pecuniary value while short-circuiting the necessity for productive labor.[5]

Commentators on Brazil have claimed that gambling, with its reliance on luck and its antirational bent, constitutes a flight from modernity or, some have said, a critique of it. Probably the most famous of all Brazilian intellectuals, the sociologist Gilberto Freyre, describes the jogo do bicho and other games of chance as holdovers from Brazil's indigenous and African totemic past.[6] Yet in Brazil, as elsewhere, playing games of chance became phenomenally popular at just the moment urbanization and consumer capitalism took hold.

Only implicitly and occasionally does this book treat the jogo do bicho as part of a global urge to gamble that accompanied urban modernization, although those interested in games of chance in other parts of the world will find a compelling counterpoint in Brazil's immensely popular animal game. Instead, I place the jogo do bicho in the context of the world of criminalized yet ubiquitous popular practices—unlicensed petty commerce and Afro–Latin American religion, for instance—that is, itself, a trademark of modern, urban public life throughout Latin America and across the globe. Until recently, most readers would likely have found paradoxical the assertion that such popular customs are part of, rather than antithetical to, "universalism, scientific rationality, the rule of the market, [and] the demands of the state"[7]—in other words, modernity. In the twenty-first century, the observation that popular practices like dissident forms of folk religion and the jogo do bicho are the products of modernity rather than a refuge from it has become something of a truism. Building on the rich body of work from many disciplines that has made it possible to consign Freyre's conception of the jogo do bicho to history as a classic relic of early twentieth century social theory, this book takes the link between informal practices and modern, urban public life not as its concluding argument but as its starting point.[8]

Revisiting Figueiredo's case illustrates some of the complexities of the jogo do bicho's early encounter with the state. According to his file, an anonymous informant had tipped off the police about Figueiredo's jogo do bicho operation. In an apparently illegal search of his home police confiscated seventy-eight lists written on scrap paper (now preserved in the National Archive of Brazil) balled up with twenty-nine *milreis*, about nine dollars. He was arrested "*em flagrante*" for violation of article 367 of the Penal Code, which criminalized playing or dealing in unlicensed games of chance.

After posting bail and leaving police custody about two weeks later, the accused presented his defense, charging that the police had "no proof whatsoever" of his guilt. Figueiredo, or more likely his court-appointed lawyer, claimed "the accused was in his home, not so much as thinking about any prohibited games when [his] home was invaded by the police district chief and other conspicuous local authorities, who appeared there because of an accusation. The house of the accused contained neither criminal evidence nor stolen objects. The accused is a reputable man who has lived for more than eighteen years in that same house without ever being bothered by the police." The search, he argues, was unjustified:

> There is no evidence that these fragments of paper contain references to any game whatsoever, and the amount of 29 *mil reis* is not even the sum of money written on those pieces of paper. But even if I were to admit that these pieces of paper really do relate to some sort of prohibited game, I would ask: is there some legal position that prohibits any citizen from having in his own home, on his household altar, as many game tickets as he wishes? Of course not. And since the accused was at home, which absolutely is not a gambling den, and since he had not been conducting any business whatsoever with those game

tickets, the apprehension of these tickets and the imprisonment of the accused would not be less than an act of violence!

"To continue with your original thinking, *o Doutor Delegado*," he wrote, sarcastically using the honorific title doctor, "would indeed have arrested the Saints on the Altar as gamblers playing the jogo do bicho!" Two days later, the judge reached a resolution: the prosecution had presented insufficient proof that a crime had occurred, and since "the jogo do bicho cannot be verified without the direct concurrence of at least two persons . . . I absolve the accused."

This outcome was far from unusual. During the first thirty-five years the game was played only about 4 percent of bicho cases ended in a conviction.[9] Most often, judges based their acquittals on a lack of incriminating evidence or on the police's failure to follow procedure. As Figueiredo's case demonstrates, defendants, police, and judges all had a great deal of space in which to maneuver, and maneuver they did. Figueiredo used the very informality of the game to his advantage by referring to the "fragments of paper," which, he insisted, failed to prove a crime had occurred. The judge decided to dismiss the charges even in the face of clear evidence the defendant had been involved in the forbidden lottery.[10]

Legislative debates, citizens' letters denouncing gambling dens and houses of prostitution, and political speeches of the late nineteenth century demonstrate a surprising level of uniformity in their antivice rhetoric. They all called upon authorities to uphold what their authors claimed was a timeless, agreed-upon principle that games of chance threatened social order. Yet compelling evidence shows a lack of consensus within Brazilian society as to whether the state should permit and regulate popular practices like the jogo do bicho or place them beyond the pale of legality and punish their participants as criminals.[11] After all, the state ran its own lotteries; why not just regulate and tax the jogo do bicho? Some within the government voiced dissenting opinions regarding the law's harsh treatment of games of chance. Opposition to the criminalization of the jogo do bicho also came from members of the urban entrepreneurial class, who installed the city's first large-scale public amusements: the entertainment impresarios long rumored to be the first jogo do bicho bankers, men who helped finance illicit games of chance and encouraged their expansion. Many agents of the state, too, diverged from the official anti–jogo do bicho creed, as they skimmed the profits in a tradition of corruption still present today.

Above all, men and women of all socioeconomic classes and ethnic backgrounds showed their approval of the jogo do bicho simply by buying and selling chances to win. While most players left no written record of their interaction with the jogo do bicho, such cultural artifacts as published tip sheets, popular songs, and plays featuring the game bear witness to its broad popularity in the decades after its inception.[12]

Popular writings on the jogo do bicho have long marveled at its longevity and popularity in the face of police repression. The game's omnipresence in the city even today attests to the failure of attempts to eradicate it. Yet despite the apparent impunity of most ticket buyers and sellers, in reconstructing the first half century of the game we can see its criminalization unfolding. This process allows us to trace shifts in conventional wisdom and new modes of social interaction, which the changing urban environment of the late nineteenth and early twentieth centuries brought about. The intervention of the law in the jogo do bicho, equivocal as it often was, had a profound impact on the historical development of the game and on urban society.

It is instructive to compare the policing of urban public life in Brazil's early First Republic with the sumptuary laws of medieval and early modern Europe, another type of law that, in retrospect, seems an ineffectual, even frivolous, attempt to defy reality. Sumptuary statutes variously forbade the wearing of certain colors, fabrics, and accessories and limited the use of such finery as decorative studs on a horse's bridle to the aristocracy. By regulating and even criminalizing certain types of outward appearance perceived to threaten the status quo, these laws aimed to suppress ostentation and control custom by managing consumption. When obstacles to the socioeconomic mobility of the poorest classes began to abate with the breakdown of the feudal order in late medieval Europe, the dominant classes utilized the law to enforce normative values.[13] Official control of consumption patterns thereby established or upheld social hierarchy. Generally understood historically as a means of compensating for the loss of the ability to distinguish people by class, sumptuary laws also had an antifraud intent: one's outer attire must truthfully represent, rather than obscure, one's inner essence.[14] As in late medieval Europe, the disappearance of hereditary legal differences in Brazil after independence from Portugal, the establishment of the Republic in 1889, and especially the end of slavery sent tremors of anxiety through those with an interest in maintaining the socioeconomic status quo. Laws that criminalized popular practices like the jogo do bicho limited private expenditure in the public realm and transformed it into an issue of public order.

The history of the persecution of petty gambling that my book tells gives credence to the legal scholar Alan Hunt's recent revision of the conventional understanding of sumptuary law. It is commonly believed that sumptuary laws "were alien to modernity" and "their disappearance provided evidence of the advancing good sense of rulers who no longer thought it desirable to seek to regulate such 'private' matters as what people should wear." Rather than dismissing sumptuary law as a failed premodern project, as most scholars do, Hunt argues that its logic was central to state formation. In fact, he rejects the failure model: "If, as all commentators seem to agree, they were doomed to failure, why did so many legislators, rulers, administrators, judges and others continue to enact and reenact sumptuary provisions?" These regulations are the key to understanding modern governance of public life. A prevailing "sumptuary ethic" dictated that the church, the guild, the crown, and eventually the modern, liberal state must regulate consumption.[15] An analytical model that interprets rampant lawbreaking as failed social control impedes understanding of the powerful role the criminalization of everyday life played in constructing the relationship between urban Brazilians and the state.[16]

The jogo do bicho developed when criminal law played a crucial role in engineering the relationship between the state and society in Brazil. In 1888 the country emerged from over three hundred years of chattel slavery; nearly a century of monarchy ended in 1889. A new Penal Code passed in 1890 bore a special burden in the face of the difficult social realities of postabolition Brazil—a nation that was heterogeneous, vast in landmass, and carried into this new era a legacy of extreme socioeconomic disparity. The game became phenomenally popular during Brazil's gradual transition to an industrial economy and the massive structural and socioeconomic transformations occurring in the capital city. The jogo do bicho thus allows us to enter through an underground passageway, so to speak, into some crucial historical problems concerning Brazil's and Latin America's experience of modernization, urbanization, and the changing relationship between the state and society.

My analysis of the jogo do bicho's first half century of existence affords access to three closely related issues crucial to understanding the historical development of urban public life in Latin America. First, the criminalization of previously tolerated acts and the geopolitical and economic changes that accompanied the transition to a capitalist, consumer economy both point to an urban version of a process usually associated with agrarian history: the enclosure of the commons. Enclosure recalls the image of a fence interrupting the rural landscape's flowing green undulations and restricting access to the basic stuff of material survival regarded from time immemorial as common property. This fence provides a powerful metaphor for the process that this book observes in motion. Rio's inhabitants in the late nineteenth century and early twentieth needed to acquire the legal right to live, work, and purchase their daily goods in the city's increasingly privatized public spaces; those who could not were compelled to carry out such quotidian activities outside the bounds of the law. Second, the historical roots of what policymakers and social scientists would later label the informal sector—the domain of work and retail commerce—stood outside that metaphorical fence. The jogo do bicho allows one to scrutinize the broader criminalization of everyday life already underway in this period, a phenomenon that would ultimately drive most buyers and sellers in Latin America's consumer economies over the line between legal and illegal. Third, then, this book will reevaluate the legal repression of the popular classes that accompanied urban modernity everywhere in Latin America, the sometimes draconian social control policies long understood as the hallmark of the relationship between the Latin American state and society at the turn of the twentieth century.

In the late nineteenth century the farthest-flung neighborhoods of Rio de Janeiro dwarfed the urban zone in their vast territorial expanse. The tight cluster of buildings in the historical center was only beginning to crawl southward and westward. The compactness of Rio's urbanized center compared to the city's enormous hinterland puts in perspective how the agrarian and pastoral livelihoods in which residents of Rio's rural zone engaged fed a growing, hungry, and still largely rural city. If life in the outskirts of the capital still sprung from the earth, Cariocas, as Rio's residents are called, also cultivated plants and animals for consumption and harvested wild fruit from the islands of the Atlantic Forest not yet submerged in the city's rising, spreading sea of brick and concrete. Urban policy in this era, designed to modernize and sanitize the city, accelerated the pace of a social and politico-economic transformation far from unique to Rio or to Brazil: the increasing difficulty of autonomous sustenance as an inevitable effect of urbanization. In an article from the 1910s, Alfonso Henriques de Lima Barreto, the novelist, social critic, and chronicler of Rio's daily life in the early First Republic, laments that the half-century-old mango and tamarind trees in Rio's public spaces were in danger of being cut down because of the "avidity, greed, and stupidity" of the municipal authorities implementing the massive urban reform project then underway. For him, the destruction of an old tamarind tree in the suburban neighborhood of Engenho Novo that provided "a sort of oasis" for both people and draft animals was too dear a price to pay for the construction of a modern avenue.[17]

Lima Barreto's words betray a deep nostalgia for a bygone time when the city's inhabitants shared public spaces of respite and sociability, accessible to all—a commons, in the Anglo–*North* American nomenclature. In some ways, he was homesick for a land he had never visited. The utopian tableau of shady groves, shared fruit, and social equilibrium he depicts was aspirational as much as truly retrospective. Yet Lima Barreto's earthy example of urban change offers a glimpse of a broader process, one that would be invisible in the political boundaries and geological features of a map: the physical and juridical separation of the city's residents from the public resources that once sustained them. Such a process of enclosure evades the cartographic record because, unlike the paradigmatic example of the fencing in of common grazing lands with the onset of industrialization in England, in urban places the restriction of access to public spaces has been accompanied by an equally significant process of enclosure, albeit an abstract one.[18] In this era in Rio few people relied on food hunted and gathered from the urban *selva*; the transition to a cash economy was by then thorough and complete. Yet in the shrinking physical space in which unpropertied Cariocas improvised a living, a nexus of state regulations restricted their choice of profession. The state handed control of public goods like transportation and utilities to private business interests and ceded dominion over individual enterprises and indeed entire sectors of the economy to monopoly concessionaires.

Innumerable scholars have considered enclosure beyond the specificity of the sheep pastures of early modern England. The scientist-turned-social-theorist Garrett Hardin's prescriptive discussion of the "tragedy of the commons" largely set the terms of the debate in the late twentieth century. Hardin and the rational-choice social science that his work helped to set in motion held that public resources must be enclosed to save the public from its avaricious self-interest.[19] E. P. Thompson revisited the process of enclosure in early modern rural England and traced social and legal conflicts over the use of the commons to show how the law acted to mystify its role in cementing socioeconomic inequalities.[20] Neoliberal writers who came to dominate the discussion have pointed to the disappearance of the commons everywhere, depicting it as an unstable form of ownership and rights regime.

Recent scholarship on contemporary Latin American cities has shown the protracted results of the restructuring—what I call enclosure—of modern urban public life over more than a century. Latin Americanists have sidestepped the debate over the chaos or sustainability of the commons by focusing on the contemporary effects of its erosion. Social scientists examining cases throughout the Americas have studied the loss of public ownership and oversight epitomized by the new "walled city."[21] Yet little is known about the origins of this process.

In late nineteenth-century Brazil, the urban commons was less a legal designation than an empty space or a gray area in the law. The state constitutionally guaranteed all citizens the right to trade as long as they did not impede public circulation or violate other existing laws. Large-scale structural and ideological changes in the last quarter of the century moved the government to favor modernizing the city through the signing of concession contracts with large companies.[22] This trend influenced city planning in the area of petty commerce and its offshoot, the jogo do bicho, as well as in the construction of intraurban transportation networks, improvements in the port, and the gutting and reconstruction of the city center.[23]

With the reorganization of urban public life, which amounted to enclosure of a metaphorical common, urban dwellers found themselves paying money for goods and services they had previously acquired free of charge or had not needed or desired. The privatization and monetization of public life in Rio around this time extended to many dimensions of people's daily lives. Because of the city's sprawl and suburbanization, for instance, residents needed to travel longer distances to the center of city and to pay for public transportation, which was privately owned. The enjoyment of leisure time became something one purchased, for example, in amusement parks, popular theater, cinemas, and cabaret performances.

In sum, the process of enclosure in Rio involved both privatization and regulation. Regulation sometimes comprised consolidating buying and selling into contained markets, otherwise restricting trade, and the criminalization of some types of trades. Ironically, the new, public interest in some activities acted to privatize them.[24] Public domains formerly outside the state's purview now attracted official attention. The criminalized jogo do bicho was a creature of this transition.

A process of urban enclosure did indeed occur as the nineteenth century became the twentieth in Brazil. Still, to emphasize the expropriation of resources and rights is to underestimate the importance of the persistent existence of people who continued to carry on their trades and livelihoods in technically illicit fashion.[25] Despite the legal and politico-economic sea changes of the time, Cariocas did not stop gleaning fruit from trees, raising pigs in the streets, and claiming for the public domain spaces that were increasingly funded, owned, and controlled by private interests. We can most usefully understand enclosure as part of a cycle of informalization. Those left outside the metaphorical (or actual) fence were not merely swept aside. Jogo do bicho dealers, unlicensed street vendors, and other participants in Rio's nascent informal economy were entangled in a struggle over de facto rights and access to resources and became part of the way both the state and the market operate.

As practices that either evade or defy state regulation but also, otherwise, occur legally, the street vendors and jogo do bicho dealers I describe fall within the definition of the problematic, yet irresistibly useful term *informal economy*. Even someone unfamiliar with the term can conjure a vivid image of the worldwide urban phenomenon it describes: the scores of street vendors who sell candy to passengers on buses and trains, for instance, or the children who proffer rags to wipe the windshields of cars stopped at intersections. Scholars and policymakers who study this realm of petty commercial life that operates outside legal bounds have amassed a stockpile of terms, none of which suits my purposes. The "parallel" economy, the stock geometrical metaphor often used to describe this economic realm, fails to capture the phenomenon this book reconstructs. The relationship between officially sanctioned behavior and actual, popular practice in the marketplace simply defies any neat characterization, as this relationship developed along the convoluted lines of the mutual involvement of tradition, legal codes and regulations, and an extralegal system that utilized the channels of law.

Even while the difficulty of fixing this concept in language attests to its elusive nature, it would be untenable to deny the significance of the fact that over 12.87 million Brazilians do work that the state does not officially recognize as such, and that an estimated 9.47 million businesses in Brazil today are not legally registered (Brazilian Institute of Geography and Statistics, 1997). An earlier article in a law journal states that the underground economy of Brazil "is estimated at thirty-five percent of Gross Domestic Product" and is "reputedly the second largest . . . in the world."[26]

A problem of anachronism arises too: to designate a realm of informal commerce is to posit a category of behavior and experience that would have had little meaning to the people of Rio in the late nineteenth and early twentieth centuries.[27] Petty commerce in the era before retail buying and selling became fully formalized in fixed locations like retail stores evades present-day classifications. The conventional way of understanding the urban informal sector presupposes that it emerges only in the context of a highly developed consumer economy or within an advanced industrial capitalist socioeconomic structure. Perhaps because of the difficulty in discerning the appropriate manner of studying these activities without imposing anachronistic analytical categories, almost nothing is known about the historical development of the unregulated buying and selling of goods. What I describe here heuristically as informal trading encompasses much of public commercial life during this era in Rio. The terminology would not appear for almost a century, but events and policies in the late nineteenth century lay the structural and epistemological foundations for the economic transactions that would later fall into this category. One might say that this examination of the jogo do bicho reveals the prehistory of the informal sector, inasmuch as the official perception of its problematic nature was what summoned it into existence.

The concept of the informal economy came out of the concern with economic development and underdevelopment in the global South. In a study published in 1970 Keith Hart used the term *informal* to describe unlicensed petty entrepreneurs in Ghana. Much of the theorizing about the informal economy has come out of Latin America. As early as the 1950s Brazilian thinkers had debated the presence of a dual economy in terms that anticipated Hart's writing on the presence of an economic sector that operated outside the purview of the law. Brazilian social scientists, most famously the economist Ignácio Rangel, wrote about the "duality" or "duplicity" of Brazilian economic life and culture, a legacy of colonialism; the slave plantation (*fazenda escrava*) had been subject to two distinct bodies of law, one internal and one external to the plantation.[28] The sociologist Alberto Guerrero Ramos similarly described two economies, one focused on internal and the other on external relations of production. "But," he writes, "the law of duality, as it is called, can be generalized to all aspects of Brazilian life." These social theorists believed that Brazil's legal culture was imprinted by the pluralism and divided loyalties born not only of a weak colonial state, but also of a tradition of impunity.[29]

In Latin America in the second half of the twentieth century, ideas about what Hart would call the informal economy changed in tandem with developments in social science and policy concerning urban poverty. After the extreme material dearth Latin American urban populations experienced in the 1950s and 1960s, "classic marginality theory" emerged, encompassing two divergent approaches to understanding modern poverty and uneven economic development: waning modernization theory and ascendant dependency theory.[30] Policymakers and scholars, primarily from a Marxist orientation, saw the informal economy as the outcome of deepening class and racial inequalities. Observers of the multitudes of underemployed and illegally employed proclaimed the existence of an "industrial reserve army" that forced down all workers' salaries and kept workers in a permanent state of exploitation. The discussion came to rest on the question of whether the capitalist economy "would be able to absorb" this "reserve army."[31]

By the seventies and eighties it became clear that the informal sector was a permanent part of the urban socioeconomic landscape. It no longer made sense to characterize those who labored illegally as marginal to the mainstream economy, but rather to define an informal sector that existed outside legal regulation.[32] As the debate about marginality in cities in Latin America and elsewhere in the so-called developing world reached full florescence in the 1970s, persistent critiques of the concept of marginality led to the idea that the unregulated underclass was intricately connected to the formal economy. The question of how to absorb the reserve army of urban poor into the mainstream economy and polity was now beside the point because the urban economy had thoroughly absorbed them. Mainstream social science redefined participation in the informal economy, like constructing and living in *favelas*, urban shantytowns, as a creative coping mechanism; marginal practices were construed not as the problem but as the solution.[33]

The concept of the informal is only slowly beginning to emerge as a category of analysis in the consumer as well the labor market. Contemporary academic and policy debates have centered on whether the burgeoning number of unlicensed workers and merchants arises from some "cultural shortcoming" (older, usually rather invidious explanations); on the inefficiency of the law and its failure to recognize and support the grassroots capitalist productive capacity of its people (neoliberal arguments like that of the Peruvian economist Hernando de Soto, which called for greater protection of private property and a streamlining of state intervention in private enterprise); and on the injustices of capitalism in creating a perpetual urban underclass (antineoliberal).[34]

In the 1890s the underlying economic conditions in which the nascent informal economy and, within it, the jogo do bicho, grew would look familiar to those who have studied the region's contemporary cities: a growing migrant population, shortages of affordable housing in the city center, and a volatile export economy. The socioeconomic upheavals of the late nineteenth century and early twentieth increased the supply of jobless Cariocas. Bitter political conflict among factions of the agrarian oligarchy, the army, and the navy marked the political transition from monarchy to republic. Intermittent civil war caused high administrative costs in the new government and contributed to inflation. Financial speculation and an expansionary monetary policy struck the new Brazilian republic in 1890 and caused economic turbulence well into the twentieth century. One side effect of the inflation brought on by economic turmoil was industrial and commercial expansion as well as increased protection of domestic production. Growth in agriculture and an enormous wave of foreign immigrants also stimulated productive industry by providing both capital and labor.

Rapid industrial and urban expansion in the context of political and economic instability benefited local elites and the growing bourgeois sectors, but affected the growing urban proletariat adversely. The cost of living shot up, aggravated by immigration, the increased demand for consumer goods by the new rich, and the government's tendency to prioritize the slumping export economy over increasingly impoverished wage earners.[35] Internal prices tripled between 1889 and 1898 as the government expanded credit to agriculture, the money supply increased rapidly, and exchange rates deteriorated. Food production decreased because of an agricultural crisis in the hinterland, which further damaged the domestic market and drove food prices up. Rents skyrocketed. In real terms, a family that previously survived on a daily wage of four or five milreis now struggled with their six or eight milreis.[36]

A tight labor market and material dearth helped to precipitate a proto-informal sector in the early First Republic, but its causality and historical importance cannot be reduced to economic factors. Simultaneously, laws and law enforcement defined the boundaries of the permissible to the detriment of the many who followed their ingenuity rather than the letter of the law in finding an occupation. Those who made a living in these professions demonstrated their willingness to risk fines and prison terms to sell goods illicitly. Yet evidence shows that sellers of jogo do bicho tickets ran a relatively low risk of legal reprisals for their illicit occupation. Police, *bicheiros* (jogo do bicho vendors), fruit stand operators, and other petty vendors acted in an uncoordinated and accidental confederation to create a trade network that was only partially submerged. The close-to-the-ground view of the informal economy that the jogo do bicho's history affords allows us to transcend mechanistic models of what some have called "extralegal normativity."[37]

Probing the complex relationship between the law and those compelled perpetually to act outside it forces one to consider further the problematic nature of the term *informal economy*. As critics have pointed out, its useful-ness is limited by the fact that in cities throughout the world unregistered work and commerce make up nearly all economic activity, in certain cases some 80 percent of gross domestic product. What do we do when the underworld is in fact the world? To differentiate between formal and infor-mal is to impose the state's vantage on the experiences of the millions of workers and consumers who participate in these market relationships; the criticism of the analytical model that limits its vision of the popular econ-omy to the formal/informal dyad should be taken seriously.

Yet crucial to understanding the development of informality is the fact that its illegality matters, not just to the state, but also to the people subject to state power. In other words, one cannot separate people's perceptions and experiences of the popular economy from the illegality of a growing segment of these market transactions. In using the trajectory of the jogo do bicho to reconstruct a small corner of the developing informal economy, I argue that such illegal or semi-illicit forms of trading were the precursors to the massive informal economies of today. In tracing this history one can see where the licit and the illicit diverged. Tracing the development of the informal economy reveals the history of contingency of criminality, a topic of current interest in the study of Latin America—but, as we will see, one that has led scholars to take for granted some crucial aspects of the elite "civilizing mission" that marked this period in cities throughout Latin America, aspects that themselves deserve to be held up to scrutiny.

Workers and consumers who participated in the informal sector are undocumented in two senses: they operated illegally; and they typically left no written records of their activities. In this way, the jogo do bicho differs from the city's myriad other forms of unlicensed commerce. The repression that drove the lottery underground also made its history uniquely visible today. The judicial archive brimming with arrest records of buyers and sellers of the jogo do bicho may be unusual among urban Latin America's other doubly undocumented workers, yet the judicial and police repression of popular practice would be immediately intelligible to anyone familiar with this moment in the region's history.

Present-day scholars disagree about the extent to which Latin America's late nineteenth-century urban modernity was state-led, imitatively Europhilic, or leavened by an acute interest in national folk cultures, but most concur on the illiberal, antipopular nature of the politics that brought it about.[38] Nineteenth-century Latin American republics shared a postcolonial dilemma: how to incorporate a diverse population, the majority of whom had been juridically unequal and culturally denigrated for centuries, into the nation's faltering embrace. By century's end, national leaderships' ambivalent, eclectic take on liberalism, the uneasy coexistence of enduring colonial legal codes and practices alongside new, republican ones, and deep cultural anxieties about rural barbarism had left their imprint on the legal culture of the region's cities.[39] Jurists, law enforcement workers, and political leaders in Latin America's prepopulist era still generally dismissed the so-called social question of how to address the plight of the working classes as a matter for the police.[40] Scholarship on Porfirian Mexico, for example, a case analogous to republican Brazil, has shown that a subtext of moral panic behind urban modernizers' battle cry of "order and progress" underlay the obtrusive interference of the state, particularly the police, in the lives of the urban poor.[41] Studies of the uglier side of the *belle époque* in Latin America include gambling, vagrancy, prostitution, and drinking among the practices marked by class and race that the state criminalized as part of the authoritarian politics that accompanied urban modernization.[42]

The Latin American elite's "enlightened intolerance" of certain manifestations of popular culture and the enforcement of public propriety through often tyrannous and discriminatory policing were hardly innovations of the late nineteenth century.[43] Yet during this period judicial archives burgeoned as policing apparatuses grew and some customary rights became criminal offenses.[44] The increases in arrests for certain infractions were a symptom of social change, one whose meaning scholars have debated.[45] Revisionist scholarship and the interdisciplinary thinking that the law and society field has facilitated have opened up the interpretive possibility that a perceived "decline of propriety" resulted not from any absolute change in popular behavior, but from the state's tendency to pass more repressive, antipopular laws.[46] Whether the number of accused criminals taken into police custody rose because the class interests of the elite forced a shift in the criteria for arrest or because of a surge in the number of people who misbehaved, fear of public disorder still holds unquestioned explanatory power in analyses of the criminalization of vernacular practice.

Almost immediately after the first bettors began to buy jogo do bicho tickets in the early 1890s, talk of the dangerous masses arose in legislative debates, bureaucratic correspondence, and judicial writing that established the legal basis for its criminalization. Arrest records show that the city's rapidly growing poor population alone suffered the legal repercussions of this activity in which both rich and poor avidly participated. The jogo do bicho is but one example of many of how the livelihoods and avocations of the popular classes aroused official suspicion even though they directly threatened neither life, limb, nor private property. The official reaction to the jogo do bicho suggests how the roots of modern social control grew tangled around what Thompson calls "the class-bound and mystifying functions of the law."[47]

Yet the ostensibly inevitable link between normative public order and the thoroughgoing repression of popular practice requires deeper inquiry. Even an axiomatic belief that class conflict characterizes modern society would not obviate the need to reconstruct the minute steps by which the jogo do bicho passed into the realm of the legally forbidden, for the historical significance of this repression derives as much from its ambivalence and failures as from its persistence.[48] Such policies as vagrancy law and the repression of popular practices have typically been interpreted as the state's attempts to dragoon the masses into wage labor and to create a disciplined laboring class.[49] Yet, as I show, the state itself described its efforts in multiple ways, ways that included but were not limited to the desire to press the nascent working class into disciplined service. The state's social control project can explain official repression, but it fails to explain both the impunity and persistence of illicit activities and the cultural and social impact of the throngs who found themselves on the wrong side of the law.

The state's "proliferation of rules" produced a working definition of the public good that was fragmentary, tentative, and open to interpretation by the vast numbers of state and nonstate actors who acted on it.[50] Scholars have noted the paradoxical, somewhat counterintuitive phenomenon that occurs within this contested and negotiated definition of the public good: the creation of criminality. As Pablo Piccato shows in his study of the social construction of a crime wave in early twentieth-century Mexico City, the jogo do bicho did not begin as a unitary, distinct practice; its criminalization brought it into existence by both joining disparate, informal lotteries under a single criminal nomenclature and creating an illicit source of income for police.[51] But beyond reversing the causal arrow between criminality and policing, as critical historical studies of the law have done, one needs to show how official anxieties about public disorder emerged as part of a process of "legal marginalization" of the urban poor.[52]

The political elite in Brazil saw the nation's capital as a critical front in the country's sporadic war between civilization and perceived barbarism. But fear of the unruly masses and the need to press them into service in the nascent proletariat took hold along with fear of political disunity and unrest. Concerns over public order grew in this period, shaped by existing class and racial fears, political anxieties, and, in circular fashion, the process of criminalization itself.

The jogo do bicho emerged during the First Republic, the rather deceptive name given to the period from 1889 to 1930. The country had abolished slavery in 1888 and, a year later, the sixty-seven-year-old period of monarchical rule known as the Empire ended. The promise of change in the patronage-based political system provided hope for some, such as the incipient workers' movement in Rio. But the political map of Brazil was redrawn so as to exclude the vast majority of Brazilians from active citizenship and access to social power. In 1930 only about two million of the Brazilian population of some thirty million could vote. Republican rhetoric lifted straight from the French Revolution was accompanied by repression that hearkened back to another French political phenomenon: the counterrevolutionary Paris of Georges Haussmann after 1851. In fact, the engineer Francisco Pereira Passos, the mayor of Rio from 1902 to 1906, is remembered as the "tropical Haussmann." Rio, the political capital, the site of the republican military takeover, and the home of many of its national heroes, held a special place for the patriots of the Republic. It was the unrivaled cultural and economic center of the country and the site of the greatest promise—and the greatest predicament—of political participation in Brazil's modern history.

Though marginalized in the city's polity, Rio's poor and working classes were the target of intensified surveillance. When slavery ended, punishment and the maintenance of public order became heightened public concerns. The issue of public order in the city was made more pressing by the explosive growth of the population and the flood of immigrants, mostly impoverished people from southern Europe and internal migrants from rural areas. In 1890 Rio had a population of about 520,000, and by 1906 it had swelled to over 810,000.[53] Worry over the retrogressive force a large, unruly populace could exert on the capital intensified because of a preoccupation with presenting the country as modern, both to bolster nationalist morale and to attract foreign investment and immigration.

The economic and cultural importance of Rio derived largely from its status as the capital of the new federalist Republic. The Constitution of 1891 provided for the creation of a Federal District in the middle of the vast plateau in the interior state of Goiás.[54] The capital would not move from Rio de Janeiro to Brasília for another sixty-nine years. Yet even as Rio reveled in its political, cultural, and economic ascendancy, the federal legislature ratified plans to demote it. This decision reflected a spatial solution to the social tensions arising in the city and the country as a whole. In the apt words of the historian Nicolau Sevcenko, "The intention of the political factions [that resolved to move the capital to the interior plains of Brazil] was to separate politics from history, for the purpose of making the ruling classes immune to the growing social tensions of the day. It was a means of privatizing politics, and of distancing politics from the public scene."[55]

One of the rationales for moving the Federal District was public security. According to a proposal published in 1907 that urgently called for the relocation, the recent military revolt in Rio's Fort Santa Cruz stood "in the heart of every Brazilian patriot" as a painful reminder "demonstrating the critical need for a measure that, once and for all, will save the government of the country from the agitations in the barracks and in the streets." As the words of this jurist and those of many commentators show, moving the capital city aimed to save the government from political agitation. He called for the implementation of "what then would be the most prompt and efficient measure that could be taken to protect the country from anarchy and the rule of political bosses [*caudillismo*], or at least make difficult the implantation of these tremendous evils among us."[56]

The fears of the urban elite bore a certain logic. Rio had been the scene of various types of political violence during its days as the Imperial Court, when the population was far less dense and heterogeneous than it was at century's end. Tumults and uprisings there punctuated the nineteenth century. The slave rebellion of 1835 in the northeastern city of Salvador da Bahia fueled a fear that reverberated in Rio until abolition in 1888.[57] The new Republic hardly brought social peace and political stability to the country. As the site of the military coup that overthrew the emperor and the seat of the military government in power from November 15, 1889, to 1891, when the first civilian president assumed office, Rio witnessed waves of violence and aggressive political repression for a decade after the Empire. Many of the most serious disturbances occurred in Rio, especially a naval revolt and a palace war that deposed the new president. In April of 1892, the vice president, acting as president, reacted to a military demonstration calling for new elections by decreeing a state of emergency and ordering the imprisonment or exile of several congressmen to "remote parts of the national territory."[58] In 1898 soldiers returning to Rio from the infamous campaign against a messianic religious community in the northeastern city of Canudos created further unrest. In an attempted presidential assassination in the wake of this turmoil the minister of war, Marshal Machado Bittencourt, was killed. A state of emergency was reinstated, and members of Congress were again imprisoned and exiled. The early years of the First Republic saw vexing questions of public order that pitted the intellectual elite's pride in the country's modernity and dedication to the rule of law against their fear that the country was being torn apart from within.[59]

Policymakers' and intellectuals' assessment of their country at the dawn of the new Republic also sounded notes of optimism. Most notably, this national "Brazilian problem" brought down to the municipal level involved the beautification of the city. The architects of the massive urban renewal of Rio were motivated by civic pride and aesthetic concerns as well as by anxieties about public order and health and the ever-present need to attract foreign investment. Urban reforms were not new to the republican period. Projects designed to improve the urban landscape in the 1870s and 1880s included new building regulations, widening of streets, reclaiming of coastal terrain through landfills, construction of a lushly landscaped promenade along the coast (Passeio Público), and the repair and reconstruction of houses. By the late 1880s any resident of Rio with a small amount of money could ride a tramway or railway line to most parts of the city.

The civilian presidential administration of Manuel de Campos Salles in 1898 marks a watershed in the establishment of a stable government and the initiation of a period of urban demolitions and dramatic reforms that would come to be known as the "putting under" (*bota abaixo*). Campos Salles's handpicked successor, Francisco de Rodrigues Alves, ascended to the presidency in 1902 on a platform of reforms in the Federal District that included a dramatic remodeling of the city and a sanitation campaign. The public sanitation drive addressed the problem of disease and hygiene but also had powerful, albeit indirect, social connotations.[60]

In December of 1902, Rodrigues Alves appointed Passos as mayor of the Federal District.[61] The four years of his administration, known to his detractors as the "Passos dictatorship," transformed the landscape of the city. The mayor waged an epic battle against backwardness.[62] His policies were a paean to an aesthetic widely shared, at least among those residents and admirers of the capital whose words are preserved in print.[63] Planners and administrators looked to Europe and especially to Haussmann's Second Empire renewal of Paris and the related "elitist methods for urban development and social control."[64] Officials ordered the demolition of tenement houses (*cortiços*), said to breed disease, criminality, and social conflict, forcing working-class and poor residents to relocate to far-flung areas of the city. The construction of a wide, Parisian-style boulevard, Avenida Central, inaugurated on November 15, 1905, involved the demolition of 641 stores. Avenida Beira Mar (Seaside Avenue) required the massive destruction of cortiços in the city center and of warehouses in the maritime districts of Candelária, São José, Santana, and Santa Rita.[65] Public statues were erected, streets widened, and scenic avenues constructed along the seacoast. The Passos administration closed public fountains, where people had gathered for over a century to wash clothes and collect water. Open-air retail vendors were shut down in favor of forms of commerce that officials could more easily tax, regulate, and contain.

The features of republican urbanism may be summarized as having four principal characteristics. First, it included the privatization of most public utilities, such as electricity, gas, and the mass-transit system. Second, it instituted the deregulation of meat and food staple provisions, whose oversight passed from the auspices of colonial-era local jurisdictions to large, often foreign-owned corporations. Third, it involved the development and annexation of the surrounding suburbs. Finally, in the spirit of the shift toward laissez-faire capitalism, under the new urbanism the government abandoned some licensing requirements and adopted a policy of noninterference in large business enterprises. These changes went hand in hand with a new neglect of the less fortunate, a neglect ideologically reinforced by social Darwinism and French positivism, which valued the progress of society guided by a "scientific-minded and determined vanguard."[66]

The preface to the census taken in the Federal District in September 1906, while the city was in the thick of the Passos reforms, is a narrative bursting with pride at Rio's growing grandeur. The virtual tour of the city begins with a description of rua Primeiro de Março (First of March Street), one of Rio's colonial nuclei, which had transformed from a small, dirt trail in the sixteenth century into a center of commerce and *flânerie* in the early twentieth. Rua Primeiro de Março was a "commercial street with a great deal of movement"; several narrower roads ran perpendicular both to it and to the recently opened Avenida Central. The smaller streets, in turn, were transected by other narrow streets. Together, they formed "the immense and compact commercial neighborhood of the city, and they have a picturesque aspect because of [this area's] originality, its movement, its appearance of a tumultuous marketplace that fills these streets with the clamor of street cries, the rolling along of vehicles, the agitation of pedestrians, the variegated colors of the shop signs."

The government publication describes one of these bustling narrow streets in the city center as being especially interesting: "The rua do Ouvidor . . . despite its narrowness, [is] the principal artery of the urban center, full of sumptuous shops, and so replete with people that at certain times of day it becomes difficult to cross the street. It is the street on which everyone meets. Someone once gave it the name, quite appropriately, 'The Open Air Club,' and not even the opening of the Avenida Central, which crosses the rua do Ouvidor, has managed to diminish its prestige as the favorite street." From there, the narrative proceeds down other narrow streets leading north and westward toward the Praça da República (Republican Square), commonly known as the Campo de Santana, and then to the rail station, Central do Brasil, the initial point of the network of train service that linked the vast, growing suburbs with the old, central city.[67]

The anonymous writers of this preface to the government census went beyond the prosaic rendering of numbers and pie charts that the rest of the document contains. Knowing that the document would be preserved and read as reference material for generations, they used the opportunity to take stock of the Federal District's demographics and also of its built environment and human geography. As the narrative weaves through busy streets and pushes past the urban multitudes that walk them, one glimpses the range of venues that would contain and constrain the city's public life. The public policies and private initiatives that sought to transform public spaces into quasi-private "Open Air Clubs" had only mixed success.

These stretches of asphalt, grass, and stone, these falling trees, deepening rock quarries, and rising walls of granite, brick, and wood will play a major role in the story of the jogo do bicho. On the glamorous rua do Ouvidor clandestine lottery operations flourished between the stores that sold English haberdashery and French perfume. The Avenida Central saw surges of antigambling police initiatives invade the private clubs believed to be gambling dens, forcing them to move to more distant neighborhoods. Wandering jogo do bicho peddlers fought over turf on the Campo de Santana; men and women walked from that square to the nearby Central Station and bought train tickets with counterfeit money. And in Vila Isabel, a new neighborhood at the western edge of Rio's sprawl, the commercial entertainment venture of an urban developer and concessionaire turned the culture of popular gambling into a criminal underworld with intricate connections to the police, shopkeepers, and citizens.

The first two chapters of this book describe the criminalization process that brought individuals like Carlos Figueiredo, the accused bicheiro introduced earlier, into contact with the justice system, and the larger social process that made such popular practices as the jogo do bicho into crimes. Chapter 1 outlines the origins of the jogo do bicho and the events that caused authorities in early Republican Rio de Janeiro to begin to view the game as a threat to public order. Through a historical process uninhibited —in fact, abetted—by petty gambling's juridical ambiguity, police targeted the jogo do bicho almost immediately after it was invented. Chapter 2 lays out the legal and practical concerns behind the promulgation of the criminal legislation related to the jogo do bicho. The unusually high rate of acquittal in cases of illicit gambling resulted from the wide discretionary power judges and police exercised. Extrajudicial policing practices and judges' failure to prosecute gambling offenders bear witness to the formation of an embedded system of informal justice that would characterize Brazilian urban public life in the twentieth century.

Evidence abounds that petty gambling had already become part of the daily life of the Federal District by the time of Figueiredo's arrest. The changing commercial landscape of the late nineteenth-century city had created an infrastructure that facilitated the purchasing of tickets to the many lotteries, both licit and illicit, which at this time became one of the most pervasive of Caroica cultural practices. Chapter 3 shows how the game developed in tandem with urban popular commerce in Brazil, arguing that the cultures that formed around the jogo do bicho were shaped by the structure and ethos of the popular, or informal, marketplace. Chapter 4 considers how money itself became crucial to the spread of the game and its criminalization and how it was both a token and a vehicle of mass culture and public life. Chapter 5 explores the cultural and folkloric aspects of the game, presenting an alternative to essentialist explanations of the Brazilian people's predilections for purportedly fetishistic aspects of the jogo do bicho, such as its system of dream interpretation, its animal symbolism, and players' superstitious dependence on the vagaries of chance. The popular tales, magazines, and forms of expressive culture that commented on the jogo do bicho demonstrate that its cultural meanings grew together with its illegality.

By 1917, a turning point, the jogo do bicho had become both an informal culture industry and a partnership between police, impresarios, and individuals involved in the game. Chapter 6 draws some conclusions about the importance of the game to the development of Brazilian urban society and legal culture. This historical moment was marked both by violent crackdowns on popular culture and labor organizing and by police corruption. Despite police repression, urban dwellers had not reached a consensus about whether the law should permit or forbid the immensely popular animal game. Debates in the daily press continued throughout the 1910s and 1920s regarding its proper legal treatment. Although it generated consternation in some corners, the jogo do bicho continued to penetrate urban society and spread to other parts of the nation. The chapter emphasizes the ironic social and cultural worth of this illicit practice; it describes a period of harsh, centralized repression of popular gambling in order to contrast the game, which functioned reliably well, with a society in which, from the perspective of the nonelite majority, little else did.

The state became powerful and effective enough to enforce antigambling laws. If only suggestively, the epilogue considers the persecution and persistence of the jogo do bicho into the late twentieth century. This concluding backward glance describes how far the game had come by then in terms of its ubiquity, its unquestioned importance to society, its structural connections to urban popular culture, and the advanced repressive apparatus the state used against it.

The trajectory of the jogo do bicho makes it possible to trace the symbiotic relationship between law enforcement and popular practice. Over time, waves of repression came mainly as a result of the leadership of one or another aggressive, doctrinaire, or ambitious official. The lawyer Armando Vidal Leite Ribeiro, for instance, as *delegado* (police district chief) undertook the "kill the animal" (*mata-bicho*) campaign described in chapter 6. Yet there is another trend: the gradual institutionalization of the jogo do bicho as an illicit partnership between renegade police and citizens acting in the criminalized urban underworld that had come about as the result of police intervention. The repression of the jogo do bicho was not originally, or ever, really a moral or legal question. Rather, it manifested the state bureaucracy's perceived need to regulate behavior, which itself derived as much from a desire to increase tax revenues and to punish wayward police as from a preternatural fear of the popular classes and their folkways. Moral and legal questions were pulled into the discussion and soon became intertwined with the political, social, and economic ones in an impossibly tight and complex knot. This uneven, accidental collaboration between agents of the law and the people forged the link between authoritarian repression and urban public life that many have come to see as a natural and organic feature of the urban landscape.

1

ORIGINS OF THE *JOGO DO BICHO*

It is my duty to address here the great question with which you have charged me. All my hope is that the action the Mayor's Office takes will, like a bath of brilliant light upon the Zoo, wash off the long-standing and most ugly stain of gambling and vice, thus acting in the name of the public good, popular education, and the progress and re-nown of your Nation.—Letter from a police official to the mayor of Rio de Janeiro, 1903

No one knows for certain how the illicit lottery called the jogo do bicho began in Brazil.[1] Many believe the Baron de Drummond thought of it first. For others, the baron's business partner, a booking agent of Mexican origin, invented the scheme. Others suppose it had always been around; the baron and his downtown bookie, they say, just capitalized on a practice often identified as perhaps the world's second old-est vocation.[2] As soon as it began in the early 1890s, the jogo do bicho caught the authorities' attention. Spilling outside the borders of the city zoo where it originated, the jogo do bicho would cross, strain, and reify the vague line between legal and illegal.

As the country's new national leadership shed what it re-viled as an outdated regime of slavery and monarchy in 1888–89, it sought to implement a modern nation through the law. In the Penal Code of 1890 lawmakers included articles that aimed to control what today is called vice and increasingly defined popular practices like the jogo do bicho as affronts to the public good.

The authorities initially characterized the animal game as wrong only because of a fragile legal consensus; within a decade those same authorities and some ordinary citizens, too, were treating it as universally iniquitous. That shift in conventional wisdom was both fueled and justified by the state's authoritarian attempts to control a heterogeneous urban population that perennially appeared to threaten the stability and progress of the new Republic. After the first bettors began to buy tickets, instantly talk of the dangerous masses filled legislative debates, bureaucratic correspondence, and judicial writing, which established the legal basis for the criminalization of the lottery. Yet the jogo do bicho bore a relatively tenuous connection to class fears in these early years. This chapter and the next investigate how political and judicial authorities in the Brazilian capital, Rio de Janeiro, came to notice, scorn, and criminalize the jogo do bicho, and thus will reveal a glimpse of the historical process that linked order with repression in urbanizing, republican Brazil.

Alongside the ideological and philosophical reasons for outlawing popular practices like the jogo do bicho, passions and interests fueled the continuation of the game on a day-to-day basis.[3] A legal apparatus that imposed fines and prison sentences on those who practiced the game quickly formed. Police officers began to apply the previously little-used antigambling articles of the Penal Code as early as 1896.[4] Yet at the grass-roots level of everyday justice, judges, police, and citizens learned to negotiate their immediate interests both through and around the law.

What urban social changes caused the jogo do bicho to become a crime in the 1890s in Rio, the city of its origin? The persecution and the persistence of the game stemmed from the conflict over control of two closely related resources: urban space and the revenue generated by retail commerce carried out there. While industrialists and the state acted to enclose, both figuratively and literally, the spaces of petty trading during Rio's *belle époque*, citizens sought work, commerce, and leisure outside the narrowing realm of the permitted. Multitudes of urban Brazilians thus entered the wrong side of the law while moving barely an inch. Changes in the way the state managed the resulting social conflicts called for new juridical relationships, which in turn altered the public spaces and social life of the city and the terms of the debate concerning the public good.[5]

By the first decade of the twentieth century, the intricate urban geopolitics and social history behind this shift in the jogo do bicho's official status disappeared in the blinding light of putatively universal legal principles. In describing the trajectory of the jogo do bicho, what folklorists, chroniclers, journalists, and the occasional scholar have recounted is the story of the game's departure from the confines of the site where it is believed to have originated.[6]

HOW THE ANIMAL GAME ESCAPED FROM THE ZOO

In the 1870s the young João Baptista Vianna Drummond, later to become the Baron de Drummond, left his small-town home in the province of Minas Gerais for the Imperial Court. The future baron parlayed the pocketful of change his father had given him into a small fortune, immersing himself in the various forms of financial speculation of his day. He played the stock market, formed an investment partnership with the most powerful banker in Brazil, the Baron (later Viscount) de Mauá, and acquired a major share in the newly privatized interregional railroad system. And then he became involved in a new type of speculation: the purchasing and developing of land at the periphery of the city.[7] Like many wealthy, urban liberals, Drummond supported the abolitionist cause, and he named his first major real estate project—the first planned urban residential neighborhood in Brazil—Vila Isabel, after Princess Isabel, who was associated with the movement to end slavery.[8]

Vila Isabel was created in 1872 when Drummond's company, Companhia Arquitectônica, purchased land from the imperial family on which a plantation called the Fazenda do Macaco (Monkey Estate) had once stood. The neighborhood was carved out of two parishes, Engenho Novo and Engenho Velho, whose names derived from Jesuit sugar mills (*engenhos*) that had occupied the site before the order's expulsion in 1759 led to the transfer of its lands to the Portuguese crown. The Jesuit owners of Fazenda do Macaco abandoned their property in 1761. For the long century to follow, the *fazenda* was left to ruin, save for the harvesting of the wild fruit and animals that flourished there, free to anyone willing to venture this far into Rio's hinterland. This region of the city still consisted of rural settlements when Drummond purchased the land. As early as 1838 mule-drawn trams had transported people and produce from the area south- and eastward to the center of Rio, but this corner of the city was still only dotted with country homes and the occasional small farm. The sprawling city would annex it fully by century's end, slowly replacing the overgrown flora of the former plantation with iron railway tracks, concrete plazas, and modest houses and shops that would serve the city's vertiginously growing population.[9] A large

TABLE 1 Population Growth in Rio de Janeiro by Neighborhood, 1870–1906

NEIGHBORHOOD	POPULATION IN 1870	POPULATION IN 1890	POPULATION IN 1906
Sacramento	24,429	30,663	24,612
Candelária	9,239	9,701	4,454
São José	20,220	40,014	44,878
Santa Rita	23,810	43,805	45,929
Santana	32,868	67,533	79,315
Glória	18,624	44,105	59,102
Engenho Velho	13,195	36,988	91,494
Lagoa	11,304	28,741	47,992
Gávea	—	4,712	12,750
Santo Antonio	17,427	37,660	42,009
Espirito Santo	10,796	31,389	59,117
São Cristóvão	9,272	22,202	45,098
Engenho Novo	—	27,873	62,898
Irajá	5,746	13,130	27,410
Jacarepaguá	7,633	16,070	17,265
Inhaúma	7,190	17,448	68,557
Guaratiba	6,918	12,654	17,928
Campo Grande	9,593	15,950	31,248
Santa Cruz	3,445	10,954	15,380
Ilha do Governador	2,594	3,991	5,616
Ilha de Paquetá	1,260	2,709	2,283
Maritime	Not indicated	4,359	6,108
Total population	235,381	522,651	811,443

Source: República dos Estados Unidos do Brasil, *Recenseamento do Rio de Janeiro (Districto Federal) realisado em 20 de setembro de 1906.*

textile factory, Fábrica Confiança Industrial, constructed there in 1878 along with workers' housing that accomondated over a thousand residents pulled workers into the neighborhood.[10] By the 1890s, this swathe of former farmland west of Rio's historic center would become the fastest growing part of the city. Between 1870 and 1890, Engenho Velho almost tripled in size, and it grew by 146.36 percent between 1890 and 1906. In the same period Engenho Novo's population increased by 125.66 percent.[11]

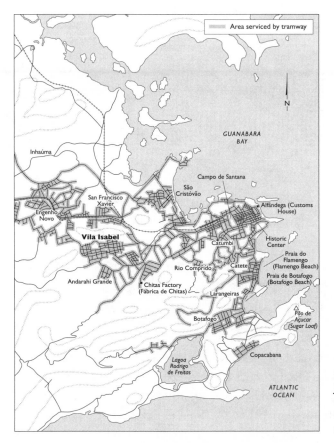

MAP 2 Rio de Janeiro, showing expansion of tramway lines, ca. 1880.

Fresh from a sojourn in Paris, the baron and his associates at the Companhia Arquitetônica hired an architect to lay out the streets of Vila Isabel in a grid of clean lines and right angles and to crown the new neighborhood with a wide boulevard reminiscent of those in the capitals of Europe. On this plot of land, he also built the Jardim Zoológico de Vila Isabel in 1888, a zoo sanctioned by special accord with Rio's municipal government and intended to keep both domestic and exotic animals for the amusement and edification of the Brazilian people, the beautification of the city, and the improvement of Brazilian livestock. This contract guaranteed Drummond not only the privilege of transforming two hundred thousand square meters of land into the city's first zoo, but also an annual government subvention of ten *contos de reis* (over fifty-four hundred dollars) to cover maintenance costs, an exemption from all municipal taxes for the term of the contract, and a promise that the city would prohibit similar establishments for twenty-five years.[12]

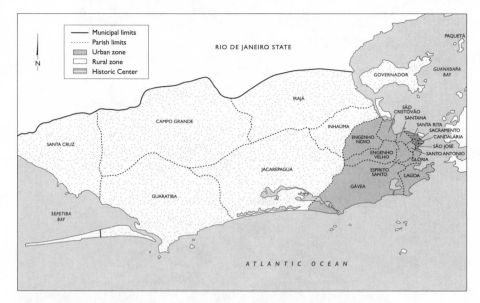

MAP 3 Greater Rio de Janeiro metropolitan area indicating parish jurisdictions, ca. 1900.

With the fall of the Empire and the establishment of the First Republic in 1889, the Baron de Drummond's fortunes took a turn for the worse. Just one year earlier, Drummond had been honored with both a baronetcy and public monies to support his zoo.[13] Now the zoo was threatened with closure amid budgetary crises and antimonarchical fervor marking the new Republic.

Drummond requested a concession from the city government to operate a game that, it was hoped, would raise the zoo out of insolvency without depleting the city's coffers. In his lengthy petition to the Police Council, Drummond argued that the zoo was destined to become the "best in the world." Moreover, the games he proposed to establish there were a "useful institution" that would benefit the people of the Federal District and by extension all of Brazil. As long as they are "well regulated and moralized," Drummond explained, these "recreational games . . . will greatly benefit the community without those nefarious annoyances that tend to appear, such as, for example, lotteries and betting on races . . . and the multitudes of gambling houses that infest this city." The government agency replied favorably, stating that "what the petitioner proposes to do is to develop a pleasant distraction within reach of the people; with games, it is true, but these games do not present a threat to public hygiene under the conditions

FIGURE 2 "Vila Isabel, ca. 1900." Photograph by Augusto Malta, Courtesy of Museu de Imagem e do Som, Rio de Janeiro, MIS, F-005695.

FIGURE 3 "Street in Vila Isabel with Streetcar, ca. 1910." Photograph by Augusto Malta, Courtesy of Museu de Imagem e do Som, Rio de Janeiro.

he proposes. . . . On the contrary, they would bring about great physical, moral, and intellectual advantages." Less than two weeks later, the petition was approved.[14] The Municipal Council signed a new contract with Drummond in October of 1890 granting him permission to establish a new business: "public, legal games" subject to police oversight and contained within the zoo. The document bears a small detail that foreshadows the trajectory these games would soon take: atop the sentence that reads, "The Municipal Council concedes to the Company the right to establish . . . public games" a government official inserted the word *licit*, purposefully handwritten in black ink beside the word *public*.[15]

Construction for these "public" and "licit" games began immediately and included facilities for spectator ballgames called *boliches* and *frontões*, early forms of commercial amusement. By July of 1892, among these public diversions was a raffle that turned the very act of entering the zoo into a game.[16] For the first time, visitors paid an admission fee, one milreis, rather than entering for free. Their tickets doubled as a chance to win a cash prize at a daily raffle. Every ticket bore the image of an animal, and early each day the baron himself would randomly select one of the twenty-five animals printed on the tickets. At five o'clock each afternoon he revealed to the public the lucky *bicho* by raising the image he had picked to the top of a tall pole near the entrance of the zoo. The winners of what was then called the *sorteio dos bichos* (animal raffle) would each take home a cash prize of twenty milreis, twice the daily wage of, for example, a shoemaker.[17]

Rio's newspapers began to report on the immense popularity of the game in July of 1892.[18] Soon, existing public transportation could no longer handle the number of people traveling to the zoo, and the *bonde*, or tramway system, added new runs in the direction of Vila Isabel. Describing the mounting number of passengers riding the tramways, an official of the Companhia Ferro-Carril da Vila Isabel in 1893 stated that "the increase in passengers we see this month was attributable to the game in the Zoological Park."[19] The folklorist Hugo Pedro Carradore relates that the animal game proved such a sensation that Drummond had to call the police to restore order when the crowd, seeking to purchase chances to win, surged at the gates.[20]

Those wishing to play the sorteio dos bichos soon did not need to find transportation to Vila Isabel. On July 12, 1892, a week after the raffle was instituted, a newspaper informed readers they could purchase their game tickets not only at the the zoo but also at a designated address on the city's

FIGURE 4 Ticket to the Jardim Zoológico de Vila Isabel (ca. 1895), also used to play the animal raffle. Courtesy of Museu de Imagem e do Som, Rio de Janeiro. Reproduced in Benchimol, *Pereira Passos*.

main shopping street, the rua do Ouvidor.[21] Private businessmen set up a ticket booth on Praça Tiradentes, one of Rio's busiest squares, to sell admission tickets to the zoo that included round-trip transportation on the bonde plus a chance to win a cash prize at the end of the day.[22]

Drummond likely established these points of sale himself to augment the flood of income his sorteio dos bichos was generating. In doing so, his moneymaking scheme strained the limits of the official permission he had obtained and began to take the form of the illicit lottery recognizable to any Brazilian today. In apparent violation of his contract, Drummond may have set up partnerships with people who were running gambling operations in the center of the city.[23] Some commentators on the history of the animal game believe he joined forces with Manoel Ismael Zevada, who ran a small, independent lottery outfit downtown called the *jogo-das-flores* (flower game), in which players would select a number corresponding to a type of flower.[24] The baron and his associates may have substituted the twenty-five animals of the sorteio dos bichos for its predecessor's flowers. With this variation on a familiar theme, a new, unofficial lottery was born. Some evidence suggests that the force behind Drummond's animal game may not have been the elusive Zevada, but the renowned commercial amusement entrepreneur Luiz Galvez, to whom Drummond appears to have subcontracted the games at the zoo in 1894–95.[25]

FIGURE 5 Cartoon dramatizing controversy over the Baron de Drummond and the jogo do bicho (1896). Source: Instituto Histórico e Geográfico Brasileiro, Rio de Janeiro, *Revista Illustrada*, ano 21, no. 718 (1895), n.p.

FIGURE 6 "Here in the city, despite the police's prohibition, the jogo do bicho continues almost like before. One only hears, 'The donkey won!' 'The camel won!'" (1895) Source: Instituto Histórico e Geográfico Brasileiro, Rio de Janeiro, *Revista Illustrada*, ano 20, no. 692, n.p.

Drummond himself does not deserve all the credit—or blame—for the transformation of the animal game into a citywide clandestine lottery. The entrepreneurial impulses of an unnamed cast of hundreds converged in the spread of the jogo do bicho. Small business owners mounted their own jogo dos bichos operations independent of Drummond and the zoo, games in which players bet on the outcome of the animal lottery and shop owners banked the lottery themselves. Independent bookmakers are thought to have begun buying large quantities of jogo do bicho tickets at officially authorized outlets and then reselling them, probably along with those of other lotteries, in their shops.[26] By 1895 lottery "bankers," or *banqueiros*, unaffiliated with Drummond were taking bets of their own on the outcome of the drawing at the zoo and paying the winners out of their own earnings. Between 1892 and 1895, when the authorities closed down the animal lottery at the zoo, these small lottery operations neither registered with the city government nor suffered police persecution. But in the three years after Drummond introduced the animal raffle, references to jogo do bicho tickets being sold among other consumer goods appear in both bureaucratic correspondence and popular media, such as newspaper chronicles. An anonymous letter to the chief of police in January 1895, three months before the city rescinded its contract with Drummond, reports that a shop in the central neighborhood of Flamengo was selling "*bichos* for the Zoo" in addition to tickets for prohibited "foreign lotteries."[27] Downtown booking agents, small stores, market stands, and kiosks set up in public spaces throughout the city offered chances to win cash by selecting the lucky animal.[28] By the mid-1890s, the animal game had escaped from the zoo.

It did not take authorities long to notice the jogo do bicho and remark on its patent illegality.[29] Although press coverage of the animal game had been uncritical, an official letter condemning the lottery at the zoo appeared in the police blotter column of the daily newspaper *O Tempo* less than a month after the game began. The letter, written by the second police district chief (*delegado*) to the chief of police, calls for police intervention to put the sorteio dos bichos out of business. Although the games appeared "deceptively innocent according to the initial simple description of them that was offered" in Drummond's petition, in practice

one can verify that they indeed have the character of actual gambling, which is manifestly prohibited. The tickets offered for sale carry the purely aleatory hope of a cash prize, and the holder of the ticket only wins the prize if he has the good fortune to select correctly the name of the species of animal that is raised to the top of a pole. This type of amusement is prejudicial to the interests of the unwise, who are naively seduced by the deceptive hope of uncertain lucre. It is precisely a true game of chance [*jogo de azar*] because winning or losing depends exclusively on randomness and luck. Such a diversion cannot be tolerated any longer. . . . I thus would order the director of the Jardim Zoológico to suspend immediately the continuation of the above-mentioned game, under penalty of prosecution under articles 369 and 370 of the Penal Code.[30]

In February of 1893, an agent of the municipal treasury wrote an internal memo that contains additional clues about what was occurring at the zoo and how some local authorities had begun to take umbrage. Examining the original contract with the owner of the zoo, this bureaucrat remarked that Drummond and his company had not fulfilled their legal obligations. The zoo, he complains, did not correspond to the original proposal and was not on par with other zoos of its kind. It had failed to acquire new animals and could not take care of even those it possessed. Furthermore, it had neglected to hold the required zoology classes and maintain the grounds.

Not only had the management at the zoo not realized any of these improvements, but, worse, "the games [for which the company was granted a concession] have been degraded by prohibited, illegal games, by an animal lottery [*uma loteria de bichos*] or drawing, in which the names of animals or birds are substituted for numbers, and with a 20% profit for the Company." Although the municipal government had given permission for games to take place, the memorandum reads, city officials had not anticipated the form they would take: "If the Company were to establish games, they would have to have been those established in all other countries, and not games of chance depending upon luck . . . which are prohibited in all times by Roman law and in our own Penal Code already in force before the contract went into effect, but whose date matters little since these activities are against the law in general." His colleague responded in agreement, "I have visited similar establishments in Europe, and in these places I have never seen any games except those that are true public diversions, like children's games, animal rides, and so on, [rather than those] that carry with them the hope of winning money. Without a doubt, it was such games, and not the animal lottery, to which the contract alluded, and one

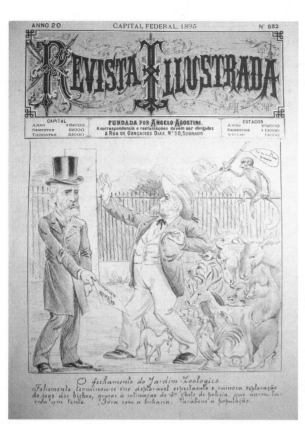

FIGURE 7 "The Closing of the Zoological Garden" (1895). Source: Instituto Histórico e Geográfico Brasileiro, Rio de Janeiro, *Revista Illustrada*, ano 20, no. 682, cover.

would therefore conclude that the contract has not been carried out." Since the zoo company had reneged on its contractual responsibilities, the municipal government would not have to fulfill its own.[31] In April 1895, in a decree issued by the Municipal Council, the city rescinded its contract with Drummond and called for an immediate cessation of the "illicit games" occurring at the zoo.[32]

A law passed in January 1895 marks the first broad attempt of Rio's republican government to place strict limits on gambling. First, this law limited betting on races and other athletic events to just one day per week. The daily nature of the jogo do bicho indeed became its defining feature, thus bringing it under the legal definition of an illicit game. Second, the legislation prohibited the taking of bets for licit lotteries by intermediaries, an inglorious profession in the eyes of the law for which the Brazilians had borrowed the English term *bookmaker*.[33] Police singled out bookmakers in general for zealous repression. Under license from the mayor's office, these middlemen first sold chances to win money based on the outcome of foot and horse races that took place in the stadiums called *velodromos* and *frontões*. Bookmakers naturally expanded to sell chances for all sorts of games, including the jogo do bicho. Their strategic locations throughout the city and the growing market for games of chance boosted their popularity in the early First Republic.[34] A police official in 1894 made the first concerted attempt to separate legally Rio's *jogos de lazer* (leisure games), a sort of off-track betting operation for athletic events involving both humans and horses, from the unauthorized lottery dealers mushrooming all over the city, who sold tickets to legal raffles and lotteries side by side with illegal ones.[35] The jogo do bicho's daily operation and its reliance on intermediaries were to become the crux of its popularity and staying power.

The emergence of independent bookmakers, bankers, and sellers allowed lawmakers and enforcers to characterize the animal game occurring at the zoo as an illegal "game of chance," and these figures continued to vex authorities after the animal game detached from the zoo. As the key personages in the daily operation of the jogo do bicho, the *bicheiros* and *banqueiros* took bets from customers and paid the ones who selected the winning animal and number. These agents functioned independently of one another and did not begin to collaborate for decades. What buyers, sellers, and government officials called the jogo do bicho actually denoted a variety of clandestine lotteries that coexisted in Rio and in cities and towns nationwide.[36]

The variants of the jogo do bicho had in common a list of twenty-five animals in roughly alphabetical order, each corresponding to a number. As the game could no longer count on the zoo raffle to derive its daily result after 1895, the enterprising army of bicho merchants and bankers found other sources. Once the animal game was disassociated from the zoo, the outcome of the Federal District's licit lottery determined the winning number, and animal, of its illicit counterpart.[37] Each of the twenty-five creatures came to be associated with a "group" of four numbers representing the last two digits (*dezena*) of the first-prize number of the legal lottery. For example, those who played the ostrich, number one in the jogo do bicho, were betting that the last two digits of the winning number in the lottery would be 01, 02, 03, or 04; the eagle, number two in the jogo do bicho, would win if the victorious lottery number that day ended in 05, 06, 07, or 08.[38] One could, alternatively, bet on the last three digits (*centena*) of the winning (licit) lottery number or on one of the other many variations.

FIGURE 8 "Gambling and Bookmakers" (1895). Source: Instituto Histórico e Geográfico Brasileiro, Rio de Janeiro, *Revista Illustrada*, ano 20, n.p.

The various winning numbers in the legal lottery gave rise to multiple versions of the jogo do bicho; one derived, for example, from the last two digits of the sum of the three first prizes (the Moderno).[39] Each of these variations had its own name at the point of sale—Rio, Salteado, Antigo, and Moderno were the most common—but at the moment of arrest all went by the common denominator "the game called 'the animal game.' " By the first decade of the twentieth century, the police referred to the jogo do bicho as "a game of chance that is connected to the lottery of the Federal Capital, corresponding to specific numbers."[40]

Vendors sold tickets for this clandestine lottery in the Federal Capital at this time wherever people traded money for goods. The official lottery had itself experienced a boost in business when the jogo do bicho appeared, and licensed lottery dealers in small shops and kiosks throughout the city sometimes sold tickets to its illicit counterpart.[41] Some people operated jogo do bicho businesses out of their homes or in the collective housing where many of the city's poorer residents lived. Both in quotidian urban life and on special occasions like religious festivals, in shops, on tramway platforms, at corner fruit stands, butcher shops, squares, and factory gates public life offered myriad opportunities to play the jogo do bicho.

Anecdotally, one can reconstruct both the ubiquity of the jogo do bicho

TABLE 2 The Original Twenty-Five Animals in the Jogo do Bicho and Corresponding Numbers

GROUP	ANIMAL	NUMBERS (DEZENAS) INCLUDED IN GROUP
1	ostrich	01, 02, 03, 04
2	eagle	05, 06, 07, 08
3	donkey	09, 10, 11, 12
4	butterfly	13, 14, 15, 16
5	dog	17, 18, 19, 20
6	goat	21, 22, 23, 24
7	sheep	25, 26, 27, 28
8	camel	29, 30, 31, 32
9	snake	33, 34, 35, 36
10	rabbit	37, 38, 39, 40
11	horse	41, 42, 43, 44,
12	elephant	45, 46, 47, 48
13	rooster	49, 50, 51, 52
14	cat	53, 54, 55, 56
15	alligator	57, 58, 59, 60
16	lion	61, 62, 63, 64
17	monkey	65, 66, 67, 68
18	pig	69, 70, 71, 72
19	peacock	73, 74,75, 76
20	turkey	77, 78, 79, 80
21	bull	81, 82, 83, 84
22	tiger	85, 86, 87, 88
23	bear	89, 90, 91, 92
24	deer	93, 94, 95, 96
25	cow	97, 98, 99, 00

by the late 1890s and what was at stake in playing it. Objects related to the animal game began to appear in random places. In February 1898, police fished a small handful of paper money and a notebook containing a jogo do bicho bet out of the pocket of a man arrested for a different crime.[42] Jogo do bicho tickets began to appear among the merchandise offered for sale in kiosks that sold snacks and coffee on street corners.[43] They surfaced in less random places, too, especially in the criminal files of those arrested for

FIGURE 9 Cartoon series showing the popularity and spread of the jogo do bicho (1895). Source: Instituto Histórico e Geográfico Brasileiro, Rio de Janeiro, *Revista Illustrada*, ano 20, no. 680, n.p.

involvement in the game. Often aided by published tip sheets and an elaborate system of dream interpretation to deduce the winning animal and number, buyers themselves picked the numbers they wished to play and decided how much to spend.[44] In 1899, wagers ranged between five hundred and five thousand reis; irrespective of neighborhood, players usually chose to gamble roughly the price of a cup of coffee or up to the equivalent of a worker's daily wage.[45]

To learn the results of the day's lottery, players could return to the site where they had purchased the ticket or consult newspapers and or signs posted wherever lottery tickets were sold. The amount of the prize depended not only on how much the bettor had wagered but also on the type of game selected. The higher the risk, the higher the pay; placing a simple bet on the last two digits of the official lottery number would pay a lesser prize than playing the *centena* (the hundreds), that is, the last three digits. Individual transactions in these earliest years of the game occasioned few written records, leaving it impossible to know how much money a winning player might have taken home. The payout was likely a relatively consistent, fixed multiple of the amount wagered, as in later decades.[46] According to testimony in a case from 1907, the winner in the Antigo, a bet on the last two numbers of the legal first-prize winner, would receive twenty times the wager.[47] The records of an arrest made in 1911 show that jogo do bicho players could win twenty-three milreis for one milreis wagered in the simplest version of the game, involving just one number between one and twenty-five, and eight hundred for one bet on a combination of three numbers.[48] In 1911 eight hundred milreis was a handsome sum, the equivalent of two to four months' salary for a bookkeeper or cashier.[49]

Ties that bound players to sellers of jogo do bicho tickets, like sellers of other merchandise, straddled the commercial and the social.[50] Writers of popular literature in the early First Republic who came to incorporate the jogo do bicho into their narrative repertoire tell of the variety of relationships between buyers and sellers. Transactions took place even in the confessional booth, according to Carradore, who recounts the story of a bicheiro-priest.[51] That tale perhaps represents less a legitimate case study than a parody meant to show the hypocrisy of the clandestine lottery's detractors or the uselessness of banning it. Yet the story does demonstrate one possible scenario in which the Cariocas imagined the jogo do bicho might be bought and sold, considering its ubiquity, and the ease with which one could surreptitiously both bet and deal in the game.

Customers at the butcher shop where Manoel Pedro da Silva Junior worked as a cashier, for example, could gamble their loose change as they shopped. Da Silva Junior, a young, Portuguese-born man who lived above the shop, could neither read nor write. But he did know how to work with numbers, and that allowed him to supplement his income by selling tickets for the jogo do bicho. The arrest records reveal nothing specific about his customers, although one might surmise that they lived near the butcher shop in the neighborhood close by Praça Onze at the western edge of the city center. By late morning on an August day in 1899 at least four people had laid small bets with him as they shopped.[52] When the police entered the butcher shop at eleven o'clock in the morning that day, following the complaint of a civil servant who lived nearby and objected to his neighbor's dealing in the illicit lottery, the officer arrested him "em flagrante delicto" for selling tickets to the "so-called animal game."[53]

Jogo do bicho arrests took place at all hours of the day, but especially in the early afternoon.[54] On December 9, 1898, at two o'clock in the afternoon Manoel Joaquim Barata, a thirty-one-year-old, "currently unemployed" Portuguese man, took bets for the jogo do bicho at the door of a tavern, where he was caught "em flagrante." His pockets were stuffed with cash, and when the police apprehended him he had already made a number of sales and was apparently on his way "to drop off the money at other commercial establishments throughout the city."[55] In this city of public servants, street vendors, dockworkers, and merchants, the exchange of cash for a handwritten jogo do bicho ticket kept time with the rhythms of daily commerce.[56]

How might Rio's residents have encountered the jogo do bicho for the first time, and what might they have thought of it? Some commentators cite newspapers, proliferating at the beginning of the First Republic, as a major vehicle for the spread of the game. But low levels of literacy suggest the role of print journalism in popularizing the jogo do bicho was limited; in 1890 and 1906, respectively, 48.28 percent and 48.11 percent of Rio's population were reported to be illiterate.[57] More likely informal information networks—virtually impossible to reconstruct historically—spread the word about where to buy tickets. A public employee might have read about the jogo do bicho for the first time at a newsstand on his way home from work or perhaps heard about it from the bonde driver. A dockworker might have stopped late at night for a shot of coffee at a kiosk and been offered a ticket. On her daily shopping rounds, a domestic worker might have learned about the jogo do bicho from a hawker on the corner.

The precise origins of the cluster of criminalized practices known as the jogo do bicho may indeed be known only by those who played it in the late nineteenth century, for at its inception there was nothing remarkably new about the jogo do bicho. Rio had seen small-time gambling operations come and go for over a century, and in the early 1890s the jogo do bicho would have felt familiar to people accustomed to betting small amounts on similar games and lotteries. Whether the jogo do bicho replaced or simply took over its antecedents is unclear. The informal, illicit lotteries that had existed were often so similar to the jogo do bicho that players may not have realized they were playing a new game.[58]

Why then did the authorities come to perceive the jogo do bicho as not only noteworthy but notorious? Carradore traces the police response to the jogo do bicho back to the state's need to control the throngs of disorderly people who reportedly visited the zoo and to suppress the "people's passion" for a game that "led to real disgraces, the ruin of families, filled jails, and stained the newspaper headlines with blood, but which also turned into the joy of the people."[59] In his retrospective reflection on the origins of the jogo do bicho, written in the 1970s when the game had already been decisively labeled a crime, Carradore echoes the common belief that criminalization resulted naturally as a rational response to feverish, irrational passion. More scholarly sources tend to echo his belief that state officials suppressed certain manifestations of popular culture because they connected these practices with public disorder. Historians have examined the official treatment of popular practice in urbanizing, belle époque

Brazil in cases that parallel the jogo do bicho; a rich historiography illustrates how the state's determination to police the city created criminal acts out of such customarily tolerated practices as the martial art known as *capoeira* and Afro-Brazilian religious practice.[60] Both before and after jogo do bicho tickets became available outside the zoo, elite Cariocas' endemic fear of the "dangerous crowd" provides a too-convenient explanation of the official repression of popular practices the historiography of Brazil has established.[61]

Lawmakers and government administrators did invoke the threatening urban masses as they suppressed the jogo do bicho, but not exclusively. The flurry of bureaucratic communiqués and hours of legislative debates concerned with the disorderly propensities of players of popular games of chance in the 1880s and 1890s also show a desire to regulate everyday trading by measures short of criminal law.

It is no coincidence that Rio's authorities sprung into action against the jogo do bicho just as it moved beyond the confines of the zoo, for, as it did with all types of commerce, the city sought to draw spatial boundaries around "sporting" transactions.[62] Lawmakers delimited retail vendors' and other traders' boundaries with several overt objectives in mind: for example, to allow for the free flow of goods and people through the city streets and to uphold the concessionaire's privilege of doing business without competition in the immediate environs. The state's zealous oversight of bookmakers demonstrates that the confinement of gambling to a certain geographic space was paramount. When restricted to the running track or sports club, gambling seemed innocuous. Yet when allowed to occur wherever anyone was willing to take the entrepreneurial risk of establishing a betting house (*casa de apostos*) or lottery shop (*casa de loteria* or *loteroteca*) the state acted to limit the hours of operation and to regulate with a tighter grip, at times outlawing the operations altogether.[63] In late nineteenth-century Rio, petty gambling operators were renegade middlemen and posed a threat to the economic order. As go-betweens, bookmakers siphoned off money that flowed between customers and commercial establishments licensed to sell amusement to the people.[64] From its earliest moments, the political will to contain petty gambling spatially manifested a wish to control it economically.

The state sought to control not only the renegade petty bourgeoisie epitomized by bicheiros selling side-bets on the animal raffle and, later, on the legal lottery, but the activities of large capitalists, too. Officials were annoyed not only that unregulated versions of the animal lottery were mushrooming all over the city, but also that within a few years of opening the zoo, Drummond was reneging on his contractual obligations to maintain an educational "zoological park." He failed to replace the animals that died off, while the games of chance he had established at the margins of his contract thrived. The state's attention was fixated on the economic activities at the zoo, not on the waning animal population or the rotting meat the former baron reportedly had been feeding them. Drummond's Jardim Zoológico extended through much of the neighborhood of Vila Isabel, and he operated several hotels, restaurants, and taverns on its grounds, all under cover of the initial concession contract and its tax exemption. Municipal authorities lashed out with fines and angry letters. The historical record illustrates that it was the state's desire to share in the profits that motivated it to take action against the zoo.[65]

Lotteries were more than just a vice or even a game; they were big business. In the First Republic, the legal national lottery was a semiprivate company and a perquisite whose spoils the government granted to a favored few. The government itself had long trafficked in chance, running lotteries to fund such public construction projects as, ironically, the Rio city jail. Throughout the nineteenth century and into the early republican period, the state allowed charitable and religious organizations to operate fundraising lotteries.[66]

The national lottery followed in this tradition but was very much a creature of its time. The new government formed the Companhia das Loterias Nacionaes do Brazil in 1896 in conjunction with a private company and granted a concession to the company to run lotteries throughout the country. The directors of the lottery were drawn from "the most prominent men of the nation."[67] Scholars as well as contemporary observers have suggested that Rio's authorities colluded with the directorship of the lottery, accepting payoffs to continue their police campaigns against the jogo do bicho in the early twentieth century.[68] How directly involved the lottery interests were in determining state policing policy is unknown, but at the very least the state attempted to harness the people's propensity for petty gambling as a public finance scheme. The lottery company actively promoted its political position and, from 1917 on, lobbied vigorously for the repression of independent games of chance.[69]

Federal law stipulated that each local lottery scheme award fifty prizes. A spin of a wheel, the archetypal symbol of chance, determined the winning

FIGURE 10 Lottery shop in the Rio de Janeiro city center, ca. 1910. Photograph by Augusto Malta, Courtesy of the Museu de Imagem e do Som, Rio de Janeiro, MIS, F-008324.

number. A travel account from 1917 describes how the drawing worked: "There is a public drawing, when many spectators are present. The method is by the wheel system, the wheels corresponding to the decimal number of the total number of tickets, and these are set in motion by young girls of ten or twelve years of age; the winning number is the one formed on the wheels when they come to a stop." In 1917 the legal federal lottery cost six hundred reis, the equivalent of fifteen cents. The first-prize winner would take home "a comfortable sum," ranging from sixteen contos (four thousand dollars) to five hundred contos (one hundred twenty-five thousand dollars). There were numerous prizes in addition to first, and the "drawer gets back the value of his ticket, if he draws only the last digit of the chief winning number."[70]

The jogo do bicho cost approximately the same as the licit lottery, although players themselves could decide how much to bet and often played less. Players in the clandestine animal game faced better odds of winning than legal gamblers but stood to win a smaller sum. The jogo do bicho was not necessarily in competition with the games of chance authorized under the government's monopoly agreement. The two types of lottery gambling coexisted, at least from the buyer's perspective. The author of the travel account mused, "I have noticed as a rule, the Bicho

FIGURE 11 Extraction of the legal lottery, ca. 1925. Source: Instituto Histórico e Geográfico Brasileiro, Rio de Janeiro, *Revista da Semana*, April 13, 1929, n.p.

plungers always buy the regular lottery tickets also, as a sort of hedging."[71] While playing the jogo do bicho did not preclude buying tickets for the legal lottery, those with a financial interest in the latter perceived the two forms to be locked in a zero-sum game.

The jogo do bicho escaped from the zoo both spatially and economically in part because it was never tightly confined there in the first place. The game was part of a contractual relationship between a capitalist and the city government, which harnessed already-existing tastes, finance capital, and urban infrastructure. National and municipal authorities appear to have believed the jogo do bicho would retain its original innocuous form as it appeared in the contract. The authorities had disregarded not just the economic and social realities of the city and the common practices of its inhabitants, but also the creative disobedience of profit-seeking business owners from the corner bicheiro to the wealthy industrialist.

MERCHANTS OF CHANCE

Commercialized leisure, including games of chance, formed a characteristic part of the development and modernization of Rio in the late nineteenth century. The official reaction to the jogo do bicho occurred in the context of the state's often-frustrated efforts to control that development through its agreements and partnerships with private enterprises. Companies and individuals vied for the grand prize of a concession contract with the municipal or, in some cases, the national government to profit from the city's growing need for infrastructure: roads, housing for the poor, mass transit, and more modern and controlled forms of retail commerce, for example. State policy that aimed to crush petty gambling stemmed from official anxiety about the fissures in the concession system through which the state managed the urban retail economy. The worries over public order that tinged the jogo do bicho with a "stain of . . . vice" arose largely because of the dynamics generated within that concession system, which limited opportunities to independent business operators while it fed a process best described as urban enclosure.[72] The privatization of the physical and economic spaces of popular commerce led to the criminalization of the vernacular practices that had long occurred there.

The quintessential urban concessionaire, Drummond was primarily neither a zookeeper nor a proponent of gambling but an urban developer. The expanding urban transportation networks, which Drummond financed and helped plan, made it possible for the poor classes to move out of the city center.[73] Drummond founded and presided over the streetcar enterprise Vila Isabel Tramway Company in February of 1871 in partnership with three financiers. In 1872 he officially requested of the minister of agriculture permission to run a tramway line to the old Fazenda do Macaco, the overgrown farmland his zoo would later occupy. The recent inauguration of two nearby stations on the Dom Pedro II Railway, São Francisco Xavier and Engenho Novo, made the area attractive to Drummond's company. Aware of these first few trickles of the eventual tidal wave of urban sprawl, Drummond sought to turn this momentum toward increasing his growing fortune. By 1873 mules pulled wooden cars along the seven-kilometer stretch of streetcar tracks that Drummond's company constructed, which connected the newly named Vila Isabel with the center of the Imperial Court.[74] His transportation company went public and enjoyed enormous but short-lived success. Apparently unable to survive the transition from animal-driven to electric trams and the competition for concessions from foreign companies, the Vila Isabel Tramway Company suffered a financial downturn and was dissolved in 1889. As the mayor's office and foreign and domestic companies battled over streetcar monopolies, Drummond turned to other industries, including the growing trade in commercialized popular culture.[75]

Drummond's urban development projects benefited from his extended kinship ties to the Baron de Mauá, his enormously wealthy, well-connected friend and business associate, whose initiative and entrepreneurial activity lit the city with gas and launched the first tramway line in the Imperial Court.[76] Drummond became the chief officer of the company that would form the Dom Pedro II Railway, Mauá's most famous undertaking.[77] Drummond also seems to have owed his fortune to having married well; upon the death of his wife, Florinda Gomes Viana Drummond, in 1883, the assets belonging to the couple included one rural estate in Valença in Rio's coffee-growing hinterland, shares in several companies, two small houses in Vila Isabel, and "8 lots of land on different streets" in Rio, including one in Vila Isabel, along with a large inventory of movable property. The long list of "goods" Drummond inherited from his wife's farm included thirty-four slaves, seven of whom had apparently been manumitted but still lived and worked on the estate.[78] In short, Drummond's investment portfolio indexes the socioeconomic changes occurring in Brazil: the contradictions of a liberalizing slave economy in the years leading up to its abolition; the transfer of wealth and power from hinterland to city; and the growing consumer market in Rio de Janeiro for public goods such as mass transportation as well as such modern public conveniences as cafés, zoos, and games of chance. And immediately prior to establishing Rio's first zoo, Drummond had inherited a fortune.

Drummond had speculated in gaming establishments before starting the animal raffle at his zoo. Among other companies, he held shares in the Casino Fluminense, a genteel gambling and entertainment establishment housed in an impressive, neoclassical building in the central neighborhood of Lapa. Many outlying parts of the city had been decidedly more glamorous in the middle of the nineteenth century, and Drummond's pet real estate project, Vila Isabel, occupied the part of the city that was arguably the cradle of elite gambling in Rio. The Jockey Club, the Prado Derby Clube, and the Derby Clube Fluminense all functioned near the zoo in the last quarter of the nineteenth century.[79] The Clube de Corridas de Vila Isabel, a horse racing club opened in 1884 (later renamed the Derby Clube), ran alongside the zoo. Rio's privileged classes frequented these racetracks and gambling clubs, among whose investors and administrators were the illustrious civil engineer who would later plan the construction of the Avenida Central, Paulo de Frontin, and the eminent writer and lawyer Conde Afonso Celso.[80] By the last quarter of the nineteenth century, gambling was a perceptible force in the urban geopolitics, culture, and economy of the capital city; playing games of chance was at the cutting edge of commercialized public entertainment, which itself was at the forefront of

Rio's modernization. Neither the state nor its citizens seem to have questioned the legality of these gambling establishments; the entrepreneur hoping to profit from their popularity needed to win not a legal battle but a concession contract from the municipal government.

Mauá, Drummond, and their ilk were merchants, a class who, since the colonial era, came not from the upper echelons of the Luso-Brazilian oligarchy but from its upwardly mobile lower tiers. Even during the Empire, Brazilian entrepreneurs faced a generally inhospitable political economy, largely because of the centralized control the emperor and his Council of State exercised over all aspects of business.[81] Yet these businessmen did manage to improve their position over the course of the nineteenth century. They traded on their financial daring and political skill to purchase titles like baron and viscount, which were theirs to keep for life but not to pass on to their offspring. Immense changes in the socioeconomic structure of Brazilian society in the half century after the country won independence from Portugal in 1822, combined with the liberal proclivities of Emperor Dom Pedro II (r. 1840–89), increased the social power that members of this new merchant elite held.[82] In sheer numbers, professions like the military, the law, and engineering predominated among the Carioca urban elite of the late Empire and early First Republic.[83] Many from outside the banking professions entered the financially risky businesses of public utilities, mass transportation, public markets, and other types of urban infrastructure. These merchant-financiers took particular care to differentiate themselves from the keepers of dry goods stores and butcher shops, who had always been a characteristic feature of Rio de Janeiro but who proliferated with the first mid-century surges of foreign immigration and urban growth. A young assistant to a merchant, for example, would have preferred the term *auxiliar* to describe his profession, rather than a *caixeiro*, used to denote a simple cashier or shop boy.[84] Entrepreneurs who produced goods for domestic consumption weathered the difficult business climate of the Empire, the export economy, and the lack of any systematic development plan. By the 1880s, as they organized into an association and growing urban markets opened up profitable possibilities, industrialists gradually gained some political footing.[85]

The upwardly mobile entrepreneurs in Brazil's cities competed with each other and with foreign businesses to win public contracts and augment their wealth and power.[86] The availability of more capital in the second half of the nineteenth century enabled individuals and companies to invest more money than ever before in such collective goods as early mass transportation and, later, commercialized public entertainment.[87] Drummond's concession to build both his intraurban transportation lines and the zoo represent part of a larger trend toward the privatization of large-scale urban development. The construction and maintenance of urban infrastructure had proceeded as either a state project or a haphazard, small-scale private undertaking earlier in the century. By the last quarter of the century, however, the municipal government signed contracts with large companies to provide the city with public works and infrastructure, including docks, public lighting and other utilities, roads, and civil construction, as well as entertainment and retail commerce.

Concession-holding merchants possessed the exclusive privilege to construct and operate many of the city's vending stands, market stalls, and street-corner kiosks, which they in turn rented to vendors.[88] Concessionaires paid a licensing fee and sometimes sweetened the deal by offering funds to the public school budget.[89] Clauses in the contracts restricted hours of operation, controlled prices, and dictated where trading could occur and the range of products vendors might sell.[90] The company that built and owned most of the city's kiosks, for instance, agreed in their concession contract of 1877 to refrain from selling alcoholic beverages. In practice, the operators of these kiosks and the state mutually disregarded the interdiction against selling alcohol, as kiosk operators did a brisk business in domestic beer and local rum (*aguardente*), and the municipal chamber amassed some much-needed income from licensing fees. Only in 1889, when the city government began to license the kiosks' competitors to sell alcohol, did officials selectively begin to cite the previously ignored no-alcohol clause in the contract.[91] For its part, the government granted the concessionaire such benefits as tax relief and an effective monopoly. These contracts designated an imaginary legal fence around the market stalls owned by the concessionaire, one that kept the competition a long coin's throw away. Although much trading in the capital still occurred in small, independently owned shops and informal street vending stands, merchants who won public contracts held enormous power to determine the conditions under which Cariocas bought and sold goods. Through its authority to award concession contracts selectively to entrepreneurs in retail commerce and stipulate the terms of those contracts, and its de facto power in deciding to what degree it would adhere to the contract, the state could effectively maintain its liberal, laissez-faire politico-economic doctrine while still controlling many aspects of the consumer economy.[92]

The small-time gambling operations that tended to fall under the prohibition against games of chance in the 1880s bore a symbiotic connection to urban petty commerce. Public discussion of both gambling and the proper use of the city's public spaces for retail trading intersected, and at this intersection one can glimpse the prehistory of the social conflicts that accompanied the rise and criminalization of the jogo do bicho a decade later. These conflicts involved business competition, in the context of the state's power to bestow on some the privilege of operating free of rules and competition and to clamp down forcefully on others.

In April of 1884, the Municipal Chamber passed a decree that updated the gaming legislation passed a half century earlier: "In all public gambling houses all games involving betting with cards, dice, and roulette or any other apparatus or means destined for the same end are prohibited." Four years later, we have evidence of how the new law was applied to the daily activities on the Campo de Santana, one of Rio's largest public squares. In July of 1888, Valentim Jr. Tavaraes, the holder of a government concession to run several small retail operations, wrote a letter to the Municipal Chamber to denounce an individual "who refused to abide by an act of the municipal government in placing his market stalls [*barracas*]." Tavaraes called upon the authorities to intervene in a dispute over the use of the area in front of the military barracks on the square. "In the market stalls in question," he complained, "some gambling was established that contradicts" the new law.[93] Tavaraes's accusation is plausible, but whether the offending vendor, apparently a competitor, ran an illicit gambling operation from his market stall is less important than what it represents as an early example of the selective application of the prohibition against publicly playing for money. An accusation of illicit gambling had both moral weight and relatively low punitive stakes. Both citizens and authorities proffered it regularly.

Tavaraes's letter of complaint and hundreds like it that survive in Rio's city archive are perhaps best understood as relics of local battles in the war, mostly an epistolary one, between concessionaires, the Brazilian government, and small, independent sellers.[94] The warring parties battled over how, where, and under whose auspices the trade in staple goods for the city's population—lard, rice, building materials, cooking oil, and so on—

would take place. These conflicts set the tone for the geopolitical contests over the moral and legal high ground that would characterize the soon-to-come question of the jogo do bicho. On the eve of the First Republic the products of truck farmers from the city's outskirts found their way to market stalls, which increasingly were constructed and owned by companies with long-term (usually ten- to twenty-year) concession contracts with the municipal government. The government had much to gain by contracting with large companies rather than allowing the small sellers to occupy city squares freely. It was decidedly easier to ensure that one large company, rather than hundreds of small, independent sellers and itinerant peddlers, would comply with the requirement to pay fees. The competition for contracts was fierce, and accusations of malfeasance abounded in letters to the government and editorials in the local newspapers.[95]

Much of the public debate was framed in terms of fair competition and adherence to contractual agreements. Yet the city archive is full of documents implying that corruption occurred regularly not only in determining who would win contracts and sinecures, but also in the complicity of public officials with monopoly-seeking concessionaires wishing to suppress competition by making spurious accusations of illegal practices. Scores of letters from concessionaires in the late nineteenth century and early twentieth demand that city officials shut down small, independent fruit stands.[96] While such correspondence fetishized contractual arrangements between the government and concessionaires, irregular business practices, especially favoritism and arbitrary and selective adherence to rules, occurred both behind the scenes and on center stage.

Contenders for government contracts in Rio's marketplace relied on a rhetoric of free trade and business ethics to promote their interests; they generally refrained from invoking the dangerous masses to incite social fears.[97] It is surprising, and therefore historically significant, that entrepreneurs and public officials concerned with the regulation of petty commerce chose not to decry the unruliness of customers and independent sellers in the popular marketplace to add force to their arguments. Silences in a historical document often reflect precisely the beliefs and assumptions the writer held most deeply and therefore felt no need to articulate—yet that does not appear to be the case here. The ruling classes in Brazil in the nineteenth century frequently expressed their anxiety about the unruliness of the nonelite urban populace.[98] The concessionaires' repeated appeals for fairness reveal their greater concern with corruption and favoritism—or more accurately, their fear that their competitors, and not they, would benefit from favoritism—than with the dangerous masses.

Control and oversight of everyday petty commerce in the final decades of the Empire were pressing public matters, but they were not yet, by and large, a police matter. Various types of informal commerce, including informal petty gambling, would become police issues once they were caught up in the power dynamics the concession system created between the urban elite, the state, and the people. These sets of indirectly connected concerns —class and racially motivated fear of the supposedly unruly urban masses and desire for a share in the benefits of Brazil's modernization—would converge in the late 1880s and 1890s, when the legislative, juridical, and other public debates about petty commerce did indeed come to turn on questions of public order.[99]

In official correspondence regarding the regulation of small commerce, little changed immediately in the transition from Empire to Republic after 1889. Gradually, however, retail concessionaires' attention turned to gambling; their petitions for contracts demonstrate an implicit understanding that wherever a crowd gathered, wherever money was exchanged, people found a way to get around the rules. Promises to prohibit gambling became a stock element in contracts granted to retailers from the mid-1880s on. For example, a request from the businessman Ayes Farinha regarding the terms of a contract with the city government (Intendência) in 1891 reads as follows:

> The undersigned, a Brazilian citizen, businessman, and resident of this capital city, wishing to establish markets in various locations in this capital, under the jurisdiction of the Intendência to provide the people with various games for diversion, *none of which will be games of chance*, and to display for sale foreign products as well as those of our nascent industries, with the aim of making them better known and to imitate what is done in the principal cities of Europe and North America, does request from Your Excellency a concession for five years . . . to bring to effect this idea, paying the Intendência the requisite license fees for the markets that will be opened. (emphasis added)

The Intendência granted Ayres Farinha's company the concession to construct markets in "diverse places in this municipality . . . as long as the sale of merchandise or objects of any nature are not exchanged by means of luck, in accordance with article 367 of the Criminal Code. Games played there must not be games of chance, that is to say, they may not be games in which winning or losing depends exclusively on luck."[100] The specter of gambling haunts the subtext of another letter on this matter, dated November 20, 1891, in which a municipal official lays out the terms of the concession agreement: "The sale of products and merchandise will not be carried out by lottery or by the employment of any lottery-like means, that is, in which winning or losing depends exclusively on luck. An infraction of this clause will cause the concessionaire to incur penalties required by Article 369 of the Penal Code, the revocation *ipso facto* of this concession, and fines in the amount of 500 milreis to benefit schools and public libraries."[101] The message resounded clearly: economics of an undesirable kind was likely to occur in a popular market, and the municipal government would not stand for it. Companies signing prized public contracts were quick to position themselves defensively against "games for which winning or losing depended exclusively on luck." And the increasingly regular use of accusations of illicit games being run out of market stalls shows the subtle transformation in the uses of the rules and codes previously established to lay a veneer of fairness over the play of private interests in the Rio marketplace; business operators and agents of the state had begun to apply these codes to prevent the practice of such popular "vices" as informal gambling.[102]

Just as neither the zoo nor the gambling there appear to have been Drummond's main business interests, gambling itself was not the principal cause of the anxiety legislators and police officials had begun to express in the mid-1890s about the jogo do bicho. State regulation of commercial enterprises large and small arose from an overarching concern with the disorderly effects of competing, profit-seeking industrialists. In its endeavor to squash the jogo do bicho, the state's real goal was to control consumer capitalism itself. The state attempted simultaneously to police both powerful capitalists by way of concession contracts and the throngs of small, retail vendors who operated outside the reach of state regulations and contractual agreements. Among this renegade petty commercial sector, which grew to meet the needs of the largest consumer economy in Brazil, were the countless unlicensed street vendors and, beginning in the 1890s, bicheiros who traded in illicit lottery tickets. The genesis of a gray zone of uncontrollable entrepreneurship marked the transition from Empire to Republic. The state finally turned to criminal law as the only effective regulatory mechanism for these small entrepreneurs who operated outside the reach of government control within the concession system.

Public criticism of gambling was not motivated only by economic self-interest, and there were misgivings about the religious, philosophical, and ethical correctness of engaging publicly in games of chance. Yet it was not the morality of gambling itself that was at stake. The debates that nudged the jogo do bicho toward the wrong side of the law dwelled on other questions: tensions between competitors over fair business practices; the irrevocable power of contractual obligations; a general desire for economic stability; and small sellers' and producers' own interests in the urban petty economy. And these debates about retail trading themselves tacitly addressed even greater uneasiness about inequality, poverty, and, eventually, public order. By 1889, with the end of the Empire, vague, preexisting concerns about regulating unfair competition came to coincide with the new social exigencies the republican regime brought about. As we will see, public responsibility for dealing with matters at the intersection of petty commerce and what would come to be labeled as criminal misdemeanor (*contravenção*) ultimately fell to the police.

CRIMINALIZATION OF THE JOGO DO BICHO:
THE HISTORICAL PROBLEM

By the mid-1890s, the words *jogo dos bichos*, as the game was then known, were being spoken not only on street corners and market stalls but also in the Chamber of Deputies and police precincts. In 1896, a lengthy debate unfolded on the floor of the Federal District's Municipal Council. Addressing the council president, the council member Sá Freyre declared,

> Mr. President, having taken notice that every day gambling sporting events[103] are practiced in the Zoological Park, and taking into account the necessity to make a ruling on the request made by the proprietors of the gambling sports clubs of this Capital city, be it declared henceforth that this request positively contradicts my [earlier] ruling. . . . The Municipal Council must not forget about our fight to end the illicit games practiced at the Zoological Park, and therefore we absolutely must not consent to their request to practice the game of *pelotas*[104] there, when the law emphatically prohibits these games.[105]

Sá Freyre's reference to the "illicit games practiced at the Zoological Park" unmistakably alluded to the jogo do bicho, by then a constant topic of local political debate.

Despite Sá Freyre's unequivocal proclamation, his statement exaggerated the clear illegality of the "games practiced at the Zoological Park." Even the Municipal Council could not agree whether the games constituted a violation of the law. As both commercial establishments and public amusements, small gambling operations in the city had fallen under municipal and national regulation since the middle of the nineteenth century. These regulations were usually administered by the Ministério da Fazenda, the executive department that controlled internal trade and tax revenues in general, and under the division of the municipal government that oversaw gaming, the Office of the Interior and Statistics. Public funds earned from licensing gambling operations were supposed to be channeled into municipal coffers to pay for local expenses, such as education and public works projects. Thus it is unsurprising that legislative debates, mostly at the municipal level, began to take notice of the jogo do bicho and especially its fiscal as well as social and legal implications. The Municipal Council's discussions in the early First Republic express first caution, then annoyance, and ultimately consternation about the nature of the jogo do bicho.

The debates showed that local politicians also feared the demoralizing effects of the flagrant breeches of public contracts. A telling example of what lawmakers thought of gambling appears in the legislative annals of April 1898. A conflict of opinion arose in regard to approval of a concession contract for a small businessman wishing to install public games in the city; some lawmakers insisted the enterprise was simply a thinly disguised gambling outfit. In the ensuing debate, council members unanimously lamented the spreading popularity of gaming in the city. They noted that small businesses frequently signed concession contracts with the municipal government, only to pursue games for which winning or losing money depended on luck rather than skill or work. Some cited an interdiction against games of chance that dated back to classical antiquity. Yet the city was locked into a contract with these small entrepreneurs, and only if the authorities could prove the concessionaire had violated it could they revoke it. Sá Freyre declared, "We see that despite the fierce war we are waging against gambling in the Federal Capital, despite the fact that we seek by all possible means to pass prohibitive laws that will make gambling disappear . . ." gambling, his colleague Rodrigues Alves said, completing the sentence, "keeps getting worse and worse." Sá Freyre picked up his diatribe again: " . . . as our colleague said so well, it may keep getting worse and worse, we must not consent to allowing gambling, only thus would we not take part in and not be responsible for a practice that acts in disrespect for all that is just and honest." He continued, "The state's legalizing power absolutely should not have any part in consenting to gambling of any kind." The council must "sweep house" and "absolutely must" deny all licenses that are discernibly intended to allow gambling.[106]

In 1898, judicial practice had not yet assigned violations of "good customs and practices" like the jogo do bicho and similar games of chance corresponding articles in the Penal Code. The code did contain eight articles outlawing all types of gambling not specifically permitted by law, but the first major legislation to classify the jogo do bicho as an infraction of the law punishable under those articles was not passed until 1910.[107] The definition of such games as infractions of the law was still so subtle and uncertain as to forestall most criminal (or civil) proceedings against those suspected of playing or dealing in them. More frustratingly still, the perpetrators of these questionable games were already so nameless and diffuse as to make it nearly impossible to keep track of them. Police reports and hearsay that filtered up to lawmakers made them take notice that countless small entrepreneurs failed to give the government its cut of their profits in the form of taxes and licensing fees. The game that had begun as a raffle at the zoo arose repeatedly as an example the speech-making legislators wielded to demonstrate a worst-case scenario of a routine administrative agreement gone awry.

The legislative debates about clandestine games of chance reflected the larger issues of power and authority that stirred city politics at the time and the ongoing power struggle between the local and federal governments.[108] In the 1890s fines levied on small, private gambling businesses did not signal a punitive or moral condemnation of petty gambling per se, as they (and much harsher penalties) later would in a direct and overt manner. The importance of the fines lay in the larger question of local autonomy and in the exigency that municipal leaders felt to preserve the integrity of certain types of local power. In 1898 fiscal responsibility for a variety of local services passed to the municipality, and this stoked the debate about local autonomy and control.[109] Local political leaders were painfully aware that federal officials had been siphoning off funds officially destined for municipal coffers. Such irregularities became common in regulating the world of public entertainment and its corollary (under)world of gambling. One council member complained, "The municipality is obliged to pay 2,500 contos to the police and almost 400 contos for the local administration of justice. However, daily the civilian police invade the duties of municipal functionaries, usurping money that belongs to the Municipal Treasury. First, in the soaring fines imposed on gaming, whose destiny the Municipality does not know."[110] The issue of petty gambling struck a nerve in local authorities, who felt that the interests and needs of the nation too often overshadowed those of the city. Furthermore, in what one legislator calls "the problem of disagreement" between diverse laws that lay out duties and rights at the municipal level, it had become difficult to discern just what was permitted and what was against the law. Officials were becoming aware that this administrative and jurisdictional confusion led to the impunity of ostensibly illicit practices and opened up the possibility of police corruption.

Members of the Municipal Council disagreed on an exceedingly basic question: How—and indeed whether—to define the jogo do bicho as a crime. In response to a complaint that council member Duque Estrada had lodged regarding the disappearance of fines that federal officials levied against "Bicheiros," the name already given to sellers of the jogo do bicho, a fellow council member declared,

> My colleague Duque-Estrada, referring to fines that the Police imposed on and charged the so-called Bicheiros, claimed these fines to be contrary to the Criminal Code, which does not establish fines of this type, which can only be imposed and charged by the Municipality. On this point, my colleague made just one little error: the Code of Municipal Regulations does not impose fines of this kind, either. And even a very short while ago ... the Council of the Civil and Criminal Chamber ruled that such fines and the charging of the same for gambling violations are arbitrary. . . . Such fines are not based in any law.[111]

As these and other Municipal Council records demonstrate, various types of gambling had gone back and forth over the line between the permissible and the illicit from time immemorial, but still by the 1890s neither municipal nor federal codes had firmly established the precise legal basis for the criminalization of games of chance. Nor had jurists amassed a body of jurisprudence to compensate for this legal lacuna.[112] Predictably, the legislative debates of the early decades of the First Republic centered on the ever-vexing dilemma of regulation versus prohibition.[113] The local legislature did not reach a consensus about whether the city should allow these games and profit from them or whether such regulation would be an administrative and public order disaster. Meanwhile, to the endless chagrin of the police chief, the municipal executive continued regularly to grant licenses for lottery-type gambling operations even as the police planned campaigns to stamp out games of chance in general.[114]

Irresolute as it was, this legislative discourse had already become police practice within four years of the invention of jogo do bicho. On August 7, 1896, four neighbors from the working-class neighborhood of Engenho Velho began the day together on a public square and ended it together in the Casa de Detenção, the city jail, detained for playing the jogo do bicho. That this group of male migrants from Spain, Portugal, and Brazil's rural northeast lived on the same block and were arrested on the same square suggests that the police brought them to the precinct as a group and that they knew each other.[115] Were they a syndicate of gamblers, or friends passing time in a public square? No evidence of their guilt is offered in the scant paperwork produced that these early arrests typically produced, and the judicial authorities did not pursue the case: the four detainees were released on August 10. The day they left the jail, three more men arrested "for selling the jogo de bichos" took their places. The jail entry log reveals that men charged with gambling-related offenses were already common among the population of detainees by 1896.[116] By that same year the game that had once been a legal raffle played at the zoo had found its way into the official documentation of Brazilian juridical practice, routinely treated as an infraction of the law.[117]

The four men detained in the city jail for selling jogo do bicho tickets in 1896 were arrested within walking distance of the Jardim Zoológico. Here, near the birthplace of the animal game, the number of individuals arrested under article 367 of the Penal Code climbed in the ensuing years, though not steadily: two in 1898; eleven in 1900; six in 1902; and forty-one in 1904.[118] Arrests for playing and selling the jogo do bicho were far from confined to the environs of the zoo. Police persecution of the game fanned out throughout the city, and the number of people arrested mounted (table 3).[119] The earliest recorded arrest in Rio related to the jogo do bicho occurred in Engenho Velho in 1895, but in short order even the most distant parts of the city witnessed an arrest or two per year. For example, in Campo Grande three arrests were made in 1899. By the first decade of the twentieth century not a single neighborhood was free of jogo do bicho arrests. The pattern seen in Engenho Velho repeated itself in the city's other neighborhoods; year by year, the relatively small number of individuals arrested for jogo do bicho offenses in the city's outlying neighbor-hoods consistently mounted at a rate that roughly corresponded to the outward growth of the city. The considerable discrepancy between the number of official cases brought against jogo do bicho players and sellers and the number of persons held in Casa de Detenção for such infractions without being formally charged manifests the continued ambiguity of the game's legal status.[120] By the second decade of the twentieth century arrest statistics for the Brazilian capital suggest that the animal game had attained its characteristically paradoxical status as a ubiquitous cultural phenome-non and criminal infraction.

The legislative record in the two decades after the invention of the game makes clear that lawmakers realized that the haphazard policy regarding games of chance was already bearing strange fruit. In a speech in 1917, one municipal lawmaker said, "In spite of everything, gambling continues. Although it is restrained, gambling is not so much diminished as [it is] in a state of hibernation: gambling continues in fact with the irresistible force of habit because," the legislator continues, quoting a statement by the venerable senator Rui Barbosa about the naval revolt in 1910, still fresh in the minds of the legislators, "'one cannot resist the irresistible.'"[121] Bar-bosa's circular logic served the lesser-known statesman quoted here as evidence of the inevitable presence of gambling in the Carioca cultural landscape. Yet as the reference to the naval revolt was meant to demon-strate, moral dissolution and even chaos perpetually threatened the city. Unfettered petty gambling would create unimagined disorder, but, the law-makers feared, the arbitrary, ineffectual policing of such activities would also yield a bitter harvest. This local legislator's oblique reference to pub-lic order was more than mere rhetoric. If not always openly discussed as a facet of this problem, the question of public order had gradually merged with those of fiscal prudence and business ethics. In the first two decades of the jogo do bicho's existence, the criminality of those who engaged in the game had come to be taken for granted by many as an organic part of the law.

What happened between the moment the entrepreneurial baron dreamed up the idea to keep the zoo afloat and the day, less than three years later, when police hauled groups of men and occasionally women to the Casa de Detenção by twos, threes, and fours? How did a mundane administrative question involving the apportioning of municipal funds and business privi-leges become one of public order to be answered by the police? No single

TABLE 3 Summary of Earliest Jogo do Bicho Arrests in Selected Rio de Janeiro Neighborhoods, 1893–1906

NEIGHBORHOOD	YEAR	NUMBER OF ARRESTS FOR JOGO DO BICHO SPECIFICALLY[a]	NUMBER OF ARRESTS FOR GAMBLING, POSSIBLY JOGO DO BICHO[b]	YEAR OF FIRST JOGO DO BICHO ARREST	POPULATION OF NEIGHBORHOOD
Santo Antonio	1893	1	3	1893	(1890) 37,660
Santo Antonio	1906	12	2	—	42,009
Engenho Velho	1893	0	—	1895	(1890) 36,988
Engenho Velho	1906	17	3	—	91,494
Engenho Novo	1893	—	—	1900	(1890) 27,873
Engenho Novo	1906	21	2	—	62,898
São Cristóvão	1893	0	—	1898	(1890) 22,202
São Cristóvão	1906	53	67	—	45,098

Sources: Arrest data compiled from AN, Índices Criminais, Códigos de Fundo T8, 70, AND T7; population data come from *República dos Estados Unidos do Brasil, Recenseamento do Rio de Janeiro (Distrito Federal) Realisado em 20 de setembro de 1906.*

[a]Arrests specifically for jogo do bicho were for article 367 of the Penal Code and Decreto-Lei 2321, article 31.

[b]Arrests possibly for the jogo do bicho include those for articles 368 through 374 of the Penal Code, which applied to various types of illegal gambling.

event transformed the jogo do bicho into a juridical bête noire. In reconstructing the way in which Brazilian lawmakers and jurists responded to this popular game with moral consternation and legal suppression, one finds not a linear causal chain but a dialogue between the game's operation and the legal apparatus established to squash it.

Significantly, in the early years, the authorities' treatment of the jogo do bicho was not a case of clear-cut, thoroughgoing repression. Rather, throughout the First Republic, the police and political leadership only sporadically undertook campaigns to end the game. Political leaders spoke with vitriol of the jogo do bicho on the floor of the national legislature, and the mayor, city officials, and the heads of the police hierarchy referred to the game in language reserved for the vilest of public offenses. Many hundreds of arrests were made; the two defendants processed for illicit gambling in the neighborhood of Santo Antonio, for example, by the 1910s became scores and by the 1930s hundreds. Yet these figures constitute a small percentage of the city's population and a tiny segment of those participating in the game. The number of persons actually prosecuted for playing or selling the jogo do bicho is smaller still. Sometimes in the face of ostensibly overwhelming evidence of guilt, during this period from the game's origin to around 1917 it appears that virtually no one who was arrested for playing or dealing the jogo do bicho was ever convicted, fined, or handed a prison sentence.[122]

The idiosyncrasies of the group of people arrested for the jogo do bicho and related offenses raise questions about how the state and the people interacted through the mechanisms of criminal law. Why, for example, between 1891 and 1929, were almost three times as many persons described as being white arrested for gambling than people described as being black? Why were so many sellers arrested and so few buyers? In light of the selective nature of the legal reprisals against the jogo do bicho and its persistence despite its ostensible illegality, simply to note an elite fear of the popular classes is to miss the jogo do bicho's richest historical lessons.

CONCLUSION

Operating the "jogo dos bichos" began as a contract-granted privilege. The game's legendary creator, the Baron de Drummond, lost his monopoly when numberless unlicensed, informal vendors all over Brazil's capital began to take bets on animals associated with numbers.[123] Evidence cited here corroborates the story that holds the baron as the game's progenitor; newspapers from 1893 report that his zoo ran games of chance that, administrative documents show, soon crowded Cariocas from all corners of the city into tramway cars bound for Vila Isabel.[124] Members of Rio's legislative body discussed the dangers the jogo do bicho posed in terms of its escape from its original, circumscribed place and purpose. Popular knowledge of the animal game came to remember its beginnings in similar fashion: it became a widespread, clandestine practice only after it evaded its creator's control and the masses (re)appropriated it. The few serious studies of the jogo do bicho and the multitude of examples from the folkloric and popular literature that describe the game's origins trace this same trajectory: from legal, innocent game carried out inside the zoo to defiant vice, played throughout the city.[125] Whether they rejoice or recoil in horror at its escape from the zoo, narratives about the jogo do bicho have in common a certain implicit understanding about this moment of transition.

Yet other evidence offered here shows this story to be incomplete: the jogo do bicho is a creation not of a baronial industrialist but of the state in its interaction with the people. Acting within the wide latitude of regulatory legislation, the police interceded in the jogo do bicho and thus grouped a disparate set of informal gambling practices under the legal interdiction against games of chance as they arrested people for dealing in the "so-called animal game." The story of the jogo do bicho's escape from the zoo is a parable of its subtle, juridical transition.

Social scientists have their own sort of allegory for representing the process this chapter narrates, which the game's baronial origin myth dramatizes: criminal sociologists employ the term *moral passage*, which calls upon a metaphor of motion through space to describe how changes in the way the state interacts with the people affect society's definitions of criminality.[126] Criminal sociologists use this term to portray the abstractions of social change; it evokes the shifting nature of commonly held ideas about deviance and the process through which society designates the difference between the permitted and the illicit. When statistical evidence demonstrates an increase in the number of persons arrested for a given offense, such changes might reflect a change in behavior: *true prevalence* in criminological parlance. Alternatively, however, the increase might manifest only a greater number of arrests, not an increase in the incidence of crime. In the latter case, a moral passage has occurred; what has shifted are the criteria for arrest, not actual aggregate behavior.[127] The term captures the dynamic, fugitive nature of the line that divides licit and illicit.

The jogo do bicho did not simply move from acceptance to persecution, or from inside to outside the zoo. Its moral passage was an instrumental effect more than a moral consensus, an effect that allowed police and, acting through them, private citizens to apply the law selectively even while neither the law nor the people had yet fully recognized the game as wrong. Its illegality, once established, provided Cariocas with a modus operandi for dealing with conflicts over the uses of the city for living, working, and commerce. The jogo do bicho thus passed into the moralizing embrace of criminal misdemeanor law rather than business ethics or state regulation.

To the extent that the jogo do bicho did undergo a moral passage, the process is one of the small steps that, cumulatively, codified the distinction between the deviant and the acceptable. If deviance, in the words of one sociologist, "is about being different," then the story of the jogo do bicho's rapid transition to illegality tells the story of the production of difference.[128] We can understand the jogo do bicho's descent into the underworld, then, not so much as the result of preexisting social inequalities, but rather as defining new ones suited to and intelligible in a postabolition, republican, urbanizing age. The concept of moral passage provides a starting and not an ending point for my investigation since it tells how officialdom reclassified a popular practice as criminal but does not fathom the distance between what the law dictates and what judges, police, and private citizens actually did.

While the jogo do bicho's ubiquity ruffled many feathers it caused nothing but mild amusement to most observers. The legislature's equivocal position reflected popular uncertainty about the game. Its brazen presence became an ordinary part of urban Brazil's cultural landscape. In 1905, according to one folklorist, "with the authorization of the tramway company Companhia de Bondes Jardim Botânico, the tickets for the *bonde* had tips for which animal to play in the jogo do bicho." By the early twentieth century, Brazilians and foreign observers alike had come to perceive the jogo do bicho as Brazil's "national vice," most often with a touch of ironic affection. The newspaper chronicler Jota Efegê noted that the jogo do bicho has become such an infectious craze that he likened the possibility of an adult avoiding its allure to that of a child "elud[ing] the measles."[129] A traveler from the United States in 1917 writes, "I asked the superintendent of the municipal lodging house in Rio de Janeiro what brought the majority of the one thousand men there nightly, and he answered, 'the Bicho.' In the United States," this traveler muses, "the reply under similar circumstances would probably be 'drink,' but liquor is not the national vice in Brazil."[130]

The moral question was not irrelevant to the state's treatment of illicit gambling, but it did not neatly overlap with the official push toward criminalization. Aside from the jurists, lawmakers, and police who fought against the animal game, some within the workers' and anarchist movements voiced misgivings about the jogo do bicho and criticized those who engaged in it.[131] Rio's commercial professional associations, especially the Associação Comercial, expressed steadfast opposition to the jogo do bicho and assisted police in seeking the arrest of bicheiros.[132] Some citizens, too, acted on behalf of the state in its anti-bicho campaigns, either as informants against suspected bicheiros in ongoing criminal investigations or in denouncing fellow citizens believed to be dealing in the clandestine lottery.

As this chapter has demonstrated, the jogo do bicho threatened a variety of actors who possessed the power to enact and enforce laws to seek its demise. It challenged the legal lottery concessionaries with unwanted competition. It came to represent the disorderly tendencies in urban petty trading that commercial associations and policymakers sought to eradicate. And, in circular fashion, it seemed to confirm the elite's fears about the entropic tendencies of the burgeoning working class, their desire to attain money without working for it, and their wanton disregard for the law. The complex causality behind the early persecution of the jogo do bicho became simplified once its classification as wrong behavior became a legal fact not three years after its invention. The articles in the 1890 Penal Code and later statutes that targeted games of chance with increasing precision then became convenient tools in the hands of politicians, police, and judges. But the law amounts to much more than that which is written, and the ambivalent morality behind the establishment of this antivice legal apparatus haunted Brazilian law enforcement's ability to pursue its aims effectively.

2

THE RULES OF THE GAME

The law is an Utopia—a country that receives no visits.

—Jeremy Bentham (1843), preface to *Rationale of Judicial Evidence, Specially Applied to English Practice*

Those who played and sold chances to win the jogo do bicho persistently defied the law, often openly. In taverns and street-corner kiosks as well as in jail cells and courtrooms, one can witness the daily actions that gave shape and meaning to legal norms in Republican Rio de Janeiro. Later chapters will describe the relationships between buyers, sellers, communities, and agents of the state that formed around the jogo do bicho. This chapter puts aside momentarily the popular uses and apprehensions of the law to focus on the actions of state officials and the juridical context in which they operated.

As chapter 1 demonstrates, the state regulated the jogo do bicho in the first half century of its existence only insofar as it criminalized it; police, judges, jail wardens, and police recording clerks mediated the relationship between the government and jogo do bicho participants. The state, in other words, encountered the jogo do bicho primarily in the hundreds of arrests police made, in criminal cases judges heard, and in quotidian interactions between civil servants and criminal defendants in police stations and jails. These encounters cumulatively reveal how these actors parlayed legal doctrine into practice and, conversely, how daily reality tested and shaped abstract principles.

This chapter will first examine the legal doctrine jurists

called upon when passing laws and judging cases that led to the criminalization of the jogo do bicho. I then investigate how the operators of the criminal justice system acted or failed to act upon these laws. Although police did frequently arrest people accused of playing and running the clandestine lottery, judges ultimately acquitted most defendants, often on technicalities. The archival evidence, though scant, consistently shows that judges found fewer than one in ten defendants guilty in jogo do bicho cases that reached the judicial hearing stage.[1]

This analysis of the criminalization of the jogo do bicho hinges on its ambivalent, ineffectual criminalization, not just its illicit status. My study benefits from the work of social historians of the law who have pressed us to see beyond the "senseless and counterproductive" nature of laws that are routinely disobeyed with impunity.[2] Notably, E. P. Thompson and his Warwick School cohorts have argued that even routinely violated laws effectively protected property rights and strengthened the power of elites.[3] Echoing Douglas Hay's work, Paul Haagen finds that judicial discretion and restraint in acquitting subaltern defendants in eighteenth-century England actually increased "patterns of deference and dependence and greatly buttressed the authority of the country's ruling class."[4] Others have read persistent, wide gaps between code and practice as evidence of popular resistance or of vernacular understandings of the law that differ from the intentions of lawgivers and enforcers. Going beyond the truism that people break the law and that legal codes often represent unrealizable ideals, a wide range of scholars have used the paradox of the criminalization and persistence of popular practices as a key to unlock the hidden ways in which the law judges, and how it cements social inequalities and catalyzes social change. The observation that the Brazilian criminal justice system in the early First Republic failed to prosecute either vendors or players of the jogo do bicho and to adhere to its own rules of conduct—evidence of the proverbial gap between code and practice—is a starting point into an inquiry not just into why the law did not work, but into how we can understand its subterranean workings.

As an object of historical analysis, the disjuncture between what the law mandates and what people actually do has its pitfalls. The notion of a gap resides in a paradigmatic assumption that still underlies Western legal history tradition: the distinction between the law (authoritative, coercive, codified, and universal) and custom (organic, informal, particular), the former created by state legislation and the latter of popular provenance.[5]

But what if law and custom are not really so disparate after all? What if law is, in both form and function, an integral part of society, not something outside it? Some scholars have faulted so-called gap studies for having a simplistic, mechanistic view of legal codes, on the one hand, and of social realities, on the other, as separate phenomena and not recognizing how law and society constitute and interact with each other. In an essay published in the early 1980s, as the interdisciplinary law and society movement gained momentum, Austin Sarat criticizes the wave of gap studies in the United States. Coming out of a naïve, overreaching belief in the law's ability to enact positive change that emerged during a period of optimism in law-based social reform in the mid-1960s, scholarship that aims to understand why legal practice differs from legal codes falsely assumes that code and practice actually can be aligned. As Sarat argues, scholars need to let go of their faith in laws as "abstractly stated goals which could ever govern legal or social behavior," and even of the idea that there is any such thing as "law on the books," at least according to the traditional understanding of the law as a transparent, discrete entity from which society's divergences must be explained.[6]

The concept of legal pluralism and especially the various reformulations and refinements to which its exponents have subjected it over the last half century constitute a useful analytical touchstone in my inquiry into the ambivalent illegality of the jogo do bicho. As a subfield of sociolegal scholarship, legal pluralism describes the existence of multiple legal systems simultaneously functioning in the "same social field."[7] The concept gained currency in the 1960s and 1970s, principally to study the multiple, overlapping sets of laws in places under European colonial rule and the disjunctures between state and nonstate and colonial and indigenous legal forms and cultures in these settings. Scholars have since broadened the scope beyond colonial and postcolonial societies to examine any relationship between dominant and subordinate groups, noting that, despite their universalist aspirations, all official legal systems are met with varying degrees of compliance and compete with subaltern or dissenting views of the law.[8]

Classical legal pluralism tended to treat custom as unchanging in a manner that effectively extended the essentializing logic of nineteenth-century colonialism. Seeking to rectify this problematic conception of popular custom, the new legal pluralism of the 1980s pushed past the more static analytical categories of earlier decades, seeing the law and society not as discrete entities that act upon each other but as a complex, dialectical relationship between "official and unofficial forms of ordering." New legal pluralism's contribution was to move away from the restrictive "law-centeredness" of previous scholarship on legal pluralism, showing that "not all law takes place in the courts."[9]

But the new scholarship often misses the fact that legal pluralism does indeed take place in the courts as well. Whether positing parallel systems of law or dialectically engaged ones, the key opposition between formal and informal codes of conduct typically corresponds with a distinction between state and nonstate actors; the vast body of work on legal pluralism has largely failed to account for extralegality and irregular justice from within the ranks of officialdom.[10] Like the "new legal pluralism" scholarship of the 1980s and beyond, my examination of the criminalization of the jogo do bicho questions typologies of legal practice that place the law and custom in discrete categories. By including state actors in the realm of the informal and unofficial, I wish to take the critiques of the previously taken-for-granted analytic separateness of law and custom a step further. Popular legal practice, or "custom," refers not just to the improvisational habits of the subaltern masses. It also encompasses the practices of the operators of the legal system simultaneously working in their capacity as human beings, even in the course of their duties as state officials.

The gap between code and practice one can observe in the illicit but ubiquitous animal game indeed derived in part from popular resistance to laws widely perceived as unjust or inconvenient and from popular uses of the law. But it also came from the law itself, broadly defined, which permitted the jogo do bicho to continue while subjecting its practitioners to harassment, arrest, and censure. As Esther Cohen argues in her analysis of the criminal prosecution of insects, pigs, and other animals accused of transgressing human norms in the ecclesiastical and secular courts of medieval Europe, extralegality is evidence of a "continual interaction between popular and learned elements in the sphere of legal practice." In observing these animal trials, legal proceedings that have no basis in the formal law, Cohen sees not divergence but "integration" between popular custom and official legal practice.[11] Similarly, in a study of the policing of Afro-Brazilian religion in twentieth-century Rio de Janeiro, Yvonne Maggie finds that the discrepancy between popular and official ideas about black magic was mitigated by judges' actual belief in sorcery.[12] The study of particular cases smashes the myth of "legal effectiveness" that Sarat criticizes by showing a fine-grained view of the myriad of interests and beliefs that converge in the act of applying the pliable abstractions of legal codes.

To see beyond the truism that people tend to defy unpopular, unevenly enforced laws, then, calls for a reconstruction of "the law as practiced" within its specific historical context.[13] Brazil's past offers rich fodder for those wising to delineate the development of modern extralegality. Historians have demonstrated a long tradition of legal pluralism in Latin America and traced the genealogy of the Brazilian penchant for circumventing laws to medieval Portugal and colonial Brazil. The succession of legal regimes in Iberia left Portugal with a legacy of a notable lack of a universalist legal system; instead, a plurality of legal systems and inequality before the law were the rule. Like Spanish American colonists who uttered, "*Obedesco pero no cumplo*" ("I obey but I do not comply"), Portuguese Americans invoked their duty to defy officials in the distant metropole who promulgated distasteful rules; inhabitants of colonial Brazil could thus run afoul of specific laws while still observing in principle the sanctity of royal authority. Episodes of large-scale lawbreaking in Brazilian history, such as the illicit importation of African slaves in the mid-nineteenth century and the granting of de facto divorces prior to its legalization in 1977, suggest a tradition not just of legal pluralism but also of systematic, overt, and outright defiance of the law.[14] Compelling as such apparent continuities are, however, to generalize about Ibero-American legal culture over the long duration is to lose the specificity of historical causality. How can one relate the illicit trading of slaves in 1860 with the propensity to play the clandestine lottery in 1911 without resorting to sweeping assumptions about Brazil's legal and political culture and its supposed propensity for lawlessness and disorder? Equally important, in understanding episodes of lawlessness as evidence of a perennial disjuncture between legal codes and real life, we lose the ability to see how law and society act on and constitute each other.

The jogo do bicho emerged at a time of fundamental change in legal codes and practices, and it is in this late nineteenth-century moment that one must contextualize the brand of extralegality epitomized by Brazil's clandestine lottery. Throughout Latin America the ascent of postcolonial liberalism in the nineteenth century had made the rule of law the crucial test of a nation's modernity, justice, and viability. Nations faced the dual problem of upholding the rule of law while also imposing order, especially in the face of brewing separatist movements and perceived crime waves. In

Brazil, the factors that stimulated the increased concern with crime are well known: postabolition racial anxieties; the rise of the scientific criminology and legal medicine; the growth of cities; and the fear of social unrest owing to global agitation by workers and profound social inequality.

But the shift in legal history that most directly impacted the greatest number of persons is barely ever noticed: the ascendant importance of petty crime in policing and juridical practice.[15] At the turn of the twentieth century, official interest in petty infractions like vagrancy, begging, drunkenness, disorderliness, and gambling surged. Practices that had been illegal but tolerated as well as those that had previously been permitted fell under new criminal prohibitions. Their historical significance lies, first, in the simple fact that laws against misdemeanor offenses touched many more lives than those against felonies. Second, the powerful social effects of the rising juridical significance of misdemeanors derive from their designation as police crimes, to be dealt with primarily by the growing police bureaucracy and soldiery. Despite the difficulty in defining misdemeanors like illicit gambling and vagrancy because of their similarity to other, licit practices, the responsibility for determining whose actions lay outside the law fell on an increasingly wide assortment of criminal law workers, including not only judges but also police and bureaucrats who were now legally empowered to make judgments previously assigned only to magistrates. In Brazil as elsewhere in Latin America at this time, judges and police alike became "crucial mediators of convoluted law."[16]

Modern-day judicial discretion may have grown out of long-standing Luso-Brazilian legal traditions like patrimonialism and the *Lei da Boa Razão* (Law of Good Sense), an eighteenth-century Portuguese legal doctrine that, in effect, authorized judges to fill in lacunae in the codified law (*Ordinações*) by exercising "good human sense."[17] Yet it is far more useful to scrutinize the late nineteenth century and early twentieth, when changes in legal codes and criminal procedure throughout Latin America inserted a new level and type of ambiguity into the rule of law. In short, misdemeanor law in republican Brazil mouthed the words of republican morality while upholding discretionary power, both private and public.[18]

When one juxtaposes the increase in judges' and police officers' discretionary power with the other defining characteristic of Brazil's legal culture in this period, what might be labeled the legalization of Brazilian society, one comes to the crux of the historical importance of the persecution and persistence of the jogo do bicho. Latin American states consolidated their power in the nineteenth and early twentieth centuries, unleashing social changes. The sociological term legalization describes the process through which the state imposed itself increasingly on the lives of its subaltern subjects and the growing sociocultural importance of the legal bureaucracy in all citizens' lives.[19] New criminal procedures aimed to rationalize, nationalize, and modernize the system of criminal justice in order to create a more governable and productive society. The law formally came to order social relationships that had previously fallen within the private domain: regimes of rights, regulatory mechanisms, and the punishment and protection of people formerly under patriarchal jurisdiction, such as slaves, children, and wives. Yet a countervailing, perhaps compensatory, regulatory regime—the realm of custom, values, or substance rather than formalities—likewise swelled in importance.[20] Thus, ironically, legalization failed to produce rigorous adherence to rules and in fact generated legal informality.

Many of the actors involved in enforcing the legal prohibition against the jogo do bicho exhibited the formalism that observers frequently associate with Latin American legal culture. In other words, state officials generally appear to have held the rule of law in high esteem, at least in that they valued the appearance of adherening to just rules.[21] The state perceived a need to dignify its intended actions with laws, even though the pervasive knowledge of the impunity of state actors (like police) partially neutralized this principled adherence to due process.[22] As we will see, when police interacted with accused players and dealers in the clandestine lottery they sometimes acted in violation of the law. For their part, judges in such cases appear to have rigorously adhered to the letter of law, if not always its spirit. The legal treatment of the jogo do bicho occupies a sociological boundary between legalism and extralegality, and it is here that we can study the origins of the criminalization of everyday life.

THE LAW'S EDIFICE: MANSIONS AND SHANTIES

La doctrine du mur de la vie privée a été définitevement édifiée en ce siècle. La loi a envisagé le jeu seulement comme un péril social. (The doctrine of the wall [that surrounds] private life was constructed definitively in this century. The law has envisioned gambling only as a social peril.)

—Cited by the judge and law professor Francisco Viveiros de Castro in an opinion on gambling, 1900, Jurisprudencia Criminal

Droit positif est science du peuple. (Positive law is the science of the people.)

—Cited in an opinion written by Judge Alfredo de Almeida Russell of Rio de Janeiro, 1909

The two judges quoted above not only demonstrate their erudition but also, upon closer inspection, reveal some arresting contradictions in Brazilian law as the country entered the twentieth century.[23] Reflecting on the mixed message these two opinions convey offers some insight into the gulf between what the law dictated and how it functioned in practice in republican Brazil. As the first quotation avers, by the middle of the nineteenth century Brazilian law had come to embrace the principle of the inviolability of the private space of one's home.[24] An invisible, juridical wall separated the house and the street. Those infractions against public morality that occurred inside the sacred space of the private home did not threaten the common good as long as the house was not public, that is, as long as it was not used as a gambling den or a house of prostitution, a public house, in the parlance of the day.[25] Gambling, as the judge affirms, was a "social peril" only when it occurred in public. Viveiros de Castro, an eminent judge and law professor, differentiates licit from illicit gambling based solely upon this private–public divide. The distinction between private and public spaces was one of the principles Brazilian jurists had at their disposal when they considered when, whether, and how much to repress gambling. The recognition of these distinct domains gave agents of the law a means of applying agreed-upon, time-honored principles to the issues of public order and social policy that the question of gambling raised.[26]

The juridical basis for the division between public and private realms derived from liberal principles that arose in reaction to authoritarian rule in the ancien régime in Europe and from the perpetuation of patriarchy under the law. The home was, in effect, its own jurisdiction.[27] Being in one's home did not confer complete immunity to state power, yet crossing the threshold from street to house attenuated the state's power to arrest, incarcerate, or gather incriminating evidence. In some cases, the principle of the home as sanctuary neutralized completely the state's authority. For example, the law generally recognized the jurisdiction of the father of the family (*patria potestad*, or literally, the power of the father).[28]

The legal designation of the private domain as a sanctuary from the authoritarian state coexisted with a contradictory trend: the expanding role of the state in policing and regulating private space.[29] Something private like the health of one's body or the insides of poor peoples' homes became a public concern despite the stark separation between private and public domains in political and legal theory. As Sarah C. Chambers demonstrates for early republican Peru, in practice the "legal boundary between private and public" was ambiguous and subject to negotiation when other matters such as honor were at stake.[30] Likewise, the Brazilian state in the late Empire and early First Republic established its authority to enter supposedly inviolable private space as epidemic disease claimed thousands of lives and threatened the stability and economic viability of the nation's rapidly growing cities. Health became public because of germ and miasma theory, but also because of social theory and displaced class and racial fears expressed symbolically.[31] Far more than generically disparaging remarks, the disease metaphors officials and reformers routinely used to refer to the jogo do bicho in the late nineteenth and early twentieth centuries bore a multiplicity of meanings that alluded to the forcing of formerly private concerns into the public realm.

Even before the First Republic, the difference between legal and illegal gambling hinged on the distinction between private and public, a distinction even then difficult to apply because of the apparent moral ambivalence about the act of playing for money. The nineteenth-century Brazilian state itself operated games of chance and allowed private lotteries and other types of gambling. In the 1830s in Rio both the law and public consciousness already associated gambling with vice and economic and moral incontinence.[32] Lotteries began to proliferate in the 1840s.[33] Foreshadowing the trajectory of the jogo do bicho from legal raffle to clandestine practice to criminal syndicate, side-betting on these legal, government-contracted lotteries occurred by the 1840s and attracted the scornful eye of the authorities.[34] Throughout the century the state prosecuted and levied fines on individuals charged with operating unofficial lotteries and raffles or with allowing gambling in their taverns or running gambling dens devoted to cards, billiards, dice, or other games for money.[35] The imperial government sought to control all forms of gaming that took place in the public realm, but despite occasional letters of complaint and plenty of laws on the books it policed gaming with a soft touch.[36]

Two criteria differentiated licit from illicit gambling during this period. First, games were permitted in private homes whether or not players wagered money. As soon as one admitted a random public, the space became a *casa de tavolagem* (a gambling house) and the owner was subject to a punitive fine. As for the second criterion, the law permitted private individuals and companies to establish games in the city's public spaces, but only as long as winning those games did not depend solely on chance. In sum, the acquisition of money by sheer luck fell outside the limits of what was legally permissible in public spaces. The state designated a category of *jogos prohibidos* but equivocated on what fell within it, as horse racing and public lotteries occurred not only with impunity but indeed with the overt zeal of the city's elite.

The juridical application of the private–public divide to petty crimes like gambling reveals the unspoken and often unanticipated side effects of legal principles as they became daily practice in the capital. When one considers the doctrine separating private from public gambling alongside the reality of public life in urban Brazil at the beginning of the twentieth century, the differential legal treatment of behaviors carried out in the two spheres bears profound historical meaning. For the vast majority of Cariocas, the inviolability of the home was almost a moot point. Extrajudicial arrests occurred frequently within homes, especially those of poorer members of the urban population. Prone to breaking down doors to arrest people for misdemeanors like dealing the jogo do bicho, Rio's police defied the principle of the inviolability of the private domicile.[37]

This legal principle was of limited relevance to the lives of the capital's poor and working-class majority in the early 1900s because of irregularities in police procedure and also because the social lives of most residents occurred not behind closed doors but on the city streets. The public domain was, perforce, the space of sociability for former slaves, southern European immigrants, rural migrants, and the nascent working class. The shortage of affordable housing for the working classes in all Brazilian cities reached a crisis level around this time. The number of crowded collective residences, nicknamed *cortiços*, or beehives, for the cities' poorest horrified elite observers of the late Empire. By the end of the 1860s, the General Inspector of Hygiene in Rio estimated that the imperial capital had "642 cortiços, consisting of 9,671 rooms inhabited by 21,929 persons, of which 13,555 were men and 8,374 were women." About twenty years later, the number of cortiços had risen to 1,331, "with 18,966 rooms inhabited by 46,680 persons."[38] Historians like Sandra Lauderdale Graham, who points out that 343 residents of one tenement in Rio shared six latrines and one water tap, have demonstrated that in late nineteenth-century urbanizing Brazil the conditions under which the densely packed, impoverished population lived "precluded any ordinary standard of privacy."[39] Dwelling in such close quarters, tenants had little option of socializing in their homes.

The importance of public spaces as preferred sites of nonelite sociability also arose, in part, as a cultural legacy of three centuries of urban slavery. Making their daily rounds of the city as laundresses, water carriers, peddlers, and other day laborers, slaves found in public spaces a momentary escape from the constant surveillance of their masters and a measure of freedom of movement and association. By the 1890s, Brazil's popular classes had long established a livelihood for themselves in the city's public terrains.[40]

The tendency to honor the sacrosanct private space of one's home and permit such activities as gambling there but not in the public domain discriminated between socioeconomic classes in a manner that belied the law's avowed determination to treat all citizens equally. The activities in which poor Brazilians engaged became labeled as legally and morally transgressive; people who had the means to assemble behind a juridical "wall" of private life carried on the same activities with impunity. Gambling took on dramatically divergent meanings for poor Brazilians. While the city's wealthy and middling classes did play the jogo do bicho, they generally enjoyed de facto immunity from legal reprisals, both because police tended to arrest sellers rather than buyers and because of the class preferences built solidly into policing practice, particularly with respect to petty crimes. The principles that jurists, arresting officers, and other agents of the state had at their disposal to bring the written law to bear on the daily life of the city proved in many cases to be exceedingly blunt tools.

The legal treatment of the jogo do bicho was also marked by its appearance during the reign of legal positivism in Brazilian jurisprudence and criminal legal practice, a tendency in legal thought whose predominant feature was exactly its faith in the efficaciousness—and denial of the bluntness—of legal principles. Arising from the thought of the French philosopher Auguste Comte in the mid-nineteenth century, positivism was on the wane in Europe when it reached its apogee in Latin America, particularly in Mexico and Brazil, a half century later.[41] Gaining currency among Brazil's urban professional class, positivism became dominant in many of the country's law schools, colleges, and military academies by the early twentieth century.

Nineteenth-century Latin American positivism was especially influential in the area of criminology. As a strain of legal thought, Comte's positivism combined with the ideas of Italian penologists of the late nineteenth century and early twentieth, in particular Cesare Lombroso, Enrico Ferri, and

Raffaele Garofalo, and spread quickly to Latin America by way of published texts, intellectual circuits, international professional conferences, and the transatlantic travels of central figures of positivist criminology.

As elsewhere in the region, legal positivism as applied in Brazil was not a unified theory per se but a part of the country's eclectic approach to law. To the extent that positivism as manifested in Latin America was a philosophy at all, it was a philosophy of bureaucrats. In the extreme, contemporary revisionist historians have argued that positivism served simply as a form of social control rather than a set of ideas: a "science of the people" only in that it enabled the state systematically and efficiently to control the populace in the face of mounting class tensions.[42] The positivist approach was characterized by its categorizing tendency, by which bureaucrats and scientists would study problems and conquer them. Exactly because of its claims to scientific method, arrived at by using its typical biologically deterministic logic, positivist criminology naturalized the juridical division between public and private on the basis of differences between men and women and, more broadly, on the state's strategies for separating people into categories.[43]

The so-called positive school of criminology sought the etiology of crime through scientific means—in other words, through observable phenomena and repeatable methods. Both innate tendencies and social environmental factors like the negative influence of one's peers or a pathological family life were seen as causes of crime. Positivist criminologists emphasized the biological basis of criminality but did not hold uniform beliefs about the precise way in which one's body bore its criminal tendencies; some held that criminality and deviancy were born in a person's bloodstream, nerve impulses, or endocrine system. For positivists, however, moral fortitude could restrain even born criminals from engaging in socially dangerous acts.[44]

The positivist school of criminology sought not just to explain what caused crime but also to cure it, always with an emphasis on the individuality of each criminal subject. Its members endeavored, first, to figure out how to solve the problem of crime, using anthropometric measurements as evidence of criminal culpability. Second, they sought to punish and correct criminals appropriately according to each of their individual endowments. Third, positivist criminology turned on its distinction between occasional criminals, who could be cured, and inborn criminals, who could not. Separating occasional criminals and "criminaloids" from innate criminals thus became necessary to curb the spread of the criminal disease by making sure that the latter would not "infect" the former.

By the early twentieth century, Brazilian law had become infused with positivist legal philosophy. Legal positivism sought to cure Brazil's social ills through methodical study and the promulgation of legislation and legal procedures tailored to local reality. Positivist jurisprudence was a reaction against the prevailing trend in penology that preceded it, which jurists such as Viveiros de Castro criticized for its idealistic belief in the essential equality of all individuals.[45]

With the concept of "humanity" deriving from Compte's writings, Brazil's positivist ideologues linked the nation's progress with the incorporation of its diverse people.[46] A body of statutes, legal codes, judicial opinions, and scholarly publications of the First Republic took scientific aim against Brazil's social problems by targeting the *peuple*, or, in Portuguese, the *povo*, a politically loaded construct that suggested both a paternalistic desire to help the less fortunate and a fear of the reputedly dangerous crowd. Positivist criminology in Brazil was characterized by its activist stance toward social problems. These jurists and practitioners of legal medicine (so-called *legistas*) were much more than just bureaucrats applying the law. These "doctor-social scientists" brought about dramatic changes in the law and its application, in such diverse areas as how courts determined paternity and the imposition of civil identity cards.[47]

Adherents to this new social science sought to ameliorate living conditions for the poor and working-class majority and incorporate these groups into the national polity, but they did so within a broader structure that Brazil had inherited from the monarchical, slave-owning society the nation had only just left behind. The primary instrument of the social reformers was the law; indeed, in the early years of the First Republic there barely existed an urban social reform movement outside the legal and legal–medical professions. But in republican Brazil criminal law bore a prodigious historical burden. Between the new directives of positivist thought and the older, class-bound functions the law already filled, agents of the law confronted a paradox: their mission was to change society using a set of tools created to maintain the status quo.[48]

In effect, this paradox enhanced the local discretionary power of those charged with giving shape and meaning to criminal law in practice: police and judges. Judge Russell's reference to the popular concerns of positivist legal philosophy comes from a case that illustrates these discretionary powers and suggests their significance at the core of the justice system's interactions with the povo—indeed the state's primary communication with the majority of Brazilians.

Russell made his statement that "Positive law is the science of the people" in a judicial opinion in a case from 1909 brought before a criminal trial court in the Federal District. A young boy, "a minor of humble social condition," had been charged with vagrancy. Although the judge could have fined the boy and sentenced him to prison or to a term in the island penal colony Dois Rios, he chose leniency. Echoing the tenets of positivist penology, Russell described the boy as a product of his environment and not yet incorrigible. The judge acquitted the accused, recommending that only if the boy were to be arrested again, "exuberantly demonstrating his incorrigibility and vicious tendencies," would he be made to suffer "penal repression."[49] The science of the people in this case amounted to the judge's discretionary application of the law based upon his impressionistic belief that the boy could be redeemed from a life of crime and indeed that his actions fit the vague description of criminal vagrancy. Conversely, the boy's future recidivism could transform his profile from that of an occasional criminal to an innate one, subjecting him to hard labor and penal exile.

In sum, these two interlocking strains of doctrine—the jurisdictional distinction between public and private space and faith in the scientific ordering of social deviancy at the heart of positivist criminology—influenced how the police and the courts understood so-called vice crimes like the jogo do bicho. In the private domain, the state lost its authority, but only over certain things; citizens who committed felonies could not expect to find refuge from the law in their domiciles.[50] It was in misdemeanor cases that the private–public distinction became meaningful. Laws against such petty infractions as gambling took special aim at public life and left the world behind the walls of private life to its own devices.

Positivism in criminology, which coincided with the rise of jogo do bicho, created a moveable standard for criminality that opened up a new frontier for the discretionary application of laws against petty crime. Thinkers and officials influenced by positivism created the expectation that the law would solve social ills by studying them and that doing so created a sharply defined classificatory scheme that had the luster of scientific reasoning. This scheme involved separating types of lawbreakers and in particular segregating petty from hardened criminals. But positivist thought lacked any solid analytical space for vice crime. Positivists disavowed any moral considerations behind the identification of lawbreakers and the official sanction the state should bring against them, even for criminal categories derived from behavior labeled as sins under ecclesiastical law. The indeterminacy of criminal behavior was thus institutionalized alongside a scientific approach to social defense through the criminal law.

THE PENAL CODE OF 1890 AND THE
MEANING OF MISDEMEANOR

The Penal Code that enumerated the new Republic's criminal laws left nothing to chance. The national code had become the sine qua non of the civil law tradition that characterized all of Latin America, which felt the reverberations of the nineteenth-century transatlantic trend toward the codification of national legal traditions. The fundamental principle of the civil law tradition was that the law had to anticipate any future legal need, accommodate any possible scenario, embody society's rules, and "exalt certainty as a supreme value."[51] The jurist and statesman Rui Barbosa writes critically of the exaggerated, unrealistic expectations of the salutary effects of codification. A code, he mockingly explains, is a "miraculous talisman" designed to "exterminate uncertainties, to fix the law, to turn jurisprudence automatic," to create the "mechanical infallibility of the application of the law"—all "a futile dream." Barbosa's essay is ultimately an injunction to work toward perfection in authoring a legal code, which must be logical, precise, clear, and above all must epitomize the "conscience of its time."[52] It was understood that legal codes would have gaps. In place of the common law tradition's doctrine of *stare decisis*, which entrusts judges to fill in lacunae in the law as written through the precedent-setting decisions, civil law trusts the completeness of the law itself and the relatively mechanistic clarification and exegesis of the written law in published jurisprudential writing.[53]

Although Brazil had failed to pass a civil code until almost a century after the other Latin American republics, its Criminal Code (1830), in force during the Empire, was widely considered a model of modern juridical thought; it had served Brazil as a source of national pride, stability, and centrality of rule.[54] After the provisional government of what would become the First Republic replaced the toppled monarchy in November 1889, the new regime began discussions on the founding documents of the new regime.[55] Lawyers and jurists elaborated a new Penal Code, which passed quickly into law the following year.[56]

The jogo do bicho had not yet been invented when the Penal Code was promulgated, but this infraction would enter criminal law as the national legislature passed statutes that refined and added to the code throughout the First Republic.[57] The new game seems to have fit as easily into the Penal Code, as if Brazil's jurisconsults had anticipated its invention.[58]

But the Penal Code was far from progressive. It was "born old," to borrow one commentator's phrase, not only because it was meant to embody liberal ideas already in place in the Criminal Code of 1830, but also because it adhered primarily to classical penology, already long superceded by positivist thought in most of the world by the mid-nineteenth century.[59] Two contradictory currents of thought competed for prevalence in the First Republic. The first and older of these, classical law, sprung directly from European Enlightenment thought and sought to uphold the dignity of the individual vis-à-vis the state by way of the social contract. Adherents to the classical school held that an individual's behavior was the product of free choice, and the criminal, therefore, must be held accountable for having chosen such behavior and be punished accordingly. The counter-current from the positivist school, by contrast, envisioned criminal culpability from a radically different perspective. As we have seen, positivist penology attributed individual action not to free choice but to psychology, biology, and environment.[60] The transition from classical to positivist criminology did not take place in a consistent or clear manner.[61] The Penal Code's position between these two famously warring schools nonetheless had an impact on both its reception and its application. Criticism of the code and intermittent calls to change it characterized the fifty years it was in effect.[62] Through new legislation and various projects to reform it, the Penal Code as a body of criminal law gravitated toward the positivist thought that then prevailed among Brazilian jurists. The controversy surrounding it and its uncertain, shifting ideological position rendered the eclectic code a pliant tool in the hands of those empowered to apply its provisions.

The Penal Code reflected the acute official concern about petty crime that marked the transition from Empire to Republic.[63] Just months after the fall of the Empire, the executive and judicial branches of the new republican government discussed "the division of infractions of the Penal

Law into crimes and misdemeanors" in both juridical theory and policing practice. Republican lawyers and lawmakers criticized the outgoing Imperial justice system's manner of repressing activities believed to threaten public morality and order, notably idleness, vagabondage and vagrancy, begging, drunkenness, disorderly behavior, games of chance, and the martial art called *capoeira*. To the new republican government, the Empire's laxity regarding such affronts to public "morality and good custom" manifested the decadence of an outdated monarchical regime.[64]

Unlike the Criminal Code that preceded it, the Penal Code codified these nascent concerns by including a subset of offenses labeled *contravenções*, a term that roughly translates into English as misdemeanors.[65] The Empire's Criminal Code contained neither the term *contravenção* nor a particular section dedicated to petty crimes, yet the concept loosely existed in the definition of certain infractions and the judicial procedures mandated for prosecuting them. For example, the Criminal Code recognized a category of vice crimes for which only the consummated act, as opposed to an attempted crime, was punishable, a rule the later definition of contravenção reaffirmed.[66] Several of the misdemeanor infractions in the Penal Code had been prohibited under the previous code, while others had been informally persecuted but not officially labeled as criminal infractions.[67] The introduction of the label contravenção in the late nineteenth century did not constitute a momentous turning point in Brazilian legal history. Yet this juridical category had a powerful effect on criminal jurisprudence and policing practice; it came into regular use as a tool to categorize types of behavior—like gambling, prostitution, itinerant vending without a license, and public loitering—that many viewed as unhealthy to society, but whose fuzzy definitions gave extraordinary power to those charged with carrying out the law in everyday practice.[68]

In fact, legislators and jurists never completely agreed on including contravenções in a national penal code. In the words of one jurist, "There is no lack of people who argue that police crimes, transgressions committed by police, and contravenções should not be part of a penal code." Ultimately, the jurist argues, a federal system had no choice but to include contravenções in the Penal Code in the interest of legal uniformity on the national scale. Equally important, the modern nations on which the Brazilian system was being modeled had all decided to include misdemeanor offenses in their codes.[69] The issue of whether it was appropriate to name these petty crimes in the nation's Penal Code, rather than in municipal statutes, was never resolved; the preface to one published edition of the Penal Code of 1940 that superceded this one still questioned their inclusion.[70]

The full weight of the Brazilian judicial system came down on these types of offenses only in the decades immediately after the passing of the Penal Code of 1890. This code and related legislation classified begging, drunkenness, vagrancy, and *capoeiragem* as misdemeanors, subject to a prison sentence (*prisão celular*) or a fine or both. These laws enshrined the doctrine of free will, which held that criminals had turned away from a life of morality and good custom and opted for one of idleness. Children and adults, men and women alike could be criminally responsible for their lack of a "means of subsistence" if the judge decided they had adopted this lifestyle by choice rather than, for example, if they had suffered an injury or illness and were unable to work. In 1899, the so-called Alfredo Pinto Law, a landmark in the government's war against vagrancy, intensified the code's punitive treatment of *contraventores* and gave police district chiefs (*delegados*) considerable power over the judgment and punishment of perpetrators of misdemeanors.[71] *Termos de Bem Viver* (Writs of Good Living) came into regular use to contend with "idlers who live on begging, gambling, theft, and all types of wicked acts"; the judge could compel those found guilty of these offenses to sign this writ, which constituted a promise to acquire a proper occupation. Recidivist capoeiras and vagrants who had signed and then broken their Termos de Bem Viver received exceedingly harsh sentences of one to three years in penal colonies, located either on islands or deep in the forests of Brazil's western interior.[72]

The emerging standards for the legal treatment of petty crime did not go unquestioned. A criminal judge interested in the "problem of the repression of vagrancy," for example, labeled the correctional system deficient, ineffective, and arbitrary.[73] Some thinkers criticized the criminalization of unemployment, especially in the aftermath of slavery.[74] The contested and inherently imprecise definitions of misdemeanor infractions invited improvisation and inconsistency at every turn.

The inclusion of the jogo do bicho among the misdemeanors in the Penal Code was by no means inevitable.[75] In reconstructing how legislators and jurists came to include articles that referred specifically to gambling among the misdemeanor offenses listed in the code, doctrine provides little help. Juridical scholarship in republican Brazil barely touched on the subject of the clandestine lottery or even gambling in general, making only indirect reference to the animal game. Positivist explanations of the game trickled out in a series of legal tracts, theses, and published opinions during the First Republic. These generally presumed it to be a pathology that called for diagnosis and blamed the pathology on the natural susceptibility to vice of certain classes.[76] But the criminalization of all types of gambling not specifically licensed as legal did not follow naturally from doctrine. Proponents of positivism, with their avowed interest in recognizing the specificity of local conditions, might well have recognized petty gambling as an innocuous part of Carioca urban folk life, just as foreign travelers to Rio did in their writings.[77] In addition to a vague blanket commitment to cracking down on public disorder, the sweeping scope and exigency for foresight of the national penal code likely prompted its authors to err on the side of including articles that might never be invoked rather than omitting those that might need to be. The jogo do bicho counted among the contravenções in the Penal Code not because of any decisive predisposition against games of chance but because of the preemptory existence of several antigambling articles.

The first Cariocas to be arrested for participation in the jogo do bicho were charged under the Penal Code's generic article (no. 367), "contravenção–jogo do bicho," forbidding games of chance: "On Lotteries and Raffles: Engaging in lotteries or raffles of any kind that are not authorized by law, even if they run in conjunction with any other lottery [will incur the following penalties]: the loss to the nation of any goods and any money earned; a fine of 200$000 to 500$000" (200 to 500 milreis).[78] The federal legislature soon passed statutes that raised the stakes, adding new infractions that specified the jogo do bicho and tying involvement in it to other offenses, especially that of involving a minor in gambling and vagrancy.[79] On October 24, 1895, a new law imposed "a fine of 200$000 for commercial establishments that violate the terms of the license by running prohibited games." In 1899 legislation established penalties for violating article 367.[80] Law (*Decreto*) 2321 of 1910, the law most frequently invoked against persons involved in the jogo do bicho in the early twentieth century, was in fact a budgetary law, but it included provisions for controlling illegal lotteries buried in its thirty-first article. Each successive law increased the fine and prison sentence, reflecting the federal legislature's growing awareness of the jogo do bicho and intensifying attempts to dissuade citizens from engaging in unlicensed games that "promise a prize" and "depend on luck."[81]

The mere existence of this succession of anti–jogo do bicho laws reveals that the leadership in the early First Republic had developed a stake in the

TABLE 4 Articles in Brazilian Penal Code (1890) that Pertain to Gambling

NUMBER	INFRACTION (IN ORIGINAL PORTUGUESE)	INFRACTION (TRANSLATED INTO ENGLISH)
367	Contravenção-Jogo do Bicho	Misdemeanor-Jogo do Bicho
368	Contravenção-Loteria Estrangeira	Misdemeanor-Foreign Lottery
369	Contravenção-Jogo de Azar em Casa de Tavolagem	Misdemeanor-Game of Chance in Gambling House
370	Contravenção-Jogo de Azar	Misdemeanor-Game of Chance
371	Contravenção-Jogo: Menor de 21 anos	Misdemeanor-Gambling: Minor of less than 21 years of age
372	Contravenção-Jogo: Uso de Violência	Misdemeanor-Gambling: Use of Violence
373	Contravenção-Jogo: Uso de Fraude	Misdemeanor-Gambling: Use of Fraud
374	Contravenção-Jogo: Equiparação do Jogador com o Vadio	Misdemeanor-Gambling: Association of Gambler with Vagrant

suppression of popular practices like the jogo do bicho, even if the police had not developed a means of actually repressing it.[82] The laws gave the state reserve weapons to be used against an increasingly popular activity that some deemed threatening to the public good. However, unlike much legislation that lies unused in law books, article 367 was often invoked by police, judges, and other public officials.[83] At least as early as 1895 police were already arresting people for involvement in the jogo do bicho on the basis of these laws (table 4).[84]

Antigambling legislation referred to a practice whose very existence was difficult to define and document, though, and these laws did not have the effect that their authors had intended. Ultimately, the police had to compensate for the vagueness of the law with respect to petty crimes.[85] The most frequently cited contravenções, vagrancy, begging, and gambling, all described acts that were legal under other, qualitatively indistinguishable circumstances. Despite a half-century-long trend in professionalizing the policing of Rio, in the early First Republic policemen possessed increasing power to set policy and administer justice on the streets.[86] Although lacking any juridical or moral consensus about the illegality of these acts, a carceral regime developed to accommodate the mounting concern in some quarters with petty crime and the resulting repression by police of previously tolerated practices. This regime included imprisonment and work in agricultural penitentiaries and military presidios for "idlers and vagabonds who were incorrigible by ordinary means." New penal colonies, including the infamous Dois Rios Correctional Colony, sprung up to hold contraventores.[87] The entry logs of the Casa de Detenção, Rio's central detention center in the 1890s, demonstrate a striking increase in the number of people arrested for vagrancy and gambling.[88]

CRIMINAL JUSTICE, URBAN POLICING, AND THE FAILURE TO PROSECUTE

Although police and judicial authorities frequently called upon the anti–jogo do bicho laws passed to extend the reach of article 367, few of those arrested and processed through the judicial system on these charges were ever found guilty.[89] Examining how judges and police each exercised their discretionary power reveals a fuller picture of the jogo do bicho's simultaneous criminalization and impunity.

The rules of judicial procedure required each judge to explain the basis for his opinion in his written sentence, and at the end of each year to bind these collected opinions in a volume for posterity. The bound volumes of manuscript sentencing records, some of which survive in the National Archive, offer some insight into why the jogo do bicho endured despite the growing number of arrests for this infraction throughout the First Republic. Judge Russell's vagrancy case of 1909 notwithstanding, judges did not typically favor historians by including in the written record a lengthy discourse on penal philosophy to reveal how they themselves framed and justified their sentences. Yet one can surmise from judges' sentencing records, examined alongside other evidence, that the unusually large proportion of jogo do bicho cases that judges acquitted in the early decades of the First Republic signifies not a failure of the judicial system but the tendency of its agents to consider in detail the lives of the city's popular classes.

Minor crime cases particularly invited the exercise of discretionary judicial power, not just because of the ambiguity of the laws and doctrines to be applied, but also for professional reasons. Jogo do bicho cases tended to terminate in the trial courts rather than advance to the appellate level. Moreover, these cases generally attracted less scholarly juridical attention than other types of criminality. In the outcome of a misdemeanor trial, the stakes were relatively low in terms of publicity, judicial career building, and the contribution of the case to criminal jurisprudence.[90]

Judges' apparently rigorous adherence to procedural rules governing the production of evidence and witnesses in jogo do bicho cases as well as their exercise of discretion created certain discernible patterns. In all cases found in the archive that ended in acquittal, as the vast majority did, judges based their opinions on similar technicalities. Most judges asserted that witnesses' testimony did not suffice to prove that the activity in which the defendant had been engaged did indeed constitute a game of chance.

The sentencing records alone do not reveal just what types of evidence each magistrate actually had before him.[91] In rare instances, however, other traces of the defendants' voyage through the criminal justice system survived in the archive. In these cases, one can cross-reference the judicial sentences with the defendants' police file (*processos*), each of which contains transcripts of eyewitness testimony and often descriptions or actual samples of the jogo do bicho lists the judges saw.[92] Seeing such evidence of defendants' apparent guilt makes judges' overwhelming tendency to acquit all the more revealing. There is a striking contrast between the preponderance of individuals acquitted for playing the jogo do bicho, an infraction that presented at least the possibility of evidence (the handwritten lists), versus, for example, the relatively low proportion of individuals acquitted for vagrancy, an infraction for which the only concrete evidence was the arresting officer's testimony and the judge's impressions of the intentions and promise of the accused. This discrepancy suggests it was not a simple lack of concrete incriminating evidence that led to jogo do bicho defendants' acquittals. Rather, judges exercised discretion in a distinctively different spirit for vagrancy, on the one hand, and petty gambling offenses, on the other: in the case of vagrancy, it was used to condemn, whereas in the case of petty gambling the rigorous application of procedural rules had the (perhaps intended) effect of absolving the defendant of the supposed infraction.

Analysis of the failure of judges to prosecute misdemeanor infractions, especially the jogo do bicho, must take place along the fault lines between policing and judicial power, a rift expressed primarily in the police's contested authority to make arrests and to detain criminal suspects. A sweeping restructuring of the police took place in the First Republic, especially as the result of a law passed in March of 1907. The first professional policing school, Escola da Polícia do Rio de Janeiro, was created in 1912. The goal was to transform Rio's police officers into modern, competent professionals and to train them in the provisions of the Penal Code and criminal laws they were newly empowered to apply.[93] Even with their new, more professional profile, Rio's police experienced a tense moment in the early First Republic as they engaged in a struggle with the other, rival institutions also endowed with coercive disciplinary force. As Marcos Bretas aptly points out, Rio's "unprotected marginal classes" suffered the collateral damage as both military and civilian police, the army and navy, the national guard, and the private security force called the Guarda Noturna (Nocturnal Guard) battled for preeminence in the city streets by exercising their ability to arrest and repress. An increase in the quantity, although not the quality, of police patrolling the streets heightened the tension between police and the judiciary and created a potentially explosive disequilibrium of de facto power.[94] Courtroom sentencing, writs of habeas corpus, internal investigations, and circulation of administrative orders against illegal arrests and detentions gave the judiciary the last word on the legality of police action taken on the streets.[95] Yet the authority of the police to arrest in many ways exceeded the magistrate's authority to acquit. From the citizen's perspective, being acquitted often mattered little: one was still left with the stigma of arrest, and the time spent away from work and loved ones was irretrievably lost.[96]

The extralegality embedded in policing practice must be seen in the context of the special position police had in urban Brazilian society in the late nineteenth century and early twentieth. As both members of communities and arbiters of justice, police held far-reaching power because of their ubiquity and authority and because of the unique knowledge of local events, people, and social networks in the communities where they worked. The police station was the first place urban dwellers would call when they needed medical assistance. When citizens required a letter to gain admission to a public hospital, they went to the police.[97] The frequent arrests of beggars and the homeless illustrate vividly the ambiguity of the role of police in treating the city's poor. Municipal regulations and the Penal Code alike criminalized begging in the urban areas of the Federal District, unless the beggar was judged physically unable to work. The job of distinguishing between valid and invalid begging fell to the patrolman, who determined whether to send the accused to the asylum for the indigent (Asilo São Francisco) or to the precinct for criminal processing.

Police officers tended to act outside their official mandate in what appears to have simultaneously constituted efforts at social control and social welfare.[98] As the historians Pablo Piccato and Mark Overmyer-Velázquez have documented for Mexico's cities in the same era, during this epoch of incipient professionalization, high expectations, and increased de facto and de jure power, Rio's police proved loyal to neither the state nor the city's popular classes from which they almost invariably came.[99]

One common extralegal practice among agents of law enforcement in dealing with misdemeanors was their tendency to characterize suspects not on the basis of the suspects' actions, but on the basis of their values, predilections, and identities. For example, the reason for arrest often cited in the entry logs of Rio's city jail is "for being a habitual pickpocket," not for picking someone's pocket, or for "being a known *bicheiro*" rather than for selling tickets to the jogo do bicho. The examples in the judicial archive are legion. For instance, an Italian-born, twenty-seven-year-old postal worker was arrested "for being a gambler" near his home in the city center in June of 1894.[100] Although contrary to procedural and criminal codes of the day, arrests on the basis of one's reputation and not one's actions were an ingrained and common practice.[101]

A case in 1899 against Manoel Joaquim Barata, who worked in petty commerce, demonstrates the subtle but powerful effects of the wide latitude of police in making arrests and influencing prosecution and the commonplace extralegality built into policing practice. Barata was arrested "em flagrante" on the afternoon of December 9, 1898, leaving a tavern, where he was accused of taking orders for the jogo do bicho. The three witnesses who testified were not citizens but police officers whom the arresting officers and delegado had called upon to fulfill the legal requirement for eyewitness testimony. Although legally questionable and a frequent cause of complaint among defendants, the use of active-duty police officers as witnesses was a common practice, appearing in virtually all jogo do bicho cases. The borderline legality of the procedures in this highly representative case is revealed not only in who served as witnesses, but also in the content of their testimony. Significantly, one of the witnesses stated that the accused was a "known bicheiro." Barata signed the document indicating he understood the charges (*nota de culpa*) with an "X," an indication that the accused could not write his name, and he was sent to the Casa de Detenção on December 10, 1898. Two shopkeepers posted bail on Barata's behalf, and he left the detention center the next day. After examining the case, the judge ruled that the law required two additional witnesses to testify. The delegado indicated the two on December 27, and both of them, once again, were police officers. On January 13, 1899, Barata was found guilty and sentenced to two months in prison and fined 350 milreis. He appealed but lost and was returned to the Casa de Detenção on April 29, 1899.[102]

Police on occasion crossed the line between failure to adhere to rules of criminal procedure and explicitly illegal behavior for personal gain. From the early 1890s on, law enforcement workers utilized their knowledge of and proximity to the jogo do bicho to benefit from it, forging an enduring, unofficial relationship between the state and the animal game. Evidence of police corruption is notoriously difficult to obtain and often passes into conventional wisdom unsubstantiated.[103] One might reasonably believe that police sometimes colluded with bicheiros on the basis of the simple fact that, during the first three decades of the First Republic, so few were arrested for illegal gambling, relative to the popularity of the game. In many cases, patrolling officers' treatment of suspects in jogo do bicho infractions appears to have been conditioned by the officers' involvement in the jogo do bicho, for instance, in their demands for protection money from vendors.

The most compelling, albeit the most problematic, evidence of the illicit relationship between police and the clandestine lottery lies in the scores of accusations made by criminal defendants and other citizens. The majority of these involve the exchange of money from bicheiros for impunity. Police irregularities involved patrolling police but also higher-ranking officers, who are repeatedly accused of both taking illegal measures to incriminate defendants and accepting money to acquit them. The case in 1907 of a forty-three-year-old Portuguese man, José Maria Ribeiro, shows how police reportedly attempted to fabricate evidence to prosecute an alleged jogo do bicho vendor. After being arrested *in flagrante delicto*, Ribeiro, the police said, had received from an individual in a small grocery stand (*quitanda*) on a square called the Largo da Fábrica in Rio's Tijuca neighborhood a list of the "so-called jogo dos bichos." Speaking through his lawyer, Ribeiro insisted that "the affirmations made here are abundantly false; that the fragments of paper that were apprehended from him have the address of a friend who resides in Portugal to whom the accused owed the amount of 47 milreis he had promised to send to his friend at the address referred to there; with regard to the numbers written in pencil on the other side of the paper, the accused does not know how to explain their origins or purpose." He had "arrived in the company of his two sons today, taking them to their school, and on the way we went into the *quitanda* located on the Largo da Fábrica in order to gather kindling for his house; and that when he got there, a police officer [*comissário*] showed up and invited him to come along to the police station, where he was immediately placed under arrest." The police searched Ribeiro and found the paper with his friend's address on one side and the lists of numbers on the other. He insisted he was "not a *banqueiro* of the jogo do bicho nor was he ever one," had lived in that jurisdiction for more than twelve years, had never been arrested, and was well known by skilled, respected people. Ribeiro paid his bail (one conto and 500 milreis) and left detention to prepare his defense.

The defense Ribeiro presented rested on an audacious accusation of police corruption. The witnesses' testimony was false, Ribeiro claims; the police recruited citizens who happened to be in the precinct at the time of his arrest, and their story was "mere fantasy" designed to ascertain that a crime em flagrante had occurred. The witnesses, Ribeiro continues, are suspect: one is a newspaper vendor "who almost always testifies in these cases," and the other was a "poor unfortunate guy who, on this day, happened to be held at the police station after being found drunk on the street corner." Whether or not Ribeiro told the truth, the judge sided with him, acquitting him and returning his bail money. In the written sentence the judge voices overt disgust with the liberties taken by the police in this and other cases.[104]

A diatribe in the widely distributed working-class newspaper *Gazeta Operária* in January 1903 echoes the imputations of police irregularities of Ribeiro and his attorney. The unsigned editorial, which bears the suggestive heading "For the 'good of social morality': The *Bicho*," begins by establishing the newspaper's position against gambling and its solidarity with the official campaign to repress it: "We know that the Chief of Police has only the best intentions against gambling, especially the jogo do bicho, that disgrace introduced . . . some years ago. We are in theory against all types of gambling, for all are condemnable; none among them, however, have gained such momentum, created such disgrace, corrupted so many justice and police officials as the jogo do bicho." The editors' dismay is as much about the corruption of "justice and police officials" as it is about the popularity of the clandestine lottery:

And the misery is such and the disgrace is so great that when an honest official seeks to do something against the exploiters of this game, they are quickly advised [not to], and any honest action fails for the lack of proof. The shame and the lack of character have reached such a point that when the police catch *in flagrante* one of those miserable people who live off of this game, all of them well known, there is not one single person who will serve as a witness. When witnesses appear, it is just to say that they are not bankers of the animal game but rather very honorable 'businessmen.' . . .

Gazeta Operária addresses the Chief of Police at this moment, asking for his energetic intervention in trying to extirpate this cancer that is called the jogo do bicho, asking him also to trust neither the reporting [on this issue] in the daily press nor his own subordinates, when he tries to take action.[105]

Beyond the formulaic rhetoric of deference to a powerful public official, the publishers express faith in the police chief's ability to use his authority to bring about the rule of law. Even as they acknowledge the respectability of the top police official, they tie the "cancer" of the jogo do bicho to the workings of everyday policing. These comments derive not from firsthand experience with the criminal justice system but rather from freely circulating knowledge, which was subject to rumors, distortions, and preconceptions. Yet the newspaper's views corroborate the many similar accusations in criminal cases like Ribeiro's and may indeed point to the apparently purposeful misuse of criminal procedure. Subtextually, this editorial also reveals a glimpse of a moral economy involving police, justice officials, and the Carioca multitudes who moved between licit and illicit petty commerce. The difficulty in obtaining witnesses and therefore in prosecuting jogo do bicho cases may have been a function of the extralegal use of officers' testimony to establish that a contravenção was in progress, but it may also signal the stubborn refusal of eyewitnesses to testify against their neighbors and colleagues.

A historical reconstruction of corruption by state officials is difficult under any circumstances. Appearing in the documentary record only when denounced officially, corruption generates an archive of randomly assorted cases, each of which reflects an infinite regress of personal and professional animosities at least as much as it reflects actual behavior. One aspect of this problematic archive does reveal useful information about the juridical and penal forces through and against which the jogo do bicho spread, however: the routine nature of the accusations of police corruption in jogo do bicho cases. Characterized by their frequent appearance and by their matter-of-fact inclusion in cases against individuals with little or no social power, denouncements of criminal fraud and malfeasance by police rose to importance in the judging of jogo do bicho cases—and, in the public sphere and legislative realm, in deciding on the legal fate of the jogo do bicho—beyond any doctrinaire juridical principles. Bracketing the guilt or innocence of each police officer accused of corruption and each criminal defendant, the jogo do bicho's informal economy of accusations and acquittals itself is a crucial element in understanding the animal game's strange career.

A SEAT AT THE TABLE

The gambling misdemeanor encompassed a wide variety of games of chance, as boundless as the human imagination, the desire for easy money, and the lure of mildly subversive forms of play. During the First Republic, urban Brazilians played dice and card games like faro and monte. Cariocas played in their private homes and also frequented casas de tavolagem, public gambling houses specified in the Penal Code and half-heartedly criminalized since the beginning of the nineteenth century. The Rio police were well aware that if they were to part the curtains in houses' and shops' back rooms throughout the city, they would see people laying bets on cards and other games. Keeping a close eye on these gambling operations fell within their mandate to maintain public order and safety and to enforce regulations concerning business practices. The police self-servingly interpreted exactly what keeping an eye on gambling operations meant.

A horse-drawn wagon pulled out from where it had been parked in front of a shop on Rio Branco Avenue in April 1896, laden with the evidence: a table made of pine, two folding chairs, three large benches, and a wooden box.[106] The shop, police alleged, served as an illegal gambling den, and, in accordance with the law, they hauled away the evidence. A few days later, a local police precinct contacted the central Police Depository requesting "a chair, and a table, too." The official in charge of overseeing the objects seized from the city's raided casas de tavolagem reassured him he would receive all the furniture he needed.

The police did not view the furniture used in casas de tavolagem as mere wooden accessories to crime. The chairs, tables, and desks were also useful objects; police stations needed furniture, after all. Judging by the spate of police reports from 1896 documenting a wave of raids on unlicensed gambling establishments in the city center, police gleaned a full complement of furniture through such pursuits. Was this yet another instance of the police taking advantage of their monopoly of coercive power? Did the police apply the law with purloined furniture in mind rather than the loyal execution of their duties? It is not necessary, or even possible, to know the motivations of the patrolling police officers on a case-by-case basis to derive insights from the cumulative history of the police repression of unlicensed gambling in the early First Republic. In fact, their diversity of motivations is particularly interesting. Rio's police exercised their discretionary power along a spectrum of illegality, and stepping back from each individual case reveals an overall pattern of selective and routinized harassment.

Unlicensed casas de tavolagem make a telling point of comparison with the jogo do bicho. They were private clubs or at least interior spaces, not public areas in the same sense as the venues for jogo do bicho sales. Law enforcement had difficulty suppressing the jogo do bicho in part because the clandestine lottery lacked its own dedicated site. Almost by definition, jogo do bicho operators did not run their businesses out of gambling dens. The furtive exchange of small amounts of money for a chance to win usually took place in the course of daily commerce: on the streets, inside shops, in front of factory gates, that is, in the public domain. Bicheiros were street vendors. They plied the tramway platforms and sold dry goods in corner stores. They swept the floors of butcher shops. They ran postcard businesses and sold legal lottery tickets from street-corner kiosks. And the police soon learned to benefit from them by asking for cash, a payoff at least as useful as a chair.

The criminalization of unlicensed gambling created a system of direct, albeit extralegal, taxation; fine money and moveable property flowed from gambling business owners to the public coffers, who thereupon often appear to have simply returned to their clandestine enterprises. The frequency of arrests followed by acquittals, far from suppressing this informal taxation system, fueled it. For police, the jogo do bicho was also a form of entrepreneurship. Those who absorbed the high costs of this system were the most socioeconomically vulnerable Cariocas, who paid with their most exhaustible resource: their clean police record, and consequently their public honor.

Just as the failure to prosecute practitioners of the jogo do bicho did not mean a failure to criminalize it, the juridical and moral ambivalence about gambling in the early First Republic and the failure to prosecute players and vendors of the jogo do bicho did not mean there were not legal principles at work. Legal doctrine served to stake out a legal fiction of separate domains in which the law could and could not act, corresponding with the liberal idea of public and private spheres, and established a type of petty or so-called police crime (contravenção), as opposed to regular crime (*delito*), with particular relevance in the public sphere. Yet legal doctrine was most forceful in its equivocation over misdemeanors like vagrancy and gambling. Doctrine created the categorizing paradigm but then left a broad swath of the disenfranchised population—persons often referred to, not incidentally, as *desclassificados*—unclassifiable and thus subject to the discretion of those who wielded the state's coercive power.

How can one consider the relative unimportance of contravenção to legal theory in light of the vast prevalence of contraventores among those arrested during this period? Misdemeanors appear to have meant something to jurists and lawmakers that was quite distinct from what they signified for both law enforcers and citizens. To the former, petty criminality was weakly theorized, and the "occasional criminal" was a mere sideshow. For police officers, petty criminals were the main act; they formed the vast majority of daily incidents reported and arrests made and the bulk of the traffic in and out of the city's penal institutions. For citizens, the criminalization of everyday life—of Afro-Brazilian religion, games of chance, and public displays of unemployment—made the laws against contravenção the crux of their daily contact with the state.

The law, broadly defined, issued not just from the pens of theoreticians and jurists like Evaristo de Morais and statesmen like Rui Barbosa, but also from the writing and practices of police, judges, lawmakers, and bureaucrats. Legal codes and regulations provided guidelines. Police and judges applied them selectively, often improvising and, especially in the case of corrupt police, acting illegally in their own interest. Judges moved to correct for the troubling idiosyncrasies of the jogo do bicho's criminalization —its popularity among otherwise law-abiding urbanites and the growing tendency among the police force to collaborate with purveyors of the clandestine lottery—by acquitting virtually all defendants charged with jogo do bicho offenses. Like the technically unlawful but nonetheless frequent and ubiquitous trials of murderous or pestilent animals in medieval Europe, the jogo do bicho may have been simply "too deeply integrated into institutional legal procedures to be easily eradicated."[107] Extending this logic, the illicit lottery survived because it had also become a part of the entrepreneurial, extralegal dimensions of the policing profession.

Judges allowed the jogo do bicho to continue, if only through the exercise of their discretionary power. The frequency with which jogo do bicho defendants were absolved of their criminal charges shows that judges, as reformers, were using the latitude to acquit that petty crime cases afforded them to protest police abuses of power. As lawmakers inveighed against the jogo do bicho while judges generally acquitted the game's sellers and bankers, a cycle of official extralegality and the preaching of public morality developed.

To what degree did judicial officials understand the social context of their decisions? Their behavior seems paradoxical. On the one hand, lawmakers and judges produced codified rules of behavior that often refused to respond to social context or that purposefully defied social realities in the interest of an ideal. The thousands of men and women arrested for vagrancy under articles 399 and 400 of the Penal Code during the decade examined here bear witness to this apparent incongruity between normative social behavior and the vast population that Brazil's and Rio's judicial authorities construed as chronically straying from that norm.

On the other hand, judicial authorities seem to have understood the social context in which they operated. Government officials often expressed such understanding in the form of extralegal behavior that may have occurred at all levels but most prominently on the part of police officers who arrested citizens—or refrained from arresting them—for violating the prohibition against the jogo do bicho. Because the jogo do bicho fell into a category of infraction with ostensibly low penal stakes for the accused and low professional stakes for the judges and bureaucrats, the judicial system simultaneously regulated, stigmatized, and informally taxed the game. Although the jogo do bicho was persecuted, it was never eradicated; those who took part in it were merely consigned to an urban underworld that penologists, jurists, and, above all, police helped to create.

3

AN UNDERWORLD OF GOODS

I began by preventing the vending of cattle innards on the streets, displayed for sale on trays, encircled by the continuous flight of insects, which constituted a repugnant spectacle. I also abolished the rustic practice of milking cows on the city's public ways, . . . such scenes which no one, certainly, would find worthy of a civilized city. . . .

I also ordered the immediate capture and extermination of thousands of dogs which roamed around the city, giving it the repugnant aspect of certain Oriental cities and also gravely endangering public safety and morality.

I have been seeking to put an end to the plague of peddlers of lottery tickets who, everywhere, persecute the population, bothering them with their infernal cries and giving the city the aspect of a gambling den.—Mayor Francisco Pereira Passos, 1903

Maximiliano Felix Bahia got work wherever he could find it. In the first decades of the twentieth century, he plied the streets of the Federal District of Rio de Janeiro selling goods from a tray. It is unlikely that we, today, would know much about him had his goods not included tickets for the jogo do bicho, an infraction that landed him repeatedly in the city jail. Tickets for the jogo do bicho are just one type of merchandise circulating through the channels of petty commerce in Rio during the First Republic that the authorities neither fully persecuted nor fully condoned.

From the late nineteenth century on, the state sought to regulate Rio's marketplaces. Yet a segment of the city's petty merchants persistently evaded official regulation, and in most cases un-licensed trading occurred with impunity. Bahia's case is an enlightening exception.

A few of Bahia's own words survive, offering a tantalizing flash of insight into his life and the society of which he was a part. After one of his arrests in 1917 on the Praça da República, the *delegado* under whose jurisdiction this case fell interviewed the accused, following routine criminal procedure. A clerk recorded the interrogation:

> What is your name?
> *Maximiliano Felix Bahia*
>
> Who are your parents?
> *mother unknown, father unknown*
>
> Marital status?
> *does not know*
>
> Profession?
> *vagabond*
>
> Nationality?
> *does not know his country*
>
> Place of birth?
> *does not know his place of birth*
>
> Place of residence?
> *The Hotel of the Stars*

The clerk hastened to clarify Bahia's last response: "This means, 'the street.' "[1] The cleverly defiant nature of Bahia's response about his residence makes the truth of his testimony difficult to discern: did he really not know where he had been born? Was he truly ignorant of his marital status? But even his obscure responses help illuminate the legal and moral gray area of petty commerce and petty gambling Bahia occupied.

In the social hierarchy of petty commerce, street vendors like Bahia ranked at the very bottom. Bahia may have slept on the street, as he claims.[2] Even if he knew he was a Brazilian citizen of legitimate birth engaged in a recognized profession, he may have seen no purpose in specifying his status to the police. He may have invented the surname Bahia or perhaps assumed it after being freed, if he had been a slave. The neighborhood where Bahia was arrested was known as Pequena África (Little Africa), a place where former slaves from the northeastern state of Bahia started what became a thriving Afro-Brazilian colony.[3] Many Afro-Brazilians who settled in the neighborhood worked primarily as street vendors, a profession that allowed them to maintain their culture by supplying religious objects, dendê oil used in Afro-Brazilian cooking and rituals, and other traditional foodstuffs. Most of these street vendors appear to have been unlicensed.[4] The record does not reveal whether Bahia had official permission to sell his wares on the Praça da República.

Bahia was known in the neighborhood as a vendor of lottery tickets, but that was not his sole vocation. According to the police, when caught he was clutching a piece of white paper with the handwritten words "cat," "lion," "snake," "cow," "monkey" and a series of numbers, along with thirty cents in cash: items unambiguously related to the jogo do bicho.[5] The documents in his file disclose an increasingly complex picture of the infrapolitics of illicit commerce in republican Rio. The piece of paper bore the signature of someone named Antonio Silva. Bahia, it seems, had acted as a middleman. José Fernandes, a thirty-one-year-old Portuguese seller of sweets in the neighborhood, testified that he had known Bahia "for a long time as a vendor of lottery tickets," but that he had seen the accused crossing the square holding in his hand an easily recognizable list of the jogo do bicho. Just two days earlier, the witness reported, Bahia had told him that someone had handed him a small amount of change and a jogo do bicho ticket, entrusting Bahia to deliver the two items to the *banqueiro*, whose name is conspicuously absent from this criminal investigation.[6] Rather than deliver the funds as promised, Bahia tore up the list and kept the cash. He had flouted the system of trust on which the illegal lottery operated. Whoever denounced Bahia used the illegal status of the game to punish someone who had broken its codes. The anonymous complaint lodged against Bahia may have come from the banker whose illicit earnings Bahia had stolen, or perhaps from the buyer who had lost his or her chance to win. When the police officer attempted to arrest him, Bahia fled into the nearby train station, Central do Brasil, but was apprehended hours later, after another anonymous party tipped off a police officer as to his whereabouts.

We are left to wonder about the motives of the parties in this case. Was Fernandes, the sweets vendor who informed the police about Bahia and brought about his arrest, a competitor? or a personal enemy? or a patron of Silva, the banqueiro whom Bahia had been cheating? Was Fernandes intimidated by the police? or were they paying him to testify? How long had Bahia been cheating the banker? Amid these unanserable questions, Bahia's and the witnesses' testimony provide clues about how persons engaged in criminalized practices interacted with the state. Police pursued Bahia only with the aid of private citizens, and citizens used the police to extend their own power to bring about justice and meet their interests.

Bahia's case also dramatizes the connection between the jogo do bicho and urban street commerce. The police files of persons arrested in the late nineteenth century and early twentieth for dealing in the jogo do bicho identify them as coachmen, tanners, plumbers, electricians, and myriad other trades. Yet far and away the most numerous group among the persons processed through the criminal justice system for violating the law against games of chance were workers in petty commerce: small vendors, owners of dry goods stores, store clerks, and, to a lesser degree, street peddlers. While some dealt exclusively in jogo do bicho tickets, the majority seem to have sold other wares as well. Petty gambling in Rio grew directly out of the small commercial establishments that sold staple goods to the city's masses, for example, *botequins*, or taverns, small variety stores, and public markets in addition to the pervasive institution of street peddling. The jogo do bicho ticket itself was a commodity, and those who sold it engaged in a type of informal work.

After abolition and the beginning of Rio's era of rapid urbanization, the state sought to implement its self-conscious modernizing vision, in part, through the enactment of rules designed to control the consumer marketplace—both the economic transactions themselves and the spaces where they took place.[7] Some of these rules succeeded. As of 1903, for example, the milkman was no longer permitted to ply the streets of Rio with his milk cow in tow, kneeling to fill his bucket. The milkman was consigned to the colorful memories of such chroniclers as the popular Luis Edmundo, who, with some disdain, describes in 1938 the door-to-door peddling of milk as a quaint custom of bygone days.[8] Petty commerce in a modernizing city created a need for regulation, due to new retailing practices like fixed pricing and the complex business of supplying a growing population with staple goods that it was less able to produce for itself. A set of policies aimed at making the city more urban led to municipal legislation outlawing the raising of pigs (in 1890) and the small produce gardens (in 1904) on which many residents had long relied for subsistence and cash.[9]

Urban petty commerce in the growing Federal District created the need not only to implement rules but also to circumvent them, and many regulations that sought to modernize petty commerce were neither enforced nor followed. Consumers simply could not acquire life's material necessities under the regulations the state mandated, and many state bureaucrats and law enforcement personnel were apparently unconvinced by the urgent calls to implement a modern urban landscape by way of controlling retail commerce in republican Rio. Vendors persistently defied the city's demands to acquire a license. And bicho ticket sellers violated the law against either operating or playing any game of chance not specifically permitted and licensed by the state.

The system of urban retail commerce from which petty gambling grew occupied an ambiguous position with respect to the criminal law. Trading without a license constituted a violation of municipal regulations and carried a fine but not arrest and incarceration. Only under vague criminal pretexts like vagrancy or public disorder did renegade forms of petty commerce fall under criminal prosecution. Yet the complexities of Bahia's case show how the criminal law, albeit often in unanticipated forms, played a role in policing the nascent informal economy. A dynamic of constant negotiation governed both the jogo do bicho itself and the wider world of petty commerce from which it grew.

In the early First Republic, a segment of the retail economy would accumulate the stigma of criminality and moral danger. The underworld carved out of the city's consumer marketplace was the product of the tension between official regulation, popular practices, and persistent material necessities. Through the tandem development of popular commerce and gambling, one can observe how people improvised a living at the margins of what was controlled, regulated, licensed, and permitted.

GAMES OF CHANCE IN A CITY OF PEDDLERS:
PETTY COMMERCE IN REPUBLICAN RIO

The historian Maria Odila da Silva Dias characterizes Rio's underworld of goods as neither new to the late nineteenth-century Republic nor particular to the capital. Referring to São Paulo, she writes,

> In the middle of the nineteenth century, travellers and observers found the cost of living in São Paulo, as far as house rental and food prices were concerned, relatively moderate and easy. Their point of view was different from that of the local town women who were living on the bread line, who existed on those margins of survival which are extremely

difficult to reconstruct from written sources: served by a small clandestine trade, urban wretchedness remained a silent element in documents, full of its own subtle nuances and elusive shades of meaning.[10]

In mentioning the "silent element in documents," Dias tacitly laments
the difficulty of studying the everyday commercial activities of the urban
poor and the consequent paucity of scholarship on them. Her passage
suggests, too, that those on the "margins of survival" both perceived and
responded to material dearth in ways that often even their contemporaries
did not recognize. Much commercial activity throughout Latin America, as
elsewhere, has occurred outside the legal and moral boundaries imposed
by the state. In cities, where mainstream local economies failed to meet
popular needs, informal bartering, street vending, pawning, and gambling
proliferated despite frequent persecution. Yet in republican Rio de Janeiro
a distinctive confluence of forces and events occurred. It is no coincidence
that the jogo do bicho emerged amid Rio's social upheavals and alterations
in its built environment in the early First Republic, at just the moment it
became urgent to demarcate the formal from the informal in myriad realms
of urban society. The jogo do bicho was a phenomenon born of the abiding
impossibility of making such a demarcation in real life.

For those who made a living dealing in the jogo do bicho, the first half of
the 1910s was a troubled time. Local governance and policing were restruc-
tured in the first two decades of the First Republic. As executive power
became ever more centralized, Rio's municipal government turned its attention away from gambling. Police filled the growing institutional void
between state power and the actions of private business owners as they
took administrative control of petty gambling.[11] Prominent among these
business owners were people who invested in popular lotteries. The fore-
bears of the jogo do bicho bankers of later decades, these petty entrepreneurs came from both the new urban bourgeoisie and the ranks of the poor
and daring. Operators of businesses of questionable or precarious legality,
of which petty gambling is the paradigmatic example, were forced to contend with the police or risk stiff fines, imprisonment, or physical violence.[12]
The changing needs, interests, and state bureaucratic structure drove the
jogo do bicho further into the realm of the illicit.[13]

The same historical forces that acted on the gray market for lottery
tickets in the capital—a new administrative order and an exacerbated fear
of public disorder—also impacted petty commerce in general. Govern-

ment authorities rarely drew explicit connections between the jogo do bicho and urban retail trading, but Rio's worlds of petty gambling and petty commerce overlapped. The year of Bahia's arrest, 1917, which marked a turning point in the vigorous persecution of the jogo do bicho, coincided with the gradual, steady push to rationalize and modernize retail trading in the city's public spaces.[14]

As Brazil's busiest port city, Rio's primary function in the regional economy at the end of the nineteenth century was to receive and distribute imported goods as well as to serve as the nation's financial center and the busiest export processing entrepôt.[15] The city brimmed not only with warehouses and wholesale distribution centers but also with small retail markets to supply the growing population with staple items. Fishermen sold their catch on the beaches, and, from dawn until nightfall, vendors crossed the city on foot with cases, trays, and carts of merchandise. Medical treatment and small repairs were available in ateliers and makeshift stalls in public squares and streets throughout the city. After a play or musical revue let out, exiting theatergoers had to wade through a thick crowd of peddlers on foot and in temporary stalls selling coffee, snacks, and a variety of foods and other items to the hungry late-night crowd.[16]

The perceived need to rein in the chaotic crowd who traded goods and services in Rio's streets in the early First Republic can best be characterized not as a moral panic but as a subtle shift in policy and common sense. Those living through this quiet revolution in petty commerce, themselves, noted the change. Writing in 1917, Lima Barreto reflects on his city before the beginning of the Republic: In his boyhood, he explains, rustic outdoor markets appeared during the traditional saints' festivals each June on the square then called the Campo de Santana, located in a poor neighborhood—the same square, officially renamed Praça da República, where police would later arrest Maximiliano Felix Bahia.[17] Lima Barreto fondly remembers the scene unfolding by the smoky light of kerosene lamps. While "the virtuous newspapers of the day" railed against the gambling and popular trading of questionable legality that went on in these vending stalls, the authorities of the late Empire justified allowing these unruly popular practices to continue because of the charity they supposedly generated for the local church. "Then came the Republic," he continues, "and soon the authorities got rid of the traditional June saints' festivals. The Republic arrived, austere and stern. It came armed with Positivist Politics, with Comte, and with his accessories: a saber and rifle."[18]

Popular practice, Barreto opines, was crushed under the wheels of the Republic, and one of the principal scenes of this tragic drama was the popular marketplace. In the eyes of Lima Barreto and many of his contemporaries, the modernization that accompanied the transition from Empire to Republic consigned popular forms of trading to the margins of urban life.

Lima Barreto's observations were no doubt subjective and perhaps exaggerated.[19] The local government of the Imperial Court, evidence shows, did not have the completely laissez-faire attitude regarding the market stalls that Barreto remembers.[20] Yet the historical record does bear out his comments about the preference of government officials during the First Republic for orderly, controlled public markets rather than the more organic, chaotic ones the writer nostalgically describes.

The republican government perfected and newly emphasized, but did not originate, a state policy aimed to control urban petty commerce. While still a colony of Portugal, regulation of retail trading in Brazil's cities sought to assure the proper distribution of goods and to protect customers from vendors' potential avarice and dishonesty. Officials most tightly controlled the sale of "foodstuffs of highest necessity," which in colonial times included salt, fish, and beef. The Portuguese crown created councils (câmaras) to oversee everyday trading: weights and measures, distribution, quality, opening and closing times of stores, and the like. Laws obliged even the smallest of retail businesses to register with the municipality and pay licensing fees. Yet everyday trading proved difficult to oversee.[21]

A petty vendor in late nineteenth- or early twentieth-century Rio would have contended with laws and municipal regulations as well as administrative procedures in effect for over a century in addition to the newer, more stringent rules. Public officials weighed their ideological commitment to the unfettered right to trade one's goods against the perceived need to maintain order. Answering a colleague's question about whether to honor a merchant's request to do business in the capital city, a letter of 1902 from the attorney and high-ranking municipal bureaucrat José de Miranda Valverde cites article 72/24 in the Brazilian Constitution of 1891, which reaffirms the early nineteenth-century statutory guarantees of the free exercise of any "moral, intellectual, and industrial" profession. "However," Valverde's letter continues, "any type of work, of culture, of industry, or commerce is subject to all the restrictions within the powers of states' police, and can be prohibited if it opposes public custom, and the security and health of the citizens."[22] In hundreds of letters and decrees, lawmakers and government administrators in early republican Rio established and juridically elaborated the legal basis for the police contravention of commercial activities.[23] By the 1890s the mayor's office began routinely to respond to security concerns in Rio's street markets by referring complainants to the police.[24]

Throughout the First Republic, state regulation of the city's petty commerce reflected the perceived exigencies arising from changes in the urban cultural, political, and social landscape and built environment. The state continued to impose pure food laws and to control weights and measures. Regulations limited the hours when businesses could stay open, prevented them from functioning on Sundays, and imposed taxes. The municipal government implemented reforms, particularly during the administration of Pereira Passos (1902–6), which prohibited such practices as milking cows in the streets. State intervention in petty commerce additionally controlled the distribution of the most basic commodities; local and federal laws designated a list of *gêneros de primeira necessidade* (staples of first necessity): bread, dried meat, codfish, lard, fat, wheat flout, manioc flour, rice, corn, beans, charcoal, firewood, oil, vinegar, salt, and sugar.[25]

The positivist ideal of order and progress underlay the shift in policy toward ever-tighter control of petty commerce, but economic concerns were also a factor. Licensing requirements and the fees they entailed contributed to public coffers, and government authorities protected concession monopolies, in part because they benefited from the exchange of favors and sinecures.[26] Urban geography also influenced the state's response. Unimpeded circulation through the streets was paramount in a port city, whose wealth derived almost exclusively from the smooth flow of goods to and from the port.[27]

Seeking a better means of overseeing the trade of goods and hoping to control rampant inflation, private contractors and public officials undertook initiatives to set up *feiras livres* (public, usually outdoor markets) and large, municipal markets.[28] The intention was to enable small producers in the city's rural zone to sell their products without the intercession of middlemen. The municipal government took this initiative in direct response to the need to provide the growing population in both the central urban zone and the hinterland with affordable, basic consumer goods. Municipal and federal laws and executive orders mandated the construction of the markets, usually following an open competition for a concession contact. Requests from would-be concessionaires flooded in, promising a hygienic, orderly solution to the problem of the city's supposed dearth of retail outlets for basic necessities. Concessionaires began establishing the markets in the 1890s. In 1906, the mayor's office ordered that the public morgue be relocated, its building demolished, and the land on which it stood disinfected and transformed into a public market operated by the Companhia Novo Mercado (New Market Company), a private enterprise that had won a public concession.[29]

In Rio and other Brazilian cities, consumers and politicians widely lauded the markets. Public reaction to them reflected some of the social conflicts both in petty commerce and Carioca society as a whole. The popular classes largely supported the construction of these so-called free markets, which sold goods at generally lower prices than many other types of retail outlets. The feiras livres appealed to small vendors, too, who were locked in perpetual competiton with street peddlers. The peddlers' low overhead allowed them to sell products at lower prices, and because of their mobility they reached customers at strategic points, such as tramway platforms and factory entrances. Formalized markets completely shut out the *ambulantes* and thus gained favor with businesses that needed protection from competition with these generally illegal but omnipresent peddlers.[30]

The positive reaction to the officially controlled and sanctioned markets arose, in part, from a deep-seated distaste for the city's retail shopkeepers, who many believed were inherently predatory.[31] That sentiment may have derived from a cultural bias against Portuguese immigrants, who dominated the Carioca commercial scene and experienced discrimination from both ends of the socioeconomic spectrum.[32] The elite classes tended to blame Portuguese immigrants for Brazil's supposed national backwardness. Radical republican nationalist *jacobinos* attacked the Portuguese community, accusing them of exploiting native Brazilians through their control of retail commerce and the residential rental market, in which poorly maintained and notoriously insalubrious tenements predominated.[33] Rio's native-born poor and working-class population reacted against the Portuguese shopkeepers because of their propensity to hire their compatriots. As both tenement landlords and would-be employers, Portuguese *comerciantes* bore the stigma of exploiters of the poor.[34]

Government policies regarding petty retail commerce were part of the process already in motion since the late Empire of handing over control of commerce to large concessionaires, itself part of a trend in Latin America to consolidate economic power in private hands since the opening of trade after independence from Spain and Portugal. Changes in the Carioca marketplace replicated this global process on a minute scale. This trend influenced city planning in the area of petty commerce—and the jogo do bicho that grew out of it—as well as in the construction of intraurban transportation networks, improvements in the port, and the gutting and reconstruction of the city center. In the 1880s representatives of scores of companies requested contracts with the city for a broad range of services and construction projects. These appeals cited hygiene, modernization, and overall improvement of the urban landscape that their companies could bring to the city and promised careful oversight and regulation of residents' activities.[35] These self-promoting concessionaires were preaching to the converted, as in the last two decades of the nineteenth century the city government signed virtually all municipal improvements over to large companies.

The historian Jaime Larry Benchimol identifies several pivotal moments in this transition in 1903 when the government of the Federal District signed or renewed concession contracts granting companies exclusive rights to build and operate small markets throughout the capital. The first such contract provided for the construction of fifteen markets by a Brazilian firm, and just days later the city signed this contract over to a British concern, the Brazilian Cold Storage and Development Company. The city turned over to the company three strategically located pieces of land: on Mercado da Harmonia square, between the rua da Saude and the waterfront; on Russell Beach; and in the populous central neighborhood of Botafogo.[36] These sites had not been empty spaces, but rather had been informal gathering places for, among other activities, the peddling of goods.

Despite an official ideological commitment to a free-market economy, government-sanctioned monopolies squashed potential competition and kept prices high. As an evocative example of the impact of the government's tendency to favor large concessionaires, the historian Teresa A. Meade describes the creation of a meat monopoly in republican Rio de Janeiro: "Over the years a semilegal black market developed whereby slaughterers from Niterói and Cachoeira [in the state of Rio de Janeiro] sold meat to butcher shops outside the official monopoly at a 20 percent discount. The discount meat markets were widely accepted, and until 1902 butchers and retailers operated with few restrictions despite government regulations. Pressed to uphold profits for monopoly producers during a particularly lean period in May 1902, municipal authorities moved to close down the extralegal network and confiscate the nonmonopoly meat." This effectively brought buyers and sellers simultaneously under control, but it also stimulated an incipient informal traffic in meat. A consumer protest resulted, which turned violent.[37]

In this and other instances, one can witness the state at work staking out the boundaries that delimited the scope of its power over the popular economy. The state could "donate" public lands for use as public markets that were really private enterprises. The activities that occurred in Rio's feiras livres and other such markets were controlled by contracts, and the law interceded to force sellers and the public to adhere to them. Small producers and vendors who operated outside this concession system found themselves limited to a shrinking geographic and commercial realm, navigating the attenuated space within a growing archipelago of private "public" markets stretching from the historic center out to the most distant suburban and rural zones of the city. The juridical and administrative distinctions drawn between the public and private domains of the marketplace—and ultimately between the criminal and civil domains of the law—may not have been a cause of the formalization of informal markets in republican Rio, but at the very least it was an effect.[38]

A smattering of consumer protests in Rio during the First Republic shows residents' acute awareness of the connections between the city's structural transformations and the increasing difficulty in making ends meet.[39] Even more than consumers, sellers perceived the shifting power relations in petty commerce, as they now needed to negotiate with big companies to rent market stalls to carry out their trade.[40] The new markets neither eradicated the hordes of vendors plying the city streets nor effectively expelled them from the commercial scene; these ambulantes just lost ground in legal and social as well as geographical terms.

The rules by which vendors were supposed to operate came not just from legal codes but from other sources too. A person wishing to sell goods on the street would have been constrained by three types of law. First, state law in the form of criminal and commercial codes, federal legislation, and municipal regulations provided guidelines to protect consumers and maintain public health and safety. Second, concession contracts signed with private companies established monopolies that prohibited vendors from trading within a certain range of markets and limited access to certain types of commerce. And third, custom imposed a set of rules and implicit understandings to which both sellers and authorities appealed.[41] Agents of the state and citizens drew from these three categories of law—statutes, concession contracts, and custom—to negotiate the boundaries between licit and illicit trading.

In their prolific written requests to the mayor's office for permission to sell goods and services in the Federal District, Cariocas reveal the terms on which citizens bargained and fought for use of public spaces.[42] In one compelling example from 1905, two men signed a letter to the mayor to protest attempts to prohibit them from selling fish on the bay coast at Botafogo Beach, located in one of the city's most central residential and largely well-to-do neighborhoods. The supplicants write, "[We are] heads of our families of no means, and without [being able to sell fish on the Botafogo Beach] we will die of hunger." They wished merely to continue to sell their catch at the point of embarkation, "in the customary way," the letter pleads. Because of the reforms then underway in this part of the city, the authorities decided that these and other supplicants could sell their fish—but only in the nearby Largo de São Clemente and only after obtaining a license and paying the required fees. The petitioners' choice of words shows that appeals to custom resonated in conflicts over the use of the city's public spaces for petty vending, at least among vendors themselves. However, the resolution of this case shows that, while still a last resort for vendors dispossessed of the public spaces on which they had traded "from time immemorial," such appeals had decreasing purchase in vendors' encounters with the state.[43]

Despite officials' modernizing zeal, forms of popular trade that diverged from the government's monetary, urban planning, and social policy occurred openly. For example, the prevalence of counterfeiting offenses indicates that various types of informal specie circulated in the popular economy.[44] Traders in the petty economy also transgressed rules in ways that did not constitute outright criminal offenses. They often evaded their obligation to register with the municipal government and pay the required taxes and licensing fees.[45] Sold in freestanding lottery ticket operations, at individuals' homes, and at retail stores that also sold licit goods, the jogo do bicho was one among many microenterprises whose owners refused to comply with the requirement to hold a license and pay fees. An exceedingly large proportion of Rio's retail vendors operated outside the law and, in a manner of speaking, poached a living on the city streets.

This is not to say that Rio lacked legal retail establishments. The capital in 1889 had over 520,000 inhabitants and about 13,815 legal retail businesses: 21 photo studios, 10 toy stores, 223 bakeries, 2,076 general food stores, to name a few.[46] The number of licenses granted to commercial establishments continually increased over the next two decades. In 1905, Rio's municipal government granted 13,786 licenses for stores; in 1906 the number rose to 13,982. The number of licensed businesses without a fixed location (*volantes*) rose from 5,066 to 5,274 in that same year. In 1907, the number of businesses operating in fixed locations reached 14,553 (1,285 industrial shops and 13,268 stores), and 6,385 licenses were granted to street vendors.[47] Even officials charged with overseeing everyday retail trading knew, though, that these large numbers did not tell the full story; a study of retail commerce commissioned in 1903 by the mayor's office admits that its data is "very deficient" and that to estimate the number of commercial establishments in Rio at a "minimum of 20,000" would "not be an exaggeration."[48]

In deciding to go into business for oneself legally, the potential comerciante needed to take into account the fees he or she would owe to the government. In general, they varied according to the size and type of the enterprise. The owner of a pastry shop on the rua Uruguaiana in the city center paid 260 *milreis* to operate his business.[49] Business owners frequently owed other fees and taxes to the municipality as well. A letter from 1900 written by a music store owner on the rua do Ouvidor complained about the monthly "exaggerated sanitation tax," 10 milreis, instead of the 3 he claims he owed to cover the cost of trash removal.[50] Like other retail businesses, lottery ticket sellers needed to obtain permission to operate, register with the municipality, and pay fees. One lottery ticket shop, De Pereira da Cunha e Companhia, was obliged to pay 200 milreis in 1896.[51] Another small business owner was taxed 126½ milreis in 1899 for the privilege of selling lottery tickets and prints and posting two signs in his storefront.[52] To register legally with the municipal government, one needed a sponsor and a fixed address. A letter of 1900 from the mayor's office shows that a peddler who sold clothing was assessed (*imposto de mascates*) 150 milreis and fined 158 milreis and an additional 20 milreis for operating without a license.[53] Registration had primarily to do with the city's need to capture tax income, but it also allowed the municipality to keep an eye on who was selling what and to control the numbers and locations of vendors. The surviving correspondence between the mayor's office, the police, and small retail business owners shows that police often rescinded licenses, even after the owners had paid their fees.[54]

In the late nineteenth century, as today, Rio was a city of *camelôs*, vendors who hawked their goods in the streets and in temporary vending stands that sold small items and foodstuffs.[55] A defining characteristic of Rio's urban landscape since the colonial period, street peddlers represented both the colorful street life of *Rio antigo* and an insidious threat to public order in the eyes of both the urban elite and many petty traders who operated in fixed shops.[56] João do Rio, the urban chronicler par excellence of Rio in its belle époque, was entranced by peddlers. In his trademark melancholic, nostalgic style, he depicts the creation of a new street as the city reaches out to annex the suburbs in the period of rapid expansion in the first years of the twentieth century. He describes a region of the city, not yet a neighborhood, which contains nothing but grass and a private house. "A few creatures" pass through. Soon, the area is divided into lots, and a house begins to go up. "Then another, and another." The region is wired for electricity, demonstrating that it "already no longer goes to sleep with the first shadows [at the end of the day]. Three or four inhabitants declare that the neighborhood is sanitary and peaceful." And at last, one knows it has become a neighborhood with a distinctive style and personality: "Street peddlers enter the area, as if they were entering new territory to be conquered."[57] Ambulantes were as predictable a part of the urban infrastructure as the houses and streets that began to spread out to Rio's receding rural outskirts.

Street peddlers may have been perceived as the conquering heroes of urban sprawl and the bearers of the "enchanting soul of the streets," as João do Rio describes them, but as they themselves and the authorities knew, ambulantes also occupied the lowest position in the socioeconomic hierarchy of popular commerce.[58] Street peddling was an exceptionally accessible profession, as it demanded little in terms of start-up costs, literacy, and specialized skills, and would-be peddlers could take it up as a second or third vocation to compensate for inadequate wages. Rio's street vendors were persecuted by both shopkeepers, with whom peddlers competed for customers, and the municipal government, especially under the zero-tolerance politics of Mayor Pereira Passos.[59]

The prevalence of women, especially those of African descent, among the ranks of Rio's ambulantes illustrates how the profession served as a refuge for those not easily integrated into the formal economy. Both slave and free women had been prominent as street vendors since the colonial era; some say that the majority of *comerciantes de tabuleiro* who sold sweets and other prepared foods from trays in the streets were female.[60] Women

FIGURES 12 and 13 Street
vendors in Rio de Janeiro, ca.
1910. Original photographs by
Augusto Malta, reproduction by
Marco Belandi. Source: Arquivo
Geral da Cidade do Rio de
Janeiro, Setor de Iconografia,
Rio de Janeiro.

also occupied a prominent place in Rio's petty commerce throughout the nineteenth-century Empire. Both custom and law allowed women to own their own market stalls.[61] In some months, as many women as men requested licenses to operate market stands on such places as the busy Largo do Rosário.[62] Women in postabolition Rio often owned small businesses.[63] While still prominent in petty commerce, women were mostly driven into the informal sector in the early twentieth century, the outcome of a process underway at least since the 1850s. None of the concessionaires who built and operated the city's large public markets were women. By 1877, the owners of the corner kiosks installed throughout the city were nearly all men; women operated only 2 of the 138 kiosks functioning that year.[64] A petition signed in 1910 by sixty-four retail business operators at the New Municipal Market, all of whom were men, shows the apparent absence of women among the vendors there.[65] By the early twentieth century, women remained in petty commerce primarily as street vendors, a profession that tightening regulations and massive urban reforms increasingly drove to the outskirts of the city.

In much of the city in the late Empire and early First Republic, women of African descent predominated among the multitudinous street vendors. *Negros de ganho* (slaves for hire) had dominated Rio's urban landscape until the end of slavery in 1888. No statistical evidence exists to tell us of the precise demographics of this army of workers in the streets of nineteenth-century Rio, but travel accounts, drawings, and contemporary descriptions point to the ubiquity of female street vendors among these slaves for hire, especially as sellers of food, laundresses, and water carriers. The wave of free persons of African descent and manumitted slaves from the northeast that began to surge in the 1870s also populated Rio's street commerce. The migrants established themselves throughout the city but especially in the section known as Little Africa where Maximiliano Felix Bahia plied his trade, which encompassed the neighborhoods of Santana, Cidade Nova, Santo Cristo, Saude, and Gamboa.[66]

Historians are only beginning to uncover information about the postabolition life trajectories of negros de ganho and free persons who migrated from the northeast, but they largely agree that many were absorbed into the unregulated and undocumented world of sellers and day laborers.[67] In the section in Rio's census for 1906 that contains biographical sketches of the city's centenarians, one entry describes a woman born in Africa and apparently brought to Brazil in bondage. Her story poignantly shows how street peddling provided a haven for Afro-Brazilians, especially women:

> Henriqueta Costa, 100 years of age, widow, African, illiterate. . . . She
> was the lover of her first master who was Portuguese, with whom she
> had 3 children, all dead. Later, she married one of her employers, who
> died three years ago. . . . She currently occupies herself peddling small
> items she makes herself (like rosaries), and she is usually found selling
> in the back streets near the corner of Marechal Floriano Street and First
> of March Street, near the entrance of Market Square. She is quite strong,
> and she hears, sees, and walks well.[68]

Costa and countless other former slaves like her had worked for cash,
sometimes managing to earn enough to pay for their manumission.[69] Many
of these individuals utilized the managerial and sales skills they acquired as
free workers to enter the informal economy as street peddlers.[70] In all
likelihood, Costa did not hold a license. Rio's law enforcement mostly
ignored unlicensed street peddlers, so there was little to dissuade people
like Costa who had few other options from establishing themselves on
street corners to sell their goods.

The lack of economic opportunity for black Brazilians in the capital at
this time resulted from competition with European immigrants also seeking work as well as from prevalent racism. Lighter-skinned immigrants
entered the most dynamic sectors of the economy, like commerce and
industrial manufacturing, while darker-skinned Brazilians typically found
themselves hopelessly employed in low-earning jobs. Poor women suffered
from both a precarious economic situation and cultural restrictions on
their occupations. Having few alternatives, women entered domestic work,
retail petty commerce, and artisanal professions like sewing and producing crafts to sell on the streets. They also found work in such marginal
and socially denigrated professions as laundress, fortune teller, cabaret performer, or prostitute. Factory work provided additional jobs beginning in
the 1880s, but women received wages that barely sufficed for survival, and
the work was often brutal. Under those conditions, taking a tray of baked
goods to sell in the neighborhood square was an entrepreneurial solution,
even if the licensing fees to carry on such work legally proved burdensome.
Street vending nourished a subculture and fueled community solidarity by
supplying necessary goods and services.[71] In a census taken in the 1890s,
just over half of Rio's "economically active population" was listed under the

vague category "domestic servants, day laborers, and others," which lumped together all those unregistered, undocumented jobs that made up the city's nascent informal economy.[72]

To understand the constraints under which vendors worked, one cannot look only to authoritarian state power; as we have seen, either for lack of will or lack of policing resources, the state often left even obviously unlicensed ambulantes and *quitandeiras*, as the women who sold homemade sweets and small items in the streets were called, alone. Social divisions, too, established the boundaries within which Cariocas could work in petty commerce.[73] As individuals gravitated toward specializing in the trade of goods their compatriots or kin sold, what has been described as a "mosaic" of commercial activity developed.[74] In a newspaper essay from 1889, the chronicler Raul Pompéia writes, "Commercial Rio de Janeiro is topographically divided into curious territorial divisions of inhabitants, grouped according to an economic law of location that depends on neighborhood, which dictates like a powerful municipal legislator."[75] People familiar with the Federal District would have known just where to go to find the merchandise they sought in the narrow, colonial-era stone streets in the city center: to the rua do Ouvidor for books, jewelry, and fineries of all kinds; to the rua Nova do Ouvidor for print shops and beer gardens; to ruas da Assembléia and Uruguaiana for fresh meat; to the rua Direita for hardware. Pompéia's narrative walking tour takes him to the nearby Lapa dos Mercadores, an open space that had served as the site of the city's first outdoor market, where buyers and marketers mingled in the shadow of the Nossa Senhora da Lapa church.[76] Amid the city's numerous "mercantile clan[s]," Pompéia noticed that those involved in petty commerce, as in social life in general, aligned themselves according to familiar affiliations: "These men from their villages form their own associations, their brotherhoods, their religious and secular festivals." The marketplace served as both a mundane aspect of one's daily chores and the place where people cemented their community associations. Although he expresses disdain for the popular classes, to which he refers elsewhere as "*gentinha miuda*" (little people), Pompéia's essay offers a glimpse of the cultural geography of the marketplace.

Conflicts between vendors often had immediate causes, such as violations of honor or territorial intrusions, but also seem to have been overdetermined by ethnic divisions.[77] Certain groups—Syrians and Portuguese immigrants or Afro-Brazilian women from Bahia, for example—sold certain types of merchandise on their usual turf. Street peddlers of the same nationality tended to assemble around the same neighborhood or cluster of streets. Postabolition racism also amplified social conflicts and strengthened alliances that formed among petty vendors and their families, friends, and enemies.[78] Pulled along by these social tensions between classes, races, ethnicities, and genders, citizens could take the law into their own hands, as they did in the Bahia case. The social hierarchy of trading determined the options people could exercise in their encounters with the law. Owners of small, portable businesses had the advantage of being able to move away when threatened with police harassment.[79] Fixed retail businesses had the benefit of stability and a broader patronage network, and they formed associations to pursue their collective interests. For example, newspapers such as *União Caixeiral* promoted the cause of workers in small commerce in the First Republic. While shopkeepers and small business owners appear to have been the most important purveyors of the jogo do bicho in republican Rio, they were also the most adamant opponents of the itinerant merchants who typified the nascent urban informal economy. Although in practice their illegal status mattered little on a day-to-day basis, unlicensed street peddlers were the most vulnerable because policemen, competitors, or personal enemies could use the law to harass them or prevent them from carrying on their work. Street vendors and other merchants applied their law within the law, enforcing social, ethnic, and ethical claims.

MARKET CULTURE AND THE MORAL QUESTION

Those who called for tighter state regulation of the market articulated their demands not only in economic but also moral terms. Early attempts to regulate commerce in Brazil and elsewhere in Latin America emanated from a common belief that a commercial transaction was pregnant with potential danger. Rules against usury, for example, sought to bring commerce in line with ideals of public virtue and diminish the possibility of cheating customers and trafficking in stolen goods. As the historian R. Douglas Cope notes in his study of the marketplace in late colonial Mexico, petty commerce has long represented a social realm ruled only by "dissolute liberty" and frightfully impossible to control.[80] In urban Brazil, demands to control petty commerce on the basis of absolutes of right and wrong public behavior expressed anxieties about the uses of public space. Politicians, state bureaucrats, wealthy capitalists, and common citizens alike intervened in the public conversation about the looming immorality of the city's public market places and thus fueled the process of urban enclosure.[81]

Private individuals in the late Empire and early First Republic participated in the negotiation of normative ideas about the city as they complained to authorities about the presence of peddlers, shacks, and kiosks and the people whom these types of commerce attracted to their neighborhoods. In 1878, thirty-four residents of one of Rio's central districts delivered a petition to the Imperial city council:

> Most illustrious men of the City Council of this Imperial Municipal Chamber of the Court: The below-signed businessmen and heads-of-family come to the feet of your most Excellent Sirs to beg for the removal of a shack [barraca] on the rua da Saude 119b belonging to a certain José Lopes. It is not right that in a corner of such a picturesque square, decorated with upstanding businesses, [run by] serious and honorable men, there would appear such a disgusting shack to do business day and night nonstop, demoralizing everyone in the place with obscene words . . . drinking, and physical fighting. Since [the shack's owner] is known as a disorderly type, we thus respectfully ask for your attention.[82]

The city archive abounds with documents that use almost identical language to censure sharply this type of petty commerce.[83] With the transition from Empire to Republic, the content of these appeals did not change. Complainants aimed their caustic rhetoric at the barracas, *chapeus-de-sol* (literally "sun hats," a type of market stand), *chalets*, and other types of venues, whose varied and colorful nomenclature bears witness to the heterogeneity of the Carioca popular economy. These venues, the petitions argued, failed to meet minimum hygienic, aesthetic, and, later, security standards. Most of all, though, Cariocas criticized the presence of street-market stands on grounds of public morality. Through the discourse of propriety, public virtue, and fear of disorder, everyday people—at least those with some access to writing—voiced their concerns about commerce, financial gain, and the use of urban space. However formulaic, petitioners' words embodied more than empty rhetoric; they dipped creatively into the store of ideas and political practices available to most of Rio's population. Complaints about street vendors and peddlers and their disorderly clientele generated and rehearsed a new conventional wisdom about urban society. Such rhetoric drew urban disorder, street retail commerce, and immorality together, thus setting the terms of public debate about the urban popular economy as Brazil entered the twentieth century.

In the late nineteenth century, the appearance of kiosks on street corners and squares provided Cariocas with another place where they could buy small items in the course of their daily rounds. During its short life, this new type of structure would enter the class- and morality-inflected battles over the use of public spaces. Kiosks began to arrive from Europe in the 1870s, the initiative of Brazilian and European entrepreneurs. At first, their brightly painted, pointy roofs and ornate dollhouse shape struck some as looking out of place in the streets of the Brazilian capital. Yet they filled an important niche for residents who wished to purchase affordable convenience items like cigarettes and refreshments. Kiosks began to multiply, especially in working-class suburbs. In 1888 they already numbered about 150.[84] As they proliferated, so did the complaints against them. Hundreds of letters to the mayor's office called for their removal. According to their detractors, the kiosks attracted unseemly people who used obscene language and got drunk, polluted the urban landscape, and offended women and children.

In the mid-1880s, the Companhia Industrial Fluminense, with which the city had a concession contract, requested permission to set up a kiosk solely to sell lottery tickets. The city approved the request. Suddenly in 1884 and 1885, most of the requests to operate kiosks specifically sought the municipal government's consent to sell lottery tickets.[85]

Kiosks quickly became lightning rods for conflict over street commerce in Rio. Generalized calls not just to close down individual kiosks but to eradicate them altogether began to appear in municipal correspondence by the early 1890s. The differing opinions of the inspector of the First District of the Parish of Engenho Novo and the deputy sheriff of the First District of Engenho Velho in June 1891 are telling. In response to a citizen's complaint about a kiosk the police chief was debating whether to close, the inspector took issue with the deputy sheriff's recommendation for the suppression of kiosks throughout the precinct. "Such establishments," the deputy sheriff asserted, "are frequented by lowly people and comprise true centers of damnation, where the vices of drunkenness and gambling make themselves evident." "Consequently," he continued, "they threaten public order and tranquility because of the nature of their gatherings and their corrupt behavior." The inspector strongly disagreed, stating, "I deem it impossible to suppress this great offshoot of petty commerce that brings in

FIGURE 14 Kiosk in São Cristóvão, Rio de Janeiro (1911). Original photograph by Augusto Malta, reproduction by Marco Belandi. Source: Arquivo Geral da Cidade do Rio de Janeiro, Setor de Iconografia, Rio de Janeiro.

large sums that powerfully help the municipal coffers, thus constituting a permanent source of revenue for the municipal government. It is for this reason that the city granted them operating licenses." He concluded his written plea by reminding the deputy sheriff the job of the police was only "to maintain order when there is a disturbance" or "to prevent crime that might result from such gatherings."

The deputy sheriff sent his retort a few days later. Even though citizens who patronized kiosks were generally orderly, he reasoned, these businesses were magnets for the worst elements of the city, people who incited even tranquil types to disorder. He continued, "Not only at late hours of the night but also during the day they shelter around them a crowd [*phalange*], which is often full of vice-ridden individuals who establish gambling among themselves, cultivating their gaming in full liberty and managing to escape the vigilance of even the most scrupulous authorities." He suggested that "even though this may be a violent measure, it is one with incontestable moral and patriotic value. We must seek to eliminate these kiosks once and for all, especially in the suburbs, and particularly in this District [Engenho Velho]."[86]

The deputy sheriff and those who shared his fear of the crowd that surrounded the kiosks decided the fate of this short-lived experiment in popular commerce and public convenience. In the 1870s and 1880s, concessionaires had argued that the kiosks they wished to build would provide an important service for the city's less fortunate and secure valuable income for the city. They would offer a salutary alternative, some argued, to the street peddlers, who denied the city any share of their profits.[87] But kiosks proved to be a failed idea. The entrepreneurs who brought the kiosks to Brazil found a market not for postcards, pencils, and Pernod, but for cigarettes and *cachaça*. And by 1893, the authorities discovered that the kiosks they had permitted to sell lottery tickets were selling chances to the jogo do bicho as well.

Their demise was fast. By 1902 the chief of police himself had begun to make decisions about how late the kiosks could stay open.[88] Over the next few years requests for kiosk licenses were often granted, but references to the vice-ridden nocturnal crowds that would congregate around the kiosks were key talking points routinely used to decry their existence. In 1911 the mayor's office did not renew the expired contract with the Companhia Kiosque and on November 11 ordered the immediate evacuation of all kiosks. Groups of municipal laborers borrowed from a road conservation project demolished the nearly two hundred kiosks throughout the city. According to one of the final letters in this largely forgotten thirty-year chapter of Rio's history, the construction materials left behind as the kiosks were laid to waste were made available "to anyone who requested them."[89] Concessionaires and city officials alike had acknowledged that this form of petty commerce supplied a useful service to the Carioca people. But mounting concern about spreading vice favored the more genteel, enclosed cafés and open markets, where the flow of people made it more difficult to cluster and socialize.

While official letters about the dangers of the market-bound crowd traveled back and forth across the city, others were writing about a more rarified realm of urban retail commerce. In the magazine *Kosmos*, the following lyrical lines appeared in 1905, regaling the rua do Ouvidor, the city's elite shopping street:

> What can one say about you, gorgeous rua do Ouvidor, that might be new, interesting, or precise? Slim and svelte as a palm frond, abundant and fertile as these sacred rivers that enclose the life and the wealth of this country, commercial and narrow as the "Mercanzie" of Venice, luxurious and scintillating like the gallery of a museum, with an ardent and febrile street life like certain streets in Naples or Alexandria—you are unique, there are no adjectives that can characterize you, there is no image into which to translate you, you are the rua do Ouvidor. . . . [90]

As the contrast between this passage and the rhetoric used to vilify street-corner kiosks and their clientele suggests, commerce was socially stratified in turn-of-the-century Rio. Social hierarchies penetrated all aspects of life; they were inscribed in every building and public fountain, in every shop and bar, and in the daily acts of deference customarily demanded of the city's majority of residents. Yet it would be a mistake to assume that the powerful and the struggling lived in separate spheres. People of all walks of life shared their public space. The wealthy bought goods from street vendors, and those in the middle sectors who held more prestigious jobs, particularly as civil servants, could not count on receiving their salaries on time. Because the government closed down at midday, many of these bureaucrats were chronically underemployed and their economic precariousness left them dependent on the popular economy for affordable goods and occasional work. Daily commerce involved not parallel worlds of rich and poor, but overlapping ones.

In 1902, the rua do Ouvidor, so rapturously described as the bastion of luxury, boasted nine kiosks, the "centers of damnation" alluded to in official correspondence. Furthermore, Manoel Ismael Zevada, the Mexican believed to be instrumental in transforming the animal raffle from a local, licit game at the zoo into a citywide gambling network, ran his operation out of a storefront on the corner of the rua do Ouvidor and rua Gonçalves Dias, just meters away from the famed high-society teahouse the Confetaria Colombo, where the intelligentsia mingled and drank imported beverages.[91] The exclusivity of the city center and in many ways its urbane glamour in general existed mostly in the wishful imaginations of the ruling classes. In documents linking petty commerce with immorality and disorder, however, one can witness the construction of the idea, if not the reality, of separate spheres of rich and poor. According to their logic, certain "types" would agglomerate in public spaces, letting loose abhorrent words and spreading vicious habits among the innocent but impressionable masses.[92] Clustered around kiosks and milling about fruit stands in the squares and fish stands at the docks were people playing games in which cash or valuable prizes could be won with no skill or work. With the increasingly popular jogo do bicho ramifying through the channels of petty commerce, the amorphous complaints against petty gambling of previous decades found a new, sharply defined form. The moral concerns about the jogo do bicho arose not because it was a type of gambling, but because it was a type of commerce.

THE JOGO DO BICHO AND POPULAR COMMERCE

The Rio police collected data in 1913 during what was perhaps the first thorough, citywide anti–jogo do bicho campaign, and their efforts give us a rare detailed snapshot of how the game spread. That year all but one of the twenty-nine police precincts (*delegacias*) had at least one and as many as thirty points of sale for the jogo do bicho.[93] Farther from the city center, increasing levels of informality in the modes of sale of jogo do bicho tickets throw into stark contrast the varying ways in which people obtained goods. In peripheral neighborhoods, tickets were sold in botequins or by ambulantes or at *pontos de bicho*, impromptu stands set up in the street. In the city center, by contrast, players purchased tickets at established commercial operations like food markets, lottery ticket shops, and in the growing number of commercialized public entertainment establishments such as cinemas, casinos, and amusement parks.

In February of 1913, a fifteen-year-old boy named Aristides, white and, according to police records, "without any profession," was taken into police custody. He attended school and knew how to read and write, add, subtract, and multiply; he was able to distinguish coins and paper money; and he had "a good notion of those things commonly seen in ordinary life." In the judge's estimation the boy possessed a normal mental state for his age, "which permits him to distinguish between right and wrong," and the state could therefore hold him accountable for the crime for which he had been arrested: selling tickets for the jogo do bicho in the tobacco shop where he worked as an assistant.[94]

The jogo do bicho arrest records reveal that small shop owners, shopkeepers, and clerks who worked in Rio's many dry goods and similar types of stores often had one foot in the commercial underworld and the other in legal retail trading. Most individuals arrested for illicit gambling between 1890 and 1917 are registered in the entry log of the city jail as "comerciante," a term that ranged in meaning from shopkeeper to operator of a small street market stand.[95] Evidence from arrest records and the entry logs for the city jail indicate that multitudes of small merchants in republican Rio either specialized or dabbled in selling tickets for the jogo do bicho. The data summarized in tables 5 through 9 demonstrate that 106 of the 230 cases sampled were men who worked in apparently small-scale retail commerce. Unsurprisingly, many of them were Portuguese immigrants, who, as we have seen, dominated the commercial scene.[96]

On a July day in 1896, four men of ages ranging from twenty-eight to forty-four, all natives of Portugal, were arrested and detained for selling tickets to the jogo do bicho. The men's relationship to each other is unclear, but the coincidence of their arrests allows one to examine dealing in the jogo do bicho as a vocation that Cariocas fit into their lives, as workers and entrepreneurs. The oldest of the men, a forty-four-year-old single white male from the city of Porto, was arrested "for not exercising an honest profession, working in the sale of tickets for the bicho." A second detainee's profession, like that of the youngest of the group, a twenty-eight-year-old, white, married male, is recorded as "cashier." The third of the immigrants jailed that day, a thirty-nine-year-old single white native of the Portuguese city of Aveiro, is registered in the entry log as a "seller of tickets." In language identical to that which appears in the other cases, the log notes he had been arrested "for not exercising an honest profession and for working in the sale of jogo do bicho tickets." The fourth man, with no profession listed, was arrested "for being a seller of jogo do bicho tickets and for being unemployed."[97]

It is significant that the recording clerk who registered these men on their way into the detention center listed some of them as lacking a profession. The young Aristides in the case cited above, although working as a store clerk at the time of his arrest, was likewise recorded in the judicial files as "without a profession." In this and many other arrest records for those accused of participating in illicit commerce, being employed was not always synonymous with having achieved the respectability of holding a recognized occupation. The arrest records of those whom police apprehended as jogo do bicho vendors demonstrate that, to the authorities, such employment was tantamount to a sort of working vagrancy. As a police

TABLE 5 Professions of Persons Detained for Jogo do Bicho and Other Gambling Offenses, 1896–1929

PROFESSION OF DETAINEES	NUMBER OF DETAINEES[a]	PROFESSION OF DETAINEES	NUMBER OF DETAINEES
retail commerce (*comerciante*)	92	pay-receiver/cashier (*cobrador*)	1
worker (*trabalhador*)	16	plumber	1
"no profession"	11	artisan	1
businessman (*negociante*)	10	theater artist	1
store clerk (*caixeiro*)	9	chauffeur's assistant	1
laborer (*operário*)	9	small boat operator (*catraeiro*)	1
shoemaker	6	driver	1
stone mason	6	weaver	1
baker	4	tanner	1
cook	4	messenger	1
barber	4	sewer (*costureiro*)	1
carpenter	4	guilder	1
cigar maker/seller	3	lottery ticket business owner	1
not indicated	3	electrician	1
ticket vendor	3	street peddler	1
tailor	3	(illegible)	1
former police officer	2	stone mason's assistant	1
painter	2	employee in city jail	1
entrepreneur (*empresário*)	2	notary/copyist	1
public servant employee	2	stoker	1
stevedore	2	photographer	1
sailor	2	founder	1
carrier (*carregador*)	2	Civil Guard from the state of Minas Gerais	1
cart driver	2		
coachman	2	war veteran	1
chauffeur	1	small farmer (*lavrador*)	1

Source: Data compiled from the extant manuscript entry logs of Rio de Janeiro's city jail from 1890 to 1929, APERJ, série Casa de Detenção.

[a]The distribution of cases by year is as follows: 1 from 1891; 3 from 1893; 21 from 1894; 1 from 1895; 30 from 1896; 7 from 1903; 4 from 1904; 1 from 1909; 8 from 1913; 2 from 1914; 8 from 1915; 36 from 1921; 22 from 1922; 20 from 1924; 23 from 1927; and 15 from 1929. No female detainees arrested for gambling offenses were found in the surviving jail entry logs. Of 230 cases, 181 were indicated as relating to the jogo do bicho and 49 were indicated as simply "gambling" or not specified.

TABLE 6 Workers in Commerce Arrested for Offenses Related to Gambling, 1896–1929: By Age

AGE	TOTAL[a]	COMERCIANTES[b]
not indicated	2	2
under 25	73	35
25–35	90	46
36–45	37	16
Over 45	28	14

Source: Data compiled from the extant manuscript entry logs of Rio de Janeiro's city jail from 1890 to 1929, APERJ, série Casa de Detenção.

[a]The distribution of cases by year is as follows: 1 from 1891; 3 from 1893; 21 from 1894; 1 from 1895; 30 from 1896; 7 from 1903; 4 from 1904; 1 from 1909; 8 from 1913; 2 from 1914; 8 from 1915; 36 from 1921; 22 from 1922; 20 from 1924; 23 from 1927; and 15 from 1929. No female detainees arrested for gambling offenses were found in the surviving jail entry logs. Of 230 cases, 181 were indicated as relating to the jogo do bicho and 49 were indicated as simply "gambling" or not specified.

[b]Those categorized as working in commerce include the 113 in this sample identified when registered in the jail as having the following professions: "comerciante" (shopkeeper); "caixeiro" (cashier/shop clerk); "vendedor de bilhetes" (ticket seller); "empresário de loterias" (lottery ticket business owner); "vendedor ambulante"(street peddler).

official noted in 1899 in the case of a man accused of dealing in the jogo do bicho, the defendant earned his "subsistence by means of this occupation which is prohibited by law, and thus it would be necessary not just to punish him but also to oblige him to take a serious profession."[98] These documents reflect the ambiguous conventions about what qualified as a legitimate profession, as well as the often arbitrary, extemporaneous assessments of the bureaucrat who recorded the information.

José Maria Ribeiro, a man arrested repeatedly for selling jogo do bicho tickets, exemplifies how sellers of clandestine lottery tickets fit in with the world of Rio's petty commerce, often in multiple ways through the course of their lives. Nicknamed Paciência (Patience), the Portuguese-born Ribeiro, a forty-seven-year-old single man, seems to have been a successful businessman when he appeared in the criminal files in 1904. In the tavern he owned in the Vila Isabel neighborhood, where the jogo do bicho had emerged roughly a decade before, police arrested Ribeiro and charged him with dealing in the clandestine lottery. Three witnesses testified that Ribeiro was known in the neighborhood as a jogo do bicho dealer, and the arresting officer asserted that he found the incriminating lists

TABLE 7 Workers in Commerce Arrested for Offenses Related to Gambling, 1896–1929: By Marital Status

MARITAL STATUS	TOTAL[a]	COMERCIANTES[b]
Not indicated	3	0
Single	137	60
Married	79	46
Widowed	11	7

Source: Data compiled from the extant manuscript entry logs of Rio de Janeiro's city jail from 1890 to 1929, APERJ, série Casa de Detenção.

[a]The distribution of cases by year is as follows: 1 from 1891; 3 from 1893; 21 from 1894; 1 from 1895; 30 from 1896; 7 from 1903; 4 from 1904; 1 from 1909; 8 from 1913; 2 from 1914; 8 from 1915; 36 from 1921; 22 from 1922; 20 from 1924; 23 from 1927; and 15 from 1929. No female detainees arrested for gambling offenses were found in the surviving jail entry logs. Of 230 cases, 181 were indicated as relating to the jogo do bicho and 49 were indicated as simply "gambling" or not specified.

[b]Those categorized as working in commerce include the 113 in this sample identified when registered in the jail as having the following professions: "comerciante" (shopkeeper); "caixeiro" (cashier/shop clerk); "vendedor de bilhetes" (ticket seller); "empresário de loterias" (lottery ticket business owner); "vendedor ambulante"(street peddler).

under a bottle. Ribeiro's defense was that "the lists they found were not new but old, because more than 15 days ago he had stopped selling the so-called jogo do bicho but had forgotten to remove these lists, which he had not even remembered." After the usual formalities, the judge acquitted the defendant for insufficient evidence.[99]

Ribeiro was arrested again *em flagrante* for selling jogo do bicho tickets in August 1908. This time he listed *negociante* (businessman) rather than comerciante as his profession. This more distinguished professional identity stands in odd contrast to his downward social mobility. Police apprehended Ribeiro at 2:00 P.M. as he "loitered without a destination" on a street corner not far from the tavern he had once owned. The police investigation reveals that Ribeiro now had "no means of subsistence . . . or profession, craft, job, or legal and honest occupation in which to make a living" and that "he had been earning the minimum amount of money required to purchase necessities from the so-called jogo do bicho." Several witnesses used language identical to the arresting officer's in incriminating Ribeiro as not only a bicheiro but also a vagrant. Protesting his innocence and defending his character, the accused testified he "has a legal, honest occupation," namely, performing various tasks in his old profession in

TABLE 8 Workers in Commerce Arrested for Offenses Related to Gambling, 1896–1929: By Nationality

NATIONAL ORIGIN	TOTAL[a]	COMERCIANTES[b]
Brazil	119	63
Region not specified	63	46
Federal District	22	9
State of Rio de Janeiro	15	4
State of Pernambuco	4	2
State of Bahia	4	1
State of Minas Gerais	4	0
State of Alagoas	2	1
State of Paraiba do Norte	2	0
State of São Paulo	1	0
State of Ceará	1	0
State of Pará	1	0
Portugal	76	36
Italy	29	12
Spain	10	1
Syria	1	0
Austria	1	0

Source: Data compiled from the extant manuscript entry logs of Rio de Janeiro's city jail from 1890 to 1929, APERJ, série Casa de Detenção.

[a]The distribution of cases by year is as follows: 1 from 1891; 3 from 1893; 21 from 1894; 1 from 1895; 30 from 1896; 7 from 1903; 4 from 1904; 1 from 1909; 8 from 1913; 2 from 1914; 8 from 1915; 36 from 1921; 22 from 1922; 20 from 1924; 23 from 1927; and 15 from 1929. No female detainees arrested for gambling offenses were found in the surviving jail entry logs. Of 230 cases, 181 were indicated as relating to the jogo do bicho and 49 were indicated as simply "gambling" or not specified.

[b]Those categorized as working in commerce include the 113 in this sample identified when registered in the jail as having the following professions: "comerciante" (shopkeeper); "caixeiro" (cashier/ shop clerk); "vendedor de bilhetes" (ticket seller); "empresário de loterias" (lottery ticket business owner); "vendedor ambulante"(street peddler).

commerce, "working as an office assistant in various shops." He "was a negociante who conducted his business poorly and today works as a book-keeper." To defend himself against the charges by demonstrating his re-spectability he submitted receipts in his name for the payment of rent. The judge dropped the charges.[100]

Four months later, in December 1908, when Ribeiro once again found

TABLE 9 Workers in Commerce Arrested for Offenses Related to Gambling, 1896–1929: By "Skin Color"

"SKIN COLOR"	TOTAL[a]	COMERCIANTES[b]
Not indicated	2	1
White	168	95
Nonwhite	57	17
Morena	15	4
Pardo claro	2	2
Pardo	26	7
Pardo escuro	6	2
Fula	2	0
Preto	6	2

Source: Data compiled from the extant manuscript entry logs of Rio de Janeiro's city jail from 1890 to 1929, APERJ, série Casa de Detenção.

[a]The distribution of cases by year is as follows: 1 from 1891; 3 from 1893; 21 from 1894; 1 from 1895; 30 from 1896; 7 from 1903; 4 from 1904; 1 from 1909; 8 from 1913; 2 from 1914; 8 from 1915; 36 from 1921; 22 from 1922; 20 from 1924; 23 from 1927; and 15 from 1929. No female detainees arrested for gambling offenses were found in the surviving jail entry logs. Of 230 cases, 181 were indicated as relating to the jogo do bicho and 49 were indicated as simply "gambling" or not specified.

[b] Those categorized as working in commerce include the 113 in this sample identified when registered in the jail as having the following professions: "comerciante" (shopkeeper); "caixeiro" (cashier/ shop clerk); "vendedor de bilhetes" (ticket seller); "empresário de loterias" (lottery ticket business owner); "vendedor ambulante"(street peddler).

himself in police custody, his fortunes appear to have worsened. Police entered the dry goods store in the Tijuca neighborhood where Ribeiro lived and found him holding a "notebook with writing on it [that] makes it exactly clear this was meant for the so-called 'jogo do bichos.' For on its pages are written all of the days of the week except Sunday, [the only day] on which the aforementioned 'jogo dos bichos' is not played." The police officer declared he had "apprehended this notebook from José Maria Ribeiro, commonly called 'Patience,' today at about two o'clock in the afternoon on rua Barão de Mesquita number 60 in a dry goods store owned by Firmino José Alves," Ribeiro's boss and a key player in the case.

The arresting officers and several witnesses asserted the accused was, in fact, a jogo do bicho vendor. Ribeiro was a "known vagrant," one claimed, "not having an occupation and making his living exclusively from gambling, for which he has already been arrested"; that "the accused stations himself in the aforementioned dry goods store with the aim of arranging buyers of the so-called jogo dos bichos." A witness echoed the policeman's statement, labeling Ribeiro a known vagrant who lives exclusively from gambling, "arranging customers in his name or for third parties for the raffle known as the 'jogo dos bichos'; this is public and notorious, such that the accused, when arrested, had in his possession a notebook with writing" that could only be for the jogo do bicho, "for in the same notebook only the weekdays are mentioned, on which the jogo do bicho is played, missing only Sundays," when it is not. When he went into the store, the witness continues, the accused tried to hide the notebook just before the police took him into custody.

In response to the accusations, Ribeiro testified that he had been in the store of Senhor Alves, where he did odd jobs. Seeking relief from the stifling summer heat, Ribeiro had come out from behind the store counter and perched in a chair when two unknown men appeared, men whom he now knows were police officers who had come to search the store. The police search turned up nothing related to the jogo do bicho except some coins, Ribeiro coyly asserts, but they took him to the precinct anyway, "for reasons he did not know." Ribeiro claims that the notebook confiscated in his possession was "exclusively for personal notations"—but, that he did not wish "to indicate just what notations these were." The judge set bail at a hefty 1 *conto* and 500 milreis, which Ribeiro managed to pay in short order.

In late January 1909 Ribeiro presented his formal defense to the court. For many years he had his own dry goods business, he explains, but today works for multiple establishments, including the store where he had been arrested. His arrest was baseless, he insists, as was the accusation of vagrancy. The judge reviewed Ribeiro's file and acquitted him once again, citing not only improper arrest procedures, as was normally the case in jogo do bicho cases, but also a key document the defendant had supplied: a letter from his employer, the negociante and fellow Portuguese national Firmino, affirming that Ribeiro was his employee.

Ribeiro's case illuminates the economy of clientelism that functioned in the world of petty commerce that already underlay the jogo do bicho in its earliest decades.[101] The decisive letter of support from Firmino suggests that the shop owner was not just Ribeiro's employer but his patron. Without Firmino's assistance, Ribeiro likely could not have posted bail and would have languished in the crowded, disease-ridden city jail for weeks while awaiting a hearing. One wonders how Ribeiro might have repaid Firmino's favor. Ribeiro's case shows how a bicheiro could be a lone businessperson but also be knitted into a hierarchical, interdependent urban community of comerciantes by way of favors, temporary employment, fines, and bail money. Throughout the five-year period these three cases span, Ribeiro's involvement in the jogo do bicho appears to have continued despite—or perhaps because of—his changing professional fortunes.

The preponderance of white, Portuguese, male shopkeepers and shop workers among those arrested for selling jogo do bicho tickets hints at how the game's selective persecution occurred along the lines of existing social tensions. As we have seen, Rio's Portuguese community carried the stigma and burden of their dominance over petty commerce. The endemic hostility toward Portuguese shopkeepers offers a way of contextualizing the seemingly eccentric arrest patterns for the jogo do bicho during this period.[102] These comerciantes and caixeiros linked the licit and illicit worlds of commerce in the Federal District. Individuals caught up in the social and ethnic tensions in the realm of petty commerce would make use of the possibilities an explicitly illegal activity in their midst offered.

Street vendors were equally important in the story of the growth of the jogo do bicho by means of the city's petty commerce. Both ubiquitous and only sporadically regulated, vendedores ambulantes were the perfect conduit for the illicit traffic in informal lottery tickets in late nineteenth-century Rio. Beginning in the 1880s, when the government of the Imperial Court began to grant licenses to street peddlers wishing to sell lottery tickets, these vendors were quickly absorbed into the busy scene of peddlers hawking their wares that had become an iconic feature of the city. Because of their mobility and visibility in the city's public spaces, peddlers quickly increased lottery ticket sales. By the mid-1880s, so many lottery ticket peddlers filled the train stations, streets, and embarkation points on the docks that they elicited a series of official complaints registered in the documentation of the Municipal Chamber.[103] Ultimately, these complaints and the municipality's efforts to control ambulantes who sold lottery tickets were in vain. The product they sold had become a staple of daily life for multitudes of people, and the peddlers themselves had become an indispensable part of the commercial infrastructure.[104] Ordinances passed in the early First Republic proved equally ineffectual, but they do serve as evidence of lottery peddlers' persistent presence.[105]

Why were the prodigious numbers of street peddlers in the First Republic not commensurately reflected in the police archive of jogo do bicho cases? The occasional arrest record of an itinerant jogo do bicho vendor makes evident that vendedor ambulante was an occupation many undertook off and on throughout their working lives, but which not all identified as their "profession" when it came time to fix their working identity in police files. In one case from 1907, the thirty-nine-year-old Alberto José Dias Chaves, according to police records a man "without a profession" but "known to be a bicheiro ambulante," was arrested on the tramway platform on rua São Francisco Xavier.[106]

That same year, police apprehended another jogo do bicho defendant, Euclides Ribeiro, on a square in the North Zone of the city, "when he sold a jogo do bicho ticket to a minor." The defendant, the police testified, "is a jogo do bicho street peddler, having no other profession." Echoing the improbable yet often effective defense other accused bicheiros commonly proffered, Ribeiro insisted that the lists of numbers and monetary values clasped in his hand at the moment of his arrest had nothing to do with the jogo do bicho. Just as vehemently, he disavowed "street vendor" as his profession; rather, he represented himself as a more respectable "employee in commerce." Lacking bail money and evidently the patronage ties to call upon a colleague, friend, or countryman to post bail for him, Ribeiro spent several days in the Casa de Detenção before the judge ultimately acquitted him.[107] At least for some Cariocas like Euclides Ribeiro, "ambulante" may have denoted less a profession per se than a strategy for economic survival. Individuals changed and alternated roles—from shopkeeper to itinerant bookkeeper, from cashier to bicheiro—according to their immediate needs and resources, leaving the historical record vague as to the occupational niche of those who ran the animal game.

In addition, the relatively few ambulantes arrested for selling jogo do bicho tickets can be understood only if one considers whom the police actually did arrest: primarily Portuguese comerciantes and the cashiers and shop assistants who worked for them. Police viewed shopkeepers as likely targets of arrest because, unlike the poorer merchants who plied the streets, comerciantes in fixed locations were likely to have a full till from which the officer could draw his informal salary.[108] A predominantly white, largely Portuguese population of accused bicheiros filed in and out of the Casa de Detenção from the late 1890s on.

The story of the peddler Maximiliano Felix Bahia, our rule-proving exception, reveals the breach in the system of regulation and control of Rio's petty commerce that draws our attention to its subterranean workings. In stealing the earnings he was supposed to have delivered to the jogo do bicho banker, Bahia attempted to break free from the system through which the game operated. The anonymous complaint against Bahia and his eventual arrest demonstrate how the system closed in to discipline him. The game's illegality could become a tool at the disposal of those who dealt in it. Bicheiros' engagements with the law furnished individuals with useful resources but also stained them with the stigma of criminality. The jogo do bicho evolved in a commercial world whose inhabitants already had developed elaborate means of evading burdensome aspects of official regulations. Rent by social tensions and operating according to a logic that often defied the law, the world of petty commerce was the perfect medium in which the jogo do bicho would become institutionalized as a normal yet illegal part of Carioca society. Like popular commerce, the game formed along the disjunctures between official expectations and the demands of everyday urban life.

By the 1910s, individual shopkeepers and store clerks were not the only ones selling bicho tickets; in trying to end the jogo, Rio's law enforcement also documented larger, more sophisticated enterprises. Some, like the Portuguese shopkeepers described here, operated legitimate retail businesses alongside the clandestine lottery. In 1918, for example, police investigated a licensed social club that had been running a pawn shop linked to a jogo do bicho business: customers playing the illegal lottery would leave household items as security.[109] In another case in the same year, the highest echelons of the Federal District's police pursued their suspicions that the Transoceanica Company, a travel agency that purportedly sold vacation cruises by way of a lottery, was a covert jogo do bicho operation.[110] Cases like these imply that persons at all levels of retail commerce freely experimented with a variety of means of selling goods and services. The sale of goods by the turn of a wheel, which Lima Barreto describes nostalgically in the passage cited above, and other creative approaches to petty trading continued well into the twentieth century. These types of commerce were neither extinct, as Lima Barreto laments, nor atavistic, as the reforming urbanists, politicians, and engineers believed. The jogo do bicho grew as part of an emerging, vast realm of commerce that spilled prodigiously over both sides of the divide between the licit and the illicit.

CONCLUSION: THE GOOD, THE ORDINARY, AND THE INVENTION OF THE UNDERWORLD

In republican Rio, in the eyes of many Brazilians, the unregulated buying and selling of lottery tickets and other "idiosyncratic forms" of commerce were inexorably linked with criminality and disorder by the early twentieth century.[111] Indeed, today it may seem odd to discuss gambling as commerce rather than as urban vice.[112] The notion that petty gambling practices such as the jogo do bicho are so firmly and exclusively associated with the urban criminal underworld is telling; such is the legacy of the way in which petty gambling came to be viewed at precisely that historical moment, and it serves to remind us of the power of the law to naturalize social categories and to forge a new common sense over time.

For João do Rio, the journalist and canonical poet of the city in the first decades of the First Republic, the city itself was a many-headed, many-souled creature. His repeated references to the street peddlers who populated each corner and whose cries filled the tramway platforms show the ubiquity of these individuals in the elite urban imagination.[113] Reading these accounts against the grain, we can also see how those engaged in petty commerce defied the norms that Brazil's elite imposed either by administratively phasing out or by criminalizing outright the types of petty commerce on which the majority of the population depended both for work and to buy basic supplies they could not produce themselves. In an essay entitled "Pequenas Profissões" (Little professions), João do Rio reflects on street peddlers and their woeful, yet somehow admirable, position in Brazilian society. Addressing the companion with whom he wanders the streets, the author asks, "Did you admire that street peddler?" His companion replies, "I did admire a refined 'con man.'" The author, in turn, exclaims, "Oh! My friend, morality is a question of one's point of view. That gypsy [peddler] is part of an army of wretches, into which the conditions of life, or one's own temperament, in the end, one's fate, drags so many people. Remember the 'La Romera de Santiago,' the poem by Velez de Guevara? In it, he has some verses that express well what these creatures are:

These are working men
who are needy and seek
in this manner to better their lot
plying the streets."

In the course of João do Rio's essay, he describes for his companion the panoply of urban types that compose the "little professions" that arouse such sympathy and curiosity and, at times, moral consternation. Among their ranks are the "hunters," who gather and slaughter cats, bringing the skinned carcasses to restaurants to be cooked and sold as rabbit. There are the gypsy fortune tellers, the gleaners of garbage and scrap metal, the sellers of goods lifted from hotel rooms, the "*selistas*," who deal in stolen or counterfeit official seals. The writer and his companion muse about the street vendors who specialize in reselling castoff cigar bands, with which tobacconists fit their cheap cigars to sell them under false pretenses. The chronicle is a poignant testament to the inventiveness of buyers and sellers in the city's subterranean market.[114] It also demonstrates the ambivalent attitude of elite commentators on this underground population and their trades, which were both necessary to the survival of the city's poor majority and inimical to the orderly progress of the nation and its capital.

The arrest records of those whose lives brushed up against the law enforcement apparatus reveal not only the persecution of popular modes of behavior but also the freelancing that went on between the cracks of what was permitted. People circumvented or openly defied the law as they bartered, passed counterfeit currency, and bought and sold tickets to clandestine lotteries, to name just a few of the practices recorded in the judicial archive. From the perspective of those who sold this merchandise, engaging in such commerce may have seemed like a much more tempting career than working in a factory or under a supervisor, especially to those who had experienced coerced labor under a slave regime. Those who bought this merchandise were simply trading cash or goods for products, not engaging in a momentous act of defiance. We can only speculate whether extra value accrued to these commodities because they were illegal. The jogo do bicho, for one, seems to have gained added cachet because it was against the law.

Petty gambling was a completely normal aspect of daily life; it occurred not in back alleys but in dry goods stores and the kiosk coffee stands that punctuated the city's street corners. It spread through networks already articulated through the petty economy. When in the early twentieth century petty gambling became a question of public order and morality, its integral connection to both the city's popular market and its powerful concessionaires faded from the debates in the local and national legislature and the courtrooms and police precincts. Although over a century of criminalization and police corruption have ensconced illicit lotteries like the jogo do bicho in the world of organized crime, such practices are inseparable from the realm of petty commerce in which they originated.

4

PLAYING WITH MONEY IN REPUBLICAN RIO DE JANEIRO

Come, come, shiny dawn, regenerating and tender, bring us solace
and hope amid all these dark ruins and colossal, still smoking pieces of
rubble, which have long attested to the disgrace and wickedness that
descend on man in his anxious desire for riches and pleasure and in
the foolish ravings of the most undignified and degrading passions.

—Visconde de Taunay, *O Encilhamento* (1893), on the Rio de Janeiro stock market

In 1896, the year the first groups of buyers and sellers of jogo
do bicho tickets began to populate the Rio de Janeiro city jail,
the animal game was within the reach of all but the utterly
penniless, just as it is today; to play it, one needed as little
as 100 *reis*, the price of a half kilo of potatoes.[1] Likewise, to
establish a business in selling jogo do bicho tickets, one required only a measure of daring, a basic level of numeracy,
some small corner of the city where one could set up shop,
and sufficient funds to pay winning customers the customary
twenty-odd times the money wagered.

As I have shown, the jogo do bicho could have attained
neither its iconic popularity nor its criminal status without
the petty commercial infrastructure that made it part of the
capital's daily life. The clandestine lottery also depended
upon another conduit: money itself. For many urban Brazilians, a monetized economy made it both necessary and
possible to improvise at the margins of the permissible. Tracing the contours of urban Brazil's vast, barely submerged
underworld of unregulated trading involves analysis of not

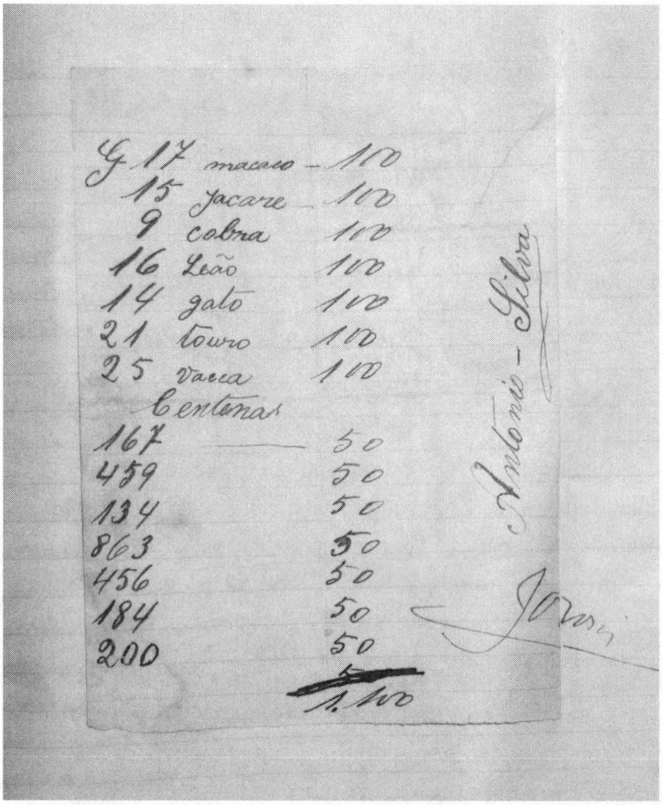
G 17 macaco — 100
15 jacare 100
9 cobra 100
16 Leão 100
14 gato 100
21 touro 100
25 vacca 100
Centenas
167 — 50
459 50
134 50
863 50
456 50
184 50
200 50
1.100
Antonio - Silva

FIGURE 15 A list of jogo do bicho bets, apprehended from a suspected vendor (1917). Source: Arquivo Nacional, Rio de Janeiro, 3ª Pretoria Criminal, 6Z-3589.

only the merchandise sold and the types of retail outlets but also the medium of exchange. This chapter places the animal game's playful approach to money amid the wide spectrum of penuniary improvisation in which urban Brazilians engaged, which straddled both sides of the law.

Just as the jogo do bicho spread through the city, the Federal District was rocked by another kind of gambling fever: a period of intense, largely disastrous financial speculation known as the Encilhamento. Both contemporaneous observers and retrospective commentators have remarked that the air in Rio practically scintillated with the promise of quick money.[2] The Carioca intelligentsia of the early First Republic utilized the jogo do bicho to condemn the questionable financial practices epitomized by the Encilhamento. But a critical examination of these apparently parallel phenomena—popular and elite gambling—suggests the enduring power of the views created by reformist, crime-fighting authorities, who envisaged the jogo do bicho as a unified practice and a vice instead of as everyday commerce. The intertwined histories of elite and popular forms of playing with money force us to question the artificial division between *jogo* and *negócio*, between play and business, that underlies both historical and contemporary conceptions of the social history of the turn of the twentieth century. I argue for a different explanation of the popular tendency to play with money, one rooted in the jogo do bicho's ordinariness as part of petty commerce, in which legal and illegal trading were virtually indistinguishable.

RIO DE JANEIRO, CAPITAL OF SPECULATION

The Visconde de Taunay, the latter-day Brazilian aristocrat and prolific chronicler of his times, opens his novel *O Encilhamento* (1893) with a scene of urban tumult. A "rather caustic" sun shone on the narrow, crooked streets built to conduct people and goods from the port to the old center of the city, now the federal capital of the new Republic. The suffocating heat "mattered little," Taunay writes, "to the agitated and noisy multitudes that filled the whole block from Alfândega Street to Primeiro de Março Avenue."[3] The density of the stirring crowd was such that even when carts attempted to pass, the mass of people made little attempt to part to allow the "heavy vehicles" through. Based on Taunay's first few lines, the reader might anticipate a demonstration or popular religious festival, common topics of urban chroniclers of the day. But at the center of the action stands the Banco do Brasil, the country's primary emission bank.[4] The tension in the novel arises not from a political uprising or a popular festival of particular exuberance but from frenzied trading in the stock market.

Most sophisticated Brazilians would have identified the phenomenon to which the title, *O Encilhamento*, refers. In the horse racing slang of the day, *encilhamento* denotes the moment of preparation just before the horses spring upon the track and also the tumultuous meeting place where bettors, horse owners, and others gathered before a race. By the 1890s, journalists and literary writers in Brazil had embraced a new common usage of this gambling jargon. The word came to describe the surge of rampant financial speculation in Rio's stock market (*Bolsa de Valores*), which lasted from about 1889 to 1891. In his memoir, the jurist Evaristo de Morais recalls, "The Republic came and with the Republic the Encilhamento. There was a profound transformation in this country. There was a fever, a madness.

Money spread itself around here in a real flood. One was given the impression that everyone had gone insane."[5] This short but momentous speculation boom broke and made fortunes. It provided the Carioca cultural imagination with abundant fodder to nourish conceptions of global capitalism, urban decadence, and public irresponsibility taken to a worst-case extreme.

As the novel begins, Taunay presents a nameless, faceless crowd engrossed in frenzied trading. The "compact mass" of people form ever-recombinant groups in the streets in "isometric movements." Taunay harnesses the power of this scene to purely visual imagery, a blur of bodies, hats, and pushcarts. But soon his opening narrative pans over to the center of the action, and the silent film showing carts rolling past the crushing, impatient crowd turns noisy:

> From time to time, tortuous channels opened up through which, wriggling out of the group, brokers and middlemen[6] hurriedly stole away, lightly and cleverly. There were an incalculable number of middlemen, of all ages, eyes glaring, bathed in sweat, with their hats fallen over the napes of their necks and handkerchiefs tied around their throats like a baby's bib, shouting buy, sell, without specifying just what they wanted to buy or sell. "Two hundred *Repúblicas*," one announced with an insistent and strained shout. "How much?" "83." "It's a deal." And notes were written quickly on little pieces of paper or on men's false shirt cuffs, which were already covered with figures, while people exchanged a thousand rough hand signals in the air, simple blinks of the eye, which initiated big business deals, or above all concluded them.[7]

Taunay's scene calls to mind another type of gambling that employed numbers hastily written on scraps of paper: the jogo do bicho. Taunay may not have intended to refer to the clandestine lottery, yet here and elsewhere the author winks at the reader, alluding to this markedly less distinguished type of gambling.[8] The novel affectionately lambastes the naive greed of the cadre of amateur financiers who huddled sweating in downtown streets hoping to pocket the spoils of capitalism. From a knowing, somewhat cynical stance, the narrator describes these men's attempts to let wealth beget wealth and hints at the socially destabilizing effects of earning money without the discipline and material productivity of work.

The Bolsa de Valores in Rio developed out of Brazil's external market for coffee and the new breed of elites made wealthy by the expansion of the crop in the southeast of the country. The gradual replacement of slave with free wage labor beginning around the 1850s liberated capital previously invested in slave labor and increased the circulation of money in Rio's economy. The city's stock market, at first organized informally, eventually came under self-regulation and moved from the street to its own meeting space, located close to the Customs House and the Imperial Palace. The use of intermediaries to facilitate encounters between buyers and sellers became institutionalized, as the stock market came to include the trade in commodities and currency from an ever-broader range of places in Brazil and Europe. Brazilian law in the last decades of the Empire moved toward a liberal permissiveness of financial speculation, and Rio's stock market increasingly shed the strictures of state regulation.[9]

With the proclamation of the Republic in 1889, the nation's new leadership adopted measures that resulted in a complete opening of the economy to foreign capital, permission for private banks to emit money, a new liberal body of commercial law, and the creation of a modern stock market, centered in the Bolsa de Valores. The establishment of emission banks and the relatively easy credit that was part of the new republican financial regime facilitated the creation of a plethora of newly minted companies. The elite and middle-class entrepreneurs who established these businesses did so not for the purpose of agricultural, commercial, or industrial production but rather, with the official blessing of the state, to exploit the "floating values" of stock shares.[10] These policies aimed to divert any surplus money held in private hands to buy shares in companies and therefore to finance the growth of Brazilian industry.

Inflation rose from a negative rate of −16.1 percent in 1887, the year that marked the beginning of the speculations with bank titles, to a rate of 84.9 percent in 1891, at the height of the Encilhamento.[11] The Encilhamento ruined many prominent capitalists of the late Empire. A new generation of arrivistes entered Rio's financial and social scene, people who had accumulated wealth virtually overnight in the early years of the new republican regime.[12]

In a newspaper chronicle of 1896, Joaquim Maria Machado de Assis used the jogo do bicho to register his disgust with these arrivistes, who had been attracted to his beloved city by the Encilhamento's promises of fast and enormous lucre. Constitutional debates in 1891 made real the possibility that the federal capital would be relocated; Machado was dismayed that Rio's powerful seemed not to care that their city was about to be abandoned to the avarice of the financial markets: "No one took action, . . . no one in the city of Rio de Janeiro complained about anything when the Constitution came up for discussion, no one brought to the attention of the legislature the city's past, nor its present, nor its probable future, and no one discussed the question of whether capital cities are or are not works of history, no one said a single thing, they simply purchased debentures, which were the bichos of the day."[13]

The author's allusion—"the bichos of the day"—to the immensely popular yet illegal game calls into question the civil rectitude of elite society by comparing financial speculation to its evil twin, the jogo do bicho. Machado dramatically contrasts capitalist finance, which many believed would propel the capital into the modern era, and the jogo do bicho, often held to be atavistic and antithetical to the modernization of the city.

The similarities Machado de Assis and his contemporaries noted between petty gambling and high finance were intentionally ironic and absurd: who, after all, would mistake the poor *bicheiro* for the wealthy, besuited financier? Yet the damning comparison in some ways was earnest. As other historians have documented for other parts of the world at this time, the questionable ethics and social impact of financial speculation caused grave concern early in the First Republic.[14] As another of Rio's chroniclers writes in a volume of verse published in 1926, the "voracious Encilhamento" threatened to devour the city under the provisional government, until the military dictator Marshal Floriano Peixoto ascended to power and decided "to resolve the crisis . . . always having morality on his mind."[15] *Speculation* had become shorthand for recklessness, economic chaos, lack of accountability, and a greedy disdain for the commonweal.[16]

Why was the Encilhamento so troubling to some observers? Taunay's novel depicts financial risk taking in the securities market as a metaphor for the unsettling psychological effects of the loss of individuality effected by modern urban life; the feverish trading in the Bolsa de Valores reduced both goods and people to infinitely interchangeable units.[17] Moreover, the Encilhamento was characterized by the involvement of amateur investors. The speculation boom devolved into "madness" in part because anyone with sufficient cash and some nerve could invest in securities or participate in the creation of the hundreds of spurious companies established, most of which folded.[18] Commentators condemned the practice of speculation by mocking the pretension of people who dabbled in banking but had no business doing so. In the preface to *O Encilhamento*, Taunay writes,

Each citizen became an incorporator and a director of banks and companies; those who yesterday did not even have the slightest capacity to run a grocery store of the most limited proportions, now placed themselves suddenly as directors of high finance; every citizen removed himself from his own profession to play the market, and Rio de Janeiro's marketplace metamorphosed in the blink of an eye into a Monte Carlo casino, but with one difference: in Monaco there is just one prince and many rules in the casino, and here there are many princes and impostors abound.

The self-criticism of certain members of the elite class with a penchant for satire and the hypocrisy of the authorities, who allowed some types of gambling and condemned others, reinforce our already ample knowledge of the antipopular bent of the republican oligarchy.[19] The simultaneity and apparent correlation between the two types of gambling may seem to present an interesting way to confront the perennial problem of how to study class divisions and interactions in Latin American urban society.

Yet we cannot take at face value the frequent comparisons between jogo do bicho players and vendors, on the one hand, and stock market financiers, on the other. The likenesses that the intelligentsia noted between patently dissimilar kinds of gambling served particular elite purposes. When viewed from the ground up, it becomes clear that the jogo do bicho bore little resemblance to the speculation occurring in the Bolsa de Valores. Neither sellers nor players of the jogo do bicho courted risk; they sought to avoid it. Most players bet very small amounts of money on the variants with the highest odds of winning. Ticket buyers were not playing off fluctuations in prices or currency values because the game operated daily, and players had only three days to cash in their winning ticket. As an illegal business enterprise, it did function for sellers as a hedge during hard times against poverty and unemployment—but this was because it was *work*, not because it was play. In other words, for the poor and middling classes, the risk management institution of choice was not gambling but participating as buyers and sellers in the nascent informal economy as a whole.

The illicit lottery is most fruitfully seen as a practice rooted in the highly heterogeneous money economy as it had been developing in the late nineteenth century, and in particular in an already-existing popular tradition of purchasing goods by means that today might be considered rather eccentric—especially by way of raffles (*sorteios* or *rifas*). The kind of playing with money that made the jogo do bicho illegal was in fact a normal, everyday feature of the modern popular economy of the early First Republic.

A PLAGUE OF PAPER

In May 1918, the Rio police closed down the headquarters of the Club dos Excentricos, one of the city's many creatively named private social clubs.[20] The club's owner and director, Salvador Panno, had operated a clandestine pawn shop for some years, but he also stood accused of running a jogo do bicho business out of his putatively legal organization, allowing bettors to exchange jewelry and other portable goods—no questions asked—for cash that the customer would, in turn, spend on a chance to win the equally clandestine animal game. Panno was undeterred by the increasingly aggressive police harassment as officials sought to shut down his club. One of his former employees who had fallen into the authorities' clutches denounced his boss, explaining how Panno and his accomplices continued to take bets for the jogo do bicho. To circumvent police surveillance, an employee simply leaned out the window of the Club dos Excentricos and lowered a basket suspended on a string to the tavern on the ground floor, where customers would place bets in the privacy of the bathroom and send them back up in the basket. The employee's testimony, combined with the flurry of tickets discovered during a search, gave police cause to shut the club's doors definitively as they carted off to the precinct wooden tables, decks of cards, and other items. Panno paid a moderate fine (two *contos*), and so, in the end, some of his allegedly ill-gotten gains cycled back to the public coffers.

The money that passed through the Club dos Excentricos—out of players' pockets and through the bathroom window, and from the illicit pawn shop to the customer's hands and then right back to the shop in exchange for jogo do bicho tickets—traveled a path that was not eccentric at all. Panno's story reveals how licit and illicit commerce were seamlessly integrated in early twentieth-century urban Brazil. In some illuminating ways, this case illustrates how the jogo do bicho typified popular participation in the money economy. Cash guaranteed every stage of the transaction as well as the legal rights and responsibilities of the accused and mediated all aspects of public life. Second, daily commerce required the use of money, but people used it in creative, often illegal ways. Finally, money was largely untraceable. Constant attempts by the police to use not only coins and bills but also ledger books and other accounting records as evidence for the prosecution in jogo do bicho cases almost always met with failure. As in the other rare but extant cases where a judge actually did find a jogo do bicho defendant guilty, Panno's prosecution is the exception that proves the rule.

Money, although new to some of Rio's residents as the dominant or sole means of providing themselves with material goods, had become prevalent and in fact indispensable by the 1890s in Brazilian cities. Cariocas did compensate for perennial cash shortfalls with food and raw materials gleaned from the urban commons; but, as noted, the commons had become increasingly inaccessible to those accustomed to making use of its fruit, firewood, and social space, as the state began to criminalize this type of sustenance.[21] City dwellers worked for wages, which they received in monthly or, more likely, daily allotments of cash.[22] By the late nineteenth century, Cariocas had largely acceded to the consensus that paper was worth gold and metal was worth bread.

The fact that nearly all urban Brazilians were already entrenched in the cash economy did not mean they would have experienced money as completely transparent and straightforward. The jogo do bicho money trail weaves in and out of the other, predictably eccentric and sometimes less than legal means of transmitting value that, despite their ubiquity, are difficult to reconstruct historically; the jogo do bicho, like counterfeiting, the other, related case this chapter will explore, produced police documentation that allows us the rare opportunity to trace the winding trajectory of money as it circulated in the popular economy.

Social historians who have described the complicated popular sentiments and the sometimes draconian official reaction to monetary crimes like counterfeiting have shown that money is never only about itself.[23] In modernizing urban Brazil, money was not just an inert container of value but also an icon of the orderly operation of the economy. The power and authority to make money conferred control of the flow of wealth. As it circulated from hand to hand, money also conveyed enormous value as a symbol of national integration. In the expansive, loosely federated Republic, money was one of the few tangible pieces of evidence of centralized, national authority.[24]

The government sought a monopoly on printing fiduciary money only belatedly. A plurality of types of currency served as media of exchange in the late Empire and early First Republic: particularly bank notes from different emission banks and treasury and promissory notes. By turns the economy in the late nineteenth century and early twentieth suffered massive emissions and contractions in the money supply. A brief examination of the state's experimentation with the economy during this time suggests how, although most likely inured to money as an instrument of trade, Cariocas are unlikely to have taken for granted its stable or unique value.

The First Republic inherited a national economy that was undermonetized because of slavery and the persistence of a patronage economy fueled by favors and influence as much as by money. Yet urban residents of all classes, including enslaved persons, had held and traded much of their wealth in cash since the early nineteenth century. The economic growth and development of banking were consequences of the coffee export economy and of slavery and its abolition. When British abolitionists in 1850 succeeded in pushing through the international treaty banning the African slave trade, they surely did not envision the ironic results of the act in the coffee-growing Paraiba valley. Practically overnight, the slave-owning planters of this area saw their human chattel increase massively in value. This opened up more possibilities for the expansion of financial credit and helped touch off the Paraiba Valley's boom decade of 1850–60. The demise of the coffee plantocracy began at the end of that decade. As the region moved toward monoculture, planters grew dependent on middlemen for the cash they now desperately needed to purchase necessities they could no longer produce for themselves.[25] Meanwhile, urban bankers profited from the planters' weakness. The creation of banks made possible more capital investment, the expansion and reorganization of credit, and the emission of more money.[26] The location of both Brazilian and foreign banks in cities strengthened the prestige of Brazil's urban centers, as the economic power of the rural planters, who depended on the banks for loans, diminished.[27]

Since the middle of the nineteenth century, the Brazilian government had dealt with deficits and foreign debt by emitting more money, a subject of heated debate in the last decades of the Empire.[28] Echoing the monetary controversies that characterized the nineteenth-century political economy in much of the world, Brazilian policymakers, merchants, and intellectuals argued furiously over what kind of wealth would back the country's circulating currency. Beyond such purely economic concerns as the international value of Brazilian currency and the stability of the domestic economy, at stake in these monetary debates were such fundamental questions as the balance of private versus state authority to issue money and the broader issue of public trust that the convertibility of paper money implies.[29] Despite the arguments of those who opposed what one commentator in 1861 called "the plague of paper currency," Brazil would eventually adopt a paper-backed currency and drift away from the hallowed gold standard.[30]

In the 1850s the Brazilian government first granted a monopoly on the emission of bank notes to the private Banco do Brasil but then extended the privilege to other banks. After a scandal involving the private banking sector's abuse of this privilege, the government began issuing money in 1866. In 1888 the state gave up its monopoly with the passing of the *Lei Bancária* (Banking Law), which created a system of imperial, provincial, and municipal emission banks.[31]

In the final years of the Empire and beginning of the Republic, gold and silver coin virtually disappeared; bank notes replaced metallic circulation as the mainstay of the economy. Meanwhile, the steady increase in nickel and bronze coin attested to the fact that coins had become merely a means of making change, rather than a medium of exchange or useful repository of value. Economic historians of Brazil have shown that, as elsewhere, the country's economy tended toward decreasingly "material" money. Bank notes, only reluctantly accepted at first, gradually came into general use, replacing metal currency in most everyday transactions.[32]

In an economy now reliant on immaterial forms of money, the First Republic was characterized by an ongoing politico-economic tug of war over monetary policy. By turns, a series of local, semiprivate monopoly banks, one central emission bank, and the Treasury had responsibility for the circulation of currency during the first decade of the new regime.[33]

The new Republic's provisional government under General Deodoro da Fonseca inherited ongoing debates about monetary policy and the problem of currency stability, exacerbated by the postemancipation increase in wage labor. Monetary reforms came early in the new Republic. To attract foreign capital and workers, the government considered it essential to attain a stable foreign exchange rate and prices. The policy through much of the decade was one of deflation and devalorization of Brazilian vis-à-vis foreign currencies.[34] The so-called Rui Barbosa reform passed in January of 1890, named for Brazil's finance minister, dramatically increased the amount of paper money in circulation and momentarily returned Brazil to a mid-nineteenth-century system in which local provincial banks printed currency. The government soon reinstated a centralized system of currency emission. Through the various phases of monetary reform, the swollen money supply created a brief, illusory sense of prosperity. In 1890–91, the circulation of paper money increased by 75 percent; the amount of money in circulation between 1888 and 1891 more than doubled.[35]

The reforms, far from stabilizing growth and currency, brought about the very opposite. The increase in the money supply and easy credit helped instigate the speculation frenzy of the early 1890s. Foreign exchange rates fell precipitously, and galloping inflation diminished the value of money. As public revenues exceeded expenditures, the government printed even more money. Fiscal instability undermined the new Republic's morale while worsening the privation of the urban poor and working classes.[36]

Political opposition to Barbosa led to policies that worsened the Brazilian economy, leading to an army revolt that brought down the government in November 1891. Economic hardship was compounded by a worldwide depression in 1893 that drove coffee prices down and wreaked havoc with Brazil's foreign debt. The stock market nearly crashed, and the cost of living increased by 60 percent between 1895 and 1898.[37]

There followed more waves of reform and monetary experimentation. After Manuel Ferraz de Campos Salles assumed the presidency in 1898, a period of economic stabilization followed until about 1906.[38] Among the measures the Campos Salles administration took was to suspend specie payments and to retire from circulation and burn large quantities of paper money.[39] By contrast with the massive earlier inflation, price levels fell by 15 percent in 1899–1900, devastating commerce, closing banks, and provoking bank runs.[40] The diminished money supply and the end of the world depression caused the value of the *milreis* to double.[41] After briefly experimenting with a return to the gold standard in 1906–13, excessive public spending and a rising national debt during the administration of President Hermes da Fonseca induced the Treasury to resort to an "old expediency": it issued inconvertible paper money, ultimately forcing the government to contract a large foreign loan.[42]

In the 1890s states and municipalities began to emit their own notes for use in small-scale transactions and for making change. Local banks began to emit coupons called *vales*, or even simply to falsify notes. At the end of the decade, the federal government "prohibited the circulation of these homespun notes and coupons" and ordered the massive minting of nickel coins.[43]

What did people carry in their pockets, and how did this limit or expand their possibilities for purchasing goods? By the 1850s, most value circulated in paper or copper money, not precious metals.[44] An English traveler reported in 1886 that copper coinage predominated throughout Brazil while in Rio, "the money [consisted] of nickel tokens" of relatively small denominations.[45] By the late 1890s, cash rather than barter or self-sufficiency was a way of life for the average city dweller. Much of this cash was already in the form of paper. A sample of persons who were arrested in 1898, for example, virtually all carried cash in their pockets. In addition to the pocket watches, lottery tickets, and occasional trinkets found in suspects' pockets and meticulously catalogued, there were paper money and coin in varying amounts: the paper money could be as much as 70$000, but it was rare for someone not to have bills in the amount of 1$000.[46] The value of this money, however, fluctuated wildly; between 1887 and 1912, the cost of living increased 940 percent.[47]

In sum, the monetary roller-coaster ride and the multiple types of money in circulation, along with volatility of prices and cycles of inflation, made this a chaotic moment in Brazil's monetary history. Although a requisite part of everyday economic life, paper money had not yet been effectively brought under the government's administrative or legal control.[48] The extreme fluctuations in the value and supply of money, salaries, and prices impacted everyday workers and consumers. Rio's residents adopted creative means of contending with such challenges as cyclical cash shortages, massive unemployment, and the frequency with which poor and middle-class people were forced to live on promised rather than real wages. Shopkeepers and petty vendors most likely extended credit to customers routinely.[49] One could purchase goods (and in some cases small businesses could pay workers' salaries) with promissory notes—both real and falsified—and vales.[50] Pawning, short-term labor contracts, and informal work like selling tickets for clandestine lotteries enabled people to get enough money for daily necessities. And forms of petty retail vending that diverged from the modern cash-and-carry model abounded.

The many varieties of illicit vending and gambling prohibited in the digests (*Consolidações*) of the Penal Code of 1890 bear witness to the diversity of kinds of selling that occurred and the law's futile attempts to outpace the creativity of sellers and buyers. Sorteios were used for the purchase of everything under the sun. For example, the Penal Code prohibited, among many other items, "Raffles of bonds and other obligations of the Union [that is, the federal government], the states, and the municipalities" and "the sale of merchandise or real estate, by way of a sorteio, according to the respective regulation, as long as there is no distribution of money, nor of conversion into money the titles selected by lottery."[51] In short, lotteries were more than just playing with money; they were a way of buying merchandise. The sorteios police targeted served as popular entertainment: they prolonged the process of acquiring household essentials, turning it into a low-stakes game of chance. Above all, popular sorteios transformed an unfortunate situation into a more pleasant one: poor and working-class people who could scarcely afford the vertiginously rising prices of basic goods could risk small amounts of money for the chance to buy merchandise at a low cost.

In his 1917 essay discussed in chapter 3, Lima Barreto gives a wonderful example of such popular games of chance used to purchase basic goods. Recounting his memories from his boyhood in the late Empire, he describes the small shacks (barraquinhas) built on the Campo de Santana during the traditional June religious festivals. I remember well, he continues, "that the public powers of the time tolerated this type of fair, characterized by rough-hewn roulette wheels, because the business owners operated under the pretext that the money they would take in would be used to finish the repair work on the local church. . . . The virtuous newspapers of that time always argued against those events. They clamored against the unstoppable gaming that went on in those little shacks." He explains that what occurred there was, indeed, a sort of gambling: "The merchandise was gained by luck, which took place in a kind of game of roulette, called pinguelim, or some other such name, with a certain number of tickets available at low cost. In general, there were different types of fowl . . . but there were other things that one could win: hogs, sheep, goats, lace, bowls, etc."[52] In this literal animal game, people could both enjoy a social experience and buy necessities in a way that circumvented their prohibitive cost.

In fact, selling merchandise for money but by means of chance was a common feature of the petty commercial landscape, not only in the late Empire but also into the early twentieth century. Lima Barreto comments that the republican government criminalized the vending shacks and expelled them from the Campo de Santana. But they did not disappear; when he wrote this crônica in the 1910s, similar types of vending at popular fairs called mafuás had been cropping up in suburban neighborhoods. The multitudes arrived at these markets on foot or on bondes from other suburbs to socialize and try to obtain goods—sheep, chickens, bottles of perfume—

"by means of luck" ("*por meio da sorte*"). At the end of the evening, the crowd dispersed. The author comments on the "parade of . . . people, the majority full of disappointment, but a good part of them unpretentiously carrying ducks, turkeys, chickens, and oinking pigs." Laden with livestock and tired from the day's outing, some raffle winners would miss the bonde, only to be arrested by the police on their long walk home, "who would take them for chicken thieves, and carry them off to the police station."[53]

The archive documents the existence of numerous *clubs de sorteios*, private clubs that customers would join as members. The arrangement allowed retail business owners legally to sell their "members" a chance to buy such goods as foodstuffs and travel packages. The clubs' legality followed a circular logic that depended simply on whether their requests to obtain licenses to operate had been approved or rejected. The Club Americano, formed in 1913 and listed as a travel agency headquartered in the historic center, was granted permission to operate a retail business and make its sales "by way of sorteios" in accordance with the law.[54] Members paid a small amount of money—just one milreis—for a chance to win a trip to Minas, São Paulo, or even Argentina or Uruguay, thus bringing the cost of travel "within the reach of all." Police District Chief Armando Vidal, beginning the most vigorous anti-bicho campaign the city had ever seen, became obsessed with the notion that this was a thinly disguised jogo do bicho operation: what the owners called installments, he insisted, were actually bets. A roll call of distinguished jurists and senators offered written opinions (*pareceres*) on the case, and it was judged that the Club Americano had done nothing illegal. It had been licensed to sell tickets for trips "*mediante sorteio*" ("by means of a raffle"), and had done just that. We will never know if the Club Americano was mounting a jogo do bicho business in the guise of a legal sorteio, or if the long list of similarities between the club and the jogo do bicho Vidal painstakingly laid out in the inquest was the imaginative product of his personal obsession with the "moral sanitation" of the Federal District.[55] But the documentation does point to the ubiquity of games of chance, particularly the sorteio, as a creative means of selling goods and services and to the near impossibility of distinguishing legal from illegal types of selling.

BAD MONEY INTO GOOD

The money economy, instead of standardizing trade, created new forms of improvisation, many technically illicit, which became functionally normal

—a phenomenon familiar to generations of observers of the informal economy.[56] The practice of trading in cash, enforced by federal economic policy and criminal law, certainly narrowed the range of activities that could occur in the popular economy.[57] Yet the cash economy also broadened the field in which people could improvise—cash is uniform, anonymous, and infinitely convertible. Much academic writing about money emphasizes the strangeness and alienation that characterize the collective experience of the gradual but global, macrohistorical process of monetization. Money became a universal symbol of the abstraction of value and a troubling reminder of how, in the now-common jargon of semiotic analysis, a sign can become unmoored from its signifier.[58] The need to trade metal alloys or pieces of paper for life's necessities may indeed have struck a segment of Rio's population, especially rural migrants and former slaves, many of whom had been marginalized from the money economy, as strange and new. In general, though, evidence fails to show that money mystified urban Brazilians of the protoindustrial era. On the contrary, one might say the abstraction of symbol from reality gave people something to play with. Money's reason for existing is its alienability.[59] Its anonymity became a vital element in the semi-illicit transactions that had become part of people's everyday lives. Mute and without memory, money told no tales. Pawned goods like the jewelry police scooped from Salvador Panno's safe formed part of a natural cycle of laundering money as it flowed silently through sequences of transactions, irrespective of their legal status.[60]

Workers and entrepreneurs in petty commerce, and notably among them jogo do bicho vendors, were crucial intermediaries in this cycle of turning good money into bad and then back again.[61] During its first decades the jogo do bicho operated in a decentralized fashion. Financed mostly by individual sellers, establishing a jogo do bicho business required little or no initial investment.[62] Bicheiros, as noted, were primarily workers or small business operators in petty commerce who received cash from customers and used it to pay their personal expenses or to reinvest in their other businesses: lottery shops, dry goods stores, taverns, and the like. The bills and coins that bettors paid them accumulated in vendors' pockets, cash tills, and other, less expected places. The jogo do bicho trade also momentarily transformed this money into figures recorded in the small notebooks that, along with a pencil and the cash itself, were the only tools of the bicheiro's trade.

Money must be understood not only as the cash itself but also as the way in which it was represented and documented. Police tried to use bicheiros' ledger books, like the cash and the tickets themselves found at the alleged crime scene, to incriminate them. In a case from 1907, Euclides Ribeiro, a *vendedor ambulante* (street peddler) was arrested on the Largo do Matadouro "when he sold a jogo do bicho ticket to the minor Antonio Gomes." Police claimed to have witnessed Antonio delivering to Euclides "a jogo do bicho list and two milreis." Ribeiro, police said, worked as an "itinerant jogo do bicho peddler, having no other profession." A search of Euclides turned up 74,800 reis as well as twenty jogo do bicho lists. He defended himself by claiming he was "an employee in commerce and not a bicheiro" and denied that the lists in his hand had anything to do with the illicit lottery. The two defendants reiterated a version of the counteraccusations common in jogo do bicho cases, accusing the police of inventing charges, harassing innocent citizens, and engaging in criminal malfeasance. At the heart of Ribeiro's and Gomes's defense was their assertion that the lists could not have been part of a jogo do bicho exchange. How could the illiterate young Antonio, they asked, have written them? "And furthermore," the defense statement reads, "all of the lists in this case are just dirty paper in little pieces," with penciled notations that anyone, "even perhaps the arresting officers, who were also witnesses in this case," could have written. The police "are incapable, because of a lack of authenticity, of providing material proof of the infraction of article 367 of the Penal Code." The judge, citing a long list of procedural irregularities, acquitted.[63]

In most arrests related to the jogo do bicho, the wads of money sellers and buyers stuffed in their shoes, behind cupboards, behind statues of Catholic saints on an altar served as the primary evidence in the criminal case. Despite seemingly clear evidence of guilt, however, cases were often dismissed because of this very same money. For example, José Gomes de Oliveira was arrested in 1907 when a minor gave him a jogo do bicho list, which the police found on him along with some money and pieces of paper "with the following words: alligator, four hundred, snake, two hundred, butterfly, one hundred reis, donkey, two hundred reis." A certain Bernadino de Rocha paid the five hundred milreis on his behalf, and Oliveira was freed on bail and eventually acquitted.[64] The case of José Maria Ribeiro discussed in chapter 3 shows how money was both the crux of the criminal investigation and its undoing. Ribeiro, a man whom police caught at least three times selling jogo do bicho tickets, stood accused in 1908 of "stationing himself in [a dry goods store] with the aim of arranging buyers for the so-called jogo dos bichos." The police officers' search yielded just some coins and a notebook with numbers recorded in it, which the accused claimed was "exclusively for personal notations, not wishing to indicate just what these notations were."[65] As in scores of similar cases preserved in the archive, the defendants in these two cases argued that the money proved nothing, and the judges, as in almost all cases, agreed. The inability to prove ownership of money was the bicheiro's most powerful ammunition. Accused bicheiros and their defense lawyers knew very well that money, and money transformed into dirty little pieces of paper, were anonymous and difficult to trace. The fact that the names of seller and player were on the handwritten scraps apparently was immaterial.

Monetization was a basic, unspoken assumption of Brazilian criminal law by the late nineteenth century. Particularly in *contravenção* cases like the jogo do bicho, money, not loyalty, guaranteed the most important steps in the legal process: posting bail money and paying the fine. Money also guaranteed the extralegal actions routine in jogo do bicho cases, such as the payment of protection money to police and payoffs to witnesses. Monetary sanctions gained importance at the end of the nineteenth century as jurists and police focused their energies on misdemeanors like unlicensed gambling, by definition almost always punishable by fines rather than prison sentences. The prevalence of the fine was a sign not just of a fully monetized economy, but also of the differential levels of participation in it: nearly everyone arrested in a jogo do bicho case who could pay the *fiança* (bail) was soon released "to defend oneself in liberty."[66] Those who did not have money approached a patron or family member. Those who had neither the money nor the social standing to borrow it were held for indeterminate, often lengthy periods in the Casa de Detenção.

The jogo do bicho relied on the circulation of cash. As the case of Panno's pawn shop illustrates, bettors needed to transform even resalable goods into money before they could play and to do so in person. The police files of jogo do bicho cases tell fascinating stories of the secret lives of bank notes as they passed from mother to son, to neighbor, to the owner of a *botequim*. In such a heterogeneous economy, the use of money cannot simply be taken for granted. It marked the jogo do bicho as explicitly part of the anonymous, public realm, one largely mediated by *pequenos comerciantes* who wavered in and out of legal businesses.[67] But the animal game was also part of a system that depended on the integration of the multiple forms of value and exchange people used. After all, the jogo do bicho ticket bore two signatures: the buyer's and the seller's. The game fused personality and impersonality, intimate society and mass culture.

Like the jogo do bicho game ticket, paper money carried the signatures of government or issuing bank officials who vouched for its value and promised to pay on demand. Counterfeiting, an all too tempting opportunity offered by economic confusion and made possible by creativity and nerve, shows vividly the extent to which urban Brazilians questioned the value and authenticity of money.[68] If the jogo do bicho teetered on the edge of legality and social acceptance, counterfeiting was beyond the pale. The tenacious attention authorities paid to its suppression provides additional insight into the slippage between licit and illicit forms and uses of money the jogo do bicho epitomized.

Why *moeda falsa* would threaten the state, both economically and politically, is no mystery. Counterfeiting had been a crime in the Alfonsine and Philippine codes of the colonial era as well as in the Criminal Code of 1830, in force throughout the Empire. The Philippine Ordinances stipulate transportation (*degredo*) for "the purchase or use of counterfeit money, in an amount less than mil reis." Counterfeit gold or silver currency brought higher penalties.[69] Throughout the nineteenth century officials cast a careful eye on counterfeiting suspects and allocated administrative resources to surveilling and prosecuting them.[70]

Echoing the metaphoric reference to disease and sickness afflicting the national body used in talking about the emission of paper money, Sylvio Romero, a preeminent Brazilian intellectual of the early twentieth century, laments the persistence of counterfeiting: "One of the plagues of our economic system is the habit of fabricating false currency. And this leprosy is not something new: on the contrary, it is quite old. The annals of national criminality are full of many cases of this kind."[71] Police, jurists, and government officials battled counterfeiting in the first two decades of the twentieth century: it appeared as an infraction in the Penal Code of 1890; the Naturalization Law of 1908 excluded from naturalization foreigners convicted of counterfeiting.[72] A ministerial annual report presented to the president of Brazil in 1907 noted the special treatment moeda falsa received in the early First Republic. The report states, "With respect to the introduction of counterfeit money into circulation and its production, the police authorities continue to exercise active and severe vigilance for the repression of this criminal industry."[73] Participants in the 1917 police convention that took place in Rio ardently discussed counterfeiting as among the most significant criminal matters of the day.

From a policing perspective, the facility with which individuals could try their hand at emitting their own currency particularly troubled authorities. Printing fake money required neither expensive, highly sophisticated equipment nor a large space in which to carry out the crime. In 1917, Albino Mendes, in prison for counterfeiting, was investigated when "materials and instruments used for the fabrication of counterfeit money," along with various partially made bills, were found in his cell.[74] It was usually citizens in the course of their daily shopping or vending who first detected counterfeit bills or coins. Counterfeiting often seems to have been an amateurish operation: the bogus bills were quite visible to the naked eye.[75]

Accusations of counterfeiting appear frequently in the daily report logs of police stations, often prompted by the suspicions of the sales clerks or business owners who had received the money.[76] In December 1903, two men walked into a shop in the distant suburb of Guaratiba. They picked out some small manufactured goods (*fazendas*) that cost 13$200 and paid the shopkeeper with a 200$000 note, enough money to buy a thousand kilos of lard or two thousand kilos of bread or to pay an electrician for a month.[77] The shopkeeper soon realized the note was false and hurried to the police station to file a formal complaint. Police arrested the two culprits, the matter was handed over to a judge, and the chief of police opened an inquiry within a month.[78] In another case, this one from 1907, the cashier at the Derby Club complained to the police that he had received moeda falsa.[79]

The amounts involved varied, as did the places where the bills surfaced, but not surprisingly counterfeit money appeared wherever money changed hands. Certain pockets of the consumer economy, such as small dry goods stores and especially the intra- and interurban transportation network that radiated across the greater urbanizing area of the Federal District, fell victim. Police documents reveal that a vast counterfeit economy surfaced in the city's railway network in the early twentieth century. In the decade between 1886 and 1896 almost three million people rode the Central train line, alone.[80] Counterfeit bills were found so frequently in the till of Central Station and the far-flung stations connected to it that the station's administrative office printed special stationery for reporting and investigating these bills. Finding moeda falsa was a routine part of the administrative duties of a string of bureaucrats that began with the railway station manager and extended to the police and eventually the Caixa de Amortização (Amortization Bank).

A spate of documents from 1908 to 1909, for example, from the directorship of the Estrada de Ferro Central do Brasil report to the chief of police that a *cedula falsa* (counterfeit note) of such and such denomination (almost always twenty or ten milreis) was found in the daily cash earnings of such and such railway station. Letters from 1909 report bills and, less frequently, coins found in train stations across the greater Rio area, all part of the Estrada de Ferro Central: a four-hundred-milreis note was found in April in Mangeira and another in Engenho de Dentro.[81] In 1915 and 1916, too, letters report moedas falsas being found in the daily earnings of stations of the Central do Brasil, each and every month, mostly one-milreis coins with the occasional small-denomination bill. Again in 1918, another wave of documents cites cedulas falsas found among the daily cash intake at the many rail stations. In police documents covering April and May 1918 every rail station along the Central line was represented.[82] These voluminous, detailed police files demonstrate the amount of time and money law enforcement expended on counterfeiting, most of which was spent on authenticating suspected false money of exceedingly small value and on the nearly impossible task of searching for the perpetrators.[83]

A report of 1907 in a police investigation into the criminal responsibility for a false note of fifty milreis voices frustration over the difficulty of following the counterfeit money trail: "This Police precinct (*Delegacia*) has expended all its efforts in its attempts to determine who deserves criminal responsibility" for the counterfeit money that gave rise to this investigation. But these efforts have been frustrated, the documents read, because the depositions gathered lack enough proof to incriminate anyone. The scores of pages of declarations made in the course of this investigation tell the story of the trajectory of a single banknote, a story whose exquisitely detailed middle is sandwiched between a generic beginning and end: the fifty-milreis note came from and was about to return to the street. In April 1907 a man named Celino was playing pool in the tavern owned by a certain Joaquim. A minor named João, whom Celino knew by sight, appeared. João asked Celino to change a bill of fifty milreis, a request Celino denied. João then suggested that Celino simply keep the bill in question, stay in the tavern, and use it to pay his bar tab; João would receive his change when it was time to settle the bill at the end of the evening. After the first round of drinks, Celino removed the folded note from his pocket and handed it to the cashier, who delivered the change to João. When he returned to the tavern the next day, Joaquim gave Celino a piece of his mind; the bill, he said, was counterfeit. João, sought out and interrogated by police, asserted that he had been given the bill by his cousin José Lopes. The police took José to have a word with Joaquim. João went to the police station, accompanied by a civilian police officer (*Guarda Civil*) who did not know if the note under investigation was indeed the same one João had given him. When police questioned João, he corroborated Celino's declarations, adding that José had told him he had found the bill on the street in front of the botequim. José's testimony confirmed that he had indeed given his cousin the note in question and that he had found it on the street. The arresting officer affirmed what the three suspects had said but concluded that his testimony "clarifies nothing." While the police had ascertained definitively that the bill was false, they found it impossible to prove that either João or José had violated article 241 of the Penal Code, which stipulates penalties for the crime of fabricating or passing moeda falsa.[84] The fake fifty-milreis note had come "from the street": public life was awash in untraceable, anonymous cash, and the note in question had come from this undifferentiated money stream.

This case is typical: those accused of passing counterfeit bills often argued that they had received the bill from a *desconhecido* (an unknown person or stranger), and the suspects usually succeeded in freeing themselves of all charges on these grounds.[85] The few cases in which police did pursue their accusations of passing counterfeit money demonstrate how the anonymity and public nature of urban commercial life gave police as well as the accused a certain latitude. In November of 1909 Casimiro de Carvalho appeared before the Secretaria de Policia do Distrito Federal bearing the paperwork intended to prosecute him for multiple criminal charges. "I present you with Casimiro de Carvalho," the letter from the chief of police read, "in whose possession was found a false note in the amount of 20$000, which accompanies him. I recommend that you initiate legal proceedings against the same, since this individual remains detained also as a disorderly person and a pickpocket [*gatuno*]." The police records leave unclear many of the circumstances of his arrest, calling into question its legitimacy. How could the police have known Carvalho had a counterfeit bill inside his pocket? They may have fabricated the moeda falsa charge or even planted the bill on the accused for lack of other evidence to detain him. Police would likely have known that "being a pickpocket and a disorderly person" had no juridical standing; the only legitimate basis for a criminal case is an accomplished act, not a state of being (see chapter 2).[86] The origin of this bill "in the street," to use the language from the previous case, did not absolve Carvalho; his status as a known criminal in the eyes of the police managed to turn good money into bad.

CONCLUSION

In the early First Republic, the capital city's *homens novos* guzzled a strange cocktail: the excitement of social mobility through material wealth, mixed with moral trepidation about the avarice of easy money. Invectives about the jogo do bicho, uttered in the service of distinguishing good capitalist financial dealings from bad, helped strengthen the campaign to wipe out the game. One might even say that the critics of the Encilhamento quoted above also each did their small part to "invent" the jogo do bicho as a widespread, unified criminal practice by assuming the game's moral and legal wrongness in their influential published writings. But if we limit our understanding of the jogo do bicho to its repression and supposed dissonance with elite culture and republican morality, we will miss the opportunity it provides to glimpse at aspects of urban public life and economic culture that have been otherwise lost in time.

Following the lead of the new generation of Brazilian historians, we also must see beyond the problematic analytical category of popular culture, which in its traditional iterations flattens the diversity of popular practice while artificially dividing it from elite culture, the state, and the materiality of life. Those who dealt in the jogo do bicho certainly traded in abstractions like hope, dreams, and hunches concerning which animal and number to play. But the game was also very much about real money, money changing hands, moving from person to person. Multitudes touched any one milreis note. Money physically crossed class lines and circulated promiscuously; it offers a useful way to think about popular participation in public life. Like the barraquinhas at the popular festivals of this period analyzed in recent works by Martha Abreu and Maria Clemetina Pereira Cunha, the small vending shacks where people bought goods by means of the technically illegal sorteios were "rehearsals," not just for mass culture but also for mass consumption, preparing people to enter the collective through quasi-legal—or what would later be called informal—means.[87]

■

5

LIVES OF THE PLAYERS

The Muse of the Streets is the Muse that flourishes in back alleys and springs up in city squares, between the noise of the masses and all the nervous anguish, it is the egalitarian Muse, the Muse of the people, that undoes all the gravest facts and turns them into popular ballads, it is the only Muse without pretensions for she is renewed with Life itself. If Brazil is the land of poetry, its great city is the warehouse, the junk-dealer, the customs house, the thrift shop, the grand emporium of poetic forms. In this Cosmopolis that is Rio, poetry sprouts among the most heterogeneous classes. . . . Wherever a man goes, there he will find waiting for him, definitive and stubborn, the Muse. If you take a modest tram, you will find a tip for playing the jogo do bicho written in verse on the back of your ticket.—João do Rio

Culture is ordinary, that is the first fact.—Raymond Williams, "Culture Is Ordinary" (1958)

As the twentieth century was beginning, Marcelo da Silva's lottery shop did a brisk business. The shop was located on the rua do Ouvidor in Rio's center amid the fading glamour of the street's perfumeries and sellers of French, leather-bound volumes, and da Silva took advantage of the steady stream of passersby as well as those buying lottery tickets—licit ones—to accumulate a large clientele for his illegal jogo do bicho enterprise.[1]

In the popular imagination those who tried their luck at the jogo do bicho at da Silva's lottery shop would have fit under the wide umbrella of what Edmund Burke and his generation called "a people out of doors."[2] The eighteenth-century euphemism classifies the masses who participated in the public life of the city according to their use of the city's public spaces rather than to the amplitude of their financial resources or patronage ties. Yet the term communicates social distance with great, if telegraphic, clarity. Such nomenclature implies separate societies for the city's well-off and poor populations, suggesting that the common folk claimed the street as their domain.

"A people out of doors" helps us think about Rio de Janeiro around the turn of the twentieth century. Brazil's literate classes referred to the non-elite urban public as the *povo* or sometimes, more disdainfully, as *a gente miuda* (the little people). In the capital city, the spatial connotations of "a people out of doors" would have been both derogatory and not; Rio's pride of place revolved around its bohemian nightlife, urbanity, and incipient consumer culture.[3] To be out of doors was to be modern and cosmopolitan. For Rio's poor majority, however, existence out of doors was a necessity as much as a choice.[4] Until the late nineteenth century, the city's poor classes found their entertainment in the urban commons, mostly free of charge. But, as previous chapters have shown, the urban commons was undergoing a process akin to the enclosure of its rural counterpart: the assertion of private ownership of and usufruct rights to land and other public goods previously recognized as collectively held closed off possibilities to those who had neither the economic means to buy valuable public resources like land or concession contracts nor the social power to challenge public life's new breed of private owners in court. Completing the cycle, the law cemented the new social and economic relations the process of enclosure generated. The jogo do bicho's early history is part of this macrolevel process, as its customers were consigned to a legal and cultural underworld even though they engaged in a trade that occurred daily all over the city—and very much above ground. Out of doors, the animal game's players traded in illegal lottery tickets, discussed the game, and scanned the urban terrain for signs that might foretell the winning animal and number.

The question of how and when culture became public precedes the issue of enclosure, a concept that assumes the prior existence of common resources that devolved to private control. In considering what the analytical category of public culture might have meant to people in early republican urban Brazil, we must first acknowledge that *public* bears two distinct meanings. First, it is political and jurisdictional, referring to the domain of state power, which acts in the name of the collective; as such, public power is distinguished from princely power, on the one hand, and the private, intimate, or domestic sphere, on the other. Second, what one can designate as public culture was literally public life, that which took place outdoors and in the self-organized domain of freely circulating ideas and people.[5] Even before the populist cultural politics of the mid-twentieth century swept vernacular practices such as Carnival celebrations and popular arts and crafts into the national state's tutelary embrace, culture had become public in both senses in cities throughout Latin America. The state encouraged culture through its relatively limited patronage of the arts but mostly discouraged it through the criminal law.[6] The Brazilian state wielded its republican morality in the form of legal interdictions designed to control superstition, police cultural values, and promote public order.

In this context, the idea of enclosure relates to the shifting balance of control over shared resources between the state, private industry, and different sectors of the population. While historians of late nineteenth- and early twentieth-century Latin America have not employed the term *enclosure*, they have depicted this process in action. For instance, Martha Abreu describes how the dominant tendency among Rio's intellectual and political elite was to attempt to contain (*cercear*) the popular festivals in which the *mestiço* crowd took part in the city's public spaces, precisely to prevent them from becoming "symbols of [Brazilian] nationality," which, in fact, they did by the 1920s and 1930s.[7]

Historians of modern, urban Latin America have also shown how interdictions that amounted to enclosure were formative of public culture. To partake of shared public spaces and resources meant to subject oneself to state surveillance.[8] Yet one could diminish the risk of arrest by paying admission to public life and culture. The commercialization of leisure entailed the commodification of morality itself: in other words, the contingency of decency and respectability upon one's ability to enter the ever more enclosed realm of commercialized public life.[9]

Just as the jogo do bicho took shape as part of the city's increasingly regulated petty commerce, it was also part of regulated, commercialized, and massified popular culture whose development coincided with the game's rise, spread through the city, and criminalization. The early twentieth century witnessed the incipient development of public amusements like music halls, theatrical spectacles, and early cinema as a wage-earning working and middle class formed. By the early 1920s an elaborate infrastructure of urban commercial leisure and a mass culture had emerged. Over this period Cariocas of diverse socioeconomic backgrounds used the city's street corners, taverns, shops, and tram platforms to play games in which winning or losing depended exclusively on chance.

Jogo do bicho players in Rio's public spaces constituted a people out of doors in another, related sense: the jogo do bicho money trail, such as it is, leads to the intersection of the *submundo* of gambling and the above-ground culture industry. Amusement parks, live entertainment venues, and eating and drinking spots, newly accessible to Cariocas of the nonelite classes, not only presented opportunities to buy and sell tickets to the jogo do bicho but also were owned, run, and financed by capital that cycled through the illicit animal game. As the informal dimension of the culture industry, the jogo do bicho suggests how what may appear to have been marginal was in fact central to the development of commercialized entertainment. Players could not have fully fathomed the extent of this link between the world and the underworld. However, the communal and ritual-laden manner in which they played the jogo do bicho, and the ideas about risk, luck, and legality expressed in the cultures that the game generated, reveal people's collective awareness of this connection. Root and branch, public culture bore the effect of laws against petty crime.

IN SEARCH OF THE ONE WHO GOT AWAY

On March 3, 1911, the Rio police arrested a twenty-eight-year-old male shopkeeper named Laureano Domingues and a forty-year-old female cook from Rio's hinterland named Felismina together, *em flagrante delicto*.[10] In the middle of the afternoon, the police claimed, Laureano had brazenly sold Felismina a chance to win at the jogo do bicho. When arrested he had in his hands two tickets for the jogo do bicho and 65,400 *reis*, while Felismina held the smaller sum of 2 milreis.[11] Witnesses confirmed details of the alleged transaction. Despite the stack of jogo do bicho lists stapled in the *processo* as evidence, the judge acquitted the defendants on April 19 because of procedural technicalities.

The police took Laureano into custody again about seven months later in a lottery shop located at his home address, in the act of selling jogo do bicho tickets to "a woman who managed to get away."[12] The two jogo do bicho lists he clutched in his hand as he was arrested—one of which, according to a witness, he had "received from the hands of a woman"—

proved insufficient to prosecute him for dealing in the animal lottery. The judge acquitted him a few days later.

Laureano spun through this revolving door at least four more times. That same year he was arrested yet again, together with two men and two women, and then again in 1917, 1926, and 1933—at the entrance to the lottery ticket shop where he worked, in the street, and at the entrance to a tavern, every time under similar circumstances.[13] We cannot know why the police pursued Laureano while so many others in his profession consistently evaded arrest. Whatever the reason for Laureano's relative misfortune, his sizeable criminal file makes it possible to trace his career as *bicheiro*.

Laureano's multiple arrests yielded for the police a plentiful harvest of jogo do bicho buyers, too. His criminal files reveal that his customers included primarily adult, working-class women—cooks, seamstresses, domestic and factory workers—ranging from twenty-three to forty years of age. But these customers seem to have been caught in the net, so to speak, and although police do identify some by name, most wriggled free with apparent ease. The density of jogo do bicho businesses throughout the city and the game's enormous, indiscriminate popularity imply that Laureano's customers would have included men and women who lived or worked in the immediate environs of his lottery shop and ranged across the spectrum from young to old and, depending on the neighborhood, well-off to poor.

Describing the demand side of the jogo do bicho obliges us to speak in the conditional—to muse about who Laureano's customers "*would have included*"—in the interest of historical accuracy, for their individual identities remain largely hidden. Attempts to reconstruct their lives are frustrated by a paper trail that thins to nearly nothing. The anonymous female buyer who got away may have benefited from the officer's slow reflexes, but likely he had little interest in arresting her at all. The rarity of arrests of buyers and the frequency with which police reports allude to nameless buyers who evaded arrest even as the officer apprehended the seller offer at least circumstantial evidence that antigambling policing largely turned a blind eye to the game's customers.[14]

Over the first decade of the jogo do bicho's existence, arrested buyers and sellers alike appear in the judicial archive. Local regulations, the Penal Code of 1890, and other federal legislation regarded the buying and selling of chances to win illicit games of chance equally illegal. Yet as police involvement in the game became systemic and the federal antivice legal apparatus became more formalized, the law came to consider selling the graver offense.[15] By the early twentieth century, buyers haunt the criminal files as little more than phantasms; in their infrequent appearances, they tend to remain anonymous and bear no material importance in the case against the sellers. The arresting policemen paid them fleeting, if any, attention. To the extent that officers earnestly aimed to suppress this activity, it would indeed have made more sense to pursue the vendor who sold to hundreds of people, rather than pursuing a single customer. And to the policeman augmenting his salary with protection money, sellers were the easier target.[16]

Jogo do bicho players did leave behind other artifacts that tell of their social and cultural lives and reveal their multitudinous numbers. The game saturated urban folklore in the late nineteenth century and early twentieth. Players figure in published stories, urban folktales, plays, songs, and pamphlets produced in Rio and other Brazilian cities of the First Republic. Later, compilers of such artifacts of folk life produced works that celebrate the game and the colorful rascals who bought and sold tickets; some even include tips on how to play and win.[17] One can easily imagine, then, why few scholars have taken such sources seriously. Yet these renderings of the jogo do bicho in the form of popular stories and pamphlets, musical revues, and ephemera in the great Ibero-American chronicle tradition do more than just fill in the blanks of the judicial archive with evidence about who played the jogo do bicho and how. They also reveal what is at stake historically in the study of the taming of chance in late nineteenth- and early twentieth-century urban Brazil. Rather than dispense with the folkloric evidence about the lives of the elusive players of the illicit lottery, one should examine stories about the jogo do bicho in the context of a broader interest among collectors of Brazilian folklore in what they generally interpret as a deeply Brazilian fascination with games of chance.

Jogo do bicho players had a rich, varied repertoire of traditions of divination to choose from as they tried to predict the winning animal and number by means of hunches and augury, as we will see later in this chapter. But we cannot explain why people played the game simply by pointing to the age-old rituals of luck in which they participated. Players' engagement with chance took on meanings particular to their place and time.[18]

Without assuming any direct causality, it is instructive to place jogo do bicho players' reliance on chance in the wider cultural context of the early

First Republic, where luck determined a number of enormously important outcomes. By 1916 a draft lottery decided who would serve in the military.[19] Popular practices and rituals reinforced the centrality of luck as a determinant in one's life.[20]

The folklorist Affonso Arinos noticed the recurring theme of random luck in the legends, stories, and ballads of Portuguese as well as African and indigenous or syncretic origin that he collected in the 1910s. Popular Catholicism, as practiced in both the city and the countryside, was also replete with fortune telling and ritual games of chance. Calling to mind the raffle drawings in Rio's popular markets described in chapter 4, Arinos writes, "The most impressive part of the night of [the festival of] Saint John is the one about luck [das sortes], when, tired of the fireworks, the dances, and the celebrations, the celebrants gather around a large table, after tasting the traditional Saint John cake and corn pudding [canjica] . . . , they go to consult the book of destiny." Festivalgoers read fortunes by putting egg white in a cup of water, passing it over the campfire, and reading the formation on the water's surface. Arinos documents popular ways of looking for signs of love, happiness, life and death in nature: "A thousand other sortes come from the ancient 'Oracle of the Ladies,' which, on this night, would reveal destiny." Other means of foretelling the future, in which the daring could flirt with demonic forces, were less "galante." Arinos witnessed these at the Festival of Saint John and also heard word of them in the songs of troubadours from the rural north who, "in characteristic verse, put in the mouth of a famous goat, the description of a duel with the Evil One."[21]

The flirtation with witchcraft and devilry that "das sortes" implied also appears in the writings of other contemporary commentators on Brazil's urban folk traditions. Drawing on both his own journalistic observations and the work of collectors of Brazilian traditions like Arinos and (Alexandre José) Mello Moraes Filho, João do Rio included witchcraft in his As religiões no Rio (The religions of Rio), a survey of nonconformist religious practices that to him represented the fascinating underbelly of urban life.[22] Commenting on the enormous power witchcraft and sorcery held over the Brazilian people and demonstrating its association with Afro-Brazilian culture, João do Rio writes, "Many people probably don't believe in witches, or in wizards, but nobody has lived in Rio without entering the dirty houses swirling with the wicked indolence of black men and women." The fear of and belief in feitiço (sorcery or witchcraft) unifies all Cariocas, he asserts, regardless of class and ethnicity: "*Feitiço* is our vice, our pleasure; it is degeneration." Rio "crawls with *feitiçeiros* [sorcerers], spread out over the whole city from the port to the Estrada Santa Cruz."[23] Listing the feitiçeiros with whom he had been in contact, João do Rio writes, "All these people live well, in plentitude, *and play the jogo do bicho* like [the Camdomblé priest] Oloô-Teté. They leave money when they die, sometimes fortunes greater than a hundred *contos*, and they mock the names of eminent persons in our society, between advice given to prostitutes and sips of rum [*parati*]." Eminent members of society are drawn to feitiçeiros because of their power to give "riches, palaces, and eternity . . . to move distance with a simple mixture of blood and herbs."[24]

It is not by chance that the famous journalist mentions the jogo do bicho. Writers like him and Arinos were both exemplars and theorists of the encounter between elite and popular culture.[25] As we have seen, at just this moment the criminal law had come to mediate this relation and to police the boundaries, however ineffectively and equivocally, between high and low. Describing the foreboding places where priests perform Afro-Brazilian sorcery between hobnobbing with the city's elite and quaffing strong liquor, João do Rio makes a point of adding that the police also "visit these houses."[26]

Chance, luck, and divination were associated not just with mildly heretical, but tolerated, folk superstition but also with secular criminality; *feitiçaria*, illegal under the Philippine Code that held force until 1830, was criminalized again under the Penal Code of 1890.[27] A universe of morality and danger surrounded games of chance. Jogo do bicho players did not risk losing only the game; tinged by an illegality so arbitrary that its juridical determination seemed subject not to the science of modern criminology but to the law of chance, many popular practices involving *azar* or sorte also involved the gamble of whether one would be arrested.

Elite writers were ambivalent about the moral and social consequences of gambling. A telling example comes from the novel *A Condessa Vésper*, an early work by the naturalist writer Aluísio Azevedo, originally published in a series of pamphlets in the early 1880s. Azevedo expresses the disapproval of gambling collectively held by his generation of bourgeois literary bohemians, who strived to construct a national culture.[28] In the moral ecology of Azevedo's novel and others of its kind, a propensity to gamble signals a person's almost certain swift decline into dissolution. When Azevedo's character Gustavo develops an obsession with gambling, he loses all proper inhibition, his will to succeed, and eventually his job. He becomes "careless, lazy, subservient, and depressed" and combs the city's gambling houses, finding ways to wager with others' money when he no longer possessed means of his own. But the author colors the novel's events in shades of ambivalence; later in the story he describes a glamorous evening out that included casino gambling at the baccarat table.[29] The condemnation of gambling served multiple and often contradictory allegorical and symbolic purposes: loss of control, moral lassitude, and ultimately hope. Gambling and misgivings about its rectitude also spoke of hypocrisy: not just elite hypocrisy but moreover the social contradictions that beset a modernizing Brazil.

As we have seen, legal and policing conventions came to categorize the jogo do bicho as a misdemeanor, punishable by fines and prison sentences. Yet even when laws forbade the jogo do bicho in black-and-white absolutes, there was no magnetic north to orient moral compasses. Law enforcement and citizens alike followed antigambling laws selectively at best. If not the law, what other codes would have shaped views about gambling among Rio's populace? Neither in doctrine nor in practice did the Catholic Church edify the morally confused, as it never actually forbade gambling.[30] Popular religious festivals almost always included games of chance.[31] Conceptual maneuvers even allowed the Church to operate its own lotteries to raise funds for charities, construing them as a lesser evil compared to other games of chance because of these church lotteries' financial rewards and their supposedly controlled form.[32]

Although neither of the traditional arbiters of public morality, the Church and the law, enunciated a clear opinion, Cariocas of the early First Republic would have overheard moralizing about gambling, like an ambient sound from which one cannot turn away.[33] Social theories, juridical writing, and elite literary production of the era reflected a stewing unease about the seemingly universal fascination with games of chance in the capital. Reformist politicians and jurists railed against gambling in general for the damage it did to the character of the worker and to the nation. In remarkably similar terms, some working-class activists, especially anarchists, warned workers away from gambling dens as they did from bars and bordellos, listing o jogo among vices like alcohol and promiscuous sex that threatened to distract them from the class war at hand.[34] Not until the 1930s did writers like Gilberto Freyre articulate what had by then solidified into conventional wisdom: the assumption that gambling manifests an explicitly nonmodern, irrational impulse and that the poor were easily duped into parting with their money. Gambling was associated with laziness and defiance. Because most Brazilians lacked social mobility they turned to the gaming table and the street-corner bicheiro for hope. The game, Freyre and his latter-day followers said, was as ingrained in Brazilian culture as cultural tendencies like racial harmony and primal impulses like totemic belief systems.[35]

Knowledge of the arbitrariness of the animal game's illegality suffused both popular and elite culture; urban Brazilians—both easedroppers on and participants in these moralizing discussions—put their knowledge of the game's wide popularity in the face of its illegality to various uses. The jogo do bicho's criminal status deterred very few from either buying or selling but did have an impact on the game. With respect to law enforcement, the multitudes of players who got away were within shouting distance but out of arm's reach. As a symptom of the process by which urban Brazilians increasingly needed to purchase admission to public life, police repression thus became part and parcel of popular culture, infusing forms of cultural expression with an understanding of this repression. Police wielding clubs, closing down voluntary associations, and smashing guitars became common in popular songs, pamphlets, and plays.[36] The forms of public expression that used the jogo do bicho as a theme assumed that the illicit lottery was a meaningful and ordinary part of urban life. The stories about petty gambling that circulated during the jogo do bicho's earliest decades were ambivalent in their moral leanings, fears, and desires; they grew out of the game's interaction with the law and reflect all the fascinating contradictions of that encounter.

Popular tales about activities officially considered criminal, such as a slave's pilferage of food, offer tactical lessons to the audience by passing on pragmatic information about not only how to perform the act, but also how to get away with it.[37] Repeated stories about illicit activities serve to normalize them, to call into question their official status as deviant behavior. When combined with such sources as the few arrest records that document the existence of players, popular stories about the jogo do bicho suggest how the players who evaded the law were part of a shared urban culture nurtured in the city's streets, shops, new amusement parks, jails, and police stations—a culture not reducible to the game's criminalization but not separable from it either.

Casual references to the jogo do bicho throughout the First Republic provide a sort of accidental census whose results we find scattered in innumerable fragments of the city's daily life: its journalism, librettos of popular musicals, lyrics of popular music, political cartoons, and chap-books. These cultural artifacts refer to the jogo do bicho with a familiarity that takes for granted its broad recognition. Imprecise as it is, this body of documentation is precious. Through interpolation, we can imagine the game's sheer ubiquity and growing importance as a locution in the lexicon of Carioca daily life.[38]

The images and representations of the jogo do bicho show that its popularity transected Rio's class hierarchy. The illicit lottery's appearances in the mainstream press help us to establish a baseline for its level of acceptance within middle-class, literate society. In the magazine *O Malho* for April 1904 a cartoon signals the readership's familiarity with the game and the ambivalent sentiments it inspired.[39] Although the piece never mentions the jogo do bicho, its title, "Bis-charada," winks knowingly at the reader in a punning reference to the illicit lottery.[40] The cartoon depicts a calendar showing the next six days of the current month, framed by the caption, "Calendário de Zé Povo" (Calendar of Joe Regular), which ex-plicitly associates the game with the popular classes. Several lines of verse name the Catholic saints celebrated on each day and offer two gambling tips by listing, beside each saint's names, a pair of the jogo do bicho's twenty-five beasts. Despite the implication that the calendar reflected Joe Regular's view of the week ahead, the gambling tips appear with no further explanation. The magazine's relatively well-to-do, literate audience evi-dently knew the game existed and also how it operated. The cartoon gently disparages the clandestine lottery by associating it with the unsophisti-cated tastes of Joe Regular. To some readers it may have served as an indictment of jogo do bicho players by emphasizing the sinfulness of their idolatrous worship of the game's animals. But the cartoon's humorous iconoclasm runs both ways, aiming not just at the jogo do bicho but also at a polite society that bristled at the game yet avidly—religiously, even— played it. Readers may well have made use of the gambling tips too.

Literary and folkloric remnants of the jogo do bicho's importance as a cultural point of reference in republican Rio are as heterodox as the city's

FIGURE 16 "Animal Puzzle: Calendar of Joe of the People" (1904). Source: Instituto Histórico e Geográfico Brasileiro, *O Malho* (April 2, 1904), n.p.

population itself and appear too sporadically to reveal minute changes over time. Yet it is possible both to generalize about the period as a whole, and to arrange elements of these plays, pamphlets, chronicles, and other sources into a common typology. From the first mentions of the jogo do bicho at the dawn of the 1900s through the early 1920s, the stories uniformly emphasize the promise of salvation through winning and the particularly communal and urban setting that makes winning possible. Usually with the assistance of family members or neighbors, it falls to the protagonists of these stories to pay attention to signs that might portend the winning number and animal. Through a combination of persistence and acumen, players might win at the jogo do bicho, thereby improving their socioeconomic condition and vindicating all their previous anguished attempts to win.

The most distinguished writers of the early First Republic published accounts that dramatize both winning and losing at the jogo do bicho. The game provided fodder for the likes of Machado de Assis, who in 1904 published a short story entitled "Jogo do Bicho" that tells of the unrelenting hope of Camilo, a low-level public servant whose life becomes entrenched in the animal game.[41] Alongside his nonjudgmental recounting of Camilo's involvement with the illicit lottery, Machado de Assis expresses concern about the social effects of the game, depicting his protagonist as living on the verge of material ruin because of his fixation. The story reflects the author's sensitivity to naturalist detail and moral complexity, and he neither mocks the desperate aspirations of the poor nor moralizes decisively about petty gambling.

Machado de Assis's tale guides the reader through the succession of frustrations, joys, and reversals of fortune Camilo experiences as a result of his obsession with the jogo do bicho. The story celebrates certain attributes both personal and communal, especially faith, patience, familial solidarity, a willingness to listen to friends' advice regarding which animals to play, and a keen ability to pay attention to signs and trust one's intuition. The dramatic element of this and other stories about the jogo do bicho derives from the uncertainty of the outcome and the individual's quest to have correctly identified the winning animal. But in these tales winning does not radically alter people's lives; it simply enables them to survive. Camilo at story's end is just where he was at the beginning: relatively happy and relatively poor. He risked a small amount of money and won a commensurately modest sum. The profit from a successful gamble on the jogo do bicho would suffice to purchase a gold broach and a pastry, not a tract of land. Nonetheless, Machado's story reveals, the game possesses an element of danger, as the promise of wealth tends to lead to obsession.

Published stories about salvation through winning in the jogo do bicho also appear as early as 1904 in newspaper chronicles of daily urban life, a typically Brazilian hybrid genre halfway between journalism and literature.[42] In a piece Lima Barreto published in 1915, he tells of an acquaintance who wrote social and fashion columns in a high-end newspaper called *A Vida Chic* (The Chic Life). When the newspaper sank into financial trouble and forced the man to find employment writing for a downscale jogo do bicho newspaper, *O Palpite*, his fortune changed. He gave a woman a jogo do bicho tip, a *"palpite,"* that paid off and "won love; something he could not gain in the elegant section of the newspaper."[43]

Stories about the jogo do bicho in the First Republic not only celebrate the possibility of deliverance but also moralize about the social cost of playing. Someone named Rachel wrote her name and the date—November 14, 1912—in careful script in the inside cover of a *folhetim* entitled "Death of the Bicheiro," a rare exemplar of a genre of popular, ephemeral literature of which few others survive.[44] The pamphlet's first lines hearken back to a golden age of social order before the fall of the Empire in 1889:

> In the time of the monarchy
> Men took great care
> The poor had money
> Which they even threw in the trash
> Men didn't have to pay taxes
> And women didn't play the jogo do bicho.

The verse continues in the same nostalgic, finger-wagging mode; the declaration of the Republic in 1889, the author explains, brought the social decay epitomized by the animal game's wide popularity:

> But then came the Republic
> And it soon brought with it despair
> The rich had no more peace
> The poor had no more money
> Only three things gained [with the beginning of the Republic], for one
>   the house
> For two, taxes, and three the [jogo do bicho] banker.

Men play here
Women play there
The mother-in-law plays, the brothers-in-law play
And whatever children they have,
Dreaming about a tip of which animal will win
They go and gamble away whatever money they have.

The next twenty-six lines decry the dangers of playing the jogo do bicho: a man "damned himself" by spending his entire spectacular fortune on the game; he stopped short of gambling away his wife only because "nobody wanted her." The addict used elaborate means to interpret his dreams to decide upon the winning animal. Despite the scolding tone of the first verses, this cautionary tale is also a lighthearted acknowledgment of the popular acceptance of the jogo do bicho. The compulsive player suddenly falls ill because of an erroneous gambling tip. When the neighborhood priest comes to hear his last confession and, later, the specter of Death appears in his house, the gambler greets these visitors expecting them to have tips on which animals to play. A monk then appears to warn him that gamblers are consigned to join the suffering, moaning souls in hell. The protagonist responds, "Tell me, father, will the bull or the donkey win?" When the monk calls upon the dying man to have faith, the gambler insists with his last breath, "I believe in the bull and the donkey / the alligator and the monkey." After the gambler dies, the monk proceeds immediately to bet two hundred milreis in the jogo do bicho, taking the gambler's death-bed utterance as a sure sign. The humor in this story, as in many narratives about the jogo do bicho, lies in its irreverence. In this case leavened by the pervasive anticlericalism of the early First Republic, the story juxta-poses sanctimonious religiosity with the ubiquitous but forbidden lottery, thus highlighting the hypocrisy of official attempts to suppress the jogo do bicho.[45]

The male jogo do bicho addict, often depicted in a satirical mode that recalls "Death of the Bicheiro," made occasional appearances as a character type in the popular literature of the First Republic. The poet and journalist Olavo Bilac wrote a short story in the first decade of the twentieth century about a man given over to a compulsive jogo do bicho gambling habit. Bilac's protagonist suffers from moral degeneracy because of his unfettered desire to play the illicit lottery. But the gambler also plays the game as a means to an eminently pragmatic end; the character takes shape not as a

Leandro Gomes de Barros

A MORTE DO BICHEIRO
E
O Boi Mysterioso
(5ª VOLUME)

A VEN[
RUA DO ALECRIM

A morte do bicheiro

No tempo da monarchia
Os homens tinham capricho,
Os pobres tinham dinheiro
Que botavam até no lixo.
Homem não pagava imposto
Mulher não jogava bicho.

Então chegou a republica
Trouxe logo o desespêro
Rico não teve mais paz
Pobre não viu mais dinheiro,
Ganha trez, um para casa
Dois para imposto e banqueiro.

O homem joga de um lado
De outro joga a mulher,
Joga a sogra e as cunhadas
E os filhos que tiver,
Com socho palpite e certeza
Vai-se o dinheiro que houver.

FIGURES 17 and 18 Pamphlet: Leandro
Gomes de Barros, "Death of the
Bicheiro" (1911). Courtesy of the Casa
de Rui Barbosa, Rio de Janeiro, Coleção
Literatura de Cordel, CRB.

mindless addict, but as a small capitalist striving to improve his material conditions. In frustration, the man exclaims, "I certainly don't know why it is that the police persecute the jogo! Do I not have the right to spend my own money, which is mine, just as I please? The prohibition against [the jogo do bicho] is an attack on individual freedom! It is violence against my independent will! An infraction against constitutional principles!"[46] Bilac is asking implicitly, If earning money is acceptable, why is the victimless act of playing the jogo do bicho not considered an honorable endeavor? The man's anger at the hypocrisy of the law that punishes those who wish to earn money through the jogo do bicho may not straightforwardly represent the author's views. Yet this statement and Bilac's story as a whole ring with sarcasm and moral uncertainty about the law and the petty crimes it punishes. Bilac understands the perfect sense the game makes to those who play it and the consequent preposterousness of the law that disallows it. As the author of "Death of the Bicheiro" does, Bilac derides the gambling addict even as he ridicules the idea of effectively suppressing the game. The public consumption of these narratives adds another layer of ambivalence to their meaning; once unleashed before a mass audience, even stories that moralize about correct public behavior take on a life of their own and are open to interpretation in diverse and dissident ways. And especially volatile are the meanings transmitted in a piece that, however moralistic on one level, makes people laugh.[47]

The scofflaws, tricksters, addicts, and socially immobile dreamers in stories, plays, and songs of the republican age flouted the law with eyes wide open and often with great flourish. Jogo do bicho players portrayed in the literature and folklore of the day—sometimes in caricature and sometimes in subtler shades—would very likely have reminded the public of an archetypal figure then of great currency in urban Brazil: the *malandro*.[48] In the First Republic, this male scoundrel figure, characterized by his distaste for work and his agility in circumventing rules, appeared in popular song, theater, and common parlance.[49] He emphatically shunned the industrial work ethic and lived off the labor of others and his money-earning schemes —a propensity demonstrated, among other things, by his gambling habit. The malandro assumed his place of importance in Carioca expressive culture in the context of a surge in interest in the underbelly of urban life as shown in prison diaries, police blotter journalism, and journalist–*flanêurs* who chronicled the urban underworld; emerging forms of popular theater, especially the *revistas do ano* (annual revues), also dramatized both the city's scandalous causes célèbres and quotidian events.[50] This roguish figure embodied the associations between urbanity and criminality that characterized the turn of the twentieth century.

"Out of doors"—on street corners, in taverns, and the like—the malandro broke rules with joyful abandon in plain sight of those assigned to enforce them. Contemporary scholarship generally interprets representations of the omnipresence of criminal types in urbanizing Latin America as expressions of horror and fascination with the city's subterranean spaces and cultures that reveal a bourgeois anxiety about the fragility of state power.[51] Such interpretations assume exclusive elite authorship of the malandro archetype, overlooking the possibility of an exchange of culture between the literate bourgeoisie and the popular classes. This does not mean that we should simply read these representations as a mirror of reality. Certainly, the urban scoundrel served different ends for different audiences. Shifting the focus from elite (mis)representation, though, allows one to read through the malandro figure a popular understanding of the criminalization of everyday life.

In his foundational essay of modern Brazilian literary criticism entitled "The Dialectic of *Malandragem*," Antonio Cândido locates the prototype of the malandro in Manoel Antônio de Almeida's protorealist novel *Memórias de um Sargento de Milícias* (1854). At the heart of this novel and the times it reflects Cândido identifies a dialectical tension between order and disorder. Satirical literature, he argues, functions to show that antithetical sets of concepts like legality and illegality, truth and falsehood, morality and immorality are reversible and that apart from ideological rationalization antinomies coexist in a curious "twilight zone" (*lusco-fusco*).[52] Contrary to the prevailing understanding of the protagonist of this novel, Leandro, as a "picaro in the tropics," Cândido reinterprets him as a trickster figure.[53] Unlike the characters in such early European picaresque novels as *Don Quixote* and *Tom Jones*, Leandro was not of humble and naive origins, and he did not learn from experience. Instead, he was naturally endowed with a tendency toward roguishness and trickery.[54] This archetypal figure, whose innate guile enables him to prevail at the story's end, plays with the idea of the born criminal. A born malandro can make the most of his disposition, in this case by becoming someone who "lives by his luck." Representations of *malandragem* in novels like Almeida's *Memórias de um Sargento de Milícias* and in less erudite media present a figure who draws his power from the tension between order and disorder and public virtue and public vice.[55]

The malandro represents a sort of organic, vernacular understanding of what is, today, a foundational understanding in the critical history of the law: that criminality is socially constructed. Depictions of the jogo do bicho player, like the recurrent figure of the malandro, embodied a popular awareness of the gap between legal mandate and daily reality and ridiculed legal and moral codes that purported to govern a people who share a common understanding that the rules outlawing such conventional practices as the jogo do bicho were made to be broken. The Carioca public consumed and repeated narratives about petty criminality, and in particular tales about how criminality meant not just breaking the law but finding a modus operandi for living with it.

If jogo do bicho players' criminality derived not from the inherent wrongness of their act but from their encounter with the law, then the differential arrest patterns for men and women may have helped to produce a distorted image of the jogo do bicho as a masculine undertaking: the malandro was an explicitly male figure, as were most of the literary and folkloric representations of jogo do bicho players and sellers.[56] The popular mythologies concerning this urban underworld of gamblers, tricksters, scoundrels, and male antiheroes portray a cultural ecology in which women were all but extinct.

In the period I study those arrested for jogo do bicho offenses were indeed almost always men. Not a single woman accused of gambling-related offenses appears in the extant entry logs of the Casa de Detenção that list women detainees. Only 3 cases involving female defendants were found among a sample of 473 cases.[57] Women did work as jogo do bicho sellers, often behind the scenes and apparently far less frequently than men (see chapter 3). But men and women played the jogo do bicho in equal numbers. The police disinterest in players in general led to the rarity of female jogo do bicho defendants and to their absence from most literary and iconographic representations of criminality associated with the game.

Although the judicial archive and literary record give the impression that the jogo do bicho was a masculine world, other evidence reveals that women were, in fact, heavily involved in the game. Gambling tip sheets were often directed at women.[58] Matter-of-fact references to women playing the game occurred in cartoons and popular stories and plays. And a close look even in the judicial archive reveals some otherwise hidden information. For example, cases against accused bicheiros often contain the original tickets seized upon their arrest. The buyers' names handwritten on these tickets include as many Marias and Joanas as Josés.[59]

Iniciação zoologica

— Diga, Lili, já lhe ensinaram na escola que especie de bicho é o elephante?
— Já, mamãe; é o grupo 12...

FIGURE 19 "Zoological initiation: 'Tell me, Lili, have they taught you in school what type of animal [*bicho*] the elephant is?' 'Yes, Mommy, it's group 12.'" (1922) Source: Associação Brasileira da Imprensa, Rio de Janeiro, *Dom Quixote*.

Women's position in public life in the early First Republic partly explains why women are an elusive presence in the written record that illicit petty gambling left behind. The Constitution of 1891 enshrined liberal, republican values and the idea of equality before the law. The language of the Constitution failed to define sharply what citizenship and equality meant and employed vague language with respect to gender, using the generic masculine pronoun to refer to all human beings. Jurists consistently interpreted "*todos* [all] are equal under the law" in a literalist fashion, taking *todos* to denote all men, rather than all persons. Women were denied active citizenship and could neither vote nor hold public office until well into the twentieth century.[60]

The wife stood as the moral foundation of the bourgeois Brazilian family, which ideally was united, introverted, and hierarchical. While patriarchal authority reigned in the home, a woman's honor was automatically suspect in the street, where she was under the surveillance not of the family but of the state. As women, especially middle-class women, increasingly became a presence in Rio's public life, they were burdened even more with the "anathema of sin."[61] Positivist criminological doctrine reinforced the idea that only meretricious women breached the private–public divide between house and street, a move that would sully a woman's honor and make her into a criminal.[62] Once in the public realm, women, like men, were subject to the discretionary power of the police to arrest and harass. For instance, although prostitution was not illegal in Brazil at this time, women suspected of prostitution or found in the street without a chaperone were regularly arrested for vagrancy. Yet women were held criminally responsible for a generally narrower range of acts than men because of gender stereotypes, restricted social roles, and the idiosyncrasies of policing practice.

Beyond the de facto impunity of male and female jogo do bicho players, women were impacted less by the criminalization of the game in part because of gendered ideas about work and idleness. The Penal Code's fear of idleness and disorder was rooted in part in elites' dread of organized labor and the burgeoning, unruly urban poor. Jurists linked illicit gambling to the litany of complaints they leveled at the supposed dangerous classes: their foul language, the social and economic costs of the loss of their labor, and the moral danger of their presence in the streets. The stock antigambling and general antivice discourse of republican moralism in this period referred generically to male criminals. In calling for action against popular gambling, jurists, politicians, and citizen petitioners also decried the dissolution of the Brazilian family, the focus of much public attention and anxiety as an endangered institution whose strength would be necessary to the new Republic's success. Gambling doubly threatened the social order anchored by the nuclear family: it would drain money away from families and promote earning money without work. Juridical theses, administrative documents, and legislative debates about gambling almost never mentioned the woman of the family, except as the victim of her husband's reckless, amoral behavior.[63] Even foreigners commenting on this subject took no notice of women's participation in the jogo do bicho and criticized it for its threat to the nation's virility.[64]

Women players and tipsters (*palpiteiras*) do appear in popular stories and journalism—not as criminals but as proper ladies. In newspapers that published tips in response to readers' queries, much of the correspondence came from players with female first names preceded by the feminine honorific title *Dona*, as in "D. Julita," or "D. Roza de Oliveira." Women were also

FIGURE 20 "Reading *O Bicho*." Source: Acervo da Fundação Biblioteca Nacional, Brazil.

frequently depicted in their role as augurs of the game's winning outcome.[65] Success in the jogo do bicho came not completely by accident but from a player's attentiveness to signs, which often meant deferring to the insights of experts. The cartoon "Lendo *O Bicho*" (Reading *O Bicho*) shows a glamorously attired woman walking down a busy city street reading *O Bicho*, a newspaper dedicated to the animal game. An onlooker informs a companion that the woman is "a distinguished purveyor of jogo do bicho tips" (*uma distincta palpiteira d'O Bicho*).[66] A nonconfrontational type of gambling, the jogo do bicho did not necessarily threaten female decency. It could be mediated through family members and played in the course of running daily errands.[67] Under certain conditions, the popular imagination allowed a space for respectable women to join in the jogo do bicho as tipsters and as players, although not as vendors. While the malandro was an explicitly marginal male, fortune was a refined lady.

As interpreted through contemporary folklore and literature, the lesser criminalization of women in the jogo do bicho helped fashion a mythical, exclusively masculine urban underworld. Cariocas' complex take on petty criminality expressed caution as well as delight in defying arbitrary rules. By way of a general fascination with the urban underworld and the archetypal malandro character's many reiterations in popular and elite cultural expression, a characteristic element of the widely shared ideas about the world of petty gambling was its masculinity.

In reality, Cariocas of all generations and, as we have seen, both sexes played the jogo do bicho. Belying the assertions of jurists and politicians that gambling destroyed family life, husbands and wives, parents and children collaborated in playing the game. Children provided tips, had a special role in deciding which animal to play, and acted as intermediaries for elder family members.[68] Minors often appear to have accompanied adult relatives or employers to place their bets, and parents routinely sent minors out to buy tickets. The shopkeeper named José Gomes de Oliveira, as noted in chapter 4, was arrested and charged with illicit gambling and involving a minor in prohibited gaming when he "received from a minor . . . a list for the so-called animal game" in 1907.[69] Police allowed the minor to "disappear" but testified that he had been playing the jogo do bicho, a charge Oliveira vehemently denied. The defendant protested the ridiculousness of asserting that the child was a jogo do bicho player when "he barely even knew how to say 'mommy.'" The defense is less than credible, not only because of the recognizable jogo do bicho lists that the archived criminal file still contains, but also because children did indeed play the clandestine lottery. The existing cases provide strong evidence of the normality of minors' involvement on both sides of the jogo do bicho transaction.

Neither work nor leisure for the players, the jogo do bicho took place amid one's daily rounds and was part of an emerging way of using the city's public spaces. A simple but important detail is that the game did not have its own special site. Another case involving a minor, from 1911, illustrates this point and demonstrates the dense social networks that ramified through the marketplace, facilitating the buying and selling of tickets. Police arrested two persons in a lottery shop on Avenida Central, one of the grand avenues constructed just a few years earlier. The police claimed a minor had entered with a jogo do bicho list and a wad of money in the amount of six milreis, on his way to place a bet. One of the witnesses, a fourteen-year-old shop assistant, testified that "the previous day at 1:30 in the afternoon a woman named Carolina So-and-So [Carolina de Tal], who lives in the apartment [sobrado] over that restaurant [casa de pasto], approached the knife sharpener Antonio Marques da Silva. She gave him a package that had one jogo do bicho list and three two-milreis coins. She went to give the package to Antonio, who told her he was going to the lottery ticket shop and would deliver [the package] there. . . . Antonio then left to deliver the package, as Carolina had ordered him to do." Only later did the witness discover that Antonio had been arrested in the lottery ticket shop when he arrived to deliver Carolina's list and money. A second witness offered identical testimony. Antonio's itinerant job made him a perfect go-between in the jogo do bicho. He walked from shop to restaurant to home honing the blades of knives and scissors and, it appears, conducting money and jogo do bicho tickets from buyer to seller, and perhaps augmenting his income with a percentage of the proceeds.[70]

Jogo do bicho players in the early twentieth century engaged in practices that still characterize the game today, including the crucial one of determining the winning animal and corresponding number. Derived from the most random of events—the spin of the wheel of the daily federal lottery—the winning jogo do bicho numbers and animals materialized everyday out of a universe whose logic was accessible only to those who were both lucky and perceptive. The procedures used to decide which animal and number to play embraced the impossibility of knowing the future for certain and set players in sympathetic vibration with their world.[71]

At first glance the element of luck may appear to be private and primarily asocial. The game did indeed operate on a suprasocial level; at the moment a player lay down her money, the decision regarding which animal or combination to play was a lonely one, and she alone could collect the earnings or absorb the loss. The jogo do bicho's symbolic and expressive power conformed to the idiosyncratic shape of each person's mind, soul, and memories. Yet chance acts in the social realm, too. Players shared betting tips with friends, family, and their extended community, and the drama of winning and losing gained powerful public cultural meaning. To decide which animal or number to play and then buy the ticket, often through such convoluted means as in the case of Carolina So-and-So who bet by way of Antonio the knife sharpener, was to mediate between "private enjoyment" and the shared, established "public meaning" these ordinary rituals had.[72]

The culture that formed around the game involved prognosticating the winning animal through the popular art and science of interpreting signs. Players and their families, friends, and neighbors consulted each other to identify and decipher attention-grabbing occurrences. Daily life presented myriad signs: an accident on the tramway line, a bird fallen from a tree, a fire in a neighbor's house. Players might follow a funeral cortege to note and then bet on the number on the deceased's grave. Above all, phenomena that appeared overnight in one's dream pointed to the outcome of the next day's jogo do bicho. The knowledge of how to parlay such daily occurrences into useful gambling insights diffused through the population by way of both oral tradition and *livrinhos de sonho*, or dream books.[73]

These small, inexpensively produced books offered interpretations of dreams and the corresponding number and animal to play. An oracle of the future in the hands of any functionally literate reader, this popular genre dates to the second century but found its fullest expression in late eighteenth- through mid-nineteenth-century Europe because of the era's broadening reading public and popular fascination with the life of the sleeping mind.[74] This ancient and transnational tradition merged with Brazil's native *folhetins*, chapbooks that proliferated mostly in the country's northeast and spread to Rio on a wave of rural-to-urban migration.[75]

Vendors in Rio's shops, kiosks, streets, and occasional fairs sold dream books and other printed material one could use to predict the game's outcome. In his chronicle of 1908 about itinerant booksellers in the city center, João do Rio comments on the striking popularity of dream books on sale in front of the São Pedro Theater, while the literary classics gathered dust and contorted, unsold, in the heat of the sun. He describes *testamentos de bichos*, another form of urban folk literature whose popularity, the author laments, had outstripped that of the literary masterpieces of his time. These testamentos were humorous pieces that recounted in verse the last will and testament of animals from the parrot to the mosquito. Lately, João do Rio observes, the "vendors of these testamentos have begun to sell them as *palpites* for the jogo do bicho, turning the seagull," an animal that did not appear among the twenty-five in the illicit lottery, "into an ostrich," an animal that did. He quips, "The gamblers don't read, but they empty their pockets."[76]

The word *palpite*, literally "heartbeat," was in use within two decades after the jogo do bicho began to denote an intuition about which animal would win. The corporeal allusion suggests a flash of prescience that is both fleeting and visceral. Occurrences in one's life as well as current events could generate palpites and drive people to bet on a specific number or animal. When the statesman Rui Barbosa, nicknamed "The Eagle of the Hague" for his famously forceful presence at the Hague Tribunal of 1907, died in 1923, the day his death was reported bicheiros were flooded by players betting on the eagle.[77]

A newspaper named *O Palpite* enjoyed a brief run in the first decade of the twentieth century.[78] Brazen editorial and production staffs housed in ever-relocating headquarters put out at least two newspapers exclusively dedicated to the jogo do bicho. *O Palpite*'s always "provisional" headquarters changed every few issues, one of the only hints of the illegal status of the lottery to which this newspaper is devoted.[79]

O Bicho, another jogo do bicho newspaper of the early twentieth century, ran from 1903 until at least 1915. It contained tips on the animals and in addition inspirational stories about past winners. Like the jogo do bicho itself, *O Bicho* ran every day but Sunday; its close imitation of standard newspapers in format and content gave it a surprisingly mainstream appearance for a publication promoting an ostensibly clandestine practice. This periodical and others like it contained just a few pages and cost just one hundred reis.[80] Amid installments of Alexandre Dumas's *The Count of Monte Cristo* and advertisements for health tonics and elixirs, *O Bicho*'s humorous but useful features made the paper a self-conscious advocate, guide, and partner-in-crime of bicho players. Devoid of political content, *O Bicho* only promoted the game. Advice to readers sometimes concerned the nuts and bolts of the jogo do bicho, as in the following: "Advisory to readers: There are two different lotteries running today, the one in São Paulo and the one in Candelária, and the reader should be advised that when he plays he should ask the *banqueiro* for which lottery he receives the jogo, in order to avoid crookery [*canalhismos*] on their part. In saying this, we are only doing our duty of looking after the interest of our readers."[81] Evidence of conflicts between players and sellers perennially appears in the press, shedding some light on their potentially competitive relationship. In one example from *O Bicho*, a cover article entitled "You should read this!" (*Convem ler!*) says, "*O Bicho* will always be the most accurate newspaper for palpites; it leaves nothing to be desired in that regard. Banqueiros are so afraid of this newspaper that they even advise their players not to pay attention to the tips we provide."[82] These warnings to players probably were delivered in a spirit of self-promotion as well as solidarity; *O Bicho* clearly perceived a need to justify its endeavor and compete with other jogo do bicho papers of the day, featuring sections entitled "Our Victories" and "Our Correct Choices" to celebrate when its palpites delivered.

The words *jogo do bicho* never appear in print, but the paper teems with animal allusions as well as references to betting, playing, winning money, and dreaming about bichos. The paper associated itself not with a criminal underworld but with a world of signs, luck, play, and making money. The slogan that appeared beneath the title of the newspaper is telling: "A useful and pleasant daily newspaper, dedicated to lovers of all sports and commercial advertising." The paper included a plethora of facts about the game to enable the reader-player to extrapolate in order to conjure the winning number based on amateur knowledge of probability and oneiric fortune telling of the game's results. Amid elaborate tables relating the winning numbers of past games, the paper listed palpites signed by various contributors or delivered surreptitiously in the form of personal classified ads, such as: "Accept 264 kisses and 820 hugs, from your cousin Zilda."[83]

Despite its short run and probably narrow audience, *O Bicho* and similar periodicals formed a sort of public sphere for the literate readership interested in finessing the daily outcome of this popular lottery. Rio's newspapers of record also reported on the jogo do bicho. In the early twentieth century they became attentive to urban popular culture as a way of promoting their supposedly populist aims, after making the transition from anti-republican monarchism to a populist critique of the Republic's passive-aggressive neglect of the social question.[84] Reporting on the jogo do bicho was an illicit use of one of the principal instruments and locus classicus of public culture. The *Jornal do Brasil* and the *Correio da Manhã,* two of Rio's major dailies, included features on the jogo do bicho, which passed tips on to readers and published the previous days' winning results. In the early twentieth century a range of periodicals from the mainstream press to the blossoming working-class one regularly dedicated some space to publishing jogo do bicho results and hints for how to win. Reflecting both Carioca society's diverse opinions about the jogo do bicho and the booming market for anything related to the game, these papers were overtly self-contradictory; they featured news stories that assumed the game's illegality while also publishing tips and results.[85] The papers' content concerning the jogo do bicho may well have communicated a subtle message about the game's public nature and its ordinariness alongside its illicit status.

As repression of the game intensified, its presence in the mainstream media became more coded. Palpites appeared as covert messages, often in verse, in columns with such suggestive titles as "Noah's Ark" and replete with bestial puns.[86] The allegories and puzzles in which tips were embedded were not terribly enigmatic. For instance, in 1902 an issue of the *Correio da Manhã* ran a column called "The Wheel of Fortune" that depicted a simple line drawing of two animals.[87] Having a dream or some

FIGURE 21 *O Bicho* newspaper. Source: Acervo da Fundação Biblioteca Nacional, Brazil.

FIGURE 22 Detail of *O Bicho* newspaper, showing the editors' reply to "correspondence" from female readers, ano 10, n. 114 (May 23, 1912). Source: Acervo da Fundação Biblioteca Nacional, Brazil.

other hint about an elephant did not necessarily mean one should bet on the elephant—the real animal was always several analytical levels away. While the exact interpretation was not always straightforward, the not-so-coded animal puns in the titles of these columns would have left little doubt that these were messages for players of the illegal lottery.

The *jogador do bicho* (and players of other lotteries of the day) depicted in urban popular culture was not a *vagabundo*, or bum. He worked, he did not drink to excess, he cared about his family. He was not a gambling addict per se but was afflicted by a somewhat different habit. Attentive to the point of distraction to the confusing onslaught of objects, images, and encounters that defined urban life and to the hope that came with the chance of winning, he compulsively scanned his visual world for signs, for palpites, of the jogo do bicho's outcome. As the historian Felipe Magalhães aptly argues, when authors like Machado de Assis wrote about the "new lottery," they were remarking on the birth of a new type of jogador that emerged with it.[88] This new type of player participated in a new type of public life, one profoundly marked by the rise of commercialized amusements; he or, just as likely, she was a new reader of the social, whose daily routines, practices, and ambitions accommodated the changing, shrinking public realm.

An alchemy of fun, chance, risk, hope, luck, and a measure of irreverence gave special meaning to the jogo do bicho in these first decades of its existence. The enormous cultural importance of this clandestine lottery reflected the particularities of social life in the city of its origin.[89] It drew people together in the increasingly chaotic, often alienating urban environment of the crowded capital. Ideas about which animal would win circulated through the information channels that characterized urban life, such as print journalism and urban popular culture as well as the informal gatherings on street corners and around kiosks and market stalls. The chance encounters and occurrences that typify city life both mirrored and fed the rituals that came to characterize the game. The jogo do bicho developed not as a lonely quest for unearned money but as a community affair and a phenomenological communion between a player and his or her urban environment.

The collective aspiration that one could get rich fueled a useful fiction. Friends, neighbors, family members, and the jogo do bicho's random public sphere, such as the "imagined community" that read the gambling tip sheets, together engaged in a ritual exchange of money for hope, while at the same time taking part in modern consumer society.[90]

Even as powerful centrifugal forces scattered Rio's nonelite majority to farther-flung neighborhoods in the early First Republic, a centripetal force pulled them into the historic center to work, buy and sell, and relax. Customers at Marcelo da Silva's downtown store mentioned at the opening of this chapter would have included laborers on construction projects, domestic workers, and residents of nearby Morro do Castelo, among other Cariocas whose daily lives brought them regularly to the city center. Particularly in the historic center the multiple, overlapping uses of public places integrated such mundane chores as stocking up on rice, selling small livestock, and taking part in the beginnings of mass culture in the form of performed music. Notable are the multiple meanings of the word *praça* in the late nineteenth- and early twentieth-century Brazil, denoting literally the public squares so central to city planning in the Iberian tradition, as well as the figurative common space of commerce (*a praça pública*).[91]

Historians have already observed this mixing of leisure and commerce in protoindustrial Rio, but typically as part of a cycle of conspicuous consumption led by the elite and middling classes. Researchers have documented well these classes' preferenes for North American and especially European pastimes. For the Latin American urban elite, historians have shown, leisure was a means of closing ranks and cementing their position in the social hierarchy; and the state engineered nonelite pastimes to "control the passions of the lower orders and encourage rational and ostensibly modern behavior."[92] Such analyses see state repression as complicit in maintaining this separation between "decent," respectable culture and the rude practices of the masses. Beyond just closing ranks according to socioeconomic class, though, state repression of popular leisure left its mark on popular understandings of participation in public life. Examining the commercialization of popular culture in Rio brings us back around to the jogo do bicho and its centrality to the collective experience of enclosure out of doors.

Cariocas were known for their penchant for gambling by the early nineteenth century. By midcentury, small lottery enterprises proliferated as the city's expanding population and cash-infused economy encouraged this time-honored practice, as we have seen. Many lottery operations were legal at first, permitted through concession contracts with the municipal government and controlled by local ordinances and the Criminal Code.[93]

Some were sponsored by religious organizations and held at street festivals as a means of raising money for the organization.[94] Not until later in the century would Rio's increasingly monetized economy and postabolition flood of immigrants and rural migrants allow forms of popular gambling to become widespread and attract the ire of authorities.

Spending money—and indeed playing for money—was one of the entertainment options available to Cariocas in the First Republic. Wagering one's money was an aboveboard social pastime. Entertainment entrepreneurs often called their dining, drinking, and dancing establishments by the name *cassino*, a word that evoked glamour and excitement. For example, in 1906 on the central rua do Passeio two French businessmen named their newly opened *café-concerto* the Cassino Palace. In a 1921 chronicle, Lima Barreto reaffirms the popularity of playing with money, which, though tinged by its questionable morality, bespoke modernity and sophistication: "They say this is a rich person's vice. . . . Brazil much be a rich country."[95]

The development of commercial amusements marked the onset of modernity in late nineteenth- and early twentieth-century Rio.[96] Formerly the province of the minuscule, Europe-oriented elite, professional entertainment began to come within reach of the poor classes as well as the growing middle sectors, including, for example, midlevel government bureaucrats, low-ranking military officers, and shopkeepers. Day-to-day sociability traditionally had taken place inside private homes and within the family unit. Some forms of commercialized, public entertainment had begun to emerge in the last quarter of the nineteenth century.[97] Now, by the beginning of the twentieth, both cultural habit and physical infrastructure summoned people into the city's public spaces during their spare moments. A number of factors fueled the expansion of professional entertainment in the late nineteenth-century city. The emergence of a wage-earning working class provided the movie houses, music halls, and popular theaters with customers who had some money to pay the admission fee. Not only was there more money in circulation, but there was also a larger population to spend it. The number of industrial workers doubled from 1890 to 1906, and the increase in liberal professionals was of a similar magnitude.[98] The new tramway and commuter rail lines could bring residents from diverse parts of the city to take part in this incipient culture industry. A large influx of immigrants, many of whom were unmarried and without families, arrived from Spain, Portugal, and Italy and sought out public meeting places to enjoy the company of others and to meet their mates.[99] Residents still partook of free entertainment like visiting family, strolling, playing dominoes, or attending religious festivals. Time away from work, or leisure, might simply have meant time spent with one's family.[100] Carnival parades, church processions, and funerals still drew large crowds of all generations and both sexes. The commercialized entertainment that surged at this time did not replace these free types of popular entertainment; the two coexisted and interacted.[101]

Despite the precarious material conditions, the working class in turn-of-the-century Rio organized to fight for a shorter workday to allow them to enjoy leisure time. Better hygiene and health care and longer life expectancy afforded individuals cumulative gains of thousands of hours of leisure. During the second half of the nineteenth century, public parks multiplied in the Imperial Court and the seaside promenade called Passeio Público was constructed.[102] The monotony of daily life in the cramped spaces of working-class housing (*vilas*) and tenements (*cortiços, cabeças de porco, estalagens*) drove the poor classes out into the streets in search of leisure, fun, and companionship. By the first decade of the twentieth century, Rio had ample public squares, gardens, and parks for sports and recreation.[103]

The various types of public performance were particularly important features of Rio's commercialized entertainment. Genres of light theater of transnational provenance, such as the *revista do ano* (annual revue) and cabaret, took on an eminently Brazilian character and gained immense popularity.[104] In the early 1890s, in storefront exhibition spaces on the rua do Ouvidor and elsewhere, large numbers of Cariocas paid one milreis each to listen to music from a phonograph.[105] The phenomenon of affordable, paid, public performances connected consumers of popular culture with a new generation of popular culture entrepreneurs. Many of the shows, movies, and various performing arts took place around the centrally located square called Praça Tiradentes, the Federal District's entertainment center.[106] *Casas de diversões,* or amusement parks like the one installed on the grounds of Drummond's zoo, offered rides, contests, and games for a moderate entrance fee. The *Gazeta Operária,* a working-class newspaper, ran an advertisement for an amusement park called Salão Paris do Rio, inaugurated in February 1903, whose attractions included "a nautical roller coaster, various programs involving trains, a magician" and a clothing sale.[107]

On the rua do Ouvidor the omniograph, Brazil's first movie theater, opened, followed soon thereafter by a kinetograph installed nearby at Praça Tiradentes. In 1897–98 Cariocas, with a mixture of fascination and caution, watched their first films and witnessed local filming. In 1906 the first full-length film had its debut in the Federal District, which by then boasted about two dozen projection houses. Movie theaters, sometimes featuring live orchestras of "gypsies" to attract customers, drew sizeable crowds.[108] Most of the city's poor and working classes could not afford to attend the more glamorous movie houses in the newly renovated center. Yet they could dig deeply enough into their pockets to attend the lower-priced cinemas in the suburban districts, where many began to see silent movies on their days off.[109] By 1910 the rua do Ouvidor had already begun its fall from glory after the construction nearby of the grand Avenida Rio Branco, part of Mayor Pereira Passos's radical reform project. Yet the street boasted among its varied shops and restaurants two cinemas, the Ouvidor and the Kab-Kab, and eventually the Palace.[110]

A notice in the *Jornal do Brasil* in December 1894 announced, "In the salon on the rua do Ouvidor 131, the day before yesterday the kinetoscope was inaugurated, the latest invention of Edison, which is, as are all the inventions of the studious and fecund inventor, wonderful. . . . We saw a cockfight."[111] The technological wonder of early motion picture and electrical illumination figured prominently at the National Exposition in 1908, which commemorated the centenary of the "commercial and industrial emancipation of Brazil." An official write-up of the event proudly credits the film's sponsorship to a familiar name at the time: "The cinematograph Paschoal Segreto installed was a great success. He showed a film of a general view of the city of Rio de Janeiro, taken from atop Sugar Loaf mountain."[112] It is a noteworthy coincidence that the first film shown in 1894 was a cockfight since Segreto, an Italian immigrant and self-made entertainment mogul, brought cinema to Rio and was also quite possibly instrumental in institutionalizing other kinds of popular yet clandestine gambling—particularly the jogo do bicho—in the city's world of commercialized entertainment.

Segreto arrived from Salermo, Italy, in 1886 an impoverished young man. When he died in 1920 he was a restaurateur, urban developer, theater producer, boxing and jiujitsu promoter, and local celebrity.[113] By the early 1910s Segreto had transformed the area around Praça Tiradentes into a center for such popular performance genres as the *teatro de revista*. Historians of

FIGURE 23 Portrait of Paschoal
Segreto (undated). Photograph
courtesy of FUNARTE/
Centro de Documentação e
Informação em Arte, Rio de
Janeiro.

this period have tended to use the language of industrialization to describe
the effect Segreto had on theatrical production. Under his influence and
that of the other entertainment impresarios of the time, the professionalized casts and capital provided by this new breed of businessmen made
Rio's theaters into "factories of public diversions" whose repeat performances and broad appeal lent them a "production line" aspect.[114] Segreto
underwrote shows with broad appeal, both in terms of class and tastes.
After 1911, he lowered the entrance prices and thereby encouraged a notable increase in the attendance of the popular classes.[115]

Segreto's involvement in Rio's world of public amusements straddled the
licit and the illicit; this very public figure drew profits from promoting not
only theatrical spectacles but also gambling, specifically the jogo do bicho.
Circumstantial evidence adds force to a century's worth of speculation and
rumor connecting Segreto and his family enterprise to the clandestine
lottery and to more general claims that the start-up capital not only for

Segreto but also for others of his cohort, especially Giacomo Rosario Staffa and Guiseppe Labanca, came from gambling.[116] A gambling operation associated with Segreto opened in the 1890s under a suggestive English name: Bookmarker Bank [sic]. The business soon began to take bets for the jogo do bicho, and it was in banking these betting operations that many of the city's future cinema impresarios got their start.[117]

A criminal investigation following a request Segreto sent to the federal patent office in 1896 hints at his possible connection to the Carioca underworld of gambling. Segreto had solicited "the privilege of exhibiting announcements . . . reproduced on an opaque screen by way of light, or [made] dynamic by way of a magic lantern." He had indeed debuted this new gadget, an early form of a moving picture, on the rua do Ouvidor. Shortly after the patent was granted, it seems, Segreto had harnessed the magic to run a gambling operation. According to the criminal case brought against him, "Whether he was already acting in bad faith when he requested the patent, or he only discovered after being conceded the patent and found that its legal use was earning him little or no income, he transformed this machine into one of the various ways in which the infamous 'jogo do bicho' is being exploited. . . . Segreto thus established the Nocturna Advertising Agency," headquartered on the Praça Tiradentes, where he ran his entertainment empire. "He divided the number of advertisements into twenty-six sections. . . . Every night he would intentionally refrain from projecting one of the twenty-six announcements, thus making it possible [to establish a game where] winning or losing depended exclusively on luck."[118] In all likelihood, it is no coincidence that the twenty-six advertisements Segreto's magic lantern projected nightly almost matched the number of animals in the jogo do bicho. Segreto may have requested his patent with the illicit lottery already in mind.[119] The authors of the federal law passed in 1910 to replace the anti–jogo do bicho articles in the Penal Code probably had Segreto and his competitors in mind when they added a clause that defines illicit lotteries as "among the other types of raffles referred to in the foregoing paragraphs, symbols, figures, and cinematic vistas."[120]

The indications that republican Rio's new generation of popular culture entrepreneurs was the jogo do bicho's early bankers and investors, while compelling, are based largely on hearsay and rumor. Clear evidence nonetheless demonstrates that the hypnotizing technologies of the movie houses and magic lanterns were intricately connected with the underworld

FIGURE 24 Employee of Paschoal Segreto's entertainment company, believed to be his brother Afonso Segreto (undated). Photograph courtesy of FUNARTE/Centro de Documentação e Informação em Arte, Rio de Janeiro.

of the jogo do bicho in myriad ways, direct and indirect.[121] The jogo do bicho may have been many Cariocas' first contact with commercialized public amusement. New gimmicks and inventions and the excitement they could generate provided a convenient subterfuge for entrepreneurs looking to benefit from the runaway success of the animal game. Conversely, the employment and money-making opportunities the *submundo* of the jogo do bicho offered allowed entrepreneurs to earn a profit they could then invest in related endeavors, such as, in Segreto's case, boxing and early cinema. From its very start, the jogo do bicho had formed part of a universe of licit popular entertainment in which the game's famous inventor, the Baron de Drummond, was an entrepreneur, much like Segreto. The emphatic protestations of Rio's would-be entertainment impresarios in their correspondence with the city government that they would not run "games whose winning or losing depended on chance" are revealing. City and federal officials feared, often apparently with good reason, that a private request to operate a licit amusement park might have concealed a scheme to run a gambling business.

CONCLUSIONS: CULTURAL HISTORY IN THE JUDICIAL ARCHIVE

In reconstructing the cultural importance of the jogo do bicho in the First Republic, the medium, in telling ways, is the message. The historical sources described in this chapter point to the omnipresence of the jogo do bicho, its wide geographic spread throughout the city, and its significance as a cultural reference point across the socioeconomic spectrum. And yet the judicial archive demonstrates that the police arrested few people in connection with the game, relative to the multitudes who appear to have played and dealt in it. The contrast between the ubiquity of this popular, illegal practice and the relative paucity of court cases against it can serve as more than just a frustrating lacuna in the historical record. Perhaps this gap is the most dynamic and interesting place to study the interface between the state and society.

Reading the archived cases is itself a game of chance; to win this lottery is to open a file and find attached small pieces of paper with handwritten columns of numbers. These scraps of paper, original jogo do bicho tickets seized as evidence at the crime scene, represent tiny, unmediated fragments of the real world that have snuck into the judicial archive. Reading these tickets against the content of the other, narrative components that make up a criminal file, they reveal otherwise hidden insights into Brazilian urban life at the time of the jogo do bicho's mounting popularity. The written defense (auto de defesa) forms part of every criminal case; this document is one of the autos that make real-world facts into legal facts, which the judge must then use to apply the law.[122] In more than a few cases, the pieces of paper affixed with rusting metal staples to these criminal files seem to belie the defendant's ardent insistence on innocence in his written testimony.

One can remain agnostic about defendants' guilt or innocence while still gleaning rich insights from reading the case. The jogo do bicho tickets are artifacts of the precise moment when a customer exchanged his five milreis for a chance to earn one hundred or much more—or, when a customer paid her five milreis. Although the arrest records give the impression that only males bought and sold chances to win the jogo do bicho, as this chapter has shown, artifacts like game tickets demonstrate just the opposite: women were some bicheiros' best customers. The figures scrawled in pencil on these tickets also disclose such important details as how much money players were willing to risk: usually the cost of a loaf of bread in 1900. These, in turn, show what was at stake. For the cost of a dozen eggs or a bottle of cheap Portuguese wine, one stood a chance of earning twenty milreis, a sum that would momentarily fortify one's daily wage but not alter one's lifestyle.[123] In light of the low probability of arrest and the reasonable possibility of winning, it is not difficult to imagine why people would want to play.

To engage in such acts of historical imagination in attempting to reconstruct long-deceased historical subjects' experiences of playing the jogo do bicho, we need to consider the difference between studying a culture that is suppressed and a culture that is only partially suppressed. The historian Lawrence Levine closes his classic study of expressive culture among African Americans both before and after slavery with a reflection on the difficulty of recovering cultures that developed and even flourished under repression. Using a stunning metaphor, Levine likens culture to a "vital secret," a phrase he borrows from William James. James had been captivated by an essay by Robert Louis Stevenson called "The Lantern Bearers," in which the poet remembers how "he and his schoolmates used to place a bulls-eye lantern under their coats, its presence unknown to all but one other. Thus equipped, each boy would walk through the night 'a mere pillar of darkness' to ordinary eyes, but each exulting in the knowledge that he had a hidden lantern shining at his belt." This " 'vital secret' " each person carries remained hidden from public view, deceiving the outside observer, who is equipped with mere "documents" and normal sight to perceive the smoldering beauty of those parts of human culture and consciousness that " 'run underground.' "[124] When we consider these individual acts and experiences as coalescing into a shared culture, though, we see that the oppressive conditions that force individual forms of expression underground will also shape the expressive culture that emerges, in the slaves' folktales Levine recounts just as in the practice of the jogo do bicho. As we have seen, the jogo do bicho's culture may have grown underground, but its infrastructure never was.

The story told here is a part of the broad narrative of the expansion and transformation of leisure in the "long twentieth century."[125] Yet the jogo do bicho fits imperfectly within the range of activities people engaged in out of doors, which depended on a thoroughly industrialized mode of production and a sharply segmented workday. Unlike attending the cinema, playing the jogo do bicho required no extended pause in one's daily activities. Cariocas laid bets and discussed the game in the course of daily chores and even work.

Even if we cannot speak of leisure, we can indeed talk about pleasure.[126] We ignore the fun of playing the jogo do bicho at the risk of dehumanizing its players. The pleasure of those who played this game would have derived from many factors: the opportunities for socializing and conspiring with friends and neighbors, the challenge of translating an inkling of which animal or number would prevail that day into a winning bet, and the real possibility of multiplying one's money. The jogo do bicho also inspired feelings of jocularity that radiated through the population and did not depend on actually playing the game; and the fun of the game often leaned toward the comedic. Of all the many arcane elements of popular culture, humor is perhaps the most slippery.[127] Yet evidence of the crucial importance of the amusement the jogo do bicho provided is hidden in the folds of the other data historical documents more readily give up. Even the police appear to have perceived the jogo do bicho as distinctively humorous. In the criminal files the tendency of the police to place unnecessary quotation marks around the term *jogo do bicho*, often redundantly adding the word "so-called" (*"o jogo denominado do bicho,"* or "the so-called 'animal game'"), is telling. Such repeated use of quotation marks, a gesture of disdain and removal, suggests that the authorities themselves noted a certain incongruity, perhaps even silliness, in the animal game as contrasted with the seriousness of the legal proceedings that the game instigated, transcribed in florid bureaucratese.

The pleasure of the game derived at least in part from a constant play on the "popular" nature of the game, in light of the "class-bound" nature of the law.[128] As we have seen, the game's folklore took its shifting moral high ground as a perennial theme. Just as the French philosopher Henri Bergson observed in his essay on laughter, written in response to urban modernity on the other side of the Atlantic, humor derives from the contrast between the mechanical and the human, the public and private, the formal and informal.[129] In this case, humor filled the moral vacuum in the space between the law and actual behavior.

The ambivalent morality and sense of humor about the illicit animal game in popular literature is an interesting foil against which to reconsider what we know about the risk of legal reprisals players faced—or did not face, as we can more accurately say for these earliest decades of the jogo's existence. While evidence shows that the jogo do bicho was ordinary in most people's eyes, the state came to characterize it as pathological. We must keep in mind that some games of chance, including the National Lottery, which enjoyed a public concession, and other licensed lotteries, were completely legal, while the law prohibited others. The essential similarity between legal and illegal games would not have been lost on the players.

Evidence from the jogo do bicho—as well as a rich, emerging scholarship on popular legal culture—shows that people were far from ignorant of the line between legal and illegal, but they were certainly not respectful of it either. This does not imply that urban Brazilians, even those who broke the law, took it lightly.[130] While the jogo do bicho's illegality appears to have meant little to most people in instructing them that it was wrong, its criminalization did impress on them that their culture was persecuted. Police intervention and sometimes violent repression of popular culture became stock elements in popular songs and plays of the early twentieth century. The encounter between the game and the law helps us understand the genesis of a besieged realm of popular culture—one that is self-conscious of its own persecution and the pastiche of legal interdictions that developed to control it. A culture deeply influenced by these legal interdictions developed as a result; identities and alterities formed along the axis of the law's dividing line between right and wrong. The jogo do bicho—a "vital secret" and certainly an open one—etched informal culture upon the public realm.

6

VALE O ESCRITO

No jogo do bicho, vale o que está escrito.
(In the jogo do bicho, what's written down counts.)
—Brazilian proverb

If the introduction to this book had not given away the end
of the story of the jogo do bicho, one could not fault a reader
for imagining a decidedly different outcome. Given its trajectory until 1917, one might reasonably assume, for example,
that the de facto impunity of the jogo do bicho would have
led to its de jure acceptance. After all, lottery gambling was
legal throughout the First Republic. The permanence of the
jogo do bicho in the urban landscape, the nonchalant tone in
which such literary icons as Machado de Assis referred to it,
its appearance in scores of magazine cartoons and popular
plays, and its broad popularity might plausibly have softened
its detractors' resolve to eradicate it. Of course, the opposite
is true. Violent outbursts of ire toward the game punctuated
the final decades of the First Republic. Both officers of the law
and some private citizens remained determined to erase what
one jurist called "the great putrefactor" of the jogo do bicho
from the map of the Federal District.[1]

The jogo do bicho made its presence known throughout
the Federal District of Rio de Janeiro and all of Brazil gradually. Yet events in 1917 present an opportunity to isolate one
historical moment in which hidden forces were revealed. In
that year, convulsions of worker agitation and a major reorga-

nization of government administration reconstructed the political and legal playing field on which agents of the state met buyers, sellers, and bankers of the jogo do bicho. Rio's police unleashed their full repressive force against the sellers of the game, initiating an operation suggestively named the *campanha mata-bicho*, or "kill-the-animal campaign."[2] New approaches to policing also materially shaped the jogo do bicho. This chapter centers on the year 1917 as a point of departure from which to draw some conclusions about the game's persecution and persistence into the twentieth century.

The clandestine lottery, more than just surviving after 1917, reorganized itself and emerged from the period—one marked by repression and generalized, violent opposition to working-class activities—with an internal logic and code of ethics that, according to popular belief, surpassed the formal one that officially opposed it. The proverb that frames this chapter —"In the jogo do bicho, what's written down counts."—expresses the popular sentiment that the jogo do bicho was both more reliable and more legitimate than the judicial system that censured it. An interesting irony took shape as the game withstood pronounced persecution in the first decades of the twentieth century: the construction of popular confidence in the game. The proverb is a play on the words *vale o escrito*, generally written on each jogo do bicho ticket.[3] With this legalistic affirmation, in effect a bicheiro poached the technology of legitimate legal practice— the purposefully chosen written word—to transform a scrap of paper into a promissory note. For over a hundred years, these words have attested to the bonds of trust that allowed the game to function. The reliability of the game depended on the compliance of a self-policing community of individuals who together formed a business network regulated only by legally insubstantial oral contracts, promises, and customary expectations.[4]

This legendary trust in the operators of the game derived its force from an implicit contrast with the perceived untrustworthiness of the operators of the state; and for most nonelite Brazilians, the state meant the criminal justice system. As we have seen, police acted as both emissaries of state power and individual entrepreneurs. By the early twentieth century, the jogo do bicho had effectively become a clandestine public–private consortium. The relationship between police and bicheiros formed the solar center around which other actors who took part in the illicit popular economy—players, neighbors, judges, public officials, and such private-sector competitors as the National Lottery Company—rotated and which radiated the energy that fueled its transactions. In the context of the game's perpetually uncertain legal status during the First Republic, the police criminality that buttressed it effectively connected citizens in networks of patronage and clientele and sustained an economy whose currency included criminal denunciations, money, and the acquired, de facto right to operate a business on one's piece of urban territory.

A sweeping examination of police corruption in urban Brazil is outside the scope this book. Indeed, explaining police involvement in clandestine petty gambling as corruption presents more analytical problems than it solves, as it flattens the historical process of which this interaction was a part. The history of the jogo do bicho recounts the social construction of not only the urban miscreant but also the wayward public official. Police served as mediators of both the law and the idea of Brazil as a nation of laws. In the 1910s and 1920s, Cariocas were living through a moment when the professionalization of policing raised the standards of public accountability. Yet this wave of police reform inflicted on the urban masses a deadly combination of "scientific policing" and its attendant interest in record keeping and the growth of a police bureaucracy, along with the continued use of arbitrary force. Owing to the social upheavals and agitated working class in 1917–18, by the 1920s, in the apt words of the historian Marcos Bretas, "*raison d'état* had arrived in the streets."[5]

The debates and social conflicts that swirled around the still-questionable legality, persecution, and persistence of the jogo do bicho in the last decades of the First Republic implicitly concerned the broader issue of the urban populace's expectations of the state—trustworthiness, predictability, and faithful execution of duties—in the face of the arbitrary exercise of power and the everyday "banal acts of violence" many citizens experienced firsthand.[6] This is not to claim jogo do bicho vendors and entrepreneurs, by contrast, upheld a rigorous standard of trustworthiness; bicheiros and their customers were capable of placing their self-interest before their imperative to fulfill their end of a bargain. The importance of the animal game's reputation for honesty—usually borne out in reality, sometimes not—lies instead in its centrality to the construction of spaces of legitimacy: bureaucratic, legal, and economic. My broad inquiry into the complexities of trust complements the existing literature on urban policing in

Brazil in this notoriously authoritarian age, which has provided a richly detailed view of how the police have acted as an arm of the state but has left popular views of illegality underanalyzed.[7]

This chapter on the early history of the jogo do bicho touches on a vast subfield of inquiry into Latin American politics, society, and history: the study of the region's premodern economy of favors, nepotism, and seigneurial power and its continuance into the contemporary era. In a patrimonial state, governed by the rule of man as opposed to the rule of law, legitimacy derives from "adherence to tradition," rather than to legal codes. In contrast, the legitimacy of the modern, bureaucratic state comes from its functional rationality; technically speaking, networks of patronage and clientele should not be central to its operation, which turns on depersonalized authority. Yet in the characteristically hybrid patrimonial–bureaucratic Iberian imperial state and its postcolonial Latin American successors, public servants wielded seigneurial power, and private power-brokers gained de facto legitimacy by force of tradition.[8]

Historians have depicted clientelism in Brazil as a continually renewed institution that gained force with modernization instead of disappearing and that remained in a uniquely decentralized form as Brazil's particular brand of local bossism known as *coronelismo* throughout the country after the beginning of the First Republic.[9] In the classic formulation associated with the historian Victor Nunes Leal, coronelismo is generally understood as a "compromise" between public power and oligarchs from the late nineteenth century to the early or mid-twentieth.[10] Getúlio Vargas's presidency, which began in 1930, and particularly his dictatorial regime known as the Estado Novo, or "New State" (1937–45), is typically seen as replacing the diffusion of power under coronelismo with an authoritarian national state. From the nineteenth-century Empire through Brazil's twentieth-century experiment with populist dictatorship, patronage has been depicted as the most enduring and effective form of social control. Historians of Brazil and elsewhere have shown that under such a system, occasional favors bestowed on the poor and working classes lulled them into complacency and stifled the demand for real, redistributive justice.[11]

If patronage amounted to social control, then what happened to the distribution of power in Brazilian society as the traditional oligarchy withered in the early and mid-twentieth century? Historians have treated the process through which the state took up the role previously filled by "personalistic hierarchy" as one of the most significant transitions in the country's history, a process intertwined with Brazil's particular experience of the major developments of the modern era: the transfer of power from rural to urban areas and the advent of industrial capitalism. With the restructuring of patrimonial society and gradual urbanization, urban police adopted the social control role formerly reserved for *fazendeiros, coroneis,* and the rural oligarchy in general. A professionalized police force developed to fill the void left by the loss of a traditional oligarchy by enforcing a code of public conduct that police and citizens were supposed to follow.[12] Police played a crucial role in mediating this urban pact between the newly empowered state and the populace not only by doing the state's bidding in maintaining social order, but also by acting outside the law as they built networks of patronage and clientele. Studies of the police hierarchy in the Federal District have shown how day-to-day justice operated by way of personal favors and personal appeals to higher-ups.[13]

Paradoxically, then, one must look to the police to understand what connected individuals within a society in which so many lived perforce outside the law. The prepolitical social solidarity and community ties generally understood as the force that binds Brazilian public life together carry far less analytical weight here than individuals' relationships to the state by way of a subterranean social compact negotiated between police and persons who played and sold the jogo do bicho.[14] Those who held the most marginal positions in the workforce, like *apontadores do bicho*, street peddlers, and day laborers, as people outside the network of patronage relations and bosses, had always in some ways been the most mobile, free, and independent among Rio's popular classes.[15] Bicheiros in the early twentieth century did not function in Carioca society as urban coroneis, as the game's powerful bankers arguably would at century's end, when they began to shoulder much of the social welfare burden in their communities. Yet even during these earlier decades, the jogo do bicho existed within a patronage system run by the modern, bureaucratic state. As it developed, the largely extralegal urban popular economy of which the jogo do bicho was a part upended the "coronelistic compromise" between private and public power.

The complaints against corrupt cops who accepted "tips" to collude with jogo do bicho dealers and bankers that pepper Rio's administrative records from the early twentieth century attest not to a widespread public outcry against the animal game but in fact the opposite. Like the anonymous denunciation of the jogo do bicho peddler Maximiliano Felix Bahia discussed in chapter 3, *denuncias* against police appear to be the exceptions that prove the rule of regularized, normalized extrajudiciality. Likewise, the crackdown on the jogo do bicho that reached a crescendo in 1917 represents an example of the police institution's attempt to rebuke its own corruption by outlawing a practice in which it had become deeply and illegally involved. While scholars and policymakers have not ignored police corruption, they generally regard it as divergence from a norm, if not as a tenacious holdover from a premodern style of governance. My interpretation of the jogo do bicho from its watershed in 1917 through the early 1930s tells a different story. The extrajudicial actions of police officers were a central element of the routine, everyday operation of the state; the patrimonial–bureaucratic state was made and unmade daily through the encounters of its police force with the people, as together they made and unmade the law.

Ultimately, I raise the possibility that the jogo do bicho accidentally answered the so-called social question: how to create a unified, functional society out of one torn by socioeconomic disparity and tension. Lawmakers did attempt to contend with Brazil's agitated, impoverished working class after 1917.[16] Social reform designed to improve the lot of the working class came, in part, from a fear that existing social tensions might lead to upheavals similar to those in Russia, Germany, and elsewhere.[17] Yet policy designed to address the social question had mostly failed in this task. In spite of an incremental move toward social reform and government protection of the laboring classes, the final decades of the First Republic are marked by persistent denial of any conflict between capital and labor and insistence (despite ample evidence to the contrary) that workers enjoyed exemplary working conditions and fair salaries. Draconian laws to squash labor activism accompanied dismissal of the urgency of a "worker problem."[18] Meanwhile, against the backdrop of these unresolved social tensions, with the criminal law as the main interface between state and society, the perennial but unsuccessful cycles of persecution of the jogo do bicho educated a generation of Rio's petty entrepreneurs, police, judges, and citizen-bystanders in the promises and obligations that citizenship *really* entailed.

HUNTING DOWN THE ANIMAL GAME: 1917–CA. 1930

Nineteen seventeen was once erroneously called "the year in which they did away with the jogo do bicho."[19] Having withstood three decades of attempts at suppression, the game had local versions in major cities like

Salvador and São Paulo. As it had been since the mid-1890s, Rio's jogo do bicho remained a side-bet on the federal lottery until 1946, and throughout this period was a popular, inexpensive, and effectively illegal alternative to legal lottery gambling.

The rules of the game in 1917 were essentially the same as in previous decades. Players selected a number or group of numbers that corresponded to twenty-five animals.[20] The bicheiros' business day commenced in the morning and lasted until two o'clock, when the lottery drawing took place. They made payments to winners until just after four o'clock, and their "hour of rest" was from five to six.[21] Periodic police harassment interrupted the life of many a bicheiro, but overall the game operated predictably and continuously every day but Sunday; the arrest of one bicheiro meant only that customers would do business with one of the scores of others.

By the first decade of the twentieth century, the police had effectively wrested control over games of chance in the Federal District away from the executive branch of the municipal government that had traditionally held it. From 1917 on, under the leadership of Chief of Police Aurelino de Araujo Leal, campaigns against illicit gambling became the favored control mechanism.[22] Law enforcement's attempts to track progress in eliminating the game provide useful, if episodic, evidence of how much effort they expended and whom they arrested. The number of jogo do bicho arrests in 1916 mounted as the anti-bicho campaign heated up, even surpassing those for vagrancy and property crimes (table 10). The most intense phase of the campaign unfolded in 1917: in September police raided 137 jogo do bicho businesses. By the end of that month, police had shut down 638 independent operations and indicted 294 *contraventores*. Police arrested hundreds during the year and forced 868 openly functioning points of sale to close.[23] Police set their sights on all jogo do bicho operations, large and small, from the lottery shops that proliferated in the city center to the clandestine gambling businesses that operated alongside or within legal retail shops, predominantly in the peripheries. Armando Vidal (Leite Ribeiro), the powerful third auxiliary district chief and prime mover in the antivice campaigns of the 1910s and early 1920s, sent a letter to Chief Leal on September 11, 1917, reporting that the day prior the Delegado had "swept the houses where the jogo do bicho was practiced, situated on Rua Quitanda 79 and Ouvidor 137, apprehending a large quantity of lists, two staplers, and paper holders." The unusually high number of lists found at this site suggests it was one of the growing number of specialized jogo do

TABLE 10 Sample of Arrests by Month in Third Police District, July–December 1916

MONTH (IN 1916)	NUMBER CHARGED WITH VAGRANCY	NUMBER CHARGED WITH CRIMES AGAINST PROPERTY	JOGO DO BICHO (ARTICLE 31 OF LAW 2321) ACCUSED/CHARGED
July	4	12	3/6
August	15	10	13/21
Sept.	16	7	10/15
October	8	No figure reported	20/31
November	20	6	12/30
December	9	2	5/15

Source: Arquivo Nacional, Serie Justiça – IJ6 – 617 (código do fundo AM) - "Delegados Districtais," janeiro de 1917.
In the 1910s, the Third Police District corresponds with the neighborhoods Santo Antonio and Santana.

bicho businesses owned by bankers who ran and financed multiple smaller bicho operations. By April 1918 several more distant precincts informed the chief of their successful eradication of all jogo do bicho businesses in their jurisdictions.[24]

The anti-bicho fervor of 1917 was evident not only in the increase in arrests.[25] It was also marked by public discussion about the jogo do bicho at the Conferência Judiciária-Policial, a high-profile police conference held in the Federal District from May to August of 1917. Local and federal magistrates, government administrators, jurists, and police authorities convened to design a state strategy for maintaining order in the capital. The agenda ranged from the surveillance of working-class organizing to the repression of Spiritism, but an overarching concern with class tensions and the city's fragile social peace inflected the entire conference.[26] Rather than setting formal policy, the conference established nonbinding recommendations and aired social concerns before an array of Rio's most powerful public servants. In general, the conference seems to have confirmed that, except for the right of the state to impose public security, all rights, including free speech, free movement, and free association, were contingent.

The conference also affirmed the inappropriateness of gambling in a civilized, healthy, functional Brazil. The thirty-one theses elaborated in the proceedings included one on the jogo do bicho, related by Delegado Vidal,

TABLE 11 Police Campaign Against the Jogo do Bicho:
Persons Arrested and Operations Closed Down in the Federal District, 1917–18

MONTH	NUMBER OF PERSONS ARRESTED	NUMBER OF JOGO DO BICHO BUSINESSES CLOSED DOWN
August 1917	65	—
September 1917	229	638
October 1917	131	173[a]
November 1917	37	—
December 1917	17	57
January 1918	43	—
February 1918	25	—
March 1918	24	—
April 1918	18	—
Total	579	—

Source: O Imparcial, June 4, 1918.
Around 40 percent (232) of the total 579 arrests were carried out by the Third Auxiliary Police Precinct (Terceira Delegacia Auxiliar), and the remaining 347 arrests were made by the regular police precincts (delegacias de distrito).

[a] This figure is for both October and November 1917.

for whom the persecution of the jogo had become a pet cause. In the epigraph, Rui Barbosa deploys the racialized criminological discourse of his day and reinforces his words with a biological allusion to the pollution of the Brazilian "organism": "Such is gambling [o jogo], the great putrefactor. Cancerous disease of the races threatened by sensuality and laziness, [gambling] makes the people torpid, callous, emasculated, in the fibres of which the organism insinuates its proliferating and inextirpable seed."[27] Vidal then begins with a caustic condemnation that echoes Barbosa's dramatic language, leaving no doubt that gambling fell well beyond the pale of the acceptable: "Gambling [o jogo]—the great putrefactor—constitutes a permanent problem, a challenge to the attention of legislators and administrators." "That gambling is a sure source of crime," Vidal writes, "no one has a doubt."[28]

The conferees expressed the hope and expectation that all lotteries would become illegal and explored the question of which laws the authorities could most effectively invoke to prosecute jogo do bicho cases. The police and judicial experts decided that police should charge accused buyers and dealers with articles 31 and 32 of Law 2321, a verbose piece of federal leg-islation passed in 1910 mainly to establish budgetary and tax guildelines, which contained an article that defined "prohibited games." Such punc-tilious legalistic details grew in importance as the sparks of controversy generated by the jogo do bicho and its persecution ignited during the often violent mata-bicho campaign of 1917. Rio's daily newspapers, magazines, legislative annals, and official correspondence between the police and the mayor's office attest to an ongoing public debate over the anti-bicho cam-paign, a debate whose subtext expressed misgivings about abuses of state power and the need to maintain public order within the strictures of the rule of law.

The controversy over the mata-bicho campaign stemmed from its ori-gins as a local police initiative. Responding to waves of concern among police officials and special interests, in particular commercial associations and the company that ran the legal lottery, police commanders ordered their patrols to step up efforts to suppress the jogo do bicho.[29] At the top of the chain of command was Chief Leal, a Bahian lawyer with a long standing interest in the criminal mind.[30] In February 1917 as the anti-bicho campaign was getting underway, Delegado Vidal wrote a letter to Leal asking him to consider outlawing bookmakers, arguing that even the ones permitted to work the horse races habitually sold tickets to unauthorized lotteries "in the shadow of a legally obtained license."[31] Tellingly, Vidal made his appeal to the police chief, a public official who lacked the author-ity to pass legislation or to adjudicate the law. The purpose-driven, savvy Vidal unlikely erred here in his understanding of the de jure division of power. The letter offers a glimpse of how police officials enjoyed de facto liberty to set law enforcement policy where the law's intent was vague.

Even as these campaigns raged, Brazilians were far from reaching a juridical or political consensus about whether this type of gambling con-stituted a crime. Police officials blamed such juridical ambiguity for their ongoing inability to eliminate the animal game or even to make most individual gambling charges stick. In a letter of January 1917 to the chief of police, a delegado describes his fruitless efforts to "repress prohibited games, especially the jogo dos bichos," which had been "consuming the greater part" of his energies; only under "very exceptional" circumstances did jogo do bicho cases ever end in conviction.[32] In a series of editorials and interviews published in the mainstream press from 1915 to 1918, Vidal himself expressed concern with the rampant illicit gambling in Rio and the danger to public morality it presented. Decrying the lack of a legal apparatus suited to its repression, he called repeatedly for aggressive policing and legal reforms.[33] Meanwhile, in the Carioca press in 1917–18 jurists and citizens debated the issue hotly in editorials, arguing that the police and their aggressive antigambling campaign, not the bicheiros, were defying the law.[34]

The controversy escalated as accusations surfaced that not the public interest but payoffs by the National Lottery Company, the jogo do bicho's supposed competitor, had motivated the wave of police repression. In September 1917 an article in the *Jornal do Comércio* alleged that the lottery company had "founded a 'trust,'" and that the "most odious task of the persecution of [the company's] rivals is falling to the police." Editorials in Brazilian papers repeatedly used the English word *trust* in quotation marks to depict the lottery business as a powerful cartel, perhaps unaware of the forceful irony of the word's other meanings in English.[35] More evidence of police malfeasance soon emerged. In October 1917 Rio's daily *Correio da Manha* published a letter that referred to a "considerable contribution" paid by the National Lottery Company to the police to repress the jogo do bicho.[36] The director of the company, Alberto Saraiva da Fonseca, responded in the *Jornal do Comércio*, not denying but defending his actions. He had signed a contract that guaranteed him a monopoly on lottery gambling in the Federal District, he argues. In Fonseca's estimation his company had acquired the right to take matters into its own hands after enduring a frustrating, years-long wait for the state to provide "due protection" against "criminal competition."[37]

Representative (*deputado*) Maurício de Lacerda brought this scandal to the federal legislature, complaining before the Chamber of Deputies that the initiative for the unjustifiably violent anti-bicho campaign had come from the directors of the National Lottery Company in their attempts to protect their monopoly.[38] In the closing months of 1917 the federal and municipal legislatures heard speeches both supporting and condemning the campaign. Some lawmakers complained about the police's ham-fisted approach to law enforcement. Police, they argued, had been shutting down licensed businesses like shoe shiners and cigarette and cigar vendors alongside the lottery ticket sellers, an injustice to petty business owners and the cause of forfeiture of the fiscal benefits of licensing fees and taxes.[39]

Assemblyman Ernesto Garcez described on the floor of the Municipal Chamber in November 1917 his appeal to Chief Leal to carry out the "the so-called campaign against the bicho with greater discretion." "Under the pretext of the suppression of the jogo do bicho," Garcez pointed out, police "persecuted many innocent individuals, and over 300 businesses' licenses have been revoked, whose total value amounts to more than 1,200 contos de reis." He insisted that the police be more cautious and respectful of this essentially harmless and potentially lucrative local practice: "In this city the jogo do bicho has existed for more than twenty years as an inveterate custom. The people have become accustomed to it just like the Italians have to their 'lotto' and the French to their horse races." The "approximately 10,000 people [who] earn a living from this game" risk slipping into the "greatest misery from one day to the next" should the police succeed in criminalizing it. Anyone in "direct contact with the people" would understand the enormous damage of persecuting the working classes and permitting the police to continue their excesses. Garcez expressed fear that once denied the ability to practice their profession and thereby driven into poverty, thousands of workers in Rio's shadow economy might "transform from one moment to the next into the gravest elements of disorder just when we need public tranquility the most." The precise legalities of the jogo do bicho, for Garcez, were beside the point: "It is known that customs make laws, and that as a rule, laws are not made against customary practices [usos e costumes]."[40]

One of the principal arguments made for the game's legalization in the wake of the kill-the-animal campaign of 1917 reiterated the intuition that many had expressed for decades: the apparently illegal animal game was "precisely the same thing" as the "very lottery authorized by the government." The government had justified the existence of licit lotteries by mandating that their proceeds go to charity. Why not likewise channel the jogo do bicho profits to such worthy causes as "the elderly, the poor, destitute children, and so on" and thus assist "those who have been abandoned by the public powers [poderes públicos]" and whose fate was left to the vagaries of "private generosity." As proposed "in the legislation . . . by the senator from Rio, Dr. Erico Coelho," the only reasonable solution to the neediness of the Carioca people and the strained city budget alike would be to legalize and regulate the jogo do bicho.[41]

The person to whom the legislators referred here, Erico Coelho, was a doctor-turned-federal-senator with fierce republican convictions but maverick positions on such explosive topics as legalizing divorce and occultism. As a medical professor and obstetrician in the late nineteenth century, he had been the "leader of the hypnotists," a brief marginal trend in medical science inspired by popular psychological ideas from France. If the Brazilian government permitted betting on horse racing, he reasoned, what justification was there for the criminalization of the jogo do bicho? While little else is known about Coelho's unsuccessful bid in Brazil's Federal Senate to legalize the clandestine lottery in 1916–17, we do know that the career of this fascinating figure had unfolded at the borderline between "healing" and charlatanism, and between legitimate and condemned practice.[42]

The unresolved issue of the jogo do bicho's status bore powerful associations with two major questions about the role of the state. First, some lawmakers directly connected the jogo do bicho to the frustrated desire to enlarge the government's role in providing entitlements to Brazil's citizens. Second, the animal game made legislators think about the state's role in fabricating a line between forbidden and permitted behavior, whether by criminalizing the variety of occultist practices then in vogue or the underground lotteries that were identical to their aboveground counterparts. Both of these sets of concerns, in turn, led to the question of public order and to the increasingly numerous, impoverished, and potentially dangerous urban masses.

In the legislature, as in the press, many protested the overly aggressive tactics of the anti-bicho campaign.[43] A municipal legislator named Jeronymo Beretta commented in November 1917 that even those who revile the contraventores who buy and sell the jogo do bicho must decry the "tumultuous, violent, and absurd procedures the police are putting into practice under the shadow of the *estado de sítio*," or "state of siege," imposed in the Federal District just as the anti-bicho campaign was beginning in October 1917. The government had invoked emergency powers before, placing state security above individual rights and juridical norms in the wake of labor unrest. Now, in 1917, as social upheaval rippled through São Paulo, Santos, Rio, and other cities, the federal government used the pretext of Brazil's formal entrance into the war in Europe to place the Federal District under this provisional emergency politico-legal regime.

The estado de sítio to which Beretta referred haunts the background of much public discussion about policing in this tumultuous time. As another municipal legislator exclaimed, "It is perfectly well known that the honorable Mr. President of the Republic had recommended to the Chief of Police that he not permit violence during the state of siege, not even under the pretext of the persecution of gambling." One angry colleague replied that the "police chief has not abused the estado de sítio, but he would be in his rights to do so," because "we are talking here about the question of vice." Other council members insisted the police had acted moderately, reminding their colleagues that Brazil itself was in a state of siege as well as a state of war. One assemblyman cited a case in which a citizen had been arrested for selling animal tickets "when the real motivation was political." An opponent quipped, "He was a political bicheiro."[44] In this revealing attempt at humor on the legislative floor, the latter assemblyman made light of the slippage between petty miscreants and political dissidents as urban Brazil's most dangerous public enemies.

CAUSES AND EFFECTS

How can one understand the marked increase in the intensity of the repression of the jogo do bicho in 1917, despite the misgivings expressed in the legislature and in the press? Both before and after that eventful year, police and lawmakers consistently reasoned according to a certain tautological logic: the illegality of games of chance necessitated their suppression. Jurists and politicians asserted that the game threatened the sanctity of the law and warned of the hemorrhage of public revenue that would inevitably result from unlicensed commerce. In addition to these long-standing justifications for the repression of the jogo do bicho, the political and social tensions that characterized the historical conjuncture of 1917 gave new meaning to the old tautology behind its criminalization. The state of siege does not explain the suppression of popular culture in that year but points to a broader historical context in which both developed. In this context, the kill-the-animal campaign converged with and gained force from the counterrevolutionary climate that would soon grip urban Brazil. With the causes and effects of the anti-bicho campaign seamlessly intertwined, changes in policing altered the way in which the jogo do bicho operated and created the institutional infrastructure that shaped the relationship between the game and police.

As Rio's police chief, tellingly nicknamed the "Carioca Trepov" after the infamous chief of St. Petersburg's police force just before the Russian Revolution, Leal earned a reputation as a hard-line counterrevolutionary. Urban Brazil's social upheavals during the late 1910s evoked frequent references to concurrent events elsewhere in the world. The São Paulo port city of Santos became known as the Brazilian Barcelona for its labor militancy.[45] In eastern Europe and the Baltic countries agrarian and working-class revolutions were erupting. Socialism was taking hold in Germany and Hungary as well as in Russia.[46] Closer by, events elsewhere in Latin America both paralleled and influenced Brazil's social tensions. The Mexican Revolution had begun in 1910 and was still unfolding in 1917, the year the revolutionary government signed the nation's new constitution into law. This historical moment occasioned changes in ideas about the objectives and nature of urban policing throughout Latin America, as mass migration and the presence of anarchism and "new forms of collective action" added momentum to a rising wave of protest against the region's closed, oligarchical regimes and lack of equal socioeconomic opportunity for the majority of the population.[47]

The early 1900s in Brazil is generally regarded as a period of relative quiet, as the police and management aggressively suppressed the few major strikes that did occur. The workers' movement began in earnest rather suddenly in 1917, a year that was punctuated by a general strike in São Paulo and Rio aiming to increase wages and improve working conditions. On May Day members of the laboring classes poured into the street demanding improvements in their lives both as producers and consumers. Subsequently, a number of strikes erupted throughout the capital. Over fifty thousand workers participated in a work stoppage in Rio that July, and labor agitation soon followed in other cities. Workers returned to their jobs in August, the culmination of a three-month-long, unprecedented display of working-class agitation and resistance. In November 1918 textile workers in Rio went on strike again, and laborers in civil construction and metallurgy immediately followed suit. What one historian calls a "continuous wave of strikes" swept across Brazil a year later. Some believed they were witnessing another general strike or even an "anarchist *Putsch*."[48]

The vigorous police campaigns against the jogo do bicho in 1917 were not just an expression of reactionary fear of labor militancy but also an outgrowth of the republican government's gradually eroding power. Political dissent in early twentieth-century urban Brazil had many faces. Most labor activists at that time were adherents to anarchism, the movement behind the insurrection of November 1918.[49] The Russian Revolution impacted Brazilian politics and society indirectly, contributing to the formation of the influential Brazilian Communist Party in 1922, which was modeled after the Third International and made illegal within months of its founding. Military officers also formed movements to dispute the current state of affairs. From 1922 to 1926 Brazil was under martial law because of a series of rebellions, the *tenentista* revolts, that young military officers mounted against the government. A related movement of young military officers and dissident members of the elite eventually brought down the First Republic in 1930, installing Vargas in the presidency. The 1920s were also marked by public health and educational reform, and the socially critical cultural awakening of Modern Art Week, an epochal exhibition of Brazilian visual arts and literature in February 1922. Despite their striking ideological differences, these multiple varieties of reformism converged on their mutual distaste for the particularly oligarchical brand of federalism that characterized the First Republic.[50]

Changes in the composition of Rio's population helped catalyze political upheaval and created new demands on policing and governance. By the early 1920s, the elite neighborhoods in the South Zone of the city had begun their ascent; Copacabana, Leme, and Vidigal gained population as they became more accessible through the prolongation of rail lines and roads. Beautification projects and demolitions of traditional hillside neighborhoods in the city center contributed to the rise in Rio's shantytowns by then already known as *favelas*.[51] Despite a lack of public investment in the city's suburban zones, these areas to the city's north and west grew vertiginously in 1910–20, primarily to house the expanding working classes, petite bourgeoisie, and low-level bureaucrats. Some of these neighborhoods doubled or tripled in population, as, in the 1920s, massive internal migration to cities began, especially from the states of Minas Gerais, São Paulo, Bahia, and the vast rural expanse of Rio de Janeiro state that began where the capital city tapered off. The Federal District reached 1,157,873 by 1920, more than double its size in the 1890s.[52]

Growth was fueled by migrants from abroad, as well. The surge of labor activity helped to incite a pronounced fear and persecution of foreigners. As a result of labor activity around 1907, Brazil adopted measures that provided for the deportation of foreigners suspected of instigating worker agitation, which overrode the constitutional and liberal misgivings that had until then prevented passage of such laws. Brazil did not experience an increase in immigration in the late 1910s and 1920s; on the contrary, it started to diminish.[53] Yet long-standing anti-immigrant sentiments merged with nascent anticommunism and tipped federal policy. Through the 1920s the law sought more aggressively than ever to control foreign-born workers. In contrast to the rhetoric against labor organizing, those who denounced the jogo do bicho did not frame the perceived threat of illicit gambling as a foreign peril. However, in the heightened antiforeign climate, a large proportion of those arrested for the jogo do bicho were foreigners, and the retail workers and small business owners whom police typically targeted came from an economic sector dominated by foreign immigrants.[54]

Whatever connection efforts to suppress the jogo do bicho may have had to a spike in antiforeigner sentiment in Rio, the kill-the-animal campaign also was part of a broader police attempt at moralizing the city. Police interest in regulating the morality of urban culture was not new, but now it aimed at a broader range of cultural production in such emerging sites of commercial entertainment as popular theater, the cinema, social clubs, and dancing societies, which reached an ever-wider audience. Chief Vidal led a campaign for what he called the *saneamento moral* (moral sanitation) of the city that was unprecedented in scope and intensity.[55] At least sometimes the courts seem to have backed the police's "incontestable right" to regulate the city's culture industries such as sports matches and public performances, to ensure they did not "offend any person or public morality" or demonstrate "public decadence" that could "cause disturbances of order."[56] The antigambling policing wave swept away social and recreational clubs that authorities suspected of running illicit gaming operations.[57] The moral sanitation campaign included not only repression of the jogo do bicho and suspected covert gambling establishments but also other measures, such as the censorship of popular theater. A law passed in 1924 solidified a policy of censorship of films and plays and mandated the creation of a police registry of actors and performers.[58] Worried about theatrical scripts he considered offensive or deleterious to public order, Vidal took "energetic measures" to fine actors who unduly took creative license in speaking their lines and to punish playwrights who produced morally offensive material.[59] His crusade aimed not just to moralize the theater but also to promote guarantees of property rights and to stop copyright infringement and the "indecorous pillage of the works of others."[60]

To pursue their policy that turned on both the sanitation of culture and enclosure of private property, the police created a vast antivice infrastructure. The antigambling administrative apparatus that was a part of this infrastructure owed its existence to the legality of some games of chance as much as to others' illegality. As the government issued more licenses to gambling establishments, the number of public employees charged with overseeing this activity commensurately increased.

Police pursued criminal prosecutions of illegal games of chance in subtly different ways than before. The transition in policing and the nature of the antivice infrastructure are typified by the Delegacias Auxiliares (Auxiliary Police Precincts); the suppression of the jogo do bicho in the 1917 era fell primarily to this new institution. Although formed in the previous decade, Rio's police hierarchy only effectively put the Delegacias Auxiliares in place in the mid-1910s, when the overflowing number of persons arrested for misdemeanors (*contravenções*) like vagrancy and gambling and the perceived need for repression of labor activists and political dissenters drove the state to restructure its policing apparatus. To the three that already existed, federal legislation in 1923 added a fourth Delegacia Auxiliar dedicated, among other things, to repressing "anarchism and other subversive doctrines" and the crime of vagrancy, a vague, pliable infraction that could be broadly applied to prosecute political dissenters for whom no other charge seemed to fit.[61] In effect, the Delegacias Auxiliares supplied a jurisdictional and administrative solution to the problem of how to police ambiguous offenses.

Each Auxiliary Police Precinct, headed by a delegado auxiliar, specialized in a cluster of related criminal infractions. The delegados auxiliares answered directly to the police chief and in turn shared his responsibility for overseeing the work of the twenty-two district police precincts (*delegacias de distrito*), the traditional, geographical jurisdictions.[62] Delegados auxiliares held heavily disputed judicial authority—to initiate inquests and judicial proceedings (*processos*), in particular—that district police precinct chiefs did not.[63] The prestige and power concentrated in the Delegacias Auxiliares eventually caused the federal government to dissolve them in 1933. New, more subordinate police units replaced the Delegacias Auxiliares.[64] After this 1933 reform, the job of handling the perpetual perceived crime wave of illicit gambling fell to the newly created Delegacia de Costumes e Diversões (Delegacia of Culture and Entertainment), which took over the tasks of the Second Auxiliary Police Precinct.

In practice, the job of overseeing the policing of clandestine games of chance during this period appears to have straddled the Second and Third Auxiliary Police Precincts. As he organized the most vigorous campaign against the jogo do bicho to date, Vidal held a position as the Third Auxiliary police chief from 1915 to the end of that decade.[65] On occasion he accompanied police officers in their searches of suspected jogo do bicho headquarters and effected the arrests of the bicheiros.[66] As we have seen,

Vidal made sure he remained a presence in the public sphere through his editorials and published interviews.

Vidal's hands-on approach in the anti-bicho campaign probably resulted more from his personal conviction and ambition than from any specific directive, for in fact the Second, not the Third, Auxiliary Police Precinct held responsibility for suppression of games of chance in the Federal District.[67] By 1920 Vidal had shifted to the position of Second Auxiliary delegado, a post he would hold until November of 1922.[68] The move seems unsurprising in that the annual reports from the Ministry of Justice and Internal Affairs show that the highest-ranking police officials perpetually circulated from post to post. These reports never indicate the reasons for these constant reassignments, but clearly the vaguely defined and controversial nature of the infractions with which these police officials dealt placed them on the front lines of the battles between police, the judiciary, and the citizenry the over the rule of law. As we will see, the ambiguous nature of the infractions they policed, combined with their relative autonomy and power, also left the Delegacias Auxiliares susceptible to becoming involved in the very activities that they oversaw.

The Auxiliary Police Districts—first the Second and then the Third—appear to have met their goal of making mass arrests for jogo do bicho–related offenses; in fact, they effectively took over the job of policing illicit gambling in the late 1910s and early 1920s. By the end of September 1917, of the 638 independent jogo do bicho businesses, 294 contraventores were indicted, and two-thirds of these actions were taken directly by the Third Delegacia Auxiliar.[69] Meanwhile, although not yet focused on illicit gambling, the Second Delegacia Auxiliar policed recreational clubs and the entertainment industry.[70]

By the 1920s, with Vidal now at the helm, the Second Delegacia Auxiliar pursued its antigambling directive at full throttle. In July 1920 the division sent a lengthy report to Rio's police chief listing "the work performed in the interest of repressing the jogo do bicho during the first semester of the current year." Of the 172 contraventores arrested during those six months, the preponderance, 117, were carried out under the auspices of the Second Auxiliary Precinct, as opposed to just 55 in all other districts combined.[71] In 1922, the precinct boasted of 334 processos initiated, 12 for "theatrical infractions" and 97 related to the jogo do bicho.[72]

The Delegacias Auxiliares succeeded not just in arresting large numbers of bicheiros but also in prosecuting the accused and punishing them with fines and prison sentences in significant numbers. By contrast, jogo do bicho cases that originated in the District Delegacias still almost always ended in acquittal.[73] A newspaper column remarked in 1917, "The campaign against the jogo do bicho when carried out by the District Delegacias is almost always poorly done, it is really deficient."[74] Specialization allowed the jurists who headed the Auxiliary Police Delegacias and the police officers who worked under them to gain a keen understanding of the rules of evidence relevant to that particular set of infractions. These specialized police officials deftly prevented jogo do bicho defendants from getting off on legal technicalities.

The Delegacias Auxiliares assumed their preeminent role in the suppression of the clandestine lottery as part of the broader reorganization of urban policing in Brazil according to scientific principles.[75] The administrative logic that assigned certain infractions to particular policing divisions derived in part from the process of professionalization already underway in the first decade of the twentieth century throughout Latin America. The state undertook a concerted effort to transform the police from a repository of the unemployable with a massive turnover rate into a stable, highly trained force. Broader trends toward modern record keeping and administrative planning also underlie the shift in policing, relating, for example, to the first stirring of what would develop into a fully blown statistical revolution in the Vargas era, and the new science of urban planning.[76]

The creation of the Delegacias Auxiliares reflects an emerging, more scientific approach to policing not only in its administrative logic but also in its perception of the criminal subject. New police procedures placed consummate value on the precise identification and categorization of criminal suspects in the interest of both scientific knowledge and social defense.[77] In 1907, the civilian police in the Federal District began to institute a requirement that citizens carry identification cards.[78] A variety of research and investigative organs tracked criminal defendants and compiled ongoing data on them to construct profiles of criminal types and careers.

In Brazil, the idea that policing should be conducted as scientific research predates 1917. Scientific policing had come to Brazil, for instance, in the country's adoption of the method of anthropometric criminal identification called *bertillonage*. Developed by the French police reformer Alphonse Bertillon in the 1880s, this approach to forensic knowledge radically altered criminal identification techniques, which previously had been purely impressionistic and based on narrative descriptions and police officers' memories. In the late nineteenth century the Brazilian police officially adopted the *bertillonage* method of scientific record keeping, biometric measurements, and the profiling of criminals with an aim of recording precise descriptions of them, tracking their repeat offenses, and utilizing their life trajectories as fodder for future legal-medical research.[79] By the 1910s ideas about the sociobiological genesis of crime had gained currency all over Latin America, intensifying the perceived need for criminal identification techniques and institutions.[80]

The emerging predilection to view criminality as an identity rather than an act relates to a much-studied shift in criminology in Latin America, by which not just crime but also sexuality and race fell under an emerging medico-legal science.[81] A cadre of new professionals sought to rid the nation of "communists, fascists, criminals, degenerate blacks, immigrants, and homosexuals." Eugenics, which placed criminality and deviancy squarely in the realm of biology, grew out of a fear of the dire consequences of leaving the era's social tensions untreated.[82] Throughout Latin America, eugenics reached its height in the 1920s and 1930s, and in some parts of the region, new institutions devoted to it continued to form through the 1940s and later. The appeal of eugenics and of scientific approaches to social pathology generally derived primarily from their supposedly apolitical nature and their status as a symbol of cultural modernity. Adherents claimed that legal-medical science would rise above the pettiness and tumultuousness of politics and employ science to cure social ills.[83] Yet the era's politicians frequently came from the ranks of the medical profession—among them Rio's influential mayors Barata Ribeiro and Pedro Ernesto, as well as the previously mentioned federal legislator from Rio, Erico Coelho. Brazilian physicians, psychiatrists, jurists, and politicians influenced each other and interacted in a small number of professional schools and associations.

It is probably not a coincidence that, at this time, references to "bicheiros" began to appear regularly in the arrest records. Naming the jogo do bicho vendor as a bicheiro implicitly marked that legal subject with a specific, criminal-professional identity. The attention that police, jurists, and those in the field of legal medicine began to pay to specialized career criminals now known as bicheiros, rather than simply as "[persons] arrested for selling the jogo do bicho," may be related to the preoccupation with following criminal careers through the recording of *reincidencias* (recidivism).[84] The shift from act to identity that was an informal part of daily policing in the prior decade—the tendency avowedly to arrest suspects because of their reputations as a "known jogo do bicho dealer," "known pickpocket," or a "disorderly person"—had become the formalized category of bicheiro.[85] This period of vigorous policing produced a sizeable body of data; individuals' arrest histories, photographs, and fingerprints comprised a library of "known" malefactors that numbered over eight hundred, on which police could draw in the future.[86]

The parallels between the new criminal ontology of vice crime, on the one hand, and the policing of political dissenters of the 1910s and 1920s, on the other, go beyond mere coincidence.[87] The antivice infrastructure created at the beginning of the twentieth century bears direct, causal connections to the one designed to repress political dissent in the era after the first tenentista revolt in 1922. In response to the labor and political unrest of the late 1910s, from within an administrative organization tailor-made for political repression, the police took up the weapons they had honed after a decade of policing gamblers, drunks, and vagrants: new record-keeping procedures that allowed inspectors to portray certain legal subjects as anarchists and generate police files to track their life trajectories; and vaguely worded legislation and executive orders allowing them to arrest persons for committing "subversive acts" or "being a Communist leader."[88] Political policing after 1922, interwoven with the continued efforts to kill the animal game, grew out of practices and reflexes first established for the repression of petty crime. Juridically speaking, the categorical bicheiro and the political criminal were siblings.

The positivist-derived notion of the born criminal had always been inconsistent with the social reality that underlay the clandestine lottery in the first place; most jogo do bicho vendors appear to have drifted in and out of that career or used it to augment insufficient wages. From the game's inception until around 1920 the bicheiro and banqueiro who backed the operation were generally the same person.[89] Now, in the late 1920s, the profile of the typical jogo do bicho seller underwent a transformation that paralleled his image among the policing-juridical institution. The jogo do bicho went from being a job in which people dabbled to one in which people specialized, and one marked by the increasingly sinister associations that its popular nature suggested.

In short, police repression had an impact on the nature of the jogo do bicho, but the reverse was also true; while judicial and policing procedures accommodated the omnipresence of ever-elusive bicheiros, the social meanings of the game also changed in tandem with law enforcement's perspective of it. When the jogo do bicho emerged from the campaigns against it around 1917, it appears to have passed a threshold in terms of its popularity, accessibility, and acceptance across the population. Yet people involved in the jogo do bicho acquired a stigma of criminality and lost some of their appeal to Rio's middle sectors, due to their arrests and the surges of violence that sometimes accompanied the anti-vice police campaigns in the 1910s and beyond.[90]

This deepening rift between the popular nature of the animal game and polite Carioca society directly affected both the organization and the spatial arrangement of the jogo do bicho. Police could effectively pressure clandestine operations in the center of the city, given the area's density of patrolling police officers and better surveillance. In the suburban neighborhoods to the west and north of the historic center, however, the law reached less forcefully.[91] The differential policing of the center and periphery altered the geography of the jogo do bicho. After the Baron de Drummond lost his monopoly on the lottery in the 1890s, it took a decentralized form as a multitude of individually owned and operated clandestine lotteries grouped under the umbrella of the jogo do bicho. The city's many jogo do bicho businesses remained atomized throughout the early twentieth century. In the 1920s, this decentralization began to reverse itself. Although the reorganization of the clandestine lottery under a few powerful overlords would not take place for another half century, with the changes in the urban landscape and more earnest police repression the ownership of jogo do bicho businesses began to devolve to increasingly fewer entrepreneurs. This recentralization appears to have begun in the periphery of the city. While jogo do bicho vendors in the city center mostly operated out of formal businesses, especially lottery shops and jogo do bicho sales outlets, in the less capitalized working-class suburbs they continued to sell their tickets as street peddlers or as part of another small retail shop or stand. Consequently, these weaker, more atomized operations in the peripheries were more susceptible to being taken over by *donos*, or "owners," proprietors of multiple ticket outlets who would capture part of their profit.[92]

While its distribution of power conformed to the centripetal force of capitalism, the jogo do bicho continued to spread throughout the city and into the working-class suburbs. In the 1920s, the jogo do bicho became more of a presence in the suburban zones, where it played an important role in the local economy, particularly in providing jobs for persons such as minors who found few other employment opportunities.[93]

Although set in motion by police repression, this restructuring of the jogo do bicho unfolded with its own momentum as police pressure on the game waxed and waned. The anti-bicho campaign of 1917 tapered off before decade's end. A period of relative tranquility for buyers and sellers of the clandestine lottery began. The three chiefs of police who succeeded Leal did not share his intense concern with games of chance. The jogo do bicho soon recomposed its extensive network of vendors and reestablished its direct lines to the police hierarchy, which were essential to the game's survival. Gambling operations of all kinds proliferated, many disguised as Carnival societies (*sociedades carnavalescas*) and various types of private clubs. No spectacular campaigns were launched to eradicate gambling, but the repression of the jogo do bicho continued, albeit in altered form. In the absence of a centralized initiative, the repression of illicit gambling itself diffused again into the hands of arresting officers, judges, and individual police officials. Salutary personal relationships between bicheiros and police became paramount.[94]

These personal relationships had long crossed the line into police criminality. In the late 1910s, the specialized antivice policing apparatus combined with the legal ambivalence toward gambling created new opportunities for graft, challenging officers of the law, many of them poorly remunerated, to maintain their professional and legal integrity in the face of great temptation.[95] Some of them participated in the illegal game simply by playing it. A letter of September 1917 from a local district head to the chief of police, for instance, reports that a police officer had been caught in a jogo do bicho shop. While on patrol he was found in "animated conversation with the owner of the shop" and supposedly caught in the act of playing the illicit lottery. A month later police authorities suspended a second officer, accusing him, too, of playing the jogo do bicho instead of carrying out his orders to patrol a suspicious lottery shop.[96]

Police insinuated themselves into the clandestine lottery as more than just ticket buyers. Although they notoriously resisted denouncing their colleagues' illicit behavior, occasional accusations in the archive confirm the conventional wisdom that the police allowed the clandestine lottery to function and drew an illegal profit from it. A uniformed civilian police officer entered a postcard shop "where only the jogo do bicho is sold" in October of 1916, where he allegedly "asked [the store owner] for money in

FIGURE 25 Cartoon from magazine *Dom Quixote*: "Repression of gambling": "What would this be, eh boy?" "They're police officers in a jogo do bicho shop." "To arrest the jogo do bicho banker?" "No, to see which number won." *Dom Quixote* (May 26, 1920), ano 4, n. 159.

the name of functionaries of [the police precinct]."[97] In November 1917, Delegado Vidal wrote to the chief of police asking permission to strip three National Guard officers of their rank for "flagrant" involvement in the jogo do bicho.[98] In his widely read prison chronicle of 1923, the journalist Orestes Barbosa describes a bicho operation headquartered in the belly of the beast: in the Casa de Detenção.[99] To the extent that Barbosa recounted the truth, the imprisoned banker's activities imply the criminal complicity of the guards.

Another journalistic chronicle describes how, in recent memory, persons arrested for the jogo do bicho sought out " 'jail-door lawyers' [*os advogados de 'porta de cadeia'*]—as the people commonly designated them," who "had a lucrative business in the payment of bail. This is because it was exceedingly easy to put an arrested bicheiro back on the street, by way of a payment to the respective police precinct, which was mediated by the police official responsible there. . . . As soon as the criminal proceedings were over, this bail money always reverted to the lawyers, in exchange for the liberty of the jogo do bicho banqueiros." A change in the law made the jogo do bicho ineligible for bail (*afiançavel*) and ended this practice of extorting money from incarcerated bicheiros. As described both here and elsewhere, this extralegal bail system provided an income for the police who kept on eye on the "jail door" and the fraudulent "lawyers" who acted as bail bondsmen, as well as impunity for those jogo do bicho sellers and bankers with the resources to pay.[100]

A short, anonymous essay from the period called "The Inextinguishable Jogo do Bicho" describes how police and justice officials may have used personal influence to grant impunity to their protégés. In times of both tolerance and repression, policing the animal game served officers of the law as "an infallible method of extorting money from bicheiros." The exchange not just of money but of power and influence formed the extralegal nexus between police and the jogo do bicho. The essay recounts a story that exemplifies public servants' ethical dilemmas as they weighed their private interests and the vulnerability of delegados in the face of police complicity with criminal activity:

> Once upon a time, there was a *delegado* of the 14th Police District, Dr. Parreiras Horta, a poor man, somewhat philosophical, eternally stuffed into his worn-out, black morning coat. The Police Chief was Leoni Ramos, who later would become the minister of the Federal Supreme Court. Parreiras Horas . . . had initiated a criminal case involving the jogo do bicho against someone caught in flagrante delicto. Hours later, [Delegado Parreiras Horta] was summoned to the police chief's office. He went. Leoni Ramos informed him that the defendant being charged was a friend and *compadre* of a congressman [*deputado*] who was a relative of the President-elect of the Republic. This deputado, someone whom one did not want to displease, obliged him to drop the criminal charges. Parreiras Horta agreed, but said: "It's easy for your excellency to order his police documents torn up. [But] you should designate my successor right now, because I am no longer the delegado." Leoni Ramos was surprised. He had not expected this. He remained courteous, wishing to be conciliatory: "No, no, it's not like that. On the contrary. You, sir, deserve all my confidence." "Yes," tranquilly continued Parreiras Horta, in order to say goodbye and depart. "I know well. But it is you who no longer deserves my trust [*confiança*]." He quit his post.[101]

Delegado Parreiras Horta, one of twenty-three chiefs of the city's district police precincts, certainly held considerable authority. Yet the essay's emphasis on the shabbiness of Parreiras Horta's elegance underscores his socioeconomic vulnerability and the contingency of the power he exercised on the moral judgments he made. Public officials and *comerciantes* alike were subject to either upward or downward mobility. Their entrepreneurial audacity largely determined which direction they would travel.

Not surprisingly, sometimes the very police officers and officials most invested in the antivice campaigns became accomplices. In 1926 the nation's president fired Rio's police chief, Marshal Carneiro da Fontoura, nicknamed "Marechal Escuridão" (Marshal darkness) for his violent campaigns against working-class organizing. Some sources explain that the firing resulted from the police force's failure under his watch to combat the jogo do bicho. Other sources offer a different explanation for his ineffectual policing of the animal game and ultimate dismissal: Carneiro da Fontoura faced public accusations of protecting "jogo do bicho vendors, from whom it is suspected he has received gratuities."[102] His successor renewed the Rio police's commitment to repressing illicit gambling, and an anti-bicho campaign in 1926 broke the relative calm of the early 1920s. Under the auspices of the Second Auxiliary Police Precinct, police arrested 515 jogo do bicho suspects that year.[103]

The surge in anti-bicho repression after Carneiro da Fontoura's dismissal amid accusations of bicho-related malfeasance points to a telling pattern in the ebb and flow of police surveillance of the animal game. Each of the crackdowns occurred on the heels of a major public scandal implicating police in the enabling of and profiting from the jogo do bicho. Campaigns against the animal game sought the moral sanitation of the police as much as that of the city streets.

Several bursts of antigambling suppression occurred in direct reaction to public police scandals concerning police entanglement in the illegal lottery. The Rio newspaper *A Noite* contained a now-famous polemic in 1913 regarding suspected police involvement in the illicit business of gambling. The director of the newspaper accused Police Chief Belisário Távora of collaboration with those who ran illegal games of chance. One of twentieth-century Rio's first avatars of moral sanitation, Távora had crusaded against pornographic magazines and pamphlets. As a result of their alleged misconduct, the Office of the Chief of Police fired and replaced three officers. The public accusations of corruption against Távora forced him to quit his post that same year. His replacement, Manoel Edwiges, immediately initiated a campaign to suppress gambling and undertook the first major police census of petty gambling points of sale in the Federal District.[104]

The campaign of 1916–17 likewise appears to have been partly a direct result of claims of improper police involvement in the jogo do bicho. An unusual number of such accusations appear in the police and administrative documents as well as in the press, clustered around the time of the campaign. Motivated by the same desire to sanitize the police's public image and protect the police force from their employees' own venality, scandals caused police not just to initiate but also to desist from anti-bicho crackdowns. The police abruptly scaled back their violent kill-the-animal campaign at precisely the moment when the press filled with chatter that the police had been receiving money from the National Lottery Company to protect their monopoly on lottery gambling. Confronted with these allegations, the police abandoned their truculent antigambling stance and maintained a quieter demeanor concerning the jogo do bicho for nearly a decade.[105]

To the campaigns of 1913, 1917, and 1926 can be added a final example. The well-known jurist, author, and police district chief Anésio Frota Aguiar carried out an anti-bicho campaign in 1933–34. He, too, soon stood accused of involvement in the game.[106] In the mid-1930s, police increased pressure on the jogo do bicho and, by extension, their collaborators in the police force. Throughout this period, increasing police criminality led to anti-bicho campaigns to clean up the police, which in turn created more opportunities for police to become involved in and profit from the animal game. This cycle contributed to building political pressure to implement a harsher antigambling regime, which in 1946 led to legislation outlawing all forms of gambling in Brazil.

The veracity of claims of police complicity can remain an open question without neutralizing their usefulness as historical events. Many of these allegations certainly bore some truth, while others probably did not. Yet they were not uttered in a vacuum, and their peculiar distribution over time reflects both the conditions that prompted the accusers and the emerging standards against which citizens would judge public officials. The clusters of accusations that serve as primary evidence of police involvement in the jogo do bicho may signify not sudden surges of police criminality but the implementation of policies that explicitly encouraged police and citizens to denounce each other. Some individual acts of police criminality made public in the press may have been editorial fabrications, invented to dramatize editors' disgust with the violent, clumsy manner in which the police pursued their antivice campaign.[107] Even false accusations are useful, however. As the historian Luise White has argued, "Secrets and lies are not forms of withholding information but forms by which information is valorized." An account crafted for a particular audience, a lie deliberately seeks "not only to conceal, but to conceal well."[108] Particularly in the context of a criminal investigation when one's legal status is at stake, a story told is a sketch of the plausible.

"NOT AN ARREST IN FLAGRANTE, BUT A FLAGRANT LIE"

A culture of protection and complicity silenced police privy to their colleagues' misconduct. In stark contrast, jogo do bicho defendants and their lawyers seem to have considered accusing the police of wrongdoing a standard part of criminal defense. Accused bicheiros parried criminal charges with recriminations of their own against police officers and officials.

Defendants arrested in jogo do bicho cases from 1910 to 1940 exonerated themselves through strategies similar to those used in the first decade of the century. As in earlier cases like Carlos Figueiredo's 1907 arrest with which this book began, accused bicheiros in 1917 and later mounted defenses that audaciously and pugnaciously—and almost always successfully —asserted to judges that the pieces of paper found in their possession with tell-tale columns of numbers and sometimes even names of animals proved nothing. Jogo do bicho defendants still typically pursued their cases not by establishing their innocence but by delegitimizing the legal proceedings against them. Yet a host of contextual factors had, in fact, changed in the interim. The quantity of cases had grown steadily, expanding the number of people affected by the legal culture enacted in both the persecution of the jogo do bicho and its avoidance. And defendants and police now leveled their accusations and counteraccusations against the backdrop of the era's intensified political and labor repression, ostensibly scientific approach to criminology fixated on criminal profiling, emerging standards of behavior for public officials, and the widely known, entrenched police complicity that had become the lynchpin of the game's daily operation. In such a context, Cariocas undergoing criminal investigation attempted to redirect their society's righteous indignation from contraventores to the state itself and its wayward agents. The social significance of these accusations derives from neither their veracity nor their immediate material impact on criminal justice, but from their power as tools that legal subjects frequently utilized to mitigate the risk of loss or harm incurred by engaging in this illegal business.[109]

In January 1926 the Second Auxiliary Police District chief entered a lottery ticket agency in the city center and arrested a group of ten men, all employees in commerce (*empregados no comércio*), six for selling and four for buying tickets for the jogo do bicho.[110] At the scene of the arrest, the police official found lists of handwritten numbers, pads of paper, the previous day's jogo do bicho results, and some cash. Police officials escorted the defendants to the police station only to find the recording clerk absent. A former administrator named Martinez who happened to be nearby agreed to officiate in that role. Martinez left the police station for the day, taking the bail money and legal documents with him to file in the registry office. Martinez, however, absconded with the money and left the documents in a "completely disorganized" pile in his home. A judge soon dismissed the case because of "irregularities."

When police renewed their efforts to prosecute the men about two months later, the accused presented an enraged defense statement, clearly prepared by the defendants' attorney. Among other wrongful acts, the defendants' lawyer asserts, the police had used fraudulent witness testimony, solicited from "subordinate officers to the authorities pursuing the case, witnesses who play all sorts of roles." By October 1926 the judge acquitted all of the defendants, citing "grave irregularities" and procedural infractions. Among the exonerated defendants was Laureano Domingues, who as a younger man had been a party in other jogo do bicho cases (see chapter 5). In his decades-long career as a jogo do bicho defendant, Domingues had become a veteran of the judicial process and witnessed the deeply problematic policing techniques and the continued success of the assertions of police wrongdoing that had allowed him recurrently to ply his illicit trade.[111]

A case from 1939 provides another particularly colorful, yet quite typical, example of the accusations defendants leveled against police. Humberto Fassula, who was arrested for at least six jogo do bicho offenses from 1937 to 1939, was apprehended in flagrante delicto one morning carrying a list of jogo do bicho bets written in pencil, a pad of paper for the sale of jogo do bicho tickets with carbon paper, and twenty-two milreis in cash. Fassula presented his defense statement six days later: "The present criminal proceeding is nothing more than a photograph of yet another of the many and customary acts of violence by the police under the pretext of the repression of the jogo do bicho, fabricating and forging official documents attesting that the crime had occurred in flagrante delicto." The defendant further accused the police of arranging for false witnesses to testify against him, claiming this was among a host of practices—using forged arrest documents, for instance—employed by police seeking at any cost to prosecute jogo do bicho suspects. The case was dismissed.[112]

On occasion, judges echoed defendants' consternation about police misconduct. In a jogo do bicho case from 1917, the judge issued a lengthy, impassioned decision condemning not the accused but the arresting officers. The police, the judge writes, should have known better than to arrest this man. No tangible proof existed that a crime had been in progress, and the supposed jogo do bicho lists, just pieces of paper with words and numbers on them, bear neither "intrinsic nor extrinsic characteristics of tickets for a punishable lottery or raffle." This judge and others repeatedly recorded their vigorous indictments of the police in the logbook reserved for sentencing criminal defendants.[113]

In the context of these quintessentially bureaucratic documents produced in the course of low-profile cases, the wordplay and dramatic language judges and especially defendants sometimes employed to condemn police for their misdeeds is noteworthy. The language used in defendants' statements communicated more than just raw anger at the purported injustice of their arrest; the moments of theatricality may ironically evoke a sense of how routine police extralegality indeed was. While we cannot know how much input defendants actually had in these defense statements, we can reasonably interpret them as collaborations between lawyers and suspects, who shared in the rich learning experience about the realities of civic life that the experience of producing them provided.

The case of Antonio Campos dos Santos, from April 1922, exemplifies the mixture of cynicism and playfulness leavened by exasperation that characterized many accusations leveled against police in jogo do bicho cases.[114] A shop employee from the northeastern state of Pernambuco, Dos Santos resided in a "shack [barracão] with no number in the Morro da Favela [Favela Hill]," a settlement whose name would become generic for the vast archipelago of shantytowns associated with the contemporary city. Having no prior arrests but lacking bail money, the accused was removed to the Casa de Detenção. Dos Santos mounted a vigorous defense. Contrary to the police officials' testimony that they had apprehended him in the act of dealing in the jogo do bicho in the hillside neighborhood where he lived, he insisted, these arresting police officers "did not go and maybe have never gone up that hill." The defense statement argues, "What these documents demonstrate is that this is not an arrest in flagrante but a flagrant lie" (*não é uma prisão em flagrante, mas sim uma flagrante mentira*). The judge found for the defendant, who was immediately ordered released on May 11, 1922, having spent about a month in the city jail.

The judge acquitted Dos Santos on the basis of a principle that arose repeatedly in jogo do bicho cases: in order to prosecute this type of misdemeanor, the accused must be caught in the act. Evidence that the suspect played or sold tickets to the illicit lottery would not suffice; for a guilty verdict, the judge required sworn testimony that someone had witnessed the suspect committing the infraction at the moment of arrest. The special challenges that the jogo do bicho presented for criminal procedure revolved in large part around the crucial principle of the *flagrância* of the infraction. From 1917 through the 1930s defendants and judges cited flagrância more frequently than any other juridical principle.[115] Holding up this "flagrancy" standard as a reason to acquit almost always implied and sometimes explicitly was a criticism of the rashness, if not the outright criminality, of the arresting police.

Legal arguments by jogo do bicho suspects often went beyond questioning the existence of incriminating evidence to question the very existence of the crime itself. Judges and defendants repeatedly asserted that, in the words of one judicial sentence from 1917, "the papers apprehended by the authorities do not have the characteristics of a lottery ticket, punishable by the law, for on these pieces of paper one finds only numbers and signatures that the judge, in the absence of any legal process to ascertain their connection to a criminal act, can in reality not connect to the jogo do bicho."[116] Domingues's attorney perhaps said it best: in the epigrammatic words of his defense statement, "The jogo do bicho is a matter that is juridically unknown" (*o 'jogo do bicho' é causa que juridicamente se desconhece*). This appears to have been the first of many instances when Domingues was arrested in flagrante delicto, bearing a fistful of cash and several easily identifiable jogo do bicho lists. The case for the defense rested on the claim that the lists, which were attached to the criminal file and eventually seen by the judge, "are not even proof of any transaction of a game described" in the legal codes. The judge agreed.[117]

Unlike such crimes as theft or assault whose vernacular understanding closely ressembles their legal definition, the prosecution of such vague and legally contrived crimes as illicit gambling could not rest on any assumptions that witnesses even knew what it was. The accused frequently used this imprecision as a fulcrum with which to move the juridical world.[118]

Another case involving Humberto Fassula illustrates the tendency among jogo do bicho suspects to question simultaneously the integrity of the police and the very existence of the game. On August 9, 1939, at noon, police arrested Fassula em flagrante on the same spot where he had been apprehended multiple times before. At the time of his arrest, Fassula carried a pad of paper and 2$500 in cash as well as a list of jogo do bicho bets, which he attempted to tear up as the police apprehended him. Two witnesses, both police officers, testified he had indeed been caught red-handed. Once again, he denied any wrongdoing. After a few days in the Casa de Detenção, Fassula, several officials, and designated scientific research expert each presented their testimony to the judge. The expert testified that "despite being torn up, [the jogo do bicho ticket] was glued to a sheet of paper and thus reconstructed in such a manner as to make it possible to affirm that this document was a copy of a list of the jogo dos bichos, whose exclusive use is in the practice of this misdemeanor."

The centerpiece of Fassula's defense statement (*auto de defesa*) to the judge was not an assertion of innocence but a condemnation of the police. He decried the manner in which the police had carried out the investigation and expressed doubts about the two supposed eyewitnesses. Furthermore, Fassula's statement argues, while the witnesses claim that the accused "carried lists" (*transporava listas*) for the jogo do bicho, it is not a crime to carry (*"transportar"*) pieces of paper, for good measure, citing the definition of *transportar* in the standard Portuguese dictionary. Containing only numbers, he says, there is nothing on this list "that would prove the accusation true, and even less so for the list that has been torn up." Yet again, the judge agreed, acquitting Fassula one week after the arrest. Fassula's lawyer had managed to accomplish what Fassula himself had attempted in the heat of the moment of his arrest: he made the jogo do bicho list disappear. While police detectives eager for a conviction needed only a bottle of glue to reassemble the jogo do bicho ticket from its torn fragments, the judge was able to piece together an acquittal based on the deductive rationale of the law.[119]

The difficulty in convicting jogo do bicho suspects may have generated innovations in criminal procedure in the 1920s and 1930s. Police began to use the *Laudo de Exame*, an official expert report that already existed to

FIGURE 26 List presented as evidence in jogo do bicho case, torn up by defendant and glued back together by police (1939). Source: Arquivo Nacional, Rio de Janeiro, CX 168, proc: A-6320, Gal. B, Juizo de Direito da 10ª Vara Criminal.

establish the authenticity of the material facts and objects associated with a criminal case, to compensate for the recurrent problem of the inadmissibility of the jogo do bicho lists as evidence. In using this document, police asked and responded to a formulaic series of questions and thus subjected jogo do bicho tickets confiscated at the time of arrest to examinations that would establish their materiality as part of a criminal transaction.[120] By the 1930s this official examination of jogo do bicho lists was carried out by a police division called the Office of Scientific Research (Gabinete de Pesquisas Cientificas), which produced a sort of affidavit in which the office's bureaucrats, in response to a standard series of questions, affirmed statements about the objects in question. The ritualistic question and answer of the procedure counterbalanced the tenuous criminality of the jogo do bicho and its material trappings. The difficulty law enforcement had in using lists captured at the time of arrest as evidence of a jogo do bicho transaction in progress was not resolved until 1944, when a federal law stipulated that "it shall be considered sufficient proof for the criminal act any lists with either clear or disguised indications" that are used for the animal game.[121]

The vast piles of documentation the jogo do bicho's unsuccessful persecution produced demonstrate the proper functioning of the law at least as much as its failure. Jogo do bicho defendants hid from antigambling laws in a thicket of procedural rules. In the end, the rule of law prevented their prosecution, even those who appear to have been guilty. Until the early 1940s, when the federal legislature passed laws that explicitly defined games of chance and mentioned the jogo do bicho by name, the game was arguably, as Domingues's attorney said, a "matter that was juridically unknown."[122] While the animal game had conspicuously existed for decades, defendants and their lawyers realized that the official radar of the state usually failed to detect it. A combination of messy police work and potential witnesses' refusal to testify accounts for many acquittals, but the protagonists here were also criminal defendants and their legal counsel, who found a way to seize onto laws when it suited them.

It is worth pausing to consider that denunciations of police so often, and so incongruously, came in the context of criminal processos. Although far from their intended purpose, these legal documents and the procedures that produced them became a public forum for accusations of police corruption and indictments of the criminal justice system. People used their audience with higher authorities, judges in particular, to air complaints.[123] There is no evidence that judges ever followed up on these accusations of police criminality. Initial, declared intentions to investigate accusations of police wrongdoing usually lead to documentary dead ends.[124]

The finely grained portraits of the lives of jogo do bicho defendants recorded in these criminal cases likewise received fleeting, if any, attention. For crimes other than felonies, defendants did not present oral arguments; rather, judges only "heard" them on paper. Defendants appeared to magistrates as legal personae, not as flesh-and-blood human beings; they were worth only what was written.

Yet the audience for these judicial proceedings was wider than the judge who decided each case. At virtually every stage, the proceedings occurred in public. Indeed, as we have just seen, the animal game did not even exist juridically unless bystanders both witnessed and recognized it. No jogo do bicho arrest during this period ever became a cause célèbre, but each case had theatrical elements, and the interaction between judge and defendant was always a sort of public performance.[125]

The investigation of jogo do bicho suspects was, too. During the police campaign of 1917, Rio's newspapers began to list by name jogo do bicho arrestees, even before they had been prosecuted. A typical story reads, "Dr. Armando Vidal arrested in flagrante the following individuals," proceeding then to list the names of five individuals and describe where each had been apprehended.[126] The public defamation of suspects was unofficially part of the campaign, both in the routine publication of their names and, as we have seen, in the construction of criminal personae that police would use as incriminating evidence. In jogo do bicho cases in the decades after 1917, defendants' strategies and judges' legal reasoning not only reasserted expectations of public behavior, but also taught a lesson in the uses of the public realm.

An editorial signed by João Qualquer (John Anyman) that appeared on the front page of the weekly magazine *Dom Quixote* in 1920 resonates with the jogo do bicho cases cited here, even though it concerns legal rather than illicit lottery gambling. This "Anyman" reports an incident, a simple piece of police blotter news whose subtext, the writer suggests, contained messages of major social significance. Two friends had pooled their money to purchase a lottery ticket. When their number won, the ticket holder refused to relinquish any part of the one-hundred-contos prize. Police investigated whether the complainant had a right to half of the money. Given the intercession of the police, this small, banal slice of everyday life gains enormous "social and moral importance." "What," the writer asks, "does the State, represented by the police, have to do with this spat between the two gamblers?" No shots were fired, no knife drawn: "The police's job is to put people in jail," not to intervene in a dispute like this.[127]

Taking into account this era's widespread concern about police impropriety, the story can be read as a satire that criticizes police inefficiency and hypocrisy. The highly visible antivice campaigns, the premature incrimination of accused bicheiros, and the constant crossfire of accusations between criminal defendants and officers of the law all show that the police's controversial role in the management of petty crime was a matter of public concern. The editorial, published in a magazine known for its humorous social commentaries, was comical because in reality the public cared little about police intervention in legal lottery gambling. By contrast, the jogo do bicho was truly a matter of public controversy, but the question of police intervention in it was moot; police arrests of vendors and extraction of illegal profits were established facts. Even while satirizing the policing of the capital, the editorial expressed a spirit of realpolitik. Gambling, it implies, happens, and so do breaches of trust—even between trusted friends—when monetary transactions are involved. The question was, who should absorb the risk of things not going as planned?

As in the jogo do bicho cases just examined, what was in dispute here was not gambling but the proper role of police. This piece contributed to the ongoing public conversation about what fell within public and what fell within private jurisdiction. John Anyman provides a pragmatic answer to this vexing policy question; the police, he argues, should retreat from the firestorm of the citizenry's contradictory moral codes. The two friends in the story had assumed the risk of both playing the lottery and entering into an informal business arrangement. The editorial claims the two friends, not the state, should have adjudicated the matter. In effect, the editorial made a virtue out of the necessity borne by anyone who operated an independent, unlicensed, illegal business, like the city's hundreds of jogo do bicho vendors.

As historians of Latin America have shown, with the end of the colonial era in the early nineteenth century, many of the responsibilities previously held by the imperial state devolved to local authority, a process that continued throughout the nineteenth century with the construction of liberal nation-states. Local authorities' contact with individuals occurred mainly through the criminal law. The proliferation from the mid-nineteenth century through the mid-twentieth in Latin America of informal legal intermediaries like Brazil's unofficial attorneys or expeditors (*despachantes*), and their equally ubiquitous counterparts in Peru called *tinterillos*, was a symptom of this postcolonial transition.[128] Another symptom was the manner in which the police acted simultaneously as agents of the state and as private entrepreneurs. As citizens negotiated their interests at the local level, they sought control of the historical process through which not only wealth but also the possibility of loss or harm was distributed through society. The "privatization of risk" and police involvement in the jogo do bicho were two sides of the same coin.[129] Whether arrests in flagrante or "flagrant lies," the utterances recorded in jogo do bicho cases document how the parties attempted to share the risk of economic and personal harm with the police officers who both collaborated with and persecuted them. The police's apparent impunity prevented them from assuming this risk in reality. Yet bicheiros benefited from police wrongdoing, which allowed the game to proceed even as it afforded a way of nullifying the charges. Examining this shifting around of blame and legal risk sheds light on the process through which this illicit lottery became a routine part of everyday policing.

WORTH WHAT'S WRITTEN

Playing the jogo do bicho was a risky endeavor in more than one sense. It entailed wagering one's money and summoning the faith that the animal or number played would deliver a prize.[130] One also trusted the dealer to pay up if that number won: no legal recourse was available if he refused to do so.

Commentators on Brazilian culture have marveled at the reliability of the clandestine lottery. In his classic work on the sociology of games and play, Roger Caillois comments on the "scrupulous honesty" of the bicheiro.[131] Writing in the late 1930s, Stefan Zweig also testified to the reliability of these underworld figures: "In order to avoid the police checking up on [the jogo do bicho] they played on agreement. The bookmaker didn't supply his clients with tickets, but he has never been known not to pay up."[132] In 1948, in a publication lauding the jogo do bicho as the "only Brazilian reality," the writer Pedro Anísio exclaimed that the game is attacked so violently "with iron, fire, and tear gas" precisely because it is "the last redoubt of Honesty in this country." While faith in government policy and politicians' promises quickly fades, "one can have faith in the little shreds of paper that every afternoon are nailed to posts all over the city by invisible hands, giving the daily jogo do bicho results—because those little shreds of paper tell the truth, honestly, decently, heroically."[133] The idea of the honest bicheiro was so pervasive that while day-to-day incidents of the jogo do bicho rarely made the daily press, breaches of the game's honor system did. In 1941, a report about a bicheiro in Rio who failed to pay the winner appeared in the national news.[134]

The paradox of the jogo do bicho's virtuous vice had the power to neutralize moral trepidation against it. The author of a magazine article from 1938 enumerates some common justifications for the legalization of the jogo do bicho. The author comments at length on the odd nature of this vice:

It is curious that they usually allege the honesty of the bicheiros as a justification for this type of gaming. It is picturesque, then, to see how honesty can be, under certain conditions, a stimulus for vice. Since the jogo do bicho is an illegal form of gambling, everything related to it is based on promises, on tacit commitments, which are not usually broken. If the banqueiro does not pay the amount that the player won, he loses morale, that is to say, he loses the confidence of the player, and so no one would risk playing with him any more. Since the bicheiros came to be controlled by a small number of bankers, some of which were owners of newspapers and had influence in politics, these people are the first to make sure that the honesty of the bicheiros is beyond any suspicion. . . . Loyalty is a primary condition for the success of the banqueiro. Here we have an example of disfigured loyalty."[135]

Jogo do bicho dealers may indeed have earned the "disfigured loyalty" of their customers simply because they were honorable businesspeople, but their trustworthiness was also their stock in trade. They asserted their honest character not just as individuals but as a group and generally "sought to distance themselves from other 'outlaw' categories, such as thieves, murderers, and drug traffickers," according to the historian Felipe Santos Magalhães in his ethnographic sketch of bicheiros in the mid-twentieth century.[136] Their ability to attract customers hinged on their reputation of reliability, and their visibility and public accessibility made them susceptible to the ire and vengeance of cheated customers. They were deeply enmeshed in the daily lives and work of the people around them, which gave them a further stake in acting in good faith. As business owners with a steady flow of cash and access to their community, bicheiros were often in a position to do favors for their neighbors and clientele, who in turn brought them new customers, became their children's godparents, or refused to testify against them.[137]

Competitiveness also defined the relationship of bicho vendors and their customers. Warnings about dishonest bicheiros published in jogo do bicho newspapers may well have served as a means of gaining the readers' business by winning their trust, but they show that the honesty of the bicheiro was far from sacred and unquestioned.[138] When a frequently played number won, it could break the bank.[139] In this regard, the aftermath of Rui Barbosa's death is iconic (see chapter 5). Inspired by the politician's moniker, "The Eagle of the Hague," multitudes of jogo do bicho players simultaneously decided to bet on the eagle that day, which proved to be "a disaster for the bicheiros" when, as legend has it, the eagle won. Multiple sources from the mid-twentieth century report that a similar incident occurred when the elephant in the zoo fell gravely ill. Taking the creature's imminent death as a sign, bettors flocked to bet money on the elephant. The elephant won, and reportedly many jogo do bicho business owners, small-time, independent bicheiros and wealthier banqueiros alike, went out of business.[140]

The hierarchical relationships between bicheiros and their underlings and between police and those subject to their surveillance created the networks of trust that allowed bicheiros to undertake the risk of engaging in this illicit business. As the political scientist Luis Roniger has pointed out, trust thrives under clientelist social relations, existing not despite but "within the framework of precariousness" and risk.[141] The promise to pay what is written on a ticket makes sense only within a context of promises, counterpromises, and obligations more generally, to paraphrase the legal scholar P. S. Atiya. Typical promises are spoken in indirect, "general language" and are binding because of traditional reciprocal expectations rather than explicit speech acts, let alone written documentation.[142] The written promise on the jogo do bicho ticket prompts us to consider these artifacts of the criminalized lottery vis-à-vis those promises that are not committed to paper: oral agreements and tacit understandings. Why did the seller promise to pay "what is written" if the player could not recur to the police if cheated and if the ticket might serve as incriminating evidence? While serving as a convenient way for bettors and vendors to keep track of their transactions, the jogo do bicho ticket also partook of the legitimacy the written word uniquely could confer.

The jogo do bicho's nonbureaucratic nature was part of its appeal. A long passage in Hugo de Barros's memoir of 1957 dwells on the material form of the jogo do bicho ticket. The radical simplicity of the handwritten pieces of paper that had so hindered law enforcement's efforts to convict defendants captivated Barros's imagination. The ticket had no official stamp or seal—none of the elements required by Brazil's legal system to admit what is written on paper into the realm of truth. For a jogo do bicho transaction, any paper and pencil would do, and the game further benefited from "the simplicity with which one receives the . . . prizes, which have no requirements, there is no presentation of an identity card, a reservist's certificate, voter's identification card, or any such thing."[143] It would be inaccurate, though, to oppose the jogo do bicho's informal system of trust to a formal world of legalism. One could not claim the prize without a ticket. The term *"Vale o escrito"* or *"vale 3 dias"* constituted an abiding promise, a contract. Having both ritual and pragmatic value, the documentation of the promise to pay what was written rendered trust concrete, movable, and relatively impersonal.[144]

The significance of written promises in Brazilian popular legal culture bears connections to the immense importance of writing in Latin American legal culture generally. The "notarial arts" had been central to Iberian legal culture during Latin America's colonial period, and an obsession with legal documents is often considered the principal legacy of the Iberian colonial state.[145] Writing always bore close associations with both the distribution of social power and the maintenance of public trust. Scholars have shown how the Latin American "lettered city" closed ranks around the cultural elite, and helped forestall electoral fraud and other acts of public dishonesty.[146] While generations of writers about Ibero-American legal culture have demonstrated the "distance that separated the written from the spoken word," no one lived a life removed from writing.[147] In her study of Brazilian slavery in the eighteenth and nineteenth centuries, Sandra Lauderdale Graham shows the pervasiveness of notarial—or what she prefers to call "juridical"—culture among Brazilian slaves and freedpersons despite their almost complete lack of literacy. Even the unlettered had a deep and proactive engagement with the written word, as they "learned about written means by word of mouth" and used literate culture to promote their interests. Far from being a linear progression from oral to written, or from vernacular to formal, culture, the popular legal culture of writing in Brazil had long been an inclusive one that made use of intermediaries and involved vast networks of trust and obligation.[148]

The significance of written documents in the early twentieth century lies not simply in age-old Ibero-American legalism but moreover in a political and legal shift then underway. Cariocas of the nonelite classes lived beneath the darkening shadow of a city of writing rising around them. Brodwyn Fischer points out that the 1930s was a watershed in the country's legal history, in large part because of the introduction of a variety of documents that "served as formal signifiers of worthy citizenship": "work cards, marriage and birth certificates, formal property titles, formal rental contracts, detailed police rap sheets, and national identity cards" gained critical importance for Brazil's urban population during Vargas's administration.[149]

Official legal culture of the early twentieth century was a watershed in another way, one that relates to the urban sociology of trust that forms the legal–cultural context for the jogo do bicho. In the 1910s and especially the following two decades, trust had become an issue of heightened concern to everyday policing. As public concern about the police's honesty and lawfulness grew, so did police oversight of trust generally. Law enforcement's interest in such offenses as falsification of documents and various types of fraud, inauthenticity, and delusion increased notably during this period. A plethora of documents from 1917 demonstrate a flurry of police investigations of the falsification of persons and objects: official documents, such merchandise as brand-name cigars, government officials, and specially licensed or credentialed tradespersons.[150]

The official organs that oversaw the police's antivice efforts, especially the Delegacias Auxiliares, seem to have been keenly involved in policing trust. In practice, the bulk of Delegacias Auxiliares' daily work included carrying out autopsies, medico-legal examinations, and investigations: all forms of truth affirmation. Officials in the delegacias were perpetually involved in investigations of the authenticity of a vast range of artifacts whose purpose was to guarantee the legitimacy of a legal process or document—official stamps, electoral lists, checks, documents attesting to a detainee's insanity, wills, and more.[151] A First Auxiliary Police Precinct report to the Rio police's central authorities in 1920 summarizes over twenty different investigations carried out under that division's auspices. Virtually without exception, these investigations inquired into suspected instances of falsification and breaches of agreement, including defaulting on and falsification of promissory notes, counterfeiting, and falsification of a *título eleitoral*.[152]

The cases of public condemnation of bicheiros in this period tellingly involve violations of public trust, not the inherent criminality of their vocation. Especially as it began to centralize in the 1930s, the power and wealth of the jogo do bicho became associated not only with reliability but also with exploitation. A chronicle from 1940 describes a former police precinct justice official who sprung people from jail using an extralegal system of bail and ran a gang of confidence men. This "jail-door lawyer," named Vieira, fraudulently freed a number of detainees and arranged false identities for them. In exchange, they backed up his false claim to be a "Minister of the Supreme Court." The freed prisoners, all unsuccessful tradesmen turned petty con artists, became the provisioners of the city's newly rich and powerful bicheiros; the "little vagabond of a tailor" and out-of-work building contractor supplied fancy suits and real estate to bicheiros, and Vieira acted as an intermediary, pocketing a handsome income.[153]

An additional accusation of dishonesty offers anecdotal evidence to complicate the cliché of the irreproachable bicheiro. An anonymous citizen in Rio wrote a letter to President Vargas to bring a criminal matter to his attention, having opted to approach the chief executive directly rather than through the "shameful," corrupt police officials. The anonymous petitioner tells of the three Fernandes brothers who had just boarded a ship en route to Europe—one with his wife, "15 days earlier having embarked one of his lovers who spends 20 contos at a time, he had a palace built worth 300 contos, and gave her 3 cars of the latest model." One of the brothers had amassed the enormous sum of fifty thousand contos in just a few years. How? "In the jogo do bicho, and from the police," the writer explains. Four to five hundred contos per day circulated through the Fernandes's firm that ran the "Para Todos" (For Everybody) lottery, a local version of the jogo do bicho. The brothers stood accused not only of marital infidelity and profligate spending but moreover of dishonest business practices. They sold lottery tickets to "the poor people who believe in the honesty" of the transaction. The Fernandeses led customers to believe the lottery operated every day, but in fact only two lottery drawings a week were held. "They calculate the 'bichos' that they have the most of, and which they have least of, and it is this that they announce." In other words, the lottery was not really extracted at all; banqueiros systematically had been falsifying the result in order to minimize the payout. They were "living well off of the misery of others" and banking the police as well as the jogo do bicho. The writer implores the president to intercept the ship and inspect their suitcases for evidence of their wrongdoing.[154]

While there is little doubt the jogo do bicho has functioned thanks to public trust in its vendors' voluntary reliability, the trustworthy bicheiro and flawless operation of the game are the products of collective mythmaking. Discordant voices sounded amid the chorus of praise for the jogo do bicho as the country's "last redoubt" of public integrity. The perception of public trust in the game, though, is itself a noteworthy cultural phenomenon, one with material consequences. The broad concept of trust was shorthand for a host of other qualities the jogo do bicho signified, like solidarity against repressive law enforcement and a community's ability to designate its own rules autonomously of a disinterested or hostile state. Although treated today, as it was in the early twentieth century, as an inexplicable peculiarity of Brazilian urban culture, bicheiros' honesty served a multiplicity of useful purposes, as both myth and social fact. The promise written on jogo do bicho tickets derived its iconic, yet ironic, social and cultural worth from an "urban sociology of trust" founded in the legal culture generated by the complicated relationship between bicheiros and police.[155]

CONCLUSION: THE PERSISTENCE OF THE JOGO DO BICHO AND THE REACH OF THE MODERN STATE

As we have seen, the operation of the jogo do bicho utterly depended on the police. Yet defendants' testimony in these criminal cases uniformly depict police participation in the jogo do bicho as predation. It would be all too easy to understand this apparent contradiction in bicheiros' sensibility vis-à-vis the police as nothing more than the moral vicissitudes of a criminal suspect trying to avoid prosecution. This contradiction speaks to us way beyond the obvious, however, when we look past individual acts to examine the cumulative effects of these informal but entrenched practices of accusation, counteraccusation, and extralegal policing. In witnessing bicheiros' simultaneous collaboration with police and expressed distaste for extralegal policing, one is watching society construct shared conceptions about corruption alongside its construction of criminality. Likewise, as I have argued in this chapter, it is not useful to explain the jogo do bicho's perseverance despite its illegality by pointing to the practice of corruption, defined as police officials' divergences from a universal, fixed ideal. Rather, among police, jogo do bicho sellers, and customers, there were promises and implicit and explicit obligations made, breached, and enforced. The criminalization of the jogo do bicho, as an official sanction of police criminality, imposed and created certain expectations of state honesty and predictability. The history of the jogo do bicho thus brings a fresh view of the relationship between the state and the people as it developed during a period from which, most historians agree, Brazil's heterogeneous masses somehow emerged as a modern, unified national public.

In seeking an epigram to evoke the relationship between the state and society in Brazil in the first decades of the twentieth century, it is customary to dredge up the infamous proclamation of the president from 1926 to 1930, Washington Luís (Pereira de Sousa). While campaigning for president of the state of São Paulo in 1920, Luís dramatically disavowed the activist role of the state in incorporating the disenfranchised. He stated, "Worker agitation is more a question of public order than of social order."[156] Luís's words accurately summarize the first two decades of the First Republic, a period characterized by authoritarian repression of the popular classes through such varied measures as censorship of popular arts and the deportation of suspected anarchists. Those who heard or read Luís's famous campaign speech in 1920 would have understood that he was adding his voice to the era's impassioned debate around the so-called social question: how to alleviate poverty and suffering, and how to incorporate the worker into Brazilian society and promote order and peace. Luís's avowed position exemplifies politicians' denial of the social bases of worker unrest during the First Republic.[157] In today's conventional wisdom about the early twentieth century, his words still unambiguously declare that the social question called for police action rather than for intellectual consideration or legal reform.

As Brazil entered the 1930s, there was little evidence to demonstrate to the growing industrial bourgeoisie and governing elites that the capital city's poor classes had become any less dangerous than before. The transition to a new political leadership following Vargas's takeover of the national government, the so-called Revolution of 1930, created instability and new class fears.[158] The social question became ever more pressing as the global economic depression hit, migration swelled the population, unemployment increased, and favelas multiplied. The politics of the 1930s and 1940s are also characterized by the breakdown of the oligarchical order and its replacement with an urban-centric, populist politics. The Vargas era's populist reforms involved the state more directly in citizens' everyday lives, with the institution of new public welfare programs and the state's entrance into such formerly private realms as education.[159]

This transition marked by the populist incorporation of the masses also occurred in the realm of culture. Brazil's first generation of folklorists, as well as poets, artists, and amateur anthropologists scoured the countryside and urban bohemian haunts for cultural artifacts, through which they wished to replace the dry bones of precious, Europhilic culture with the beating heart of Brazil. The era's paeans to Brazilian national folk culture came from private individuals and also, eventually, official organs of the state. The impulse toward cultural pride and the official narrative of national progress also found expression in the discovery and appreciation of local, Carioca culture: its food, music, Carnival tradition, and other urban folkloric traditions. In an illustrative example, in her work on modernism in Rio in the 1920s, Mônica Pimenta Velloso points toward the cultural importance of Don Quixote among the Carioca intellectual elite as a picaresque figure that drew on the archetypal scoundrel, the *malandro*, a symbol that evoked the quintessence of subaltern, urban Brazil.[160] This surge of affection for the popular was selective. The Carioca intelligentsia's fascination with samba accompanied a campaign to sanitize samba lyrics by removing references to idleness or iconoclasm of any kind.[161] Like risqué samba lyrics, games of chance fell outside the realm of popular culture the ruling classes welcomed into the national fold.

The history of the jogo do bicho suggests that the historical puzzle of national integration of the early and mid-twentieth century cannot be solved by looking exclusively at those aspects of the cultural politics of the post-1917 years on which historians have traditionally dwelled: the education system, labor politics, and the official veneration of the popular. Populism, per se, may have begun with the administration of Rio's mayor Pedro Ernesto and Vargas's presidency, but the incorporation of the popular classes into the collective took place in a process that began earlier and includes the longer history of citizens' engagement with the state by way of the criminal law. The story of the jogo do bicho reveals that everyday policing fills in a crucial, yet untold, part of the story of that incorporation.

A growing scholarly literature shows how police in the early twentieth century in Rio, Buenos Aires, and other cities intervened in social conflicts that were not necessarily criminal, such as domestic disputes and discord between employees and bosses.[162] The police force's directive to preserve public order also gave them responsibility for Rio's abandoned children, beggars, and homeless, sick, and indigent persons, for lack of social services to provide the public assistance that would keep them off the city streets.[163] The police archive is peppered with enough cases to demonstrate convincingly that they combined their role as law enforcers with a generally informal, usually arbitrary, and often oppressive role in providing social services to the city's most socioeconomically vulnerable. Not coincidentally, it was precisely the police divisions charged with control of the jogo do bicho and other forms of vice crime, the Delegacias Auxiliares, that most explicitly took on this role.[164]

"In the jogo do bicho, what's written down counts": more than Luís's famous quotation cited above that reduced the call for social reform to a question of public order, this popular appraisal of the unique value of the promise that sustains the clandestine lottery articulates an important perspective on the Carioca people's relationship with the state as Brazil entered the twentieth century and beyond. In its jesting yet sardonic manner the proverb voices the collectively acquired wisdom on how best to maneuver in modern urban society. The story of the jogo do bicho demonstrates that the law provided an answer to the social question in urban Brazil, but in informal, unintended ways. The state responded to the social question by framing it as a question for the police. Yet the social dynamics of police repression were never limited to the enactment of laws and the application of policy, and the state's judicial power was never simply imposed from above. The law in practice was an adventitious, collaborative endeavor. Only when we redefine the law in recognition of its multiple, colloquial meanings can we reconstruct the formation of Brazilian urban society through the creative destruction of its rules.

EPILOGUE

A photograph taken in 1971 shows a group of men, their hats cocked slightly forward, leaning in toward each other. They stand and sit close together, their eyes fixed on some small, white, objects, barely visible in the blurry image. The straight-downward shadows that the men cast tell us that the photographer captured them in the middle of the day. The police, it seems, had an interest in following these men's movements and in taking repeated shots of them from far away, as we can tell from the shallow depth of field. The square where the men congregate, Praça Drummond, bears the name of the baron who had built the zoo that once stood on that plot of land.[1]

The locale of this photograph is a poignant coincidence, although the police who captured these images in 1971 as part of yet another campaign to end the jogo do bicho probably did not consider that the men under surveillance stood and sat on precisely the patch of land where the game had begun nearly a century before. In the 1970s, as in the 1910s, men and women, sitting on park benches in innumerable squares, walking on sidewalks, and standing on corners throughout Rio de Janeiro, still wrote tickets to the animal game.

Before granting permission to publish this image, the Public Archive of the State of Rio de Janeiro, which holds the police surveillance files of which it is a part, imposed a condition: the head of each person represented had to be blotted out. It mattered little that, as it turned out, the men in the photograph were just playing a game of dominoes in the park:

FIGURE 27 Police surveillance photograph of suspected jogo do bicho players (1971) (retouched in 2009 by archive to blur suspects' faces). Courtesy of Arquivo Público do Estado do Rio de Janeiro, DOPS, Secreto-94, folha 08.

showing their faces would have constituted an act of defamation prohibited by law and ethics. The same policing organ that took these pictures also tracked all persons deemed dangerous to the state, then under a dictatorial military regime. The disfigured image is an artifact of the jogo do bicho's connection to the policing of everyday life over the course of the long twentieth century, dramatizing the enduring consequences of both.

I have shown that during the period from the beginning of the jogo do bicho through the 1930s only a minuscule proportion of persons arrested for the game were convicted. Yet although judges acquitted most jogo do bicho cases during these decades, the intervention of the law had a decisive impact on every aspect of the clandestine lottery: its structure, cultural meanings, social functions, and political significance. In the period on which I focus, citizens' contact with the criminal law did not occur primarily through prison sentences but through daily interactions on street corners and city squares and in police stations and courtrooms. It occurred through the demand for protection money and the exchange of clemency for denouncing a colleague and through the way in which shared understandings of the law and its workings ramified through communities.

The complex, informal relationship between the criminalized lottery

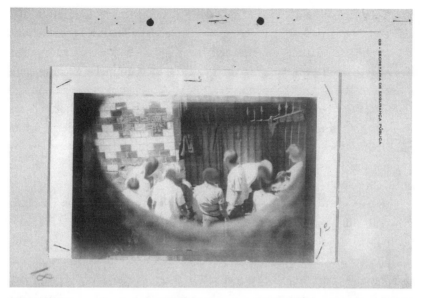

FIGURE 28 Police surveillance photograph showing suspected jogo do bicho transactions (1971) (faces of suspects retouched by archive in 2009). Courtesy of Arquivo Público do Estado do Rio de Janeiro, Brazil, DOPS, Secreto 94, folha 18.

and the state whose formation this book has documented did not simply disappear as players and especially sellers of the jogo do bicho entered what folklorists, jurists, and journalists and other commentators generally understand as the animal game's new era, which began in the 1940s. The passage of a series of laws during that time—a new penal code, its companion misdemeanor code, and a law of 1946 prohibiting most kinds of gambling throughout Brazil—is commonly regarded as marking the beginning of the jogo do bicho's true criminalization. The animal game's ubiquity and the lack of prosecutions for it until the 1940s stand as evidence of its having escaped the criminalization that befell it in the second half of the twentieth century, when, driven underground, it became a bona fide organized crime syndicate.

Or so the story goes. The history recounted in this book contests this typical narrative; in fact, the jogo do bicho's criminalization began immediately upon the game's invention in the 1890s and is inseparable from it. The laws passed in the forties did result in a surge in arrests for the jogo do bicho. Yet the era of increasing and more effective antigambling policy in the mid- and late twentieth century arose mainly from processes already long underway: the gradual strengthening of state power; perennial bursts of official attention to urban "moral hygiene"; the criminalization and consequent stigmatization of jogo do bicho ticket sellers; and the intimate, yet extralegal, relationship between the jogo do bicho and the police. Revising the conventional chronology of the jogo do bicho accomplishes more than just setting the folklorists straight. A brief look at the second half century of the jogo do bicho's existence highlights how its first half century was part of a broader process involving the making of modern, urban public life—a process characterized by the criminalization of everyday popular practices and the metaphorical and literal enclosure of the spaces of the city's poor and working-class majority.

The period 1930–45, the first stretch of the Vargas era, was relatively peaceful and prosperous for Rio's gambling industry in general, most notably the grand casinos but also games of chance of all varieties. The liberalization of games of chance in the Federal District, which began around 1932, did not result from any direct action taken by the populist president. Instead, the top-heavy structure of the federal government under Vargas made it easier for the whims of the executive to become policy and facilitated the legal functioning of casinos in the federal capital. Because of the tax revenue casinos brought in and perhaps also because of his populist posture, Rio's mayor, Pedro Ernesto, was keen on keeping the enormously popular gambling casinos legal. For similar reasons, Vargas allowed casinos to function in the Federal District by executive order until the end of his presidency in 1945. Some public figures spoke of gambling as a social phenomenon that corrupted the moral values and good customs of Brazilian society. This rhetoric formed a crucial part of the propaganda that brought about the dictatorial phase of Vargas's presidency, the Estado Novo, in 1937. Vargas never made the leap to outlaw gambling definitively, as many expected him to do.[2] However, the Penal Misdemeanor Code, passed in 1941, for the first time included an article (article 58) that used the term *jogo do bicho*, unambiguously making it a juridical entity and labeling it as an infraction of the law.[3]

The police records of 1940–41 have left a richly detailed portrait of the jogo do bicho in that year, as seen through the eyes of the state. The documents show a marked increase in convictions. In that year, for example, 783 individuals were incarcerated in Rio's prisons and penal colonies because of their involvement in the illegal lottery. The scores of anonymous denunciations against "those practicing the jogo do bicho" in the Federal District indicate both the remarkable diversity of locations where

TABLE 12 Federal Legislation Pertaining to the Jogo do Bicho, 1890–1946

LAW	DATE PASSED	NOTES/RELEVANT ARTICLE(S)
1890 Penal Code (Law 847)	October 11, 1890	See Table 3
Law 628	October 28, 1899	Articles 3 and 4
Law 2321	December 30, 1910	Article 31
Civil Code (Law 3071)	January 1, 1916 (in effect January 1, 1917)	Article 1479
Law 21143	March 21, 1932	Article 15 named the jogo do bicho
Law 241	February 4, 1938	Budgets money for oversight of gambling casinos; imposes new taxes on gambling casinos
Law 854	November 12, 1938	Article 58, Section B
Law 3688: "Lei das Contravenções Penais (LCP)"	October 3, 1941	Article 58
Law 6259	February 10, 1944	Altered article 58 of LCP; lengthy law that regulates lottery gambling (and affirms legality of the official lotteries), and specifies "prohibited lotteries" (articles 40-44) and contravenções (articles 45-60); article 58 mentions the jogo do bicho by name.
Law 9215	April 30, 1946	Prohibited all gambling "in all national territory"

tickets were sold—"in the back of an alcohol factory," "on the street corner of Domingues Lopes and João Vicente streets," "in front of Café X," for instance—and the persistence of the police in trying to root it out.[4]

Jogo do bicho arrests steadily mounted in the 1940s. Between 1942 and 1945, more than 4,200 persons accused of breaking article 58 passed though the Federal District's police precincts. These arrests and indictments were the responsibility of the Special Precinct for Culture and Entertainment

(Delegacia de Costumes e Diversões). In 1940, far fewer cases were dismissed than in the pre-1917 period. The number of acquittals decreased not because of a commensurate reduction in the number of frivolous arrests, but because the police had responded to the realities of the justice system and found routine ways around juridical procedures—a process that began decades earlier, as described in chapter 6.[5]

General Eurico Gaspar Dutra won the presidential election in 1945. Alongside an avowed commitment to return to democratic normalcy following Vargas's dictatorship, Dutra's presidency was marked by his moral crusades against certain types of behavior he considered socially harmful, such as communism, prostitution, and games of chance. In a backlash against all types of gambling, including the "elegant gambling dens" of Copacabana, Dutra and his advisors declared their intention to protect society, the family, and the popular economy by eradicating games of chance.[6] The capital remained at the center of these political and legal debates about the status of gambling in Brazil, despite their national scale. Dutra acted swiftly in the first few months of his presidency. A new policing organ called the Service for the Repression of Prohibited Games, created in March 1946, carried out 114 arrests in the first few days after its founding.[7] The president himself, the ministers of state, and Rio's chief of police met in April 1946 and agreed to pass a federal law making all games of chance illegal. At this same meeting, the officials pledged to redouble their efforts to repress communism and to prohibit demonstrations and public gatherings on International Worker's Day, the first of May, impending in just days. On April 30 a presidential decree, Law 9215, prohibited gambling throughout Brazil. Arrests for the jogo do bicho immediately spiked in 1946, reflecting a true change in the state's relationship to gambling, not to misdemeanors generally; arrests for vagrancy remained level during Dutra's presidency while gambling arrests climbed "vertiginously."[8]

One out of these thousands arrested in Rio de Janeiro in the post-1940s era bears a name familiar to us. Humberto Fassula, as chapter 6 shows, had been charged multiple times throughout the 1930s with selling tickets to the jogo do bicho. His final arrest apparently took place in 1950, and this case reveals both what had changed and what had not in the game's structure and the nature of its encounter with the state.[9] Early one afternoon, police apprehended Fassula and charged him with violating article 58 of the Penal Misdemeanor Code. As with so many other cases that we have seen throughout this book, according to the arresting officer, Fassula was apprehended em flagrante while "writing lists for bets for the so-called jogo do bicho, which were being dictated to him by an individual who managed to escape." Fassula insisted, as before, that the pencil, pad, and carbon paper did not belong to him and called the charges against him "absurd."

This case also shows some noteworthy differences in the jogo do bicho as compared with earlier decades. Some of these changes may have been particular to Fassula's own personal trajectory. For instance, unlike his previous arrests, when court-appointed lawyers had represented him, Fassula now could afford to hire an attorney, whose name and credentials the defendant made a point of mentioning in his arrest records. Other changes reflect broader patterns in the state's shifting relationship to the jogo do bicho. First, we see how the state had begun to prosecute persons charged with jogo do bicho offenses.[10] In the end, the judge found Fassula guilty and sentenced him to six months in prison and a fine of ten thousand *cruzeiros*, Brazil's new currency as of 1942.[11] Second, and probably most interesting, is the locale of Fassula's arrest. The police apprehended him not on a street corner or public square as usual, but inside a jogo do bicho *fortaleza* (fort).

The urban geography of the jogo do bicho is crucial to gaining broader historical insights from the continuities and changes in the animal game. In the 1940s and 1950s, tickets for the clandestine lottery still primarily sold in small, makeshift vending stands, or *pontos*. Yet operations had a more formal business structure than earlier, perhaps a manager and some employees, including ticket writers and salespeople, lookouts during times of heightened repression, and a banker who financed and owned the operation. At some point in the forties or fifties the illicit lottery came to be run out of a fortaleza, a fortified building or room protected sometimes by reinforced doors and basements with hidden access. As ownership of jogo do bicho businesses became concentrated in ever fewer hands, the powerful operators needed a place from which to administer their growing businesses. Safely ensconced in their fortalezas, banqueiros did their accounting and ruled their urban fiefdoms. These developments continued to force downward the risk of legal reprisals for involvement in the jogo do bicho, a process already long underway by the 1940s. Those at the top of the hierarchy conducted business in strict secrecy within enclosed, fortified headquarters, shielded from the authorities. Meanwhile, sellers out in the streets were exposed.[12] The street-corner bicheiro who bore the brunt of the game's criminalization, with his block of paper, small desk, and chair,

FIGURE 29 Police surveillance photograph of jogo do bicho betting site surrounded by barbed wire (*arame farpado*) (1975) (retouched by archive in 2009 to blur faces). Courtesy of Arquivo Público do Estado do Rio de Janeiro, Brazil, DOPS-235.

became the crucial point of contact between the game and law enforcement, on one hand, and the game and its customers, on the other. These two archetypal jogo do bicho figures—the wealthy jogo do bicho banker and the street-corner seller—with their differential susceptibility to arrest and their respective ways of occupying urban space, would typify the game up to the present day.

In the forties and fifties a new generation of banqueiros de bicho emerged. The early entertainment entrepreneurs like Guiseppe Labanca and Paschoal Segreto gradually got out of the jogo do bicho, and in their stead a group of lottery ticket and food retailers entered the scene.[13] Included among the hundreds arrested in a sweep of jogo do bicho businesses in 1940 was Victor Fernandes Alonso, a millionaire "real estate operator who owns two 5- and 10-cent stores."[14] These banqueiros claimed their own turf and often defended it through the barrel of a gun.[15] The concentration of power in the hands of bankers who used lethal violence to control certain territories may have begun as early as the thirties and accelerated in the fifties.[16]

FIGURE 30 Police photograph of jogo do bicho vendor's table (1975). Courtesy of Arquivo Público do Estado do Rio de Janeiro, Brazil, DOPS-235.

In the mid- and late twentieth century, the jogo do bicho became an increasingly entrenched fact on the ground in the city of its origin and a well-established reality in cities throughout Brazil. Law enforcement efforts wavered between tolerance and persecution and varied from city to city despite the unequivocal federal ban on the animal game codified in article 58. Local governments legalized the game from time to time, both de facto and de jure. According to the folklorist Pedro Hugo Carradore, for example, the São Paulo state government under Ademar Pereira de Barros (1947–51 and 1963–66) decided to regulate instead of expressly prohibit the game.[17] During the military rule of 1964–85, and especially during its most repressive and authoritarian phase from 1968 through the mid-1970s, the same government agencies that kept track of the regime's political opponents also watched the jogo do bicho, which they characterized as a threat to public order.[18] Notwithstanding political events of major significance, including the military coup in 1964 and the transference of the federal capital from Rio to Brasília in 1960, the jogo do bicho continued unabated.

In the 1970s and 1980s the jogo do bicho infamously grew involved with the drug traffic, although the nature and extent of the involvement is a matter of some dispute. Rio became a major entrepôt for international narcotraffic in the seventies. The relative peace of the late 1960s was broken by a series of famous murders as powerful jogo do bicho kingpins jockeyed for position. Several of the victims had known connections to the drug trade: the jogo do bicho owner Raul Capitão's son Marquinhos was murdered in 1988; the famous jogo do bicho banqueiro Osmar Khalil's son Wilson was assassinated in 1985.[19] Surges in violent crime in the 1980s related to the jogo do bicho also concerned disputes over the control of ticket sales outlets in a particular swathe of urban territory as well as the "elimination of witnesses."[20] In the 1990s, despite Judge Denise Frossard's highly publicized prosecution of a number of high-ranking jogo do bicho bankers that also exposed the involvement of the police in the game, few would claim that either the impunity of jogo do bicho bankers or the brisk trade in chances to win the game suffered a major interruption. A perennial news item in contemporary daily newspapers in cities throughout Brazil, the animal game's present-day entanglement with organized crime and corruption has taken a myriad of forms. In 2004 and 2007 massive, national scandals implicated the sitting president's top operatives, who arranged the exchange of large sums of money for government favors to jogo do bicho kingpins.[21]

Both the repression and the persistence of the jogo do bicho into the twenty-first century derive in large part from its place in the urban economy. Even as the game took its contemporary, decentralized form and individual sellers became specialized employees contracted out to wealthy, powerful jogo do bicho bankers, the illicit lottery's connection to local communities intensified. By the 1980s, Rio's jogo do bicho kingpins were household names, appearing frequently in the newspapers. Some commentators have interpreted the social initiatives the illicit lottery's principal owners and operators undertook as strategic decisions designed to enhance their standing in the communities and give them a measure of respectability. They systematically began to fund day-care centers, football clubs, and various forms of social welfare such as construction projects in poor neighborhoods: a continuation of bicheiros' former role as moneylender, *padrinho*, and confidante, but certainly, by virtue of the scale of these contemporary social welfare projects, a radical departure from jogo do bicho vendors' historic informal, small-scale roles in their communities.[22]

The social services that the jogo do bicho hierarchy provided prominently included financial support for the Carnival celebrations organized by associations called samba schools (*escolas de samba*). In the 1930s and 1940s as Rio's annual Carnival processions began to assume their modern form, the nascent samba schools were the beneficiaries of populist patronage networks flowing directly from the municipal and federal executive. This would change in the second half of the twentieth century, with privatization and later the emerging neoliberal model for public affairs. As the city and federal governments shifted financial responsibility for Carnival from public to private hands and the cost of these annual productions skyrocketed, jogo do bicho banqueiros generated community and political support and consolidated their power by funneling some of their proceeds into this quintessentially popular, large-scale community project.[23] Among the directors of the Independent League of Samba Schools (LIESA), which has held enormous power over Rio's carnival productions since the mid-1980s, there have been several persons known to be high up on the jogo do bicho hierarchy. At the same time, Rio's jogo do bicho organization grew in complexity, capitalization, and national reach.[24] That the jogo do bicho developed into a crime-syndicate-cum-social-welfare program in the seventies and eighties on the heels of the privatization of Carnival lends credence to the argument that the jogo do bicho's criminalization as well as its persistence resulted directly from the process of urban enclosure this book has traced.[25]

A revealing letter that accompanies the photographs from 1971 (see figs. 27–29) shows how far the surveillance of the jogo do bicho had come by the last quarter of the twentieth century and highlights the long-term effects of the process of criminalization. The head of a local police division (*delegado*) wrote to a higher-ranking police official to discuss the blurry images of the men in the photographs. The delegado had visited those sites depicted in the photographs, he asserts, and those men were not playing an illicit game at all.[26] This, the letter attests, was simply a group of elderly widowers from the neighborhood engaged in legal games of *sueca*, a popular card game, and dominos. Yet the men's presumed innocence did not solve the policing problem or entitle them to carry on their ostensibly legal recreational activity. The delegado writes, "It is my duty to inform you that the above-mentioned individuals were warned that they were no longer permitted any sort of gathering, due to the fact that they might confuse the authorities charged with extirpating prohibited games." The figures profiled by the police as criminal types occupied the spaces of the city to work, play, socialize, and live. This use of the city's public spaces was at times intentionally subversive, but most often the subversion was an unintentional effect of preexisting social and political tensions.

As a means of accounting for the large number of people who live outside the law in some part of their routine, everyday lives, the concept of resistance seems to provide a ready analytical solution. The study of popular resistance to domination grew in the 1980s along with rising interest in recovering instances of subaltern agency. The French cultural theorist Michel de Certeau showed that if one examines everyday life, it is possible to observe people resisting domination. The study of "how society works" beyond the confines of institutions, constitutions, and laws brings into focus a realm of activity in which people are actively opposing the control and authority of an oppressive elite.[27]

Yet in more recent decades, scholars wishing to understand the complexities of the power-laden relationship between the people and the state have begun "resisting resistance" as an analytical paradigm. While inspired by the idea of resistance as conferring agency on those doubly disempowered by their oppression and their omission from the historical record, a new generation of scholars has written critically of its flattening effect and its overreaching scope. In his critique of the overwhelming emphasis on resistance, written as this analytical approach reached its apogee in the late 1990s, the anthropologist Michael F. Brown pleads with his fellow social scientists to "do better": "For while families, organizations, and systems of production doubtless impose forms of subjugation, they are also institutions that enable. Without them, society would cease to exist, and with it, the capacity for human beings to survive. All social life entails degrees of dominance and subordination, which mirror the hierarchy intrinsic to the family and to the socialization process itself. Resistance to such power can no more explain the myriad forms of culture than gravity can explain the varied architecture of trees."[28] The resistance paradigm presupposes two camps acting against each other and provides little guidance in our attempt to understand the interactions between subjects on disparate ends of the power spectrum, even if their relationship is essentially oppositional. Nor does it help us to comprehend the variety and complexity of popular belief and action.[29] To settle upon resistance as defining the interaction between citizens and the law is to presume the jogo do bicho's criminality as a given rather than as a historical construction that developed as people both fought against and acted in concert with the state by way of the criminal law.

In seeking to comprehend the vast realm of everyday illicit activity now commonly known as the informal sector, one should look not just at domination and resistance but also at coercion and consent. In her recent study of hotel workers, the sociologist Rachel Sherman writes that withholding work and carrying out subtle acts of sabotage on hotel guests or coworkers "constituted moments of resistance, but they were also mechanisms of consent." "Unlike the concept of resistance . . . ," she continues, "the concept of consent allows us to think of workers as using their agency to participate in work rather than to refuse to participate. Explaining consent entails taking seriously the reasons that workers like their jobs and the rewards they derive from them, without losing a critical perspective on unequal social relations of appropriation." Consent can be oppositional, but it is bestowed rather than taken. Moreover, workers' local and immediate acts of resistance occurred in the context of their acceptance of broader rules of how society shall operate.[30]

As the foregoing chapters have shown, by educating people in the varied uses of money and the law, the jogo do bicho has garnered consent for both capitalist exchange and the formal legal system, rather than necessarily resisting the prevailing rules in either realm. People obeyed individual laws under compulsion and duress. But they actively acceded to the rule of law as an overarching principle.[31] In both cases, because most urban Brazilians found it virtually impossible either to be fully included or to opt out, the solution has been to create derivatives: they played with money, betting on the outcome of the lottery, and they traded in an informal economy in most ways indistinguishable from the licit one; and once arrested, they utilized the official channels of the law to wriggle free of it.

Without dwelling on the assertion that jogo do bicho vendors and players consciously defied unfair laws, one can argue that, once arrested, bicheiros and players actively pursued their idea of justice. The criminal cases I examine in this book bear witness to a version of what the historian E. P. Thompson named a "moral economy." Thompson's paradigmatic example describes the social relations between the English peasantry and rural elite in the eighteenth century, two disparate socioeconomic groups bound by a patrician model based on tacitly agreed-upon conditions: the transparency of market relations and the primacy of the needs of the poor over the interests of "dealers and middlemen."[32] As capitalism upset this paternalist modus operandi, peasants reacted to such exploitative practices as tampering with markets to create artificial scarcity with violent protests. In short,

Thompson's "moral economy" concept concerns the way in which the poor have appropriated the expectations developed under a paternalist system and used them to demand their right to sustenance as that paternalist model gave way to a more individualist and market-driven means of production. Crucially, peasants' hopes, desires, and expectations, not just their empty bellies, drove them. As they engaged in such ostensibly prepolitical actions as food riots, they acted systematically in pursuit of justice.

The moral economy concept proves especially illuminating in its relationship to the law. Just as in eighteenth-century rural England, in late nineteenth- and twentieth-century Brazil the law continually generated new "marketing offenses"; the prohibition against unlicensed games of chance was just one of these. At the same time, though, the moral economy existed not in opposition to but rather dependent upon state law. Although popular in orientation, the moral economy was never strictly informal, in the sense of occupying a world apart from officialdom. In the paternalistic society Thompson studied, the law in code and in practice held the protection of the poor as a high priority. Although initially backed by law, the moral economy's position in eighteenth-century England's legal system changed to reflect the new nexus of interests of the emerging capitalist elite class. As the historian Douglas Hay demonstrates, "legal discourse, deliberation and decision" ultimately ratified the "doctrines of political in place of moral economy."[33] The bread rioters in eighteenth-century England may not have been so community-minded or tradition-bound as Thompson supposed them to be. But their involvement in occasional bursts of civic disorder can inform my study of criminalized popular urban practice, even though the jogo do bicho caused disorder that was the opposite: mundane and everyday and only disorderly because of having been labeled as such by the police. As James C. Scott writes, the moral economy manifested itself not just as food riots but moreover as "social sanctions which operate at the community level to reinforce the claims of the poor to some measure of social insurance from their better-off neighbors":[34] like the right to claim urban space to run a business or to play a game of chance whose illegality was the product of law and politics rather than of shared community censure.

Lima Barreto, the journalist and literary writer whose words have appeared throughout this book, published a newspaper chronicle in 1915 that unearths the deep roots of the persecution of the elderly men absorbed in their daily game of dominoes on Praça Drummond some six decades later in 1971.[35] Lamenting the influx of desperate Brazilians from the countryside flooding the city of Rio, seduced by greed and disingenuous politics, Lima Barreto tells of how their fascination for the city draws them there. Their sad fate, he explains, was to become "vagabonds" in the streets. They had abandoned the "feverish marshes and implacable drought" of their hinterland homes, "believing that here [in Rio] lay El Dorado. There they left their thatch houses, their cassava, their pigs, and they ran to Rio de Janeiro to grab some money from the inexhaustible cornucopia. No one paid them any attention back there, no one wanted to improve their fortune, there in the place where the blood of their grandparents irrigated the fields." With the deep empathy that was his trademark, Lima Barreto traces their transition from poor people of the land to poor, dependent, and resourceless people of the city. The author notes in this chronicle, as he does elsewhere, that if allowed to develop their natural sense of community, the freedom to provide mutual assistance, and the ability to set their own moral standards, the popular classes could survive and thrive. Yet it appeared to him that the city offered little latitude for the exercise of those freedoms.

Lima Barreto ends his poignant *crônica* with a potent dose of his characteristic sarcasm: "O Rio civiliza-se!" (Rio, get civilized!), he writes. In reiterating this battle cry of the turn-of-the-century rebuilders and reformers of the city, the author reminds the reader of the human costs of the elites' modernizing mission. For Lima Barreto, civilization lay less in a particular place than in a type of relationship between human beings, one which he felt was about to be lost to the world. The underworld of those overlooked or plowed under by the civilizing process fascinated him because he appears to have felt it offered a possibility for Brazil genuinely to civilize itself. More than their importance as individual subjects, the prostitutes, thieves, old gamblers, police, soldiers, poor children, and vagabonds who populate his chronicles have profound meaning to the author as upholders of an all-important but endangered community. Only with the second coming of this community did Lima Barreto feel he could hope for collective success, happiness, and justice for the Brazilian nation.

Despite the cronista's tendency to feel an almost apocalyptic sorrow over the social injustice in his beloved city, the former bondsmen, tenant farmers, and village dwellers who populate his early twentieth-century urban chronicles in reality did find ways of compensating for their lack of social power. For many of them, the magic of survival turned on their ability to create new pathways through which power would flow. For the unnamed thousands who played the jogo do bicho and kept the bicheiros and banqueiros in business the game was in many ways a mere pastime. For the thousands of sellers of the illicit lottery, it provided them with a convenient means of earning a living when, oftentimes, there were few other opportunities. Historians looking for meaning and inspiration cannot justifiably construe the game as an act of resistance, *tout court*. Yet the game as it developed—as a social system, an urban culture, and an informal and moral economy—was both cause and product of an enduring struggle.

My book has aimed to recognize social conflict at the level of the everyday while avoiding falling back on an oversimplified, overly sanguine resistance paradigm. This story of the jogo do bicho's persistence despite its illegality cannot be reduced to a struggle between the state and the people as clear antagonists. It is instead a microcosm of a multifarious relationship between the people and the state by way of the criminal law. Both literally and figuratively, enclosing public spaces transformed citizens into trespassers. The historical trajectory of the animal game helps us understand the development of "extralegal normativity," on the one hand, and, on the other, the normalized police repression of everyday urban life. The story of the jogo do bicho impels us to recalibrate the tools used to analyze participation in public life: to see the informal not as idiosyncratic or marginal but as ordinary. We can thus recognize the political and creative aspects of gestures that might seem to remove people from society (in other words, to marginalize them) and in activities that seem simply, categorically to constitute radical denials of established norms. At the same time, we can see historical subjects as active participants in their world not only through their resistance but also through their cooperation and collaboration. The more than a century-long process of the criminalization of everyday life so well typified by the jogo do bicho paradoxically shows both the genesis of modern social inequality and the particular way in which Brazilian urban society cohered.

NOTES

INTRODUCTION

1. All references to this case are from AN, Série Processos Crimes, 16o Distrito Policial, June 25, 1907.
2. See, for example, Lopez-Rey, "Gambling in Latin American Countries"; Macry, *Giocare la vita*; Fabian, *Card Sharps, Dream Books, and Buckets Shops*; Wolcott, "The Culture of the Informal Economy"; Clapson, *A Bit of a Flutter*; Crespo, "Os jogos de fortuna ou azar em Lisboa em fins do Antigo Regime"; and Urrutia, " 'La tentación de la suerte.' "
3. See, for example, Pina-Cabral, *Between China and Europe*, chap. 4.
4. Reith, *The Age of Chance*, 75. See also Lears, "Playing with Money," 7–41; and Clifford Geertz, "Deep Play."
5. Kavanagh, *Enlightenment and the Shadows of Chance*; Hacking, *The Emergence of Probability*; Lears, "Playing with Money"; Reith, *The Age of Chance*; "The Culture of Risk and Pleasure," special volume of *Eighteenth-Century Studies* 33: 4; and, Macry, *Giocare la vita*.
6. Freyre, *Casa-grande e senzala*, 203–4, 244n13. See also DaMatta, "The Many Levels of Carnival," in *Carnivals, Rogues, and Heroes*, 91.
7. Reith, *The Age of Chance*, xv.
8. See especially O'Brien and Roseberry, eds., *Golden Ages, Dark Ages*; Palmié, *Wizards and Scientists*; and Glassman, *Feasts and Riot*.
9. No comprehensive statistics exist for conviction rates for jogo do bicho cases. The data used here come from a random sample of cases (*processos*) in the National Archive (AN). Case outcomes are also noted in judges' sentencing records (AN, Livros de Sentença), of which only a small number survive.
10. The processo contains jogo do bicho lists; AN, Série Processos-Crimes, T8–3467.
11. Cf. Parker, "Law, Honor, and Impunity in Spanish America."
12. Newspapers devoted to the jogo do bicho include *O Bicho* (1903–14) and *O Palpite* (1906–9); BN, Setor de Periódicos.
13. González Arce, *Aparencia y Poder*, 105. Sumptuary laws existed in times and places

other than medieval Europe, including ancient Greece and Rome, the Islamic world, and medieval Japan.

14. Goodrich, "Signs Taken for Wonders." Cf. Halttunen, *Confidence Men and Painted Women*, 42.

15. Hunt, *Governance of the Consuming Passions*, x–xii.

16. Goodrich, "Signs Taken for Wonders," 721; Hunt, *Governance of the Consuming Passions*.

17. Lima Barreto, *Marginália*, 87.

18. E. P. Thompson dates England's first enclosure act to February 1710; *Customs in Common*, 109. The origins of the gradual process of the privatization of common lands in western Europe is generally located in the seventeenth century.

19. Hardin, "The Tragedy of the Commons"; Elizabeth Blackmar, "Appropriating 'the Commons': The Tragedy of Property Rights Discourse," in Low and Smith, *The Politics of Public Space*, 49–80.

20. See especially *Customs in Common*, chap. 3; and *Whigs and Hunters*. Thompson directly criticizes Garrett Hardin for caricaturing the commons as a chaotic "free for all"; *Customs in Common*, 108.

21. Caldeira, *City of Walls*; Low, *On the Plaza*. See also Low and Smith, *The Politics of Public Space*.

22. Benchimol, *Pereira Passos: Um Haussman Tropical*, 283. This process can be traced at least to May 27, 1874, when Emperor Dom Pedro II convened the Improvements Commission of the City of Rio de Janeiro, a group of engineers that included the young Francisco Pereira Passos, who later became Rio's famous mayor; ibid., 138.

23. Cf. da Silva, *Operários sem patrões*, chaps. 9, 10.

24. As David Harvey has argued, what is interesting here is not how public space is being eroded but how it is being constituted; "The Political Economy of Public Space," in Low and Smith, *The Politics of Public Space*, 17–34.

25. See O'Brien and Roseberry, eds., *Golden Ages, Dark Ages*.

26. Rosenn, "Brazil's Legal Culture," 39. The institute's study is entitled, "A Economia Informal Urbana."

27. See Cross, *Informal Politics*, 1–8.

28. In Brazil the idea of the dual economy dates at least to the influential work of Ignácio Rangel, *Dualidade básica da economia brasileira*. See generally Smith, ed., *Perspectives on the Informal Economy*; Portes, Castells, and Benton, eds., *The Informal Economy*; and Wilson, ed., "The Urban Informal Sector." The best-known work on the informal economy is undoubtedly *The Other Path* by the neoliberal Peruvian economist and politician Hernando de Soto.

29. The Portuguese word employed to describe the dual economy, *duplicidade*, is a false cognate of the English word *duplicity* and lacks its connotations of deceitfulness. In Ministério da Educação e Cultura, *Introdução aos Problemas do Brasil*, 22–24. Max Weber's ideas, disseminated in Brazil in the writings of the lawyer and historical sociologist Raymondo Faoro, also touch on the duality of the Brazilian economy, rooted in the country's colonial political and legal culture. On the

duality between "formal legal rationality" and the social substance of the law in Weber's thought, see Wilson, "Rationality and Capitalism in Max Weber's Analysis of Western Modernity," 97.

30. Ward, "Introduction and Overview."

31. Jelin, "Ciudadanía, Derechos e Identidad."

32. Morse and Hardoy, eds., *Rethinking the Latin American City*, 17.

33. Perlman, *Myth of Marginality*; Ward, "Introduction and Overview," 185.

34. De Soto, *The Other Path.*

35. Benchimol, *Pereira Passos: um Haussmann Tropical*, 169–71; Carone, *Classes sociais e movimento operário*, 71; Meade, *"Civilizing" Rio*, 51–52; Conniff, *Urban Politics in Brazil*, 66–67; Carvalho, *Os bestializados*, 21.

36. Hahner, *Poverty and Politics*, 129–30.

37. The term *extralegal normativity* is Enrique Ghersi's; Alonso, Iwasaki, Ghersi, eds., *El comercio ambulatorio en Lima*, 13.

38. Carvalho, *Os bestializados*, 15–41; Needell, *A Tropical Belle Epoque*; Abreu, *O Império do divino*; Viotti da Costa, *The Brazilian Empire.*

39. Ramos, *Divergent Modernities*; Joseph, "Preface," in Salvatore, Aguirre, and Joseph, eds., *Crime and Punishment in Latin America*, xii–xvi.

40. Moreira, *São Paulo na Primeira República*, 27; Filho, *Questão Social no Brasil*, 28–61.

41. Piccato, *City of Suspects*; Overmyer-Velázquez, *Visions of the Emerald City*. Similarly, see Bronfman, *Measures of Equality.*

42. Olívia Maria Gomes da Cunha, "The Stigmas of Dishonor: Criminal Records, Civil Rights, and Forensic Identification in Rio de Janeiro, 1903–1940," in Caulfield, Chambers, and Putnam, *Honor, Status, and the Law in Modern Latin America*, 293–315; Carvalho, *Os bestializados*, 30–31.

43. See, for example, Viqueira Albán, *Propriety and Permissiveness in Bourbon Mexico*; Arrom, *Containing the Poor*; Holloway, *Policing Rio de Janeiro*. The quotation is from Viqueira Albán, *Propriety and Permissiveness*, xix.

44. Bronfman, *Measures of Equality*; Piccato, *City of Suspects*; Dain Borges, "Healing and Mischief: Witchcraft in Brazilian Law and Literature, 1890–1922," in Salvatore, Aguirre, and Joseph, eds., *Crime and Punishment in Latin America*, 181–210.

45. Douglas Hay, "Property, Authority, and the Criminal Law," in Hay et al., eds., *Albion's Fatal Tree*, 17–63; Langbein, "Albion's Fatal Flaws."

46. Viqueira Albán, *Propriety and Permissiveness.*

47. Thompson, *Whigs and Hunters*, 260.

48. Steven Spitzer makes a similar argument; "The Rationalization of Crime Control in Capitalist Society," in Cohen and Scull, eds., *Social Control and the State*, 312.

49. On vagrancy law in Brazil, see, for example, Huggins, *From Slavery to Vagrancy*; Mattos, "Vadios, jogadores, mendigos e bêbados na cidade do Rio de Janeiro do início do século."

50. Viqueira Albán, *Propriety and Permissiveness*, xviii.

51. Piccato, *City of Suspects.*

52. Garland, *Punishment and Modern Society*; Piccato, *City of Suspects*; Fischer, "The

Poverty of Law." The idea that penality creates delinquency, and not the reverse, was most famously developed by Michel Foucault, *Discipline and Punish*, esp. 20–21, 276–77.

53. República dos Estados Unidos do Brasil, *Recenseamento do Rio de Janeiro (Distrito Federal) realisado em 20 de setembro 1906*.

54. Ribeiro, *A Capital Federal e a Constuição da República*.

55. Sevcenko, "A capital irradiante: técnica, ritmos, e ritos do Rio," in Sevcenko, ed., *A história da vida privada no Brasil*, 619.

56. Ribeiro, *A Capital Federal e a Constituição da República*, 7–8.

57. Holloway, *Policing Rio de Janeiro*; Reis, *Rebelião escrava no Brasil*.

58. The jurist and statesman Rui Barbosa invoked habeas corpus in favor of the victims of this summary justice. His request was rejected because of the state of emergency; Marinho and Rosas, *Sesquicentario do supreme tribunal federal*, 17–18.

59. Marinho and Rosas, *Sesquicentario do supreme tribunal federal*, 18.

60. A large literature describes the early twentieth-century transformation of Rio's urban landscape. The authoritative work is Benchimol, *Periera Passos: Um Haussmann Tropical*. See also Brenna, ed., *O Rio de Janeiro de Pereira Passos*; Green, *Beyond Carnival*, 17–20; Sevcenko, ed., *História da vida privada no Brasil*, 22–33; Meade, *"Civilizing" Rio*; Rocha, *A Era das demolições*; and Rebelo and Bulhões, *O Rio de Janeiro da Bota-Abaixo*.

61. Brenna, *O Rio de Janeiro de Pereira Passos*, 20.

62. Mathias, *Viagem pitoresca ao velho e ao novo Rio*, 217–19; Benchimol, *Pereira Passos: Um Haussman Tropical*, 268–69.

63. See Brenna, *O Rio de Janeiro do Pereira Passos*.

64. Conniff, *Urban Politics in Brazil*, 7.

65. Avenida Central (now Avenida Rio Branco) was eighteen hundred meters long and thirty-three meters wide; Lobo, *A história do Rio de Janeiro*, 504–5.

66. Conniff, *Urban Politics in Brazil*, 7–8.

67. República dos Estados Unidos do Brasil, *Recenseamento do Rio de Janeiro (Distrito Federal) realisado em 20 de setembro de 1906*, xliv.

1. ORIGINS OF THE *JOGO DO BICHO*

1. The letter quoted in the epigraph is in AGCRJ, códice 15–5-62, folha 30.

2. The most rigorous history of the jogo do bicho is Magalhães, "Ganhou leva"; see also Mello, "A história social dos jogos de azar no Rio de Janeiro, 1808–1946." The game's origins are also recounted in DaMatta and Soárez, *Águias, burros e borboletas*, 59–99; and in Herschmann and Lerner, *Lance de Sorte*, 61–79. For popular literature on the jogo do bicho, see Pacheco, *Antologia do jogo do bicho*, 15–17; and Carradore, *Folclore do jogo do bicho*, 15–21.

3. I borrow this phrase from Albert O. Hirschman's classic study *The Passions and the Interests*.

4. The earliest documented arrest for involvement in the jogo do bicho dates from July 13, 1896; APERJ, CD-5626. Federal legislation in 1910 strengthened penalties against unlicensed games of chance; Decreto-Lei 2321.

5. Benchimol, *Pereira Passos*, 319.

6. See, for example, Cruz, *Vale o escrito*; Cascudo, *Dicionário do Folclore Brasileiro*; Gerson, *História das ruas do Rio*, 358–59; Hahner, *Poverty and Politics*, 215; DaMatta and Soárez, *Águias, burros e borboletas*, 59–99; Geraldo Lopes, "Quase 3 mil pontos de 'bicho' na cidade," *Tribuna da Imprensa* (October 24, 1978), Coleção DOPS, APERJ.

7. Lobo, *História do Rio de Janeiro*; Faoro, *Os donos de poder*, 433–34; Benchimol, *Pereira Passos*, 96–111.

8. Many of Vila Isabel's streets were named after Brazilian personages associated with the passage of the Law of the Free Womb (1871), which emancipated children born of slave women; Gerson, *História das ruas do Rio*, 359. One must not make too much of Drummond's devotion to the abolitionist cause; his wife, Florinda Gomes Viana Drummond, owned a slave-operated estate in the interior of the state of Rio de Janeiro, which he later inherited; AN, Inventários, Juizo da 2a Vara de Órphãos, 20 Ofício, Ano 1883, Rio de Janeiro, N. 961, caixa 4274.

9. Abreu, *Evolução urbana do Rio de Janeiro*, 41, 44; Benchimol, *Pereira Passos*, 106; Gerson, *História das ruas do Rio*, 359.

10. See Gerson, *História das ruas do Rio*. On the construction of worker housing, see Lobo, Carvalho, and Stanley, *Questão habitacional e o movimento operário*; Carvalho, *Contribuição ao estudo das habitações populares*, 150.

11. Late nineteenth-century Rio's fastest growing neighborhoods were located in the north and west zones. República dos Estados Unidos do Brasil, *Recenseamento do Rio de Janeiro*, 23–24.

12. The zoo was constructed in 1888 but had been planned since 1884; see AGCRJ, códice 15–4-62, folhas 2–3. See also DaMatta and Soárez, *Águias, burros e borboletas*, 60–62; Mello, "A história social dos jogos de azar no Rio de Janeiro, 1808–1946," 56; Benchimol, *Pereira Passos*, 111n20. One *conto* equals 1,000 milreis. At an average exchange rate of 1.85 *milreis* to the U.S. dollar in 1888, one conto would equal approximately US$540.

13. Barata and Bueno, *Dicionário de famílias brasileiras*, 879.

14. Drummond directed his appeal to the Conselho da Intendencia; AGCRJ, códice 15–4-62, folha 10. See also DaMatta and Soárez, *Águias, burros e borboletas*, 65; Mello, "A história social dos jogos de azar no Rio de Janeiro, 1808–1946," 57.

15. AGCRJ, 15–4-62, folha 10.

16. Mello, "A história social dos jogos de azar no Rio de Janeiro, 1808–1946," 58. See also DaMatta and Soárez, *Águias, burros e borboletas*, 65. The date by which Drummond had begun to run the *sorteio dos bichos* appears in Rio's daily newspapers (*Jornal do Brasil*; *O Tempo*; *Diário do Comércio*) as July 3 and July 4, 1892.

17. *Jornal do Brasil* (July 4, 1892); Campos, *Dicionário de curiosidades do Rio de Janeiro*, 147; Gerson, *História das ruas do Rio*, 359; Benchimol, *Pereira Passos*, fig. 14 (np).

18. *O Tempo* (July 16, 1892), np; *Diário do Comércio* (July 11, 1892), np.

19. AGCRJ, códice 55–4-9, folha 9.

20. Carradore, *Folclore do jogo do bicho*, 19. See also Cavalcante, *Os bicheiros*, 62; DaMatta and Soárez, *Águias, burros e borboletas*, 79.

21. "Jardim Zoológico—Prêmios Diários Sobre Animais de 20$ a 40:000$—Vendas das Entradas na Rua do Ouvidor No 129 e no Jardim"; *O Tempo* (July 12, 1892), np.

22. AGCRJ, códice 15–4-62, folha 16. The streetcar line on which these businessmen offered transportation to the zoo, the Companhia Ferro-Carril de Vila Isabel, was one of the Baron de Drummond's own development projects, and he still owned a major share in it.

23. Herschmann and Lerner, *Lance da sorte*, 68; Mello, "A história social dos jogos de azar no Rio de Janeiro, 1808–1946," 1–32; Carradore, *Folclore do jogo do bicho*, 20.

24. DaMatta and Soárez, *Águias, burros e borboletas*, 67. Hugo Pedro Carradore describes several "jogos das flores" that existed in the late nineteenth century; Carradore, *Folclore do jogo do bicho*, 17–18.

25. In 1951 Manuel Bandeira and Carlos Drummond de Andrade collected an anonymous account of the origins of the jogo do bicho which mentions "a certain Manuel Ismael Zevala [*sic*]," a Mexican national who operated a lottery shop on the rua do Ouvidor and who personally knew the Baron de Drummond; Bandeira and Andrade, *O Rio de Janeiro em prosa e verso*, 194. Marcelo Pereira de Mello points out that no researcher has ever fully substantiated the involvement of Manoel (sometimes Manuel) Zevada in the development of the jogo do bicho. Both he and Jaime Larry Benchimol cite sources that point to the more convincing story of Drummond's partnership with Luís Galvez: Mello, "A história social dos jogos de azar no Rio de Janeiro, 1808–1946," 55, 56, 62; Benchimol, *Pereira Passos*, 111n20. However, Zevada's name arises frequently enough that the possibility he played some part in the jogo do bicho's popularization should be taken seriously. The newspaper *O Tempo* identifies "sr. M. I. Zevada" as the manager of the Empresa Jardim Zoológica; (July 3, 1892), np. See also Carradore, *Folclore do jogo do bicho*, 15.

26. DaMatta and Soárez, 76; Carradore, *Folclore do jogo do bicho*, 20; Mello, "A história social dos jogos de azar no Rio de Janeiro, 1808–1946," 61.

27. AGCRJ, códice 45–2-48, "Carta anonyma sobre o jogo dos bichos e de loterias. 1895."

28. DaMatta and Soárez, *Águias, burros e borboletas*, 75.

29. AGCRJ, códice 15–4-62, folhas 14, 30; *Relatório do Ministro de Justiça e Negócios Interiores do Brasil* (Rio de Janeiro: April 1896), 153; and *Anaes do Conselho Municipal (D.F.)* (Rio de Janeiro: September 1897), 117.

30. *O Tempo* (July 23, 1892), np.

31. AGCRJ, códice 15–4-62, folhas 12–13.

32. Mello, "A história social dos jogos de azar no Rio de Janeiro, 1808–1946," 60.

33. Municipal Law (*Decreto*) number 126; see DaMatta and Soárez, *Águias, burros e borboletas*, 80.

34. Mello, "A história social dos jogos de azar no Rio de Janeiro, 1808–1946," 39–40, 42.

35. DaMatta and Soárez, *Águias, burros e borboletas*, 79.

36. DaMatta and Soárez, *Águias, burros e borboletas*, 76.
37. The game apparently continued uninterrupted after 1895, even after the raffle at the zoo ceased to exist. Owing to its decentralized nature after 1895, jogo do bicho operators reputedly utilized other sources alongside the federal lottery daily numbers, such as daily stock quotations. Cf. Fabian, *Card Sharps, Dream Books, and Bucket Shops*. Bookmakers may have invented the idea of deriving jogo do bicho winners by associating animals with the final digits of the official lottery numbers; Mello, "A história social dos jogos de azar no Rio de Janeiro, 1808–1946," 39–40.
38. Carradore, *Folclore do jogo do bicho*, 29–31; DaMatta and Soárez, *Águias, burros e borboletas*, 87–88.
39. DaMatta and Soárez, *Águias, burros e borboletas*, 87; Cooper, *The Brazilians and Their Country*, 263.
40. See, for example, AN, Notação T8 1677, 11ª Pretoria Distrito Policial (January 5, 1904); AN, Notação T8 3467, Delegacia do 16° Distrito Policial (June 19, 1908). By the mid-twentieth century one writer lists the following varieties of the jogo do bicho: "o Agave Americano, o Buraco, o Caridade, o Popular, o Elefante, o Moderno Lôto, o Nascente, o Ocidente, o Carioca, o Garantia, o Luz do Céu, o Esperança, o Estrela do Destino, o Segurança, o Ajuda de Nossa Senhora, o Talismã da Sorte, etc. etc."; "O jogo do bicho, inextinguivel," in Bandeira, *O Rio de Janeiro em prosa e verso*, 196.
41. Requests for licenses to sell lottery tickets demonstrate the ubiquity of lottery tickets sales throughout the city; see AGCRJ códices 45–4-23, 45–4-24, 45–4-27, and 23–5-26.
42. AN, GIFI 6C-30, April 1898, "Papeis sobre depositos de presos."
43. AGCRJ, 45–4-20 and 45–4-21.
44. Tip sheets include *O Bicho* and *O Palpite*; BN, Setor de Periódicos (see chapter 5). See also DaMatta and Soárez, *Águias, burros e borboletas*, 84–87. Cf. Fabian, *Card Sharps, Dream Books, and Bucket Shops*.
45. Data on the cost of playing the jogo do bicho come from testimony and evidence in criminal cases (processos); see, for example, AN, Notação OR.0822. Cost of living data are extrapolated from figures from 1911; see Oakenfull, *Brazil in 1911*, 355–57.
46. For the 1960s, see Abreu, *O submundo da prostuição, vadiagem e jôgo do bicho*, 103.
47. AN, T8.2543.
48. AN, Série Processo Crime, José Raposo do Conto Jr. e Antonio Marques da Silva, Delegacia de Polícia do 20 Distrito (1911).
49. Oakenfull, *Brazil in 1912*, 436–37.
50. AN, Série Processo Crime, T8.1755.
51. Also see the short story "Jogo do Bicho" (1904) by Machado de Assis in *Obras Completas*, vol. 2 (discussed in chap. 5 below).
52. AN, T7–0018.
53. AN, T7–0018.
54. Times of arrests are based on testimony presented in criminal cases (processos) found in the Arquivo Nacional.

55. AN, OR.0822.

56. Of the 811,443 people recorded in 1906 in the census of the Federal District, proportionally the largest professions include "unclassified industries" (26,019); building construction (31,800); commerce (62,062); domestic service (117,904); "day workers/manual laborers" (29,933), in addition to workers in the clothing industry (31,710) and agriculture (21,411); *República dos Estados Unidos do Brasil, Recenseamento do Rio de Janeiro (Distrito Federal) realisado em 20 de setembro 1906*, 104.

57. Herschmann and Lerner, *Lance de sorte*, 68–71; Meira, "O papel da imprensa no jogo do bicho (1890–1920)"; Magalhães, "Ganhou leva," 60–72. For literacy rates in Rio de Janeiro, see República dos Estados Unidos do Brasil, *Recenseamento do Rio de Janeiro (Districto Federal) realisado em 20 de setembro 1906*, 107–115.

58. Dent, *A Year in Brazil*, 240; Mello, "A história social dos jogos de azar no Rio de Janeiro, 1808–1946," 1–32.

59. Carradore, *Folclore do jogo do bicho*, 19. See also Cavalcante, *Os bicheiros*; DaMatta and Soárez, *Águias, burros e borboletas*, 49.

60. Bretas, *A guerra das ruas*; Holloway, *Policing Rio*; Chalhoub, *Trabalho, lar, e botequim*; Dain Borges, "Healing and Mischief: Witchcraft in Brazilian Law and Literature, 1890–1922," in Salvatore, Aguirre, and Joseph, eds., *Crime and Punishment in Latin America*, 180–210. Skidmore, *Black into White*, 47.

61. Brazilian historiography's emphasis on the draconian, antipopular politics of the First Republic is, in part, the legacy of the republican regime's attempts to justify its policies by pointing out the weakness and "supposed tolerance of the monarchical regime" that preceded it; Abreu, *O império do divino*, 337–38; Chalhoub, *Cidade febril*, 290–91.

62. The term *sporting* was used frequently to denote gambling activities in this period.

63. APERJ, Código de Polícia Municipal da Cidade do Rio de Janeiro, 99–101, and Posturas Municipais, September 1898.

64. Mello, "A história social dos jogos de azar no Rio de Janeiro, 1808–1946," 39–40.

65. AGCRJ, códice 15–4-33 and 15–4-63, esp. folha 14; AGCRJ, códice 15–4-62, folha 30.

66. Relatório dos Ministérios da Justiça e Negocios Interiores, Projeto n. 51, 1896, 28; Anais da Câmara, February 1, 1896, 5. See Mello, "A história social dos jogos de azar no Rio de Janeiro, 1808–1946," 33–79.

67. Cooper, *The Brazilians and Their Country*, 263.

68. See Mello, "A história social dos jogos de azar no Rio de Janeiro," 93–96; citing Mello, DaMatta and Soárez affirm his assertion, *Águias, burros e borboletas*, 79.

69. DaMatta and Soárez, *Águias, burros e borboletas*, 82.

70. Cooper, *The Brazilians and Their Country*, 259–61.

71. Ibid., 263.

72. AGCRJ, códice 15–5-62, folha 30. See the epigraph at the beginning of this chapter for the full quotation.

73. Abreu, *Evolução Urbana*, 36–53.

74. Benchimol, *Pereira Passos*, 106. Brasil Gerson dates the laying of the bonde tracks to 1875 in *História das ruas do Rio*, 359.

75. Benchimol, *Pereira Passos*, 107; Boone, "Streetcars and Politics in Rio de Janeiro."

76. Mauá's varied interests included mine speculation as well as urban development and interurban transportation; Marchant, *Viscount Mauá and the Empire of Brazil*, 3. Mauá (Irenêo Evangelista de Souza) was the executor of the will of the deceased Conselheiro Antonio de Menezes Vasconcellos de Drumond in 1874; AN, Coleção Inventarios—Juizo da 1a Vara de Órphãos, N. 252, caixa 4004, Galeria A.

77. DaMatta and Soárez, *Águias, burros e borboletas*, chap. 1.

78. AN, Inventários, Juizo da 2a Vara de Órphãos, 20 Ofício, Ano 1883, Rio de Janeiro, N. 961, caixa 4274.

79. Important gambling establishments existed in the area that would become Vila Isabel as early as the late 1840s; Leite, *Rio de Janeiro*. On the Casino Fluminense, see Needell, *A Tropical Belle-Epoque*, 65–72.

80. Gerson, *História das ruas do Rio*, 361–62.

81. Warren Dean, "The Brazilian Economy, 1870–1930," in Bethell, ed., *Cambridge History of Latin America*, 5:688.

82. Faria, *Mauá*; Barman, *Citizen Emperor*, 192; Lustosa, *As Trapaças da sorte*, 15; Costa, *The Brazilian Empire*, 53–77.

83. Needell, *A Tropical Belle Epoque*; Viotti da Costa, *The Brazilian Empire*, 172–201; Lobo, *História do Rio de Janeiro (do capital commercial ao capital industrial financeiro)*, vol. 2.

84. Faria, *Mauá*, 50–51, 68–69.

85. Emilia Viotti da Costa, "Brazil: The Age of Reform, 1870–1889," in Bethell, ed., *Cambridge History of Latin America*, vol. 6, 731.

86. Benchimol, *Pereira Passos*; Boone, "Streetcars and Politics in Rio de Janeiro"; Silva, *Operários sem patrões*.

87. Abreu, *Evoluçao Urbana*, 35; Viotti da Costa, *The Brazilian Empire*, 195, 291n33.

88. See generally AGCRJ, códices 45–4-21; 45–4-23; 45–4-25; 45–4-29; 45–5-30; 45–5-30; 45–5-31; 45–5-32; 45–5-33.

89. See, for example, AGCRJ, códice 45–4-21, folha 129.

90. See, for example, AGCRJ, códice 45–2-22, folha 109.

91. AGCRJ, códice 45–2-22, folhas 2–6.

92. Topik, "The Evolution of the Economic Role of the State."

93. AGCRJ, códice 58–3-38, folhas 20–21.

94. See especially documents related to kiosks (*kiosques*) from 1883 to 1911: AGCRJ, códices 45–4-21; 45–4-23; 45–4-25; 45–4-29; 45–5-30; 45–5-30; 45–5-31; 45–5-32; and 45–5-33. See also AGCRJ, códice 61–1-19-A2 and códice 58–3-39, folha 49.

95. Public health concerns still figured prominently in this regulation of petty commerce; AGCRJ, códice 58–3-39, folha 4; Chalhoub, *Cidade febril*; Hochman, *A era do saneamento*, 55–57.

96. AGCRJ, códice 58–3-39, folhas 38–49.

97. For another example, see *Jornal do Comércio* (January 19, 1885), np.

98. Pechman, *Cidades estreitamente vigiadas*, 303–75; Holloway, *Policing Rio*; Carvalho, *A construção da ordem e Teatro de sombras*, 232.

99. For documents that dramatically illustrate this transition, see AGCRJ, códice 45–4-22, folhas 35–41.

100. AGCRJ, códice 43-3-48; 24–8-91, folha 3. The author of this letter incorrectly referred to the "Criminal Code" instead of the "Penal Code."

101. AGCRJ, códice, 24–8-91, folha 4. The monetary figure indicated here is five hundred milreis, which in the 1880s was roughly equivalent to US$150.

102. AGCRJ, códices 45–4-23, 45–2-48.

103. What is loosely translated here as "gambling sporting events" reads in the original Portuguese *jogos de frontões*. A *frontão* (pl. *frontões*) was a form of popular amusement common in Rio at the turn of the twentieth century. See Bretas, *A guerra das ruas*, 88–92; Mello, "A história social dos jogos de azar no Rio de Janeiro, 1808–1946," 42–43.

104. The game of *pelotas* (or sometimes *pelas*) is an athletic game of Basque origin. It was popular in late nineteenth-century Rio de Janeiro as both a spectator sport and for betting; Mello, "A história social dos jogos de azar no Rio de Janeiro, 1808–1946," 45–46.

105. *Annaes do Conselho Municipal* (Rio de Janeiro, April 1898), np.

106. *Annais do Conselho Municipal*, (April 1898), 172.

107. Senado Federal, Lei 2321, December 30, 1910.

108. Benchimol, *Pereira Passos*, 257–59. See generally Evan Stark, "Gangs and Progress: The Contribution of Delinquency to Progressive Reform," in Greenberg, ed. *Crime and Capitalism*, 445–46.

109. Hochman, *A era do saneamento*; Mello, "A história social dos jogos de azar no Rio de Janeiro, 1808–1946," 33–98.

110. *Annaes do Conselho* (April 1898), 44. One conto in 1898 was equal to approximately US$163 (at a rate of 6.14 milreis to the dollar), as opposed to the higher rate in 1917 of one conto to US$273 (at a rate of 3.65 milreis to the dollar).

111. *Annaes do Conselho* (April 1898), parecer 21.

112. In the civil law tradition that characterizes the legal systems of all Latin American countries, the judiciary produces scholarship, rather than case law, as in the common law tradition, to compensate for any lacunae in the existing body of laws; Merryman, *The Civil Law Tradition*.

113. Cf. Crespo, "Os jogos de fortuna ou azar em Lisboa em fins do Antigo Regime."

114. DaMatta and Soárez, *Águias, burros e borboletas*, 81.

115. APERJ, CD-DF 5626.

116. The other infractions most common in the Casa de Detenção in 1896 include *desordeiro* (disorderly conduct), *gatuno* (pickpocketing/theft), *capoeira* (urban gangs, associated with group violence and with Afro-Brazilian men), *ofesas corporais* (assault), *vagabundo* (vagrancy), and *roubo* (robbery). Less common offenses include *por estar encontrado sem domicílio* (for being found homeless) and *ser vagabundo conhecido* (for being a known vagrant). See APERJ, CD-DF 5626. There is no record of women entering the city jail for jogo do bicho infractions in this period.

117. References in arrest records to the offense of *selling* tickets routinely mentioned

the jogo do bicho (e.g., *por vender o jogo de bichos*) by 1896. In contrast, references to the offense of *playing* the jogo do bicho most often described the arrest generically as "for gambling" (e.g., *por jogar*); see, for example, APERJ, CD-DF 5626. The Penal Code of 1890 and federal law 2321 (1910) made both buying and selling unauthorized lottery or raffle tickets a crime; Ministério da Justiça, *Código Penal dos Estados Unidos do Brasil* (1890), 8.

118. AN, Índices Criminais, 11a Pretoria, Engenho Velho (1895–1912).

119. The summary arrest data on which these statistics are based do not indicate whether the defendant was arrested for playing or selling; AN, Índices Criminais.

120. Compare, for example, the number of individuals detained in APERJ, CD-DF-5626 and the number of cases in indicated in the AN, Índices Criminais.

121. *Annaes do Conselho Municipal*, (November 1917), 281. This reference to Barbosa with respect to the five-day naval revolt in 1910 (known as the Revolta da Cibata) was surely multifaceted. Barbosa took up the case of the rebelling naval recruits, fighting for their amnesty and an end to corporal punishment in the military.

122. Evidence here comes from the few extant judges' sentencing records (*Registros de Sentença*) and a broad survey of criminal cases (*processos crimes*) in Brazil's National Archive.

123. According to Campos, *Dicionário de curiosidades do Rio de Janeiro*, 147, the jogo do bicho's spread throughout Brazil occurred soon after the game began in the nation's capital.

124. Felipe Santos Magalhães's dissertation contains the best critical analysis of the jogo do bicho's origin myths; "Ganhou leva," chap. 3. See also Mello, "A história social dos jogos de azar no Rio de Janeiro, 1808–1946," 54–64.

125. See, for example, Saldanha, *O jogo do bicho*, 7–15; Gerson, *História das ruas do Rio*, 359; Cruz, *Vale o escrito*; Hahner, *Poverty and Politics*, 215; Zweig, *Brazil, Land of the Future*, 147; DaMatta and Soárez, *Águias, burros e borboletas*, 59.

126. Huggins, *From Slavery to Vagrancy in Brazil*, 55–108. See also Gusfield, "Moral Passage"; Addelson, *Moral Passages*.

127. Huggins, *From Slavery to Vagrancy in Brazil*, 78.

128. Gusfield, "Moral Passage"; Cunha, *Intenção e gesto*; Huggins, *From Slavery to Vagrancy in Brazil*, 55.

129. Quoted in Chasteen, "The Pre-History of Samba," 39.

130. Cooper, *The Brazilians and Their Country*, 262.

131. *Gazeta Operária* n. 16 (January 11, 1903), 2; the author would like to thank Pedro Tórtima for bringing this article to my attention. On antivice concerns within the anarchist movement, see Hahner, *Poverty and Politics*, 215.

132. AN, Série Justiça, IJ^6–617 (1916–"Diversas Autoridades").

2. THE RULES OF THE GAME

1. The existing data demonstrate a higher acquittal rate for the jogo do bicho than for other infractions. For example, approximately 40 percent of all processos initiated in the city of São Paulo between 1880 and 1924 ended in prosecution; Fausto, *Crime e cotidiano*, 260.

2. Cohen and Scull, "Introduction: Social Control in History and Sociology," in Cohen and Scull, eds., *Social Control and the State*, 8–9; Haagen, "Eighteenth-Century English Society and the Debt Law," in Cohen and Scull, eds., *Social Control and the State*, 222–47; Hay, "Property, Authority, and the Criminal Law," in Hay, Thompson, and Linebaugh, eds., *Albion's Fatal Tree*, 17–63.

3. Hay, Thompson, and Linebaugh, eds., *Albion's Fatal Tree*.

4. Haagen, "Eighteenth-Century English Society and the Debt Law," in Cohen and Scully, eds., *Social Control and the State*, 229.

5. Merry, "Legal Pluralism," 875; Cohen, "Law, Folklore, and Animal Lore," 7.

6. Sarat, "Legal Effectiveness and Social Studies of the Law," 26, 30. See also Ewick, Kagan, and Sarat, "Legacies of Legal Realism: Social Science, Social Policy, and the Law," in Ewick, Kagan, and Sarat, eds., *Social Science, Social Policy, and the Law*, 1–9.

7. Merry, "Legal Pluralism," 870.

8. Merry, "Legal Pluralism"; Santos, "The Law of the Oppressed." Michel Foucault also weighed in on legal pluralism in *Discipline and Punish*; on Foucault, see Merry, "Legal Pluralism," 888.

9. Merry, "Legal Pluralism," 873–74, 876.

10. In an essay from 1988 reviewing the literature on legal pluralism, Sally Engle Merry does acknowledge that "state law is itself plural"; "Legal Pluralism," 885, 890.

11. Cohen, "Law, Folklore, and Animal Lore," 35.

12. Maggie, *Medo do feitiço*; esp. chap. 4.

13. Cohen, "Law, Folklore, and Animal Lore," 10.

14. Rosenn, "Brazil's Legal Culture," 7–8, 13–14. See also the anthropological and sociological literature on the *jeito* in Brazil (or the *jeitinho brasileiro*), a term that refers to a special talent for getting around rules; Souza, *A experiência da lei, a lei da experiência*, 83–136; Barbosa, *O jeitinho brasileiro*.

15. The social history of criminality in urban, republican Brazil has focused on violent crime; see, for example, Fausto, *Crime e cotidiano*. Sidney Chalhoub uses vagrancy cases in his influential study but derives his analysis primarily from violent crime cases; *Trabalho, lar, e botequim*. Notable exceptions include Mattos, "Vadios, jogadores," and Adamo, "The Broken Promise," chap. 4.

16. Bronfman, *Measures of Equality*, 26.

17. Rosenn, "Brazil's Legal Culture," 8–9, 12; Faoro, *Os donos do poder*.

18. Cf. Cohen and Scull, "Introduction," 9; Haagen, "Eighteenth-Century English Society and the Debt Law," in Cohen and Scull, eds., *Social Control and the State*, 222–47.

19. Salvatore, "State Legal Order and Subaltern Rights."

20. In studying the onset of Western modernity, Max Weber likewise distinguishes between the formal/rational and substantive aspects of the law; *Economy and Society*; H. T. Wilson, "Rationality and Capitalism." The phenomenon of legalization described here approximates Foucault's concept of normalization. Foucault suggests that the hierarchical, nonegalitarian "systems of micropower called the

disciplines" do not exist despite the formal equality of the law; rather, they supported the "general juridical form that guaranteed a system of rights that were egalitarian in principle"; *Discipline and Punish*, chap. 3.

21. Thompson made a similar observation in *Whigs and Hunters*. See Benton, *Law and Colonial Cultures*, 256. On legalism in contemporary Brazil, see Rosenn, "Brazil's Legal Culture," 20.

22. On a similar phenomenon in a later period, see Pereira, *Political (In)justice.*

23. The quotation can be found in AN, SDJ, Tribunal Civil e Criminal, 5ª Pretoria Criminal. Am 208 D 8890 (cd: 70), Registro de Sentenças—Crimes, 1909–1912, folha 149.

24. The classic works on the distinction between house (*casa*) and street (*rua*) in Brazilian culture are DaMatta, *A casa e a rua*; and Freyre, *Sobrados e mucambos.* See also Beattie, *Tribute of Blood*; Lauderdale Graham, *House and Street.* This principle was reaffirmed in the authoritative commentaries of the jurist Nelson Hungria on the Penal Code of 1940, *Comentários ao Código Penal*, 208.

25. Soihet, *Condição feminina*, 141–245; Overmyer-Velázquez, *Visions of the Emerald City*, 104.

26. This distinction between private and public, and between skill and luck, remains the primary way of differentiating licit and illicit gambling; França, *Enciclopédia Saraiva do Direito*, 346, 350. Cf. Chambers, "Crime and Citizenship," in Aguirre and Buffington, *Reconstructing Criminality in Latin America*, 31–32.

27. The honor of the family patriarch was at stake in the state's obligation to respect the inviolability of the home; Beattie, *Tribute of Blood*, 8–9. On nineteenth-century liberalism in Brazil, see Peixoto et al., eds., *O liberalismo no Brasil imperial.*

28. Guy, "Parents Before the Tribunals." On patriarchy and the home's designation as an inviolable sanctuary, see Chambers, "Private Crimes, Public Order: Honor," in Caulfield, Chambers, and Putnam, eds., *Honor, Status, and the Law*, 28–48; quotation is from 31.

29. Beattie, *Tribute of Blood*, 9; Carvalho, *Os bestializados*, 126–39.

30. Chambers, "Private Crimes, Public Order," 28.

31. Hochman, *A era do saneamento*; Rago, *Do cabaré ao lar*, 172–75; Needell, "The 'Revolta contra Vacina' of 1904."

32. AGCRJ, códice 45-2-42, folhas 4, 5, 7. See also Abreu, *O império do divino*, 216–19, 267–68. "Brothels and gambling joints" were clustered together in the same neighborhoods in nineteenth-century São Paulo; Dias, *Power and Everyday Life*, 135. The nineteenth-century naval code (*Artigos da Guerra*) punished gambling and drunkenness; Morgan, "Legacy of the Lash," 59–60.

33. Pereira de Mello, "A história social dos jogos de azar no Rio de Janeiro," 10–14.

34. AGCRJ, códice 45-2-42, folhas 7–9.

35. See, for example, AGCRJ, códice 45-2-42, folhas 10–12; and 45-2-47, folhas 1–3.

36. Those laws include (but are not limited to) article 281 of the Criminal Code of 1830 and colonial legislation passed on January 25, 1677; October 29, 1696; May 24, 1696; and August 6, 1770; AGCRJ, códice 45-2-42, folha 7.

37. See AN, T8-2347, Varas Criminais, 16ª Delegacia, 1907; Pechman, "Os excluídos

da rua," in Bresciani, ed., *Imagens da cidade*, 29–30. AN, T8–2347, Varas Criminais, 16ª Delegacia, 1907.

38. Rago, *Do cabaré ao lar*, 166.

39. Lauderdale Graham, "Making the Private Public," 30.

40. On *cortiços*, see Chalhoub, *Cidade febril*; Azevedo, *O cortiço*. On popular culture and nonelite sociability in republican Rio, see Carvalho, *Os bestializados*, 38–41; Abreu, *O Império do divino*; Sevcenko, ed., *História da vida privada no Brasil*, 3:132–213. On urban slavery in nineteenth-century Rio, see Karasch, *Slave Life in Rio de Janeiro, 1808–1850*; Mattoso, *To Be a Slave in Brazil*; Soares, *Devotos da cor*.

41. Zea, *Positivism in Mexico*; Raat, "Leopoldo Zea and Mexican Positivism"; Hughes, *Consciousness and Society*, 33–66.

42. Tórtima, *Crime e castigo*, 46; Salvatore, "Penitentiaries, Visions of Class, and Export Economies," in Salvatore and Aguirre, eds., *The Birth of the Penitentiary in Latin America*, 208–17.

43. Nesvig, "The Lure of the Perverse," 3; da Cunha, *Intenção e gesto*.

44. Nesvig, "The Lure of the Perverse," 4–5; Green, *Beyond Carnival*, 119–21. On positivist criminology in Brazil, see Tórtima, *Crime e castigo*.

45. Caulfield, *In Defense of Honor*, 17–47.

46. Diacon, *Stringing Together a Nation*.

47. Corrêa, *As ilusões da liberdade*, 15. See generally Salvatore, Aguirre, and Joseph, eds., *Crime and Punishment in Latin America*.

48. Bretas, *A guerra das ruas*, 31; Holloway, *Policing Rio de Janeiro*; Nachman, "Positivism, Modernization, and the Middle Class in Brazil," 7.

49. AN, SDJ, Tribunal Civil e Criminal, 5a Pretoria Criminal. Am 208 D 8890 (cd: 70), Registro de Sentenças—Crimes, 1909–1912, folha 149.

50. Where questions of patriarchal authority and female honor were concerned, though, the criminal law tended to act more like civil (or private) law; see Corrêa, *Morte em família*; Chambers, "Private Crimes, Public Order," 37–40.

51. Rosenn, "Brazil's Legal Culture," 20.

52. *A obra de Ruy Barbosa em criminologia e direito criminal*, 210–11.

53. Merryman, *The Civil Law Tradition*; Rosenn, "Brazil's Legal Culture," 20.

54. The Code of Criminal Procedure of 1832 followed the Criminal Code of 1830. On the Civil Code of 1917, see Grinberg, "Slavery, Liberalism, and Civil Law," in Caulfield, Chambers, and Putnam, *Honor, Status, and the Law in Modern Latin America*, 109–27.

55. Records of the provisional government's discussions in 1890 are found in Dunshee de Abranches, *Atas e Actos do Governo Provisório*.

56. The Penal Code was promulgated as Decreto 847 on October 11, 1890, by the Ministry of Justice, overseen by Generalíssimo Manoel Deodoro da Fonseca, head of the provisional government; *Código Penal*, Casa de Rui Barbosa.

57. Silva, *O salão dos passos perdidos*, 226n1.

58. Little has been written on the Penal Code of 1890. Exceptions include Caulfield, *In Defense of Honor*, 17–47; Borges, "Healing and Mischief," in Salvatore, Aguirre, and Joseph, eds., *Crime and Punishment in Latin America*, 181–210. On the

authorship of the Penal Code, see also the commentary in Galdino Siqueira, *Código penal.*

59. Silva, *Direito ou Punição?*, 4; *Código Penal e Legislação Complementar*, 1–3. Cf. Rodrigues, "The Idea of Responsibility."

60. Positivist, as opposed to classical, criminology held that one's physical aspect is the mirror of the soul, reflecting levels of virtue or vice; Schwarcz, *O espécáculo das raças*, 166. On racialist thinking in Brazilian criminal anthropology, see Rodrigues, *Os Africanos no Brasil.* See also Peard, *Race, Place, and Medicine*, 102–6; Skidmore, *Black into White*, 57–64; Salvatore, "Penitentiaries, Visions of Class, and Export Economies," in Salvatore and Aguirre, *The Birth of the Penitentiary in Latin America.* On judicial discrimination against dark-skinned Brazilians, see Chalhoub, *Trabalho, lar, e botequim*, 76; Adamo, "The Broken Promise," 196, 198, 201. In the First Republic, relatively few people identified as being black (*negro*) or dark-skinned (*pardo*) were arrested for the jogo do bicho in comparison to other types of crimes and misdemeanors, especially vagrancy. For data on skin color of persons arrested in Rio, see APERJ, Série CD.

61. Rodrigues, "The Idea of Responsibility." See generally Adelman, *Republic of Capital*, 165–90; Parker, "Law, Honor, and Impunity in Spanish America," 331–41.

62. A new Penal Code was enacted in 1940. See da Silva, *Direito ou Punição?*, 36–52; Ribeiro, *Cor e criminalidade*, 14–15.

63. Soares, *A negrada instuição*; Bretas, *A Guerra das ruas*; Carvalho, *Os bestializados*; and Santos, "A prisão dos ébrios," 139. For evidence of the Brazilian leadership's increased concern with petty crimes in the First Republic compared with the Empire, see the arrest figures that Thomas H. Holloway published concerning the numbers of persons arrested by military police in 1871. Only 7 of the 171 arrested in a five-month period were for vagrancy, a figure strikingly lower than any for the Republic; "A Healthy Terror," 657.

64. *Relatório* (1889), 11–12, 19–21.

65. On the Criminal Code of 1830, see Ramos, *O Indicador Penal.* For a legal definition of *contravenção*, see Naufel, *Novo Dicionário Jurídico Brasileiro*, Vol. II, 110.

66. Ministério da Justiça, *Código Penal*, 8 (art. 70).

67. The most frequently cited example is *capoeiragem*, a martial art of Afro-Brazilian origin; see Soares, *A capoeira escrava e outras tradições rebeldes no Rio de Janeiro, 1808–1850.* See also Borges, "Healing and Mischief," in Salvatore, Aguirre, and Joseph, eds., *Crime and Punishment in Latin America*, 181–210.

68. Araujo, *O Código Penal interpretado*; Von Liszt, *O Brasil na Legislação Comparada*, 64; Viveiros de Castro, *Jurisprudência criminal*, 1–14. According to Boris Fausto, 77.5 percent of all arrests in the city of São Paulo in 1892–96 were for contravenções as compared with 22.5 percent for crimes; in 1912–16, 85.6 percernt of all arrests were for contravenções; *Crime e cotidiano*, 45.

69. *Código Penal*, 340.

70. *Código Penal e Legislação Complementar*, 1–3.

71. The law referred to here is Decreto 628 de 28 de outrubro de 1899. See Santos, "A prisão dos ébrios," 147, 151. Cf. Aguirre, *Criminals of Lima*, 128–32.

72. Articles 399 and 400 of the Penal Code of 1890 define vagrancy and specify the penalty for breaking the *Termo de Bem Viver*, respectively. New measures put into effect as part of the police reform in 1907 stipulated that individuals convicted of vagrancy, after serving their sentences, would be handed a document obliging them to "take an occupation" within a specified amount of time; *Actos do poder executivo*, 750. For an example of how authorities actually utilized Termos de Bem Viver, see Senna, *Através do Carcere*, 10.

73. Figueiredo, *A contravenção de vadiagem*.

74. Santos, "A prisão dos ébrios," 160–61.

75. For an early debate on the status of the jogo do bicho, see *Relatórios do Conselho Municipal*, April 1896, 170–71.

76. Mello, "A história social dos jogos de azar," xn2.

77. See, for example, Cooper, *Brazilians and Their Country*, 262.

78. *Código Penal da República dos Estados Unidos do Brasil* (1892), 235–36. The figure 200$000 signifies two hundred milreis, or US$52 in 1892. This exchange rate of 3.82 milreis to the dollar is the annual average of the month-end closing quotations; Global Financial Data; http://www.globalfinancialdata.com. I am grateful to Gail Triner for sharing this currency conversion data with me.

79. See, for example, Decreto 6994 of April 16, 1908.

80. See Article 3, 1 Decreto 628, October 8, 1899.

81. AGCRJ, códice 45–4-23, folha 58.

82. In *Whigs and Hunters*, Thompson makes a similar argument regarding the application of the Black Act; 219–69.

83. For example, in the parish of Engenho Velho (11th Precinct), the following numbers of individuals were arrested under article 367 of the Penal Code from 1895 to 1912: 1895, 2; 1898, 2; 1899, 10; 1900, 11; 1901, 11; 1902, 6; 1903, 28; 1904, 41; 1905, 30; 1906, 17; 1907, 31; 1908, 30; 1909, 2; 1910, 10; 1911, 16. AN, Instrumento de Pesquisa: Índices Criminais, T-8.

84. Individuals may have been arrested prior to 1895, but the cases currently accessible at the National Archive extend only to that year.

85. Tórtima, *Crime e castigo*, 131.

86. Bretas, *A guerra das ruas*, 63–70. On the Empire, see Holloway, *Policing Rio de Janeiro*; Chalhoub, *Trabalho, lar, e botequim*. See generally Greenberg, ed., *Crime and Capitalism*, 482, 553–54.

87. The Colônia Correcional de Dois Rios on Ilha Grande functioned for two years before being closed for not fulfilling its objectives. It reopened in 1903 and in 1907 was judged inadequate and completely reorganized. Santos, "A prisão dos ébrios," 138; *Relatório* (1889), 19. The law stipulated fines or "prisão celular" or both for jogo do bicho infractions, which signified imprisonment in the Federal District's House of Correction. Prisoners charged with violating antigambling laws generally served out their terms in the detention center or were sent to the House of Correction instead of Dois Rios in the 1890s through the 1920s.

88. APERJ, Série CD. See also Soares, *A negrada instuição*; Bretas, *A Guerra das ruas*; Carvalho, *Os bestializados*; and Santos, "A prisão dos ébrios," 139.

89. Out of a sample of 460 judicial sentences from the manuscript sentencing records of selected trial court judges in the Federal District of Rio de Janeiro from 1906 to 1917, only 4 out of 26 cases of people accused of jogo do bicho offenses were convicted (an acquittal rate of approximately 87 percent). As a point of comparison, of the 350 vagrancy cases taken from this same sample, 107 were found guilty and 243 were acquitted (an acquittal rate of approximately 69 percent); AN, Tribunal Civil e Criminal. 5a Pretoria Criminal, Am 208 D 8898, "Registro de Sentenças—Crimes,1. 4, 1909–1912"; Registro de Sentenças Criminais 1907–1909. 5a Pretoria, Am 208 D8872.

90. Positivism's emphasis on individualized sentencing also likely encouraged judicial discretion.

91. I use the masculine pronoun advisedly; Brazilian judges during the period this book covers were all men.

92. Based on the cases analyzed here (ranging from 1909 to 1917), the reasons for acquitting the accused appear to have remained consistent over time and from judge to judge; AN, Registros de Sentença, Tribunal Civil e Criminal, 5a Pretoria Criminal, Am 208 D 8898.

93. The police reform law was Decreto 6440 of March 30, 1907. See also da Cunha, "Os domínios da experiência, da ciência e da lei"; Neder, Naro, and Silva, A polícia na Corte e no Distrito Federal, 235–36.

94. Bretas, A guerra das ruas, 53–60; the quotation is from page 53. The number of police varied and occasionally decreased due to budgetary crises, before reaching a high in 1905 (58 per ten thousand residents); ibid., 48.

95. Bretas, A guerra das ruas, 63–70. See, for example, AN, Serie Justiça—Policia IJ⁶-657, "Casa de Detenção-1918."

96. Da Cunha, Intenção e gesto.

97. Mattos, "Vadios, jogadores, mendigos e bêbados," 104; Bretas, "Daily Work in Rio de Janeiro Police Stations in the Early Twentieth Century," 10–11; Bretas, "O informal no formal"; Chalhoub, Trabalho, lar, e botequim, 28–37.

98. In 1918 police admitted 298 alleged beggars to the Casa de Detenção, all "in extreme misery" and needing medical assistance; Relatório (1918–1919), 94.

99. Piccato, City of Suspects, 41–45; Overmyer-Velázquez, Visions of the Emerald City, 64.

100. APERJ, CD-5628.

101. See, for example, Ministério da Justiça, Decreto n. 847 de 11–10–1890. As the city jail's entry logs' narrative descriptions of the reasons for arrest in the 1890s and early 1900s gave way to more objective, legalistic citations of specific laws, this practice of arresting someone for "being a known thief" or "being a known bicheiro" disappeared from the written record. However, police continued to use the informal and unsubstantiated knowledge of a criminal suspect's state of being throughout the period studied.

102. AN, OR.0822.

103. See, for example, Carradore, Folclore do jogo do bicho, 23; Cavalcante, Os bicheiros. Anonymous denunciations of police involvement in vice in Rio de Janeiro (ca.

1913) can be found in AN, GIFI 6C-424. For legislative debate on the question of police corruption in overseeing both legal and illegal gambling, see *Annaes do Conselho*, September 1897, 43–44.

104. AN, T8–2543.

105. "Para o 'bem do moral social': O Bicho," *Gazeta Operária*, n. 16 (Rio de Janeiro: 11 de janeiro de 1903), 2. I am grateful to Pedro Tórtima for bringing this article to my attention.

106. All references to the seized furniture in *casas de tavolagem* come from AN, Gifi 6C-30, "Papeis sobre moveis apprehendidos em casas de jogo."

107. Cohen, "Law, Folklore, and Animal Lore."

3. AN UNDERWORLD OF GOODS

The source of the epigraph is *Boletim da Intendência*, July / September 1903, 32–33; quoted in Benchimol, *Pereira Passos*, 277–78.

1. AN, Delegacia do 140 Distrito Policial (n. 626, Maço 2153, Galeria A, Seção de Guarda SDJ).

2. See Lobo, Carvalho, and Stanley, *Questão habitacional e o movimento operário*; Benchimol, *Pereira Passos*, 286–94.

3. Moura, *Tia Ciata e a Pequena África no Rio de Janeiro*. At the time of Bahia's arrest, criminal processos generally did not note defendants' skin color or ethnicity.

4. See, for example, Benchimol, *Pereira Passos*, 281.

5. Police arrested Bahia holding "*mil e cem reis*," or 1$100 (1.1 milreis), the equivalent of 30 cents at the average 1917 milreis / U.S. dollar exchange rate of 3.65; Global Financial Data (http://www.globalfinancialdata.com).

6. What I translate as "a small amount of change" in the original reads "*dez tostões*." A *tostão* is a nickel coin from the colonial era worth 10 reis. Although no longer in use, its name remained as slang for a small amount of money. The witness in this case probably refers to the amount of 10 reis. (When Bahia was arrested he was carrying just 1.1 milreis, so the amount that one bettor would have given him probably would have been small.) It seems questionable that a witness could have actually seen the precise amount of money handed over to Bahia.

7. Cf. Overmyer-Velázquez, *Visions of the Emerald City*, 67–69.

8. *O Rio de Janeiro do meu tempo*, 63; cited in Benchimol, *Pereira Passos*, 281.

9. Benchimol, *Pereira Passos*, 277–85.

10. Dias, *Power and Everyday Life*, 139.

11. Freire, *Uma capital para a República*, 108–9; Bretas, *A guerra das ruas*, 68.

12. Mello, "A história social dos jogos de azar no Rio de Janeiro, 1808–1946," 87. Other examples of legally ambiguous petty commerce include prostitution and the unlicensed selling of legal goods.

13. Carvalho, *Os bestializados*, 17–19.

14. Benchimol, *Pereira Passos*, 235–85. See also Bluestone, "'The Pushcart Evil'" 68–93.

15. As the Imperial capital, the port of Rio had served mainly to transship coffee from

the Paraiba Valley. In the late Empire, the port's function began to change as the market for imported consumer goods gradually supplanted waning coffee exports; Benchimol, *Pereira Passos*, 219.

16. AGCRJ, códices 58–3-38 and 58–3-35.

17. Coaracy, *Memórias da Cidade do Rio de Janeiro*, 3:187–211.

18. *Feiras e Mafuás*, 22. See also Sampião, *O Brazil mental*.

19. Sevchenko, *Literatura como missão*; Figueiredo, *Lima Barreto e o fim do sonho republicano*; Sergio Buarque de Holanda, preface to Lima Barreto, *Clara dos Anjos e outro contos*, 2d ed.; Abreu, *O império do divino*, 333–34.

20. AGCRJ, códices 58–3-32, 58–3-33, 58–3-34, and 58–3-35.

21. Renato Pinto Venâcio and Júnia Ferreira Furtado, "Comerciantes, tratantes, e mascates," in Del Priore, ed., *Revisão do Paraíso*, 95–113.

22. AGCRJ, códice 45–4-23, folhas 93–96.

23. See, for example, AGCRJ, códices 45–4-23, 45–4-20, 45–4-21.

24. AGCRJ, códice 61–4-45, folha 366; códice 45–4-21. See also Queiroz, *Os Radicais da República*.

25. AGCRJ, códice 39–4-5, folha 39 and códice 34–9-6, folhas 1–30. See also Lima Barreto, *Vidas urbanas*, 110–11.

26. Freire, *Uma capital para a República*, 108–18.

27. "Comercio em Flagrante!" *Fon Fon* (June 9, 1915), np.

28. *Código de Polícia Municipal da Cidade do Rio de Janeiro, Posturas Municipais* (September 1898), 99–101; AGCRJ, códices 61–1-25, 6–1-19A; Lima Barreto, *Feiras e Mafuás*, 26. On at least one occasion, a group of small farmers from the outskirts of the city also requested permission to build a public market; AGCRJ, códice 61–1-24, folha 43.

29. AGCRJ, códice 61–1-25.

30. AGCRJ, códices 61–1-19A-2 and 58–3-39, folha 49.

31. See AGCRJ, códices 61–1-19A, 6–1-19A2, 61–1-24. Cf. Sullivan, *Markets for the People*.

32. In 1890 approximately 30 percent of Rio's population was foreign, of which about 70 percent were Portuguese; Mattos, "Vadios, jogadores, mendigos e bêbados na cidade do Rio de Janeiro do início do século," 21.

33. Carvalho, *Os bestializados*, 21; Lobo, *A história do Rio de Janeiro*, 509.

34. Chalhoub, *Trabalho, lar, e botequim*, 114. A paradigmatic example of the exploitative Portuguese shopkeeper and slumlord is the character João Romão in Aluísio Azevedo's naturalist novel *O Cortiço*. See also Evaristo de Morais, *Reminiscencias de um Rábula Criminalista*, 15.

35. AGCRJ, códice 53–3-39.

36. Benchimol, *Pereira Passos*, 138, 283–84.

37. Meade, *"Civilizing" Rio*, 55–56. See also Faria, *Mauá*, 122.

38. Pechman, "Os excluídos da rua: Ordem urbana e cultura popular," in Stella Bresciani, ed., *Imagens da cidade*, 30–34.

39. Meade, *"Civilizing" Rio*.

40. Evidence of small sellers' awareness of these shifting power dynamics can be found in the petitions and administrative correspondence between these small entrepreneurs and the city government; see, for example, AGCRJ, códice 44–4-5.

41. Even unlicensed sellers fought government attempts to remove them from the sites where they sold their goods, appealing to their customary rights; see, for example, AGCRJ, códice 61–4-45, folha 36; 58–3-39, folha 34. For the earlier nineteenth century, see códice 58–3-33.

42. AGCRJ, códices 43–3-48, 61–1-24, 45–4-23.

43. AGCRJ, códice 61–4-45, folha 36. See also Holston, "The Misrule of Law."

44. AN, Secretaria da Polícia do Distrito Federal—233; AN, GIFI 6C-317. See also APERJ, CD-6323.

45. See, for example, AGCRJ, códice 49–4-5. For a retail vendor charged with falsifying licenses for commercial establishments; AN, GIFI-233.

46. Rosa, *Rio de Janeiro*, 238.

47. Lobo, *História do Rio de Janeiro*, 501–2.

48. Rosa, *Rio de Janeiro*, 238.

49. AGCRJ, códice 61–1-16, folha 2.

50. AGCRJ, códice 61–1-15.

51. *Anais da Câmara, índice janeiro—fevereiro* (1896), n/p. For licensing fees for the year 1917, see *Anais do Conselho Municipal* (1917), np.

52. AGCRJ, códice 61–1-15, folha 12.

53. AGCRJ, códice 61–1-16, folha 16.

54. AGCRJ, códices 61–1-16, 61–1-15; these documents cover 1900–1908.

55. On Rio's local consumer market, see Levy, *História da Bolsa de Valores do Rio de Janeiro*, 39–42.

56. Although a municipal law (Decreto 372) on January 9, 1903, banned street peddlers who sold lottery tickets in the Federal District, the practice continued; Benchimol, *Pereira Passos*, 279. On street peddlers as urban folkloric characters, see Barros and Buenrostro, *Las once y serenoooo!*.

57. *A alma encantadora das ruas*, 6–7.

58. The French traveler Gustave Aimard observes a hierarchy of street vendors in 1888, with shop owners at the top and *quitandeiras* (women in the street who sold mostly produce) from Minas and Bahia at the bottom; *Le Brésil Nouveau*, 131. Prostitutes, not mentioned here, deserve further analysis as part of Rio's street commerce.

59. Benchimol, *Pereira Passos*, 282–85. See also Stein, *Vassouras*, 85–90; Del Priore, "Comerciantes, tratantes, e mascates," 107–108; Ahr, "Peddlers and Politics in the Second French Republic."

60. Vila Rica in 1804, a town of 8,867 inhabitants, had 38 *comerciantes de tabuleiro*, of whom 36 were women, 40 percent slave and 60 percent free; Del Priore, "Comerciantes, trantantes, e mascates," 107.

61. AGCRJ, códice 58–3-38, folha 15, 17, 19, 20.

62. AGCRJ, códice 58–3-38; see documents pertaining to August 1861.

63. See, for example, AGCRJ, códice 49–4-5.

64. AGCRJ, códice 45–4-19, folha 118–34.

65. AGCRJ, códice 61–1-25, folhas 121, 123.

66. Hilária Batista de Almeida, known as Tia (Aunt) Ciata and acknowledged as a pivotal figure in the development of Afro-Brazilian culture and music in the Federal District, was part of this mass migration from Bahia to Rio in the late nineteenth century. She joined the city's budding informal economy as a seller of sweets and other items both on the street and at occasional religious festivals; Moura, *Tia Ciata*.

67. Chalhoub, *Trabalho, lar, e botequim*, 37; Gomes, *A invenção do trabalhismo*, 10; Silva, *Negro na Rua*.

68. República dos Estados Unidos do Brasil, *Recenseamento do Rio de Janeiro (Districto Federal), realizado em 20 de setembro de 1906*, 152. See also Benchimol, *Pereira Passos*, 280–85.

69. Henriqueta Costa appears to have earned her freedom only with abolition.

70. Umbelina de Mattos, interview with author (Rio de Janeiro, June 30, 1999).

71. Dias, *Power and Everyday Life*; Silva, *Prince of the People*, 42–49, 60; Engel, *Meretrizes e doutores*; Moura, *Tia Ciata*.

72. Mattos, "Vadios, jogadores, mendigos e bêbados na cidade do Rio de Janeiro do início do século," 21.

73. Lesser, *Negotiating National Identity*, 50–51. See also Geertz, "Suq: The Bazaar Economy in Sefrou," in Geertz, Geertz, and Rosen, eds., *Meaning and Order in Moroccan Society*, 142–43.

74. Clifford Geertz describes the cultural complexity of the bazaar in Sefrou, Morocco, explaining that it is "often called a mosaic pattern of social organization—differently shaped and colored chips jammed in irregularly together to generate overall design within which their distinctiveness remains nonetheless intact"; "Suq: The Bazaar Economy in Sefrou," in Geertz, Geertz, and Rosen, eds., *Meaning and Order in Moroccan Society*, 141.

75. Pompéia, *Crônicas do Rio*, 40–41.

76. Gerson, *História das Ruas do Rio*, 33.

77. Chalhoub, *Trabalho, lar, e botequim*, 104–5; Benchimol, *Pereira Passos*, 280–81.

78. Baronov, *The Abolition of Slavery in Brazil*.

79. See, for example, AN, Série Justiça—IJ[6]–599.

80. Cope, "Between Liberty and Constraint." See also Stallybrass and White, *The Politics and Poetics of Transgression*, 27–79.

81. Some examples include AGCRJ, códice 45–4-23, folhas 105–9. See also Carone, *Movimento Operário no Brasil, 1877–1940*, 15; O'Malley, "Specie and Species," 369–95, Painter; "Thinking About the Languages of Money and Race," 396–403; O'Malley, "Response to Nell Irvin Painter," 405–8; Blackburn, *The Making of New World Slavery*, 15.

82. AGCRJ, códice 58–3-38, folha 6.

83. See for example AGCRJ, códice 58–3-38, folhas 1–27.

84. AGCRJ, códice 45–4-21, folhas 161–64.

85. See, for example, AGCRJ, códice 45–4-21, folha 107. In 1891 the city stipulated that

kiosks be illuminated at night; they were allowed to sell newspapers, books, bulletins, flowers, sweets, fruits, cheeses, cigars, cigarettes, small items, coffee, soft drinks, and lottery tickets; they were not allowed to sell footwear, clothing, or haberdashery; AGCRJ, códice 45–4-22, folha 109; AGCRJ, códice 45–4-21, folhas 1–13.

86. AGCRJ, códice 45–2-22, folhas 37–38.

87. AGCRJ, códices 45–4-19 to 45–4-33. Barreto, *Vidas urbanas*, 77.

88. AGCRJ, códice 45–4-23, folha 90.

89. AGCRJ, códice 45–4-33.

90. 2:2 (February 2, 1905), np. Raul Pompéia likewise commented that the rua do Ouvidor was exclusively an elite space; *Crônicas do Rio*, 40–41. See also Kelsey, *Brazil in Capitals*, 13; Castro, *Le Brésil Vivant*, 47–53; Bilac and Bomfim, *Através do Brasil*, 314–315.

91. DaMatta, *Águias, burros, e borboletas*, 66–67. Zevada's nationality, name, and precise role in the spread of the jogo do bicho are far from substantiated in the documentary record. Even if he were a fictionalized or composite figure, popular imagination embraces unquestioningly the idea that the clandestine, underworld jogo do bicho emanated from the *haute monde* of the rua do Ouvidor. On the Confetaria Colombo, see Tigre, *Reminiscências*. For a police investigation of an alleged jogo do bicho operation on the rua do Ouvidor, see AN, IJ[6]–625.

92. Similarly, see works on urban types in early twentieth-century Rio; Barbosa, *Na prisão*; Reis, *Os Ladrões no Rio*.

93. Mello, "A história social dos jogos de azar no Rio de Janeiro, 1808–1946," 215–55. The exception was the Third Precinct, which did have five "Jogos de Salão" that operated illicitly within legal casinos on the busy streets of the commercial and entertainment district.

94. APERJ, IML 1913 (0073), Exame de idade e discernimento. The Penal Code of 1890 established a legal age of nine years for penal responsibility for both crimes and contravenções; Benácchio, "Meninos vadios."

95. Of the 230 cases of men detained for gambling offenses surveyed, 92 are listed as *comerciante*, another 10 as *negociante*, 1 as street peddler (*vendedor ambulante*), and 3 as (probably lottery) ticket seller (*vendedor de bilhetes*); APERJ, série CDDF.

96. The census for 1906 contains detailed data about the distribution of professions among Rio's inhabitants but clusters all foreigners together; República dos Estados Unidos do Brasil, *Recenseamento do Rio de Janeiro*.

97. APERJ, CD-5626 and CD-5628.

98. The judge ultimately acquitted this defendant; AN, Notação OR. 1033.

99. AN, T8.1677.

100. AN, T8.3077.

101. AN, T8.3074.

102. Chalhoub, *Trabalho, lar, e botequim*, 103–5, 114.

103. Cited in Mello, "A história social dos jogos de azar," 13.

104. Mello, "A história social dos jogos de azar," 13–14.

105. See APERJ, Código de Polícia Municipal da Cidade do Rio de Janeiro, Posturas

Municipais, (September 1898); article 235 stipulates that a person operating as a vendedor ambulante (street peddler) without the proper license will be fined and the items confiscated.

106. Chaves was first asked to pay 1:500 (1 conto and 500 milreis) in bail, which was reduced to 500 milreis, but only after he spent "almost three days detained in the police precinct." Chaves was later acquitted. Witnesses in this case give the name of the street where Chaves was arrested variously as "rua São Francisco do Xavier" and "rua São Francisco de Xavier," which appear to be misrenderings of the street São Francisco Xavier; AN, T8–2437.

107. AN, T8–2478.

108. See, for example, AN, SDJ, OR.2915. I would like to thank James N. Green and William Martins for bringing this case to my attention.

109. AN, Série Justiça, IJ⁶—645, 1a seção. See chap. 4 for discussion of the Club dos Excentricos.

110. AN, Série Justiça, IJ⁶—617 (Delegacias Auxiliares, 1a Sec. 1–6/1917).

111. I am borrowing Gavin Smith's ironic use of the term *idiosyncratic* to describe the informal sector; "Towards an Ethnography of Idiosyncratic Forms of Livelihood," 71–87.

112. On gambling as vice, see Soares, *O Jogo do Bicho*; Abreu, *O Submundo do Jogo de Azar, Prostituição e Vadiagem*. DaMatta and Soárez sought to revise the predominant view of the jogo do bicho as crime but barely touched on its relationship to petty commerce; *Águias, burros, e borborletas*.

113. João do Rio, *A alma encantadora das ruas;* on the cries of vendedores ambulantes on tramway platforms, see 43; on *músicos ambulantes,* see 65; on the appearance of *camelôts,* see 174.

114. João do Rio, *A alma encantadora das ruas,* 23–28.

4. PLAYING WITH MONEY

1. See for example AN, 140 Distrito Policial, n. 626, maço 2153, Galeria A (October 1917). The monetary unit during the Empire and the First Republic was the milréis (instead of the *real,* or "royal," the monetary unit during the colonial era). See Gomes and Kornis, "Com a história no bolso: moeda e a República no Brasil," in Museu Histórico Nacional, *O Outro lado da moeda,* 115–18; Oakenfull, *Brazil (1913),* 564–65.

2. Tannuri, *O Encilhamento,* 51. See also Romero, *A obra do Sílvio Romero,* 130. Financial speculators at the time of the Encilhamento invested primarily in securities but also in urban real estate, foreign currency, and export commodities. Although frequently mentioned in passing in works of Brazilian history, the so-called speculation fever of the early First Republic has received little sustained analysis, especially with regard to its cultural reverberations. For works of economic history that touch on the Encilhamento, see Levy, *A história da bolsa de valores;* Lobo, *História do Rio de Janeiro,* 445–69; Linhares, ed., *História geral do Brasil,* 186; Faoro, *Os donos do poder,* 509–10.

3. Taunay, *O Encilhamento,* 15.

4. The Ministry of the Treasury passed a law on January 17, 1890, that provided for the establishment of several emission banks. The Banco do Brasil dates from 1808 and is the "first Brazilian credit establishment"; Departamento Editorial das Edições Melhoramentos, *Novo Dicionário de História do Brasil Ilustrado*, 73, 241.

5. Morais, *Reminiscencias de um Rábula Criminalista*, 15. On Antonio Evaristo de Morais, see Hahner, *Poverty and Politics*, 282–84.

6. In the Portuguese original, Taunay uses the word *zangões*, which can be translated as "middlemen," as I do here, or as "runners." Taunay's *corretores* is translated here as "brokers."

7. Taunay, *O Encilhamento* 15–16.

8. Taunay (1843–1899), a monarchist and critic of the republican regime, served as a military officer and the head of two Brazilian provinces during the Empire and sat on the Brazilian Academy of Letters. He published at least twenty-one works of both fiction and nonfiction; Departamento Editorial das Edições Melhoramentos, *Novo Dicionário de História do Brasil*, 569. Although ostensibly a novel, *O Encilhamento* is populated by thinly fictionalized Carioca businessmen and politicians.

9. Levy, *História da Bolsa de Valores do Rio de Janeiro*.

10. Sevcenko, *História da vida privada no Brasil*, 15; Departamento Editorial das Edições Melhormaentos, *Novo Dicionário de História do Brasil*, 241; Topik, *The Political Economy of the Brazilian State, 1889–1930*, 18–19.

11. Lobo, *A história do Rio de Janeiro*, 458.

12. Sevcenko, *História da vida privada no Brasil*, 15.

13. Quoted in ibid., 619.

14. Fabian, *Card Sharps, Dream Books, and Bucket Shops*; Levy, "Contemplating Delivery." Arthur Azevedo also used the Encilhamento to condemn popular gambling; Mencarelli, *Cena aberta*, 242. Azevedo lost all of his money in companies that failed because of the Encilhamento; Mencarelli, *Cena aberta*, 46–47.

15. D'Almeida, *Lucros e perdas*, 24. Almeida expresses no moral opposition to gambling. He lauds the presence of horse racing in the city as "a victory of active progress" in his poem of 1924 "Hail, Linneo," addressed to Linneo Machado, then president of the Jockey Club; 46. See also Pompéia, *Crônicas do Rio*, 48; Gerson, *História das Ruas do Rio*, 361–63.

16. Brayner, *Labirinto do espaço romanesco*, 121–45. The English word *speculation* assumed its meaning of "a commercial venture or undertaking of an enterprising nature, especially one involving considerable financial risk on the chance of unusual profit" in the late eighteenth century through the nineteenth; "Speculation," *Oxford English Dictionary*, online version (dictionary/oed.com). See also Sousândrade, "O Inferno de Wall Street," in *Guesa errante*, canto X.

17. See Cronon, *Nature's Metropolis*, 97–147.

18. Many of these enterprises that mushroomed during the Encilhmento existed on paper only, but actual companies were also established. The types of businesses primarily included urban public infrastructure (such as light and power com-

panies) and the (mainly textile) factories then spreading throughout the city; Lobo, *A história do Rio de Janeiro*, 464, 479–82.

19. On the antipopular politics of the provisional government, see Lucas, "Cinearte," 25–26; Carvalho, *Os bestializados*.

20. All references to this case come from AN, Série Justiça, IJ⁶—645 (ano 1918). The club was located on Avenida Mem de Sá, 10.

21. For example, workers in the Carioca and Corcovado textile factories entered the Floresta Nacional de Paineiras clandestinely at night to extract *lenha* (kindling) in 1911. The Delegacia Auxiliar responded that "energetic provisions" be taken to prevent it from happening; AN, Polícia, GIFI, 6C-357.

22. On the remuneration of workers in Rio, see Lobo, *História do Rio de Janeiro*, 709–16. Across all professions, the majority of workers were paid *por empreitada* (by contract), fewer were paid daily, and fewer still monthly.

23. See, for example, Gaskill, *Crime and Mentalities in Early Modern England*, 123–202.

24. Gomes and Kornis, "Com a histório no bolso," 114–15. See also Piccato, *City of Suspects*, 144.

25. Stein, *Vassouras*.

26. Burns, *A History of Brazil*, 158.

27. Ibid., 149–58.

28. Faria, *Mauá*, 252.

29. In the mid-nineteenth-century monetary debate between *metalistas* (who favored the gold standard and convertibility) and *papelistas* (who, wishing to expand credit, held that paper money only needed to be commensurate with the number of actual transactions in the economy and did not need to be convertible into gold), the metalistas prevailed. Both schools favored adherence to the gold standard, although some individuals, such as Mauá, preferred "purely fiduciary circulation"; Villela, "The Quest for Gold," 79, 83, 87–88.

30. Faria, *Mauá*, 252.

31. Vieira, *Evolução do sistema monetário brasileiro*, 178; Burns, *A History of Brazil*, 149–58.

32. Ibid., 174–75.

33. Topik, *The Political Economy*, 28. On postabolition monetary expansion, see Levy, *A História da Bolsa de Valores*, 40.

34. Neuhaus, *História monetária do Brasil, 1900–45*, 15–17.

35. Topik, *The Political Economy of the Brazilian State, 1889–1930*, 30–32; Burns, *A History of Brazil*, 239–41.

36. Burns, *A History of Brazil*, 239–41.

37. Topik, *The Political Economy of the Brazilian State, 1889–1930*, 31, 36.

38. Neuhaus, *História monetária do Brasil, 1900–45*, 1.

39. A British traveler in Brazil in 1911 describes Campos Salles's "chief task" after assuming the presidency in 1898 as the reestablishment of "national credit, and to do this it was necessary to take serious measures"; Oakenfull, *Brazil in 1911*, 108. Campos Salles also, famously, negotiated a debt consolidation program with Britain in 1898 called the Funding Loan.

40. Neuhaus, *História monetária do Brasil, 1900–45*, 18.

41. Topik, *The Political Economy of the Brazilian State, 1889–1930*, 31.

42. This was the second of Brazil's British Funding Loans. Neuhaus, *História monetária do Brasil, 1900–45*, 1; Burns, *A History of Brazil*, 303.

43. The federal government ordered the coinage of 20:000:000$000 in nickel coins; Vieira, *Evolução do Sistema Bancária*, 192–93.

44. Centro Cultural Banco do Brasil, *Dinheiro, diversão e arte*, 11–16.

45. Dent, *A Year in Brazil*, 301.

46. AN, GIFI 6C-30, Caixa 7.

47. Oakenfull, *Brazil (1913)*, 560.

48. See Henkin, *City Reading*, 141.

49. See, for example, Edgard Carone's discussion of workers' banks (Bancos dos Operários); *Movimento Operário no Brasil*, 15.

50. A textile factory in São Paulo paid its workers with coupons (*vales*), which they could trade for merchandise at a type of company store; Subiroft, *A Oligarquia Paulista*, 134–40.

51. Piragibe, *Consolidação das leis penais*, 123–26.

52. *Feiras e mafuás*, 22.

53. *Feiras e mafuás*, 25.

54. AN, Série Justiça, IJ⁶—617.

55. CPDOC, AV 19.10.29. Cartas a Armando Vidal da SBAT (Sociedade Brasileira de Autores Teatrais).

56. Enrique Ghersi uses the term "extralegal normativity" to describe this phenomenon; Iván Alonso, Fernando Iwasaki, Enrique Ghersi, eds., *El comercio ambulatorio en Lima*, 69–100.

57. As Gayatri Chakravorty Spivak states in her reflections on Marx's analysis of the relationship between value and money, the "emergence of the money-form" has the effect of systematizing exchange value; "Scattered Speculations," 75.

58. This alienation of reality from the symbol used to represent it simultaneously occurred not only with respect to money but also in language and human psychology. See Shell, *Money, Language, and Thought*; DiPiero, "Buying into Fiction."

59. Lambek, "The Value of Coins," 741. On the impersonality of money as a function of modernity and its social effects, see Poggi, *Money and the Modern Mind*.

60. Thomas DiPiero makes a similar point, citing money's tendency to "disappear without a trace, leaving behind no residue of the transactions it occasions"; "Buying into Fiction," 2. On pawning, see Piccato, "Cuidado com los rateros," in Salvatore, Aguirre, and Joseph, *Crime and Punishment in Latin America*, 233–272; Francois, "Cloth and Silver." Michael Lambek describes the "laundering" (desacralization) of sacred coins by reintroducing them into circulation; Lambek, "The Value of Coins," 747. Viviana Zelizer argues that people make money their own and bring it into their own networks; *The Social Meaning of Money*.

61. Goux, *The Coiners of Language*, chap. 3; Williams, "A Kind of Grisham's Law," in *What I Came to Say*, 93–97.

62. Significantly, the person who financed the animal game was already called a

"banker" (*banqueiro*) by the early 1900s; given the small number of banks then, this may have been the only banker that most people ever encountered. See, for example, the case of Carlos Figueiredo in 1907; AN, T8.2543.

63. AN, T8.2478.

64. AN, 23 de Janeiro de 1907.

65. AN, T8.3074. For another case, see AN, O1.2589.

66. A law of 1899 stipulates that the defendant must be allowed to post bail and defend him- or herself in liberty as long as the fine is under 100$000; Decreto 3475 de 4 de novembro de 1899, article 60, no. 2. See, for example, AN, 11ª Pretoria Criminal, n. 7769, caixa 118fo. An additional law mandates that "bail shall be paid by means of a deposit of money, or precious metals or stones, or in national or municipal bonds [*apolices ou títulos da divida nacional, ou do Municipalidade*]" or the person could use real property (*hypoteca de immoveis livres de preferencia*) as security; *Atos de poder legislativo*, Lei n. 628 de 28 de outobro de 1899 (Art. 50 Sec. 50), 37. On the rise of the fine as connected to the monetization of societies, see Garland, *Punishment and Modern Society*, 104.

67. "Amid competing currencies, the use of a particular kind of money marked—and shifted—socioeconomic and political boundaries"; Colloredo-Mansfeld, "Money of Moderate Size."

68. Cf. Henkin, *City Reading*, 161.

69. Nogueira, *Pena sem prisão*, 164.

70. AN, Série Justica-Policia, IJ⁶—657; Série Justça—Gabinete do Ministro, IJ¹—1067.

71. *A Obra de Sylvio Romero em criminologia*, 130.

72. Oakenfull, *Brazil in 1911*, 154.

73. Ministério da Justiça e Negócios Interiores, *Relatorio Apresentado ao Presidente dos Estados Unidos do Brazil pelo Ministro de Estado da Justiça e Negocios Interiores, Augusto Tavares de Lyra em março de 1907*, 1:79.

74. Letter from Directoria da Casa da Correção to Chief of Police, August 24, 1917, AN, IJ⁶–625 (Série Justiça—Polícia).

75. AN, Série Justiça—Polícia, IJ⁶–657, "Moeda Falsa, 2a secção, jan.—dez. de 1918."

76. For example, for references to several police investigations regarding *moeda falsa*, see AN, Polícia-Documentos 233 (1907).

77. Oakenfull, *Brazil (1913)*, 569.

78. AN, pacote 101, colonia, 3a secção (Requerimentos), 1903.

79. AN, Polícia—233, 3a Delegacia.

80. Abreu, *A evolução urbana*, 53.

81. AN, GIFI 6C-317.

82. These documents are clustered around certain brief periods, probably reflecting concentrated bursts of police activity to investigate counterfeiting rather than the actual patterns of the occurrence of this crime.

83. The quantities of counterfeit money that authorities discovered at each station of the Estrada de Ferro Central do Brasil for a several-month period in 1915 are, by station: Estação Del Castilho (3); Est. Quintinho Bocayuva (13); Est. Lauro Muller (14); Est. Maritima (25); Est. da Matadouro (28); Est. de Santa Cruz (22);

Est. de Encantado (3); Est. da Cascadura (22); Est. de Campo Grande (14); Est. de Engenho de Dentro (1 "imitando as de nickel de quatrocentos reis," 12 of one milreis); Est. de Meyer (6); Est. de Engenho Novo (9); Est. de Sao Diogo (14); Est. de Deodoro (15); Est. de Realengo (3); Est. Marechal Hermes (5); Est. de Dona Clara (5); Est. de Mangueira (4); Est. Alfredo Maia (5); Est. da Madureira (13); Est. de São Cristóvão; Est. de São Franciso Xavier (3); Est. Engenheiro Trinidade (2); Est. de Todos os Santos (3); Est. Terra Nova; Est. Bangú (8); Est. Central (16); Est. de Piedade (17); Est. de Rio das Pedras (5); Est. Andrade Araujo (1 nickel de 400 reis); Est. "Magno" (2, one of which was a nickel); Est. Santíssimo (3); Est. Riachuelo (2); Est. da Rocha; Est. de Ancheta (9); Est. de Paciência (3); Agência Pestana; Thomas Coelho (2); Estado de Pavuna (2); Est. Bento Ribeiro (2); Est. Costa Barros; AN, Serie Justiça—Polícia—IJ⁶—576.

84. AN, Polícia—233.

85. See, for example, AN, Polícia—233.

86. AN, Série Justiça—Polícia, IJ⁶—657.

87. Abreu, *A festa do divino*, 16.

5. LIVES OF THE PLAYERS

The first epigraph comes from a collection of chronicles about Rio de Janeiro, *A alma encantadora das ruas* (1908), 173; the source of the second epigraph is Williams, *Resources of Hope*, 3–18.

1. AN, Processos crimes, T-8428.

2. Pencak, Dennis, and Newman, eds., *Riot and Revelry in Early America*.

3. Lopes, ed., *Entre a Europa e África*.

4. Soihet, *Condição feminina e formas de violência*, 151–53; Marins, "Habitação e vizinhança," in Sevcenko, ed., *História da vida privada no Brasil*, 131–87.

5. Warner, "Publics and Counterpublics."

6. On the state's patronage of the arts in the First Republic, see Mencarelli, *Cena aberta*.

7. Abreu, "Mello Moraes Filho: Festas, tradições populares, e identidade nacional," in Chalhoub and Pereira, eds., *A história contada*, 186.

8. Aguirre, *The Criminals of Lima and Their Worlds*; Piccato, *City of Suspects*; Tórtima, *Crime e castigo para além do Equador*, 129–30; da Cunha, *Intenção e gesto*; Huggins, *From Slavery to Vagrancy in Brazil*; Bretas, *Ordem na cidade*, 61–91.

9. Peiss, *Going Out*; French, *A Peaceful and Working People*; Overmyer-Velázquez, *Visions of the Emerald City*.

10. AN, OI-2625, 9a Vara Criminal, seção de guarda CODES/Judiciário.

11. Two milreis (or 2,000 reis) could buy two dozen eggs or four liters of milk in 1911; Oakenfull, *Brazil in 1911*, 356–57.

12. AN, OI-2586, 10a Vara Criminal, seção de guarda CODES/Judiciário.

13. AN, OI-2589, 10a Vara Criminal (1911); AN, 6Z-3149, 3a Delegacia Auxiliar (1917); AN, CX 270 Proc, 70m Gal. B (1926).

14. For other examples of cases against accused bicheiros that mention anonymous buyers who evade arrest, AN, ;T8.1755; AN, T8.1677; AN, T8.2543.

15. See Lei 2321 do 30 de dezembro de 1910, Article 31, Section 4, Numbers I and II, a. Cf. Crespo, "Os jogos de fortuna ou azar em Lisboa em fins do Antigo Regime," 86 fn3.

16. See, for example, AN, OR 2915, 8ª Pretoria do Rio de Janeiro, ano 1903.

17. Carradore, *O folklore do jogo do bicho*.

18. Thompson, "Folklore, Anthropology, and Social History," 253; Crapanzano, "Hermes' Dilemma: The Masking of Subversion in Ethnographic Description," in Clifford and Marcus, *Writing Culture*, 49–76, esp. 74–75.

19. The word used in Brazil for the military draft, or lottery, is *sorteio* (not *loteria*); Beattie, *Tribute of Blood*, 6, chap. 10.

20. Borges, "Healing and Mischief," 198–203; Bastide, *As religiões*, 195; Arinos, *Lendas e tradições Brasileiras*, 20–22; Hahner, *Poverty and Politics*, 351, fn 61.

21. Arinos, *Lendas e tradições Brasileiras*, 21–22, 138–39. The word *play* (*jogar*), as in to play a sport, was used to describe betting on the jogo do bicho, which has always been called the animal game instead of the animal lottery or simply animals. A fruitful comparison can be made between the jogo do bicho and *capoeira*, the martial art or dance associated with Brazilians of African descent in the nineteenth century and criminalized unofficially in the late Empire and in the First Republic. Capoeira also uses the phrase *to play* (*jogar*). Present-day practitioners of *capoeira regional* explain their use of the more innocuous-sounding *jogo* rather than *dance* (*dança*) or *fight* (*luta*) because of its clandestine nature; Chvaicer, "Embodying Difference," np.

22. João do Rio, *As religiões do Rio*, 34; Abreu, "Mello Moraes Filho."

23. *As religiões do Rio*, 35. See also Maggie, *Medo do feitiço*. The Estrada Santa Cruz is located in the western zone of the city, far from the port area.

24. *As religiões do Rio*, 36 (emphasis added). Oloô-Teté is the name of one of the *babalaôs* (priests within Afro-Brazilian religious practice) that João do Rio discusses. *Parati* (also known as *cachaça*) is a strong liquor made of fermented sugar cane.

25. Abreu, "Mello Moraes Filho," 178. See also Chazkel, "The *Crônica*, the City, and the Invention of the Underworld."

26. *As religiões do Rio*, 39–40.

27. Borges, "Healing and Mischief." See also Maggie, *Medo do feitiço*; Palmié, *Wizards and Scientists*; and Damazio, *Um pouco da história do espiritismo no Rio de Janeiro*.

28. Sevcenko, *Literatura como missão*; Chalhoub and Pereira, eds., *A história contada*; Mencarelli, *Cena Aberta*; Straccia, Fatigatti, Ferreira, Guidin, and D'Ambrosio, *O espetáculo das massas*; Borges, "Healing and Mischief," 194–95.

29. Azevedo, *A Condessa Vésper*, 381.

30. Reith, *The Age of Chance*, 5. The Catholic Church also remained silent on the issue of homosexuality, which was under intense discussion among medico-legal professionals in the early twentieth century; Green, *Beyond Carnival*, 113.

31. Abreu, *O império do divino*, chap. 6.

32. Cf. Crespo, "Os jogos de fortuna ou azar em Lisboa em fins do Antigo Regime," 89.

33. Cf. French, *A Peaceful and Working People*, 71–72.

34. Rago, *Do cabaré ao lar*, 112; Hahner, *Poverty and Politics*, 215.

35. Freyre, *Casa-grande e senzala*, 203, 244n131.

36. References to the police in Brazilian popular music appear as early as the middle of the nineteenth century; Sandroni, *Feitiço Decente*, 122.

37. Lichtenstein, "That disposition to theft," 418–19; Levine, *Black Culture*, 125–30.

38. See Maria Clementina Pereira Cunha's preface to Abreu, *O Império do divino*, 13–17.

39. *O Malho*, ano III, no. 8 (April 2, 1904), np.

40. The *charada*, often featured in magazines of the day, was a sort of puzzle composed of symbols or icons, from which the reader needed to reason out words that relayed a hidden message.

41. In *Obra Completa de Machado de Assis*, vol. 2.

42. Chazkel, "The *Crônica*, the City, and the Invention of the Underworld."

43. Lima Barreto, *Vidas urbanas*, 113–14.

44. The *folhetim* contained illustrated stories often written in verse. The pamphlets consulted for this study are found in the collection of the Casa de Rui Barbosa. I am grateful to Carolina Sanin Paz for sharing with me her personal collection of folhetins.

45. Following a period of religious liberalization in the late Empire, the early First Republic was marked by the disestablishment of the Catholic Church and republican secularism. See also "O padre que se tornou bicheiro," in Carradore, *Folclore do jogo do bicho*, 25–28; AN, Delegacia Auxiliar da Polícia, 2ª—Peças Teatrais, Caixa 70, pasta no. 1700, S/T, agosto de 1920; "A Mão Zelosa da Moral e dos Bons Costumes e o Jogo," cited in Meira, "O papel na imprensa no jogo do bicho (1890–1920)," 210.

46. This excerpt from Olavo Bilac (1865–1918) is undated; quoted in Carradore, *Folclore do jogo do bicho*, 50.

47. Mencarelli, *Cena aberta*.

48. It is uncertain when the term *malandro* came into common use. On the *capadócio*, a precursor to the *malandro*, see Elias Thomé Saliba, "A tradição cômica da vida privada na República," in Sevcenko, ed., *História da vida privada no Brasil: República*, 338–39. In a publication of 1903, the term is italicized but is not included in the book's glossary of slang terms, suggesting it was widely understood but still considered a recent coinage or foreign word; see Reis, *Os Ladrões do Rio*, 159. In 1905, a weekly publication entitled "O Malandro" appeared in São Paulo state. One should also consider the *bilontra*, a trickster-huckster figure who appeared in late nineteenth- and early twentieth-century popular theater in Rio de Janeiro and is similar to the malandro but somewhat higher on the socioeconomic hierarchy; see Mencarelli, *Cena aberta*. For parallel phenomena elsewhere in Latin America, on Argentina see Ludmer, *The Corpus Delicti*; on Venezuela, see Fernandez, "Mambíses, Malandros, y Maleantes."

49. Santiago, "Worldly Appeal," 36–37; DaMatta, "Pedro Malasartes and the Paradoxes of Roguery," in *Carnivals, Rogues, and Heroes*, 198–238; Lopes, ed., *Entre*

Europa e África, 182; Bretas, A guerra das ruas, 62–63; Zaluar, A máquina e a revolta, 149–50.

50. Abreu, "Mello Morais Filho," in A Historia Contada, 173; Lopes, ed., Entre Europa e África, 174; Mencarelli, Cena aberta; Süssekind, As revistas do ano e a invenção do Rio de Janeiro.

51. Masiello, "Melodrama, Sex, and Nation in Latin America's Fin de Siglo," in Sommer, Places of History, 134–43.

52. Cândido, "Dialética da Malandragem," 84.

53. Santiago, "Worldly Appeal," 36–37.

54. Cândido, "Dialética da Malandragem," 69.

55. DaMatta, "Pedro Malasartes and the Paradoxes of Roguery," in Carnivals, Rogues, and Heroes: An Interpretation of the Brazilian Dilemma, 198–238. Pedro Malasartes derives from the Afro-Brazilian deity Exú, a figure between the divine and the diabolical; Rosenfeld, Negro, macumba, e futbol, 53. See also Dias, Power and Everyday Life, 163. On the trickster figure's association with the market and illegality, see generally Hyde, Trickster Makes this World, 7, 203, 206–52; Brown, Hermes, the Thief.

56. Green, Beyond Carnival, 87–90; Levine, The Unpredictable Past, 59–77.

57. AN, Gifi, Polícia 233. See also Soihet, Condição feminina e formas de violência. Women were generally arrested far less frequently than men for all crimes. In Rio's Third Police District, for example, from April through June of 1907, 727 men and 49 women were arrested. In the districts and time periods surveyed, women were arrested almost exclusively for vagrancy and occasionally for theft and assault (ofesas físicas); APERJ, CD-DF 5627; CD-DF 6317; CD-DF 6336. See also Socolow, "Women and Crime," 42–3; Feeley and Little, "The Vanishing Female," 719.

58. See, for example, O Bicho; BN, Setor de Periódicos.

59. AN, T8 3467, Delegacia do 160 Distrito Policial (1909); AN, Série Processos Crimes, T8 2347.

60. Caulfield, In Defense of Honor, 26. Women gained the vote in Brazil in 1932.

61. Rago, Do cabaré ao lar, 61–116; Lauderdale Graham, "Making the Public Private"; DaMatta, House and Street.

62. Lombroso, Criminal Woman, the Prostitute, and the Normal Woman; Nesvig, "The Lure of the Perverse," 10–11.

63. See, for example, Annaes da Conferência Judiciária-Policial, 215.

64. Cooper, The Brazilians and Their Country.

65. Pitkin, Fortune is a Woman, chap. 6.

66. O Bicho, 9: 269 (23 de novembro de 1914), np.

67. Cf. Peiss, Cheap Amusements, chap. 1.

68. See, for example, Machado de Assis, "Jogo do Bicho," in Obras Completas, vol. 2. Minors' frequent involvement in the sale of jogo do bicho tickets may have resulted from the ubiquity of adolescent boys who worked as assistants in petty commerce. See, for example, AN, Série Processo Crime, T8.2347.

69. AN, T8–2478.

70. AN, Delegacia de Policia do 20 Distrito, reus: José Raposo do Conto Jr. and

Antonio Marques da Silva (1911). Cf. AN, Delegacia da Policia da 13ª Circum-scripção Urbana (Manoel José Luiz Pereira).

71. Reith, *The Age of Chance*, xiv; Hacking, *The Emergence of Probability*, 131–33.

72. I refer here to Mary Douglas's and Baron Isherwood's analysis of the cultural (shared) meaning of consumption: Goods "are the visible parts of culture"; "The main problem of social life is to pin down meaning so that they stay still for a little while. . . . rituals serve to contain the drift of meaning," not just across time but also across people; Douglas and Isherwood, *The World of Goods*, 43–44.

73. *History Workshop Journal*, no. 48 (autumn 1999); Burke, *Varieties of Cultural History*, 30; Fabian, *Card Sharks, Dream Books, and Bucket Shops*. Ralph Ellison recalled in a personal letter in 1976 that, as a child, he had read Freud's *The Interpretation of Dreams* because he had "mistaken [it] for the type of dream book used by numbers players"; Callahan, " 'American Culture is of a Whole.' " I am grateful to Adam Rothman for bringing this reference to my attention.

74. In the *History Workshop Journal*'s special issue on dream books (number 48, Autumn 1999), see Perkins, "The Meaning of Dreambooks," 105; Wigzell, "The Dreambook in Russia," 117.

75. RB, Coleção Literatura de Cordel. See also Slater, *Stories on a String*.

76. *A alma encantadora*, 47–50.

77. This story is recounted in numerous texts. See, for example, Alleau, ed., *Dicionário dos jogos*, 48.

78. BN, Setor de Periódicos. See also Lima Barreto, *Vidas urbanas: Artigos e Crônicos*. 2d ed., 113–14.

79. Director-manager Henrique Tocci, in the issue of January–July 1912, its head-quarters (*redação*) is noted as 182 rua da Alfandega (*provisoriamente*); v. 9, n. 1–146. A few months later, it had moved (to rua Primeiro de Março, 139 [provisoria-mente]). (Readers wishing to purchase back issues were instructed to go to a store at a different address: rua Rodrigo Silva.) It moved again in early June 1912: rua do Hospicio, 179 (provisoriamente). On April 3, 1912, it appears at rua da Alfandega 182. By July 1914, the masthead no longer had any address at all. One must allow for the possibility that the indication of a "provisionally located" headquarters for this newspaper was merely the publisher's joking reference to the illegality of the game, alluding to an editorial team on the run.

80. *O Bicho* ran from 1904 to 1914; the collection in the Biblioteca Nacional begins in 1907. Other than *O Bicho* and *O Palpite*, the jogo do bicho newspapers in Rio de Janeiro in the first two decades of the twentieth century included *A Mascote*, *O Talismã*, and *O Chico*, possibly among others; Magalhães, "Ganhou leva," 60–69.

81. *O Bicho*, ano VIII, no. 2 (January 5, 1911), np.

82. *O Bicho* ano VIII, no. 109 (May 11, 1911), np. See also Magalhães, "Ganhou leva," 75–76.

83. *O Bicho*, January 4, 1912, np.

84. Silva, *As queixas do povo*, 46–47.

85. Magalhães, "Ganhou leva," 60, 68–72.

86. Meira, "O papel da imprensa no jogo do bicho (1890–1920)."

87. "Roda da Fortuna," *Correio da Manhã*, (July 14, 1902), 3, cited in Meira, "O papel da imprensa," 201.

88. Magalhães, "Ganhou leva," 118.

89. Hannerz, *Exploring the City*, 209–14; Halttunen, *Confidence Men and Painted Women*; Henkin, *City Reading*, 1–38.

90. For an alternative view of the jogo do bicho as "ritual sacrifice," see DaMatta and Soárez, "Águias, burros e borboletas," 111–12.

91. At this same time, *praça* also came to refer to enlisted men in the army; Beattie, *Tribute of Blood*, 9.

92. Overmyer-Velázquez, *Vision of the Emerald City*, 31, 39. See also Needell, *A Tropical Belle Epoque*; Fanni Muñoz Cabrejo, "The New Order: Diversions and Modernization in Turn-of-the-Century Lima," in Beezley and Curcio-Nagy, *Latin American Popular Culture*, 155–65; Beezley, *Judas at the Jockey Club*.

93. Mello, "A História social dos jogos de azar no Rio de Janeiro, 1808–1946," 1–27; Abreu, *O império do divino*, 267–68.

94. AGCRJ, códice 49–8-9, folha 4.

95. *Vidas urbanas*, 262–63. This chronicle was originally published as a newspaper column on August 20, 1921.

96. See Nasaw, *Going Out*; Peiss, *Cheap Amusements*.

97. See, for example, a British traveler's description of a bullfight in Rio in 1884; Dent, *A Year in Brazil*, 192, 195. Cf. Beezley, *Judas at the Jockey Club*.

98. The number of industrial workers in Rio went from 52,520 to 115,779; Magalhães, "Ganhou leva," 27; Benchimol, *Pereira Passos: Um Haussman tropical*, 172–73. In 1872 there were 2,383 professionals and 10,712 functionaries; in 1906, there were 14,946 professionals and 30,793 functionaries; Magalhães, "Ganhou leva," 27; Benchimol, *Pereira Passos: Um Haussman tropical*, 177.

99. See, for example, Hahner, *Poverty and Politics*, 211–12.

100. See Cross, ed., *Worktime and Industrialization*, 10; Besse, *Restructuring Patriarchy*.

101. Hahner, *Poverty and Politics*, 212; Carvalho, *Os bestializados*, 38–39.

102. Medeiros, *O lazer no planejamento urbano*, 7, 210–12.

103. Rougier, *Le Brésil em 1911*, 229; Rago, *Os Prazeres da Noite*, 56.

104. Lopes, ed., *Entre África e Europa*, 22–24; Mencarelli, *Cena aberta*.

105. Süssekind, *Cinematógrafo de letras*, 34.

106. Green, *Beyond Carnival*, 23–25.

107. *Gazeta Operária*, no. 20 (February 8, 1903), np.

108. Süssekind, *Cinematógrafo de letras*, 39, 41; Araujo, *A Bela Época do cinema carioca*; Costa, *Como eu vi o Brazil*, 96. Large-scale interest in cinema did not come about until after the First World War; Medeiros, *O lazer no planejamento urbano*, 73.

109. Hahner, *Poverty and Politics*, 211.

110. Gerson, *História das ruas do Rio*, 50–51.

111. Süssekind, *Cinematografo de letras*, 39

112. APERJ (Setor Biblioteca) *Dois Rios*, 71–74.

113. Martins, "Paschoal Segreto." See also Gerson, *História das ruas do Rio*, 50.

114. Lopes, ed., *Entre África e Europa*, 23; Mencarelli, *Cena aberta*.

115. Lima, "Arquitetura do espetáculo," 119; Green, *Beyond Carnival*, 24.

116. None of the three criminal cases against Paschoal and his brother Gaetano Segreto currently available in the National Archive were related to the jogo do bicho. See AN, Varas Criminais, Catalogo Geral, Juizo da 3a Pretoria, ano 1902, no. 1249k, caixa M2278. The Segretos are parties in numerous civil cases and were processed for multiple infractions of the sanitary code; for the latter, see AN, Varas Criminais, Juizo de Feitos da Saude Pública, 6a VC, 1906. The Labanca brothers also introduced a magic lantern to the Carioca public in the populous central neighborhood Catete; Gerson, *História das ruas do Rio*, 268.

117. See generally Lima, "Arquitetura do espetáculo"; Arujo, *A Bela Época do cinema carioca*. Martins, "Paschoal Segreto," 4.

118. AN, 8ª Pretoria Criminal, 1899, OR.1055.

119. See also Viveiros de Castro, *Jurisprudencia criminal*, 314–15.

120. Lei 2321 do 30 de dezembro de 1910, article 31, section 2.

121. Empreza Paschoal Segreto (Paschoal Segreto Company) fought constantly to define the commercial amusements they operated as sporting games as opposed to games of chance. For example, in 1926 they won a court case to maintain their patented game called Rambolk, which was threatened with closure and fines; AN, Notação GIFI 8N-79, Supremo Tribunal Federal, 1683. See also Bretas, "A polícia das culturas," in Lopes, ed., *Entre Europa e África*, 245–59.

122. Corrêa, *Morte em família*.

123. Cost of living data come from Oakenfull, *Brazil in 1911*, 355.

124. *Black Culture and Black Consciousness*, 440–41.

125. Cross, "Crowds and Leisure."

126. U.S. cultural historians of the 1980s and 1990s took a special interest in recovering and historicizing the element of pleasure in cultural practice: Peiss, *Cheap Amusements*; Fabian, *Card Sharks, Dream Books, and Bucket Shops*; Lears, *No Place of Grace*. Warren Susman also emphasizes the play element in culture; *Culture as History*.

127. Beezley and Curcio-Nagy, Introduction, in Beezley and Curcio-Nagy, eds., *Latin American Popular Culture*, xii–xiii.

128. Thompson, *Whigs and Hunters*, 260.

129. Elias Thomé Saliba, "A dimensão cômica da vida privada da República," in Sevcenko, ed., *História da vida privada no Brasil*, 289–365.

130. Thompson, "Folklore, Anthropology, and Social History," 254.

6. *VALE O ESCRITO*

1. The jurist quoted is Rui Barbosa; *Annaes da Conferência Judiciária-Policial*, 215.

2. Mello, "A história social dos jogos de azar," 96–110.

3. Some jogo do bicho tickets from the 1920s and 1930s also have such variations as *confira vale 3 dias* (confirmed valid for 3 days) stamped, printed, or written on them.

4. See, for example, the Maximiliano Felix Bahia case from 1917 examined in chapter 3.

5. "Polícia e polícia política no Rio de Janeiro nos anos 1920," 30. Contemporary examples of the notion of the jogo do bicho's superior reliability abound. Brazil's largest newspaper recently labeled the jogo do bicho "one of Brazil's rare serious and respected institutions," and it is "only in [the jogo do bicho] that what is written is valid"; João Ubaldo Ribeiro, "O presidente trabalha, sim," *O Globo* (June 13, 2004).

6. Douglas Hay, "Law and Society in Comparative Perspective," in Salvatore, Aguirre, and Joseph, eds., *Crime and Punishment in Latin America*, 426.

7. See, for example, Cancelli, *O mundo da violência*; Rose, *One of the Forgotten Things*.

8. The quotations are from González Echeverría, *Myth and Archive*, 53–54. See also Faoro, *Os donos de poder*.

9. Leal, *Coronelismo*; Woodard, "Coronelismo in Theory and Practice"; Eisenstadt and Roniger, *Patrons, Clients, and Friends*, 3; Hagopian, *Traditional Politics and Regime Change in Brazil*, 15–27.

10. Leal, *Coronelismo*; Souza, *A experiência da lei, a lei da experiência*, 113.

11. Graham, *Patronage and Politics*; Da Costa, *Brazilian Empire*. Cf. Aguirre and Salvatore, "Introduction: Writing the History of Law, Crime, and Punishment in Latin America," in Joseph, Aguirre, and Salvatore, eds., *Crime and Punishment in Latin America*, 16.

12. Pechman, *Cidades estreitamente vigiadas*, 348; Holloway, *Policing Rio*; Graham, *Patronage and Politics*.

13. See, for example, Heymann, "Quem não tem padrinho morre pagão."

14. Brazilian intellectuals of the early and mid-twentieth century like Oliveira Vianna, Gilberto Freyre, and Sérgio Buarque de Holanda depicted Brazilian society as held together by a prepolitical "social solidarity" in lieu of a social contract; Pechman, *Cidades estreitamente vigiadas*, 422. See also DaMatta, *A casa e a rua*.

15. Negro, "Paternalismo, populismo e história social." See also Blok, *Honour and Violence*, chaps. 3, 4.

16. Weinstein, *For Social Peace in Brazil*, 52; Bandeira, *A Igreja católica na virada da questão social (1930–1964)*, 34–58; Carvalho, *Cidadania no Brasil*, 110–26.

17. Leme, *Ruy e a questão social*, 24, 56; Barbosa, *A questão social e política no Brasil*, xxiii; Baldessarini, *Crônica de uma época*, 9.

18. Some early steps toward social security were taken in 1923, for instance, when the federal legislature passed a law that provided pensions for railway workers. A subsequent law (in 1925) established the right to vacation time for workers; Baldessarini, *Crônica de uma época*, 8.

19. Mello, "A história social dos jogos de azar no Rio de Janeiro, 1808–1946," 89.

20. "For the simplest form of the game . . . if one of the four numbers in that group wins the National Lottery first prize, you win. If you play one milreis on the group and one in the group wins, you win 24 milreis. If you play the actual winning *decena* [tens], you win 90 mileris [about $25]. For the winning centena [last 3 winning digits], you win 900 milreis; on the last thousand, you would usually win 8 contos [$2000]"; Cooper, *The Brazilians and Their Country*, 263. Police records

also detail how the game was played; see, for example, AN, Varas Criminais, 3ª Pretoria, n. 1779, Maço 2163.

21. Cavalcante, *Os bicheiros*, 109. Only the morning jogo do bicho drawing derived from the result of the legal lottery, whereas the "afternoon and and nighttime drawing has nothing to do with the extraction of the lottery"; "As medidas repressoras: 'O jogo do bicho,'" *A Notícia* (September 13, 1917), np. The numbers for the second and third jogo do bicho drawings may have come from a special, clandestine drawing.

22. Mello, "A história social dos jogos de azar no Rio de Janeiro, 1808–1946," 92, 98. The police officials who carried out the early twentieth-century's series of anti–jogo do bicho campaigns were Astolfo Rezende (1907); Armando Vidal (1916); Renato Bittencourt (1926); Frota Aguiar and Jaime Praça (1933); and Frota Aguiar again in 1934; Magalhães, "Ganhou leva," 180.

23. Mello, "A história social dos jogos de azar no Rio de Janeiro, 1808–1946," 93, 107.

24. AN, Série Justiça IJ⁶–645 (ano: 1918).

25. Between February 2 and September 9, 1917, 68 persons were detained in the Casa de Detenção for jogo do bicho–related offenses; APERJ, CD-79.

26. *Annaes da Conferência Judiciária-Policial*; Tórtima, "Polícia e Justiça de Mãos Dadas"; Pechman, *Cidades estreitamente vigiadas*, 345–49; Salem, *História da polícia*, 100–102.

27. *Annaes da Conferência Judiciária-Policial*, 215.

28. Ibid.

29. Bretas, *Ordem na cidade*, 52; Magalhães, "Ganhou leva," 180; "Ainda a polícia e a campanha contra o 'bicho,'" *Correo da Manhã*, September 25, 1915, np. The police chief and district heads (*delegados*) had acquired the authority to prosecute certain misdemeanor cases, particularly those involving gambling with the passage of the so-called Alfredo Pinto Law (Decreto-Lei 628, de 24 de outobro de 1899); Bretas, *Guerra das ruas*, 68.

30. As a jurist and lawyer in Bahia, Leal published books on religious beliefs among the inmates in Bahia's House of Correction; see Leal, *A religião entre os condemnados da Bahia: estudo de psichologia criminal*.

31. AN, Série Justiça SJ—IJ⁶ (código do fundo AM).

32. AN, IJ⁶ 689.

33. CPDOC, Recortes de jornal: J 42. See, for example, "A campanha contro o 'bicho': Uma entrevista com o 30 delegado auxiliar," *O Imparcial*, June 4, 1918. See also Mello, "A história social dos jogos de azar no Rio de Janeiro, 1808–1946," 98.

34. Mello, "A história social dos jogos de azar no Rio de Janeiro, 1808–1946," 102–7.

35. "Uma campanha inique," *Jornal do Comércio* (September 18, 1917), np.

36. Mello, "A história social dos jogos de azar no Rio de Janeiro, 1808–1946," 108. The same allegations can be found in "O 'bicho' e a polícia," *Jornal do Comércio* (September 26, 1917), np.

37. *Jornal do Comércio* (October 27, 1917), np. See also Mello, "A história social dos jogos de azar no Rio de Janeiro, 1808–1946," 109.

38. Mello, "A história social dos jogos de azar no Rio de Janeiro, 1808–1946," 97.

The lottery company's director, Alberto Saraiva da Fonseca, called Deputado Maurício de Lacerda *o advogado dos bicheiros* (the bicheiros' lawyer) because of Lacerda's insistence that the anti-bicho campaign was unfair; *Jornal do Comércio* (October 27, 1917), np. Lacerda's motives for taking on the lottery company are unclear. He enjoyed strong worker support and was known as a "maverick spokesperson for the liberal opposition to the oligarchy"; Maram, "Urban Labor and Social Change in the 1920s," 217.

39. *Anais do Conselho Municipal*, Novembro de 1917, 284.
40. *Anais do Conselho Municipal*, Novembro de 1917, 280.
41. *Anais do Conselho Municipal*, Novembro de 1917, 281.
42. Borges, "Healing and Mischief," 191–92. I am grateful to Dain Borges for sharing his insights and research notes on this subject with me. Coelho's proposed measure to legalize the jogo do bicho is also mentioned in Bandeira, *O Rio de Janeiro em prosa e verso*, 196.
43. "A campanha contra o 'bicho,'" *Jornal do Comércio* (September 27, 1917), np. See also Mello, "A história social dos jogos de azar no Rio de Janeiro, 1808–1946," 104.
44. *Anais do Conselho Municipal*, Novembro de 1917, 281–84.
45. Silva, *Operários sem patrões*.
46. Polanyi, *The Great Transformation*, 250–51; Pechman, *Cidades estreitamente vigiadas*, 346.
47. Kalmanowiecki, "Soldados, ou missionários domésticos."
48. Barbosa, *A questão social e política no Brasil*, xxii; Hahner, *Poverty and Politics*, 280; Weinstein, *For Social Peace in Brazil*, 52–53; Maram, "Labor and the Left in Brazil, 1890–1921," 266; Meade, *"Civilizing" Rio*, 168.
49. Maram, "Labor and the Left in Brazil, 1890–1921," 266.
50. Carvalho, *Cidadania no Brasil*, 90–93, 104–5. Maram, "Urban Labor and Social Change in the 1920s," 215. According to Maram, the estado de sítio lasted until 1927. Military revolts continued into the 1930s.
51. Kessel, *O vitrine e o espelho*.
52. Dávila, "A 'mensagem' que os números da estatística brasileira querem enviar à nação," 27, 46, 56.
53. There were 239,129 foreign immigrants who moved to Rio (and 829,851 who moved to São Paulo) in 1920. There were 1,565,961 foreign immigrants in Brazil in 1920; Dávila, "A 'mensagem' que os números da estatística brasileira querem enviar à nação," 30.
54. On the expulsion of foreigners, see Hahner, *Poverty and Politics*, 265–66.
55. See, for example, AN, Delegacia Auxiliar da Polícia, 2a—Peças Teatrais. Caixa 70, pasta 1700. On Armando Vidal Leite, see CPDOC, Coleção Armando Vidal. On "social hygiene" as part of early twentieth-century scientific policing, see da Cunha, "As domínios da experiência, da ciência da lei." See also Stallybrass and White, *The Politics and Poetics of Transgression*, 135–38.
56. CPDOC, AV 22.02.01.
57. AN, Série Justiça, IJ⁶–645 (ano: 1918). See also the letter of July 12, 1917, from Armando Vidal to the Chief of Police: AN, Serie Justiça—IJ⁶ 617.

58. Bretas, *Ordem na cidade*, 76.

59. CPDOC, AV 19.10.29, Cartas a Armando Vidal da SBAT.

60. *Jornal do Brasil* (June 18, 1919), np.

61. The Quarta Delegacia Auxiliar was created by Law (Decreto) 15848 of November 20, 1922. The quotation is from *Relatório do Ministério da Justiça e Negócios Interiores*, 1923, 181. Also relevant here is Decreto 16.107 (February 8, 1923); the author is grateful to Olívia Maria Gomes da Cunha for sharing her research data and insights. The Quarta Delegacia Auxiliar took over the suppression of communism after 1926; Bretas, "Polícia e Polícia Política no Rio de Janeiro nos Anos 1920," 28, 33.

62. Bretas, *Ordem na cidade*, 159; Bretas, "Polícia e polícia política no Rio de Janeiro nos anos 1920," 28–29. Documents demonstrating the activities of the Delegacias Auxiliares in 1913 can be found in AN, Polícia—GIFI 6C-424 and AN, Série Justiça, IJ[6]–632.

63. *Relatório do Ministério da Justiça e Negócios Interiores*, 1923, 165.

64. Olívia Maria Gomes da Cunha, personal communication with author, June 18, 2008.

65. For biographical information on Armando Vidal Leite Ribeiro (1888–1982), see CPDOC, Coleção Armando Vidal, Apresentação do Índice, 537.

66. "As medidas de repressão contra o jogo do bicho na 3a Delegacia Auxiliar," *A Notícia* (October 19, 1917), np.

67. The Segunda Delegacia Auxiliar oversaw the entertainment industry, "repression of gambling," and control and censorship of public entertainment; *Relatório do Ministério da Justiça e Negócios Interiores* (1922 and 1923), 181. The Terceira Delegacia Auxiliar was responsible for the repression of anarchism; *Relatório do Ministério da Justiça e Negócios Interiores*, (1919–20), 71. It also oversaw the other Delegacias Auxiliaries, maritime police, and pawnshops (*casas de penhores*); *Relatório do Ministério da Justiça e Negócios Interiores* (1922 and 1923), 182.

68. *Relatório do Ministério da Justiça e Negócios Interiores* (1922 and 1923), 181.

69. Mello, "A história social dos jogos de azar no Rio de Janeiro, 1808–1946," 107.

70. *Relatório do Ministério da Justiça e Negocios Interiores* (1916 and 1917), 65; *Relatório do Ministério da Justiça e Negocios Interiores* (1918 and 1919), 75. The Segunda Delegacia Auxiliar was also responsible for contravening the solicitiation and traffic of prostitutes (*lenocínio*); *Relatório do Ministério da Justiça e Negócios Interiores* (1919 and 1920), 75. On the division of responsibilities among the Delegacias Auxiliares, see *Relatórios do Ministério da Justiça e Negócios Interiores* for the following years: 1916 and 1917, 65; 1917 and 1918, 68; 1918 and 1919, 75; 1919 and 1920, 71, 75; 1922 and 1923, 173, 175–77, 181–83; and 1927 and 1928, 168.

71. AN, Série Polícia-Justiça, JJ[6]–736.

72. *Relatório do Ministério da Justiça e Negócios Interiores* (1922 and 1923), 181–82.

73. Evidence here comes from judicial sentencing records for 1917–18. See especially AN, Registro de Sentença, Códices do Poder Judiciário (3ª Pretoria Criminal), AM208 D 8789, Livro no. 5. From October to December 1917, virtually all jogo do bicho

cases coming from the Terceira Delegacia Auxiliar ended in conviction, while all cases coming from the Delegacias Districtais were acquitted.

74. "As medidas repressoras: 'Jogo do bicho,' " *A notícia* (September 13, 1917), np.

75. Secretaria de Estado de Justiça, DOPS, 32; Rose, *One of the Forgotten Things*; Bretas, *Ordem na cidade*; Green, *Beyond Carnival*, 67–74; Secretaria de Estado de Justiça, DOPS: *A lógica da desconfiança*, 10; da Cunha, *Intenção e gesto*.

76. Dávila, "A 'mensagem' que os números da estatística brasileira querem enviar à nação," 45–46.

77. Pechman, *Cidades estreitamente vigiadas*, 362–72. Also see chapter 2.

78. Da Cunha, *Intenção e gesto*; Green, *Beyond Carnival*, 70–71.

79. Ruggiero, *Modernity in the Flesh*, 108.

80. Pechman, *Cidades estreitamente vigiadas*, 291–92.

81. Cristina Rivera-Garza, "Criminalization of the Syphilitic Body: Prostitutes, Health Crimes, and Society in Mexico City, 1867–1930"; and Kristin Ruggiero, "Passion, Perversity, and the Pace of Justice in Argentina at the Turn of the Last Century," in Salvatore, Aguirre, and Joseph, eds., *Crime and Punishment in Latin America*, 147–80, 211–32.

82. Green, *Beyond Carnival*, chap. 3; Stepan, *The Hour of Eugenics*, 38–39.

83. Green, *Beyond Carnival*, 70–71, 110–11.

84. Da Cunha, *Intenção e gesto*.

85. See the jogo do bicho cases in AN, IJ⁶ 785 (código de fundo AM).

86. Bretas, *Ordem na cidade*, 74.

87. See Bretas, "Polícia e Polícia Política no Rio de Janeiro nos Anos 1920," 25–34; da Cunha, *Intenção e gesto*; Olivia Maria Gomes da Cunha, "The Stigmas of Dishonor: Criminal Records, Civil Rights, and Forensic Identification in Rio de Janeiro: 1903–1940," in Caulfield, Chambers, and Putnam, eds., *Honor, Status and Law in Modern Latin America*, 295–315; Rose, *One of the Forgotten Things*, 20.

88. Maram, "Urban Labor and Social Change in the 1920s," 218–19; Chazkel, "Social Life and Civic Education in the Rio de Janeiro City Jail"; Weinstein, *For Social Peace in Brazil*, 53; Cancelli, *O mundo da violência*. For an example of political arrests in this period, see AN, Série Justiça-Polícia, IJ⁶–657 (código do fundo AM). For the surveillance and suppression of the anarchist newspaper *A Voz do Povo*, see AN, JJ⁶–736.

89. Magalhães, "Ganhou leva," 86.

90. Mello, "A história social dos jogos de azar no Rio de Janeisro, 1808–1946," 129.

91. Magalhães, "Ganhou leva," 151–153.

92. Ibid., chap. 4.

93. Fausto, ed., *História Geral da Civilização Brasileira*, vol. III: *O Brasil Republicano*, 258; Lobo, *História do Rio de Janeiro*, 520–21; Mello, "A história social dos jogos de azar no Rio de Janeiro, 1808–1946," 122, 131.

94. Mello, "A história social dos jogos de azar no Rio de Janeiro, 1808–1946," 126–35.

95. Cf. Bretas, "Polícia e Polícia Política no Rio de Janeiro nos Anos 1920."

96. These and several other accusations of police involvement in the jogo do bicho in

1917 are found in AN, SJ-IJ⁶. I use the passive voice advisedly here, as the surviving documents do not indicate who made the accusations.

97. AN, Série Justiça, IJ⁶–599.

98. AN, GIFI, GC 530. See also Bretas, *Ordem na cidade*, 147, fn7.

99. Barbosa, *Bambambã!*, 71.

100. Barros, *O fabuloso império*, 39–40. Barros refers to article 321, no. II of *Código do Processo Penal*. Additionally, Federal Law (Decreto) 21143 of March 21, 1932, article 15, stipulates that "the *contravenção* called the jogo do bicho is *afiançável* [ineligible for bail]." Likewise, Federal Law 6259 of February 10, 1944, article 59, made the jogo do bicho ineligible for bail. On "jail-door lawyers" (*os advogados da porta de xadrez*) see also Cavalcante, *Os bicheiros*, 258–62.

101. This essay is dated 1951 but may have been written earlier and refers mainly to the late 1910s through the 1940s. In Bandeira, *O Rio de Janeiro em prosa e verso*, 196.

102. USNA, Record Group 59, General Records of the Department of State, 832.00/570. "General Conditions Prevailing in Brazil," attachment to Edwin V. Morgan, Rio de Janeiro, to the Secretary of State, April 13, 1926. On Carneiro da Fontoura, see also Bretas, "A Polícia e a polícia política," 28.

103. Bretas, *Ordem na cidade*, 74–5; Magalhães, "Ganhou leva," 182.

104. Mello, "A história social dos jogos de azar no Rio de Janeiro, 1808–1946," 89–90; Magalhães, "Ganhou leva," 153; Moura, *Tia Ciata e a pequena África no Rio de Janeiro*, 116–27. This scandal in 1913 is immortalized in the song "Pelo Telefone" (1917), generally considered Brazil's first recorded samba composition.

105. Mello, "A história social dos jogos de azar no Rio de Janeiro, 1808–1946," 110.

106. AN, Secretaria da Presidência da República, Lata 527; da Cunha, "A lei da experiência, a experiência da lei," 13; Olivia Maria Gomes da Cunha, personal communication with author (June 2006). On the campaigns, see Magalhães, "Ganhou leva," 180.

107. See AN, Polícia, GIFI 6C-424.

108. White, "Telling More," 11, 14–15.

109. Gotkowitz, "Trading Insults"; Calhoun, "The Privatization of Risk."

110. All references to this case come from AN, CX 270, Proc. 70, Gal. B.

111. Fassula was apparently acquitted seven times and convicted twice. In November 1937, he was given a minimum sentence of ten days of prison and a fine of 100$000; AN, Notação Proc. n. 4794–1937. A detailed list of his arrests can be found in AN, CX 168, proc. A-6320.

112. AN, Notação Proc. n. 6383, 1939, Fundo: 20a Vara Criminal.

113. AN, Registro de Sentenças, Códices do Poder Judiciário (3ª Pretoria Criminal) AM208 D 8789; Registro de Sentenças Livro n° 5.

114. All references to this case come from AN, Notação 7147 6Z.7147.

115. AN, Registro de Sentença, Códices do Poder Judiciário (3ª Pretoria Criminal) AM208 D 8789; Registro de Setenças Livro n° 5. Cf. Magalhães, "Ganhou leva," 186.

116. AN, Registro de Sentença, Códices do Poder Judiciário (3ª Pretoria Criminal) AM208 D 8789; Registro de Setenças Livro n° 5.

117. AN, OI.2589, 10a Vara Criminal.

118. Many other examples can be found in AN, Registro de Sentença, Códices do Poder judiciario (3ª Pretoria Criminal) AM208 D 8789; Registro de Sentenças Livro n° 5.

119. AN, CX 168, proc: A-6320, Gal. B; Juizo de Direito da 10a Vara Criminal, Processo A—6320 Galeria B, Caixa 168.

120. See, for example, AN, Notação Proc. n. 6383, 1939; Fundo: 20a Vara Criminal.

121. Decreto-Lei 6259 de 10 de fevereiro de 1944, artigo 58, section 2nd.

122. See the October 1941 law, LCP—Decreto-Lei 3688, articles 51 and 57, and especially 58; and the 1944 Decreto-Lei 6259 (the February 1944 law that regulated lotteries), articles 45–57.

123. Cf. Salvatore, *Wandering Paysanos*, 187–89.

124. Cf. Bretas, *Ordem na cidade*, 151–55.

125. Cf. Graham, *Patronage and Politics*; Gotkowitz, "Trading Insults," 106–7.

126. "As medidas de repressão contra o jogo do bicho na 3ª Delegacia Auxiliar," *A Notícia* (October 19, 1917), np; from FGV/CPDOC, Coleção Armando Vidal, Recortes de jornal: J 42.

127. "A polícia proteje os jogadores," *Dom Quixote* anno 4, no. 166 (July 14, 1920).

128. DaMatta, "Pedro Malasartes and the Paradoxes of Roguery," in *Carnivals, Rogues, and Heroes*, 198–238; Aguirre, "Speaking for the Subaltern?"

129. Calhoun, "The Privatization of Risk"; Randall and Charlesworth, eds., *Moral Economy and Popular Protest*.

130. DaMatta and Soárez, *Águias, burros e borboletas*.

131. Quoted in Alleau, *Dicionário dos jogos*, 103.

132. Zweig, *Brazil, Land of the Future*, 148.

133. Quoted in Pacheco, *A antologia do jogo do bicho*, 63.

134. APERJ, DOPS, Geral-68, *O Globo* (4/9/1941).

135. From *O Observador*, no. XXXIV (November 1938), np.

136. Magalhães, "Ganhou leva," 164.

137. Cf. Wolcott, "The Culture of the Informal Economy."

138. BN, Setor de Periódicos, *O Bicho* (issues surveyed from 1907 to 1914); Magalhães, "Ganhou leva," 77–78.

139. Cavalcante, *Os bicheiros*, 109.

140. This story is recounted in numerous texts. See, for example, Alleau, ed., *Dicionário dos jogos*, 48; Caillois, *Quatre Essai de Sociologie Contemporaine*, 37–38.

141. Roniger, *Hierarchy and Trust in Modern Mexico and Brazil*, 10, 198; Hannerz, *Exploring the City*, 213.

142. Atiyah, *Promises, Morals, and Law*, 99, 103, 169–70, 177.

143. Cited in Magalhães, "Ganhou leva," 109–10.

144. See Douglas and Isherwood, *The World of Goods*, 43–44.

145. Rama, *The Lettered City*; Burke, "The Uses of Literacy in Early Modern Italy," in Burke and Porter, eds., *The Social History of Language*, 21–42; González Escheverria, *Myth and Archive*, chapter 2.

146. Graham, *Patronage and Politics*, chap. 5; Rama, *The Lettered City*, 179.

147. Rama, *The Lettered City*, 29.

148. Lauderdale Graham, "Writing from the Margins," 612.

149. Brodwyn M. Fischer, "Slandering Citizens: Insults, Class, and Social Legitimacy in Rio de Janeiro's Criminal Courts," in Caulfield, Chambers, and Putnam, eds., *Honor, Status, and the Law in Modern Latin America*, 179, 196.

150. For another example, see *Annaes do Conselho Municipal* (November 1917), 280. (Projecto n. 235).

151. AN, IJ⁶-625 (código do fundo AM, secão de guarda CODS, série justiça-policia).

152. AN, Série Polícia-Justiça JJ⁶ 736, 3a seção—Delegacias Auxiliares—November 1920.

153. Cavalcante, *Os bicheiros*, 258–62.

154. AN, SDE Caixa 5C, Gabinete Civil da Presidência da República. This letter is undated but is archived with a group of documents from the 1930s and 1940s.

155. Hannerz, *Exploring the City*, 213. See also Halttunen, *Confidence Men and Painted Women*, 42; Chalhoub, *Trabalho, lar, e botequim*, 205–6.

156. Quoted in Moreira, *São Paulo na Primeira República*, 27. See also Filho, ed., *Questão Social no Brasil*, 28–61.

157. Hahner, *Poverty and Politics*, 267–68; Luís also famously stated that "the social question is of secondary interest to the question of public order"; Moreira, *São Paulo na Primeira República*, 30.

158. Weinstein, *For Social Peace in Brazil*, 58–59.

159. Dávila, *Diploma of Whiteness*; Barbosa, "Escola e questão racial na história de Campinas (Final do Império)," 50–58; Gomes, *A invenção do trabalhismo*.

160. Velloso, *Modernismo no Rio de Janeiro*; Green, *Beyond Carnival*, 67–70; Abreu, *O império do divino*; Guelfi, *Novíssima*; Williams, *Culture Wars in Brazil*, 36–42; Sevcenko, *Orfeu extático na metrópole*, 269–74; Vianna, *The Mystery of Samba*; Sandroni, *Feitiço Decente*, 97–99.

161. Williams, *Culture Wars in Brazil*, 51, 85–88; Cohen, *The Manipulation of Consent*, 30–33; Rose, *One of the Forgotten Things*, 71.

162. Mastrofski, "Community Policing as Reform," 50, 62; Chalhoub makes a similar argument in *Trabalho, lar e botequim*. See also Bretas, " 'The Sovereign's Vigilant Eye?' "; Salem, *História da polícia no Rio de Janeiro* 106–7; Bretas, "O informal no formal," 1996, 216; Kalmanowiecki, "Soldados, ou missionários domésticos."

163. Bretas, *Ordem na cidade*, 64, 71; Leal, *Annaes da Conferência Judiciária-Polícia*. Terceira Seção, "Polícia Administrativa"; Pechman, *Cidades estreitamente vigiadas*, 345–48. See, for example, *Relatório do Ministério da Justiça e Negócios Interiores* (1919 and 1920), 71–73.

164. See especially AN, IJ⁶-625.

EPILOGUE

1. The Jardim Zoológico in Vila Isabel closed in 1941, and Rio's new zoo was inaugurated on March 18, 1945, at the Quinta da Boa Vista; Noronha Santos, *As freguesias antigas do Rio antigo*, 42.

2. Mello, "A história social dos jogos de azar no Rio de Janeiro, 1808–1946," 150–51, 167, 171–73; Decreto-Lei 854 do 12 de novembro de 1938.

3. Lei (or Código) das Contravenções Penais, Decreto-Lei 3688 de 3 de outubro de 1941.

4. APERJ, DOPS-Geral-68.

5. Magalhães, "Ganhou leva," 187–88.

6. Mello, "A história social dos jogos de azar no Rio de Janeiro, 1808–1946," 180.

7. *Relatório do Ministério da Justiça e Negócios Interiores* (1948).

8. Mello, "A história social dos jogos de azar no Rio de Janeiro, 1808–1946," 182–84; Salem, *História da polícia*, 100–102. The federal law referred to here is Decreto-Lei 9215.

9. AN, Notação Processo n. 3801, CX 1247.

10. The police investigating this case consulted Fassula's *vida pregressa*, the detailed rap sheet that was an innovation of the Vargas-era document revolution; AN, Notação Processo n. 3801, CX 1247. See also Brodwyn M. Fisher, "Slandering Citizens: Insults, Class, and Social Legitimacy in Rio de Janeiro's Criminal Courts," in Caulfield, Chambers, and Putman, eds., *Honor, Status, and Law in Modern Latin America*, 176–200.

11. At an exchange rate of 18.38 cruzeiros to the dollar in 1950, CR$10,000 equals $544; http://www.globalfinancialdata.com.

12. Magalhães, "Ganhou leva," 157–59. Out of 433 persons arrested for jogo do bicho–related offenses, not one had gone beyond primary school. Less than .005 percent of the persons arrested for violating article 58 of the Lei das Contravenções Penais from 1942 to 1958 had a secondary education or higher; ibid., 194.

13. On Labanca and Segreto, see chapter 5.

14. "Brazil Jails Gamblers," *New York Times* (November 13, 1940), 12.

15. Magalhães, "Ganhou leva," 91–92; Barros, *O fabuloso império do jogo do bicho*, 106.

16. "Guerra da contravenção já," *O Globo* (July 3, 1983), 20; Magalhães, "Ganhou leva," chap. 4.

17. Carradore, *Folclore do jogo do bicho*, 56. Decreto-Lei 204, February 27, 1967, legalized some lotteries and betting on horse races and permitted and regulated the federal lottery, placing lotteries under federal control and stipulating that they could not be contracted out as private concessions. Lei Federal n. 7.291, de 19 de dezembro de 1984, explicitly permitted betting on horse races.

18. See, for example, APERJ, DOPS, Caixa 254, f. 220. The famous jogo do bicho banker and former president of the Independent League of Samba Schools, Ailton "Captain" Guimarães served in a counterinsurgency unit during the most repressive phase of the military government. See Larry Rohter, "Brazilain Numbers Game Ties Officials to Mobsters," *New York Times* (June 7, 2007), A10.

19. Evangelista, *Rio de Janeiro*, 34–44. Some claim that the jogo do bicho is a money laundering scheme for more serious illicit activities, such as traffic in arms and drugs; *Istoé* (March 5, 2003).

20. See "Guerra da contravenção já," *O Globo* (July 3, 1983), 20.

21. Oliveira, da Silveira, and Silva, "Pathological Gambling and Its Consequences for Public Health," 5; "Bicho pagou propina a jurados do carnaval," *O Globo* (June 10, 2007), 1, 22–23; Rohter, "Brazilian Numbers Game Ties Official to Mobsters," *New York Times* (June 7, 2007), A10.

22. Evangelista, *Rio de Janeiro*, 32, 36–37.

23. Chinelli and Silva, "O vazio da ordem."

24. Evangelista, *Rio de Janeiro*, 37.

25. President Luiz Inácio Lula da Silva announced in 2007 a dramatic increase in public funding for "Rio de Janeiro's Carnival parade to reduce the influence of numbers runners and gangsters who have traditionally controlled parade groups"; "Brazil president promises funding for Rio Carnival parade groups," *International Herald Tribune* (December 8, 2007).

26. APERJ, DOPS, Geral-68 (Estado da Guanabara, Secretaria de Segurança Pública. 1 de novembro de 1971).

27. De Certeau, *The Practice of Everyday Life*; Levine, "Michel de Certeau and Latin America," in Centeno and López-Alves, *The Other Mirror*, 309–28.

28. Brown, "On Resisting Resistance," 734.

29. Diana Paton makes a similar argument; see *No Bond but the Law*, chap. 5.

30. Sherman, *Class Acts*, 9, 16, 17, 19.

31. Kahn, *The Cultural Study of Law*.

32. Thompson elaborated his concept of the moral economy in an essay in *Past and Present* in 1971. See Thompson, "Moral Economy of the English Crowd in the Eighteenth Century," in *Customs in Common*, 185–258; Randall and Charlesworth, eds., *Moral Economy and Popular Protest*, 1.

33. Douglas Hay, "Moral Economy, Political Economy and the Law," in Randall and Charlesworth, eds., *Moral Economy and Popular Protest*, 93–122; the quotation is from 94–95.

34. James C. Scott, "The Moral Economy as an Argument and as a Fight," in Randall and Charlesworth, eds., *Moral Economy and Popular Protest*, 188.

35. This newspaper chronicle ("A Volta," January 26, 1915) was republished in Lima Barreto, *Vidas urbanas*, 82–83.

GLOSSARY OF PORTUGUESE TERMS

ambulante: see *vendedor ambulante*

apontador (*apontadores*, pl.): see *bicheiro*

banqueiro (*de bicho*): individual who finances ("banks") a jogo do bicho operation

bicheiro: seller of tickets for the jogo do bicho

bicho: animal; creature; beast

cachaça: a strong, rum-like alcoholic beverage popular in Brazil made from fermented and distilled sugar-cane juice

Carioca: of or from the city of Rio de Janeiro

comerciante: someone who works in commerce, usually a shopkeeper

contravenção: misdemeanor; vice crime

contraventor: one who commits a *contravenção*

coronel (*coroneis*, pl.): local patron or boss; rough equivalent of *cacique* in Spanish America

delegacia: neighborhood-level administrative unit of police; precinct; department

delegado: head of *delegacia*

entrudo: mischievous Carnival tradition involving throwing objects, outlawed in First Republic

fazendeiro: owner of large estate (*fazenda*); member of Brazil's landed gentry

First Republic: period that began on November 15, 1889, following the fall of the Brazilian monarchy and ended with the Revolution of 1930, which ended the presidency of Washington Luis and brought President Getúlio Vargas into power

folhetim: chapbook; popular, inexpensively produced pamphlet

fortaleza: literally a "fort"; centralized, fortified, clandestine locale where jogo do bicho businesses are administered and where the day's cash intake is counted

jogatina: gambling

jogo: game; gambling

padrinho: godfather; a fictive kin relationship

palpite: tip or suggestion (e.g., of which animal to play in the jogo do bicho); literally, "heartbeat"

vendedor ambulante: street peddler

BIBLIOGRAPHY

ARCHIVES CONSULTED

Rio de Janeiro

Arquivo Geral da Cidade do Rio de Janeiro (AGCRJ)
Arquivo Nacional (AN)
Arquivo Público do Estado do Rio de Janeiro (APERJ)
Biblioteca Nacional, Seção de Periódicos (BN)
Casa de Rui Barbosa (CRB)
Centro de Pesquisa e Documentação—Fundação Getúlio Vargas (CPDOC)
Instituto Histórico e Geográfico Brasileiro (IHGB)
Museu de Imagem e do Som (MIS)

Salvador, Bahia, Brazil
Arquivo Municipal do Salvador (AMS)
Arquivo Público do Estado da Bahia (APEB)

Washington, D.C.
Oliveira Lima Library
United States National Archives (USNA)

PUBLISHED PRIMARY SOURCES

Abranches, Dunshee de. *Atas e Actos do Governo Provisório*. 3d ed. Rio de Janeiro:
    Oficinas Gráficas do Jornal do Brasil, 1953.
Actos do Poder Executivo. Rio de Janeiro: Imprensa Nacional, 1907.
Aimard, Gustave. *Le Brésil Nouveau*. Paris: E. Ventu Ed., 1888.
Almeida, A. A. Cardoso d.' *Lucros e perdas: Versos de um sexagenário*. Rio de Janeiro,
    1926.
Anaes do Conselho Municipal (D.F.). Rio de Janeiro: September 1897–November
    1917.
Anais da Câmara Municipal, Primeira Sessão Ordinária, February 27 to May 9, 1896.

Annaes da Conferência Judiciária-Policial, convocada por Aurelino de Araujo Leal. 4 vols. Rio de Janeiro: Imprensa Nacional, 1918.

Araujo, João Vieira de. *O Código Penal interpretado, segundo as fontes a doutrina, e a jurisprudência e com referencias aos projectos da sua revisão*. Rio de Janeiro, nd.

Arinos, Affonso. *Lendas e tradições brasileiras*. 2nd ed. Rio de Janeiro: F. Briguiet e Companhia, 1937.

Assis, Machado de. *Obra completa de Machado de Assis*. Vol. 2. Rio de Janeiro: Novo Aguilar, 1994.

Azevedo, Aluísio. *O cortiço*. Rio de Janeiro: F. Briguiet, 1939 (1890).

——. *A Condessa Vésper*. Rio de Janeiro: R. Briguiet, 1939.

Bandeira, Manuel, and Carlos Drummond de Andrade. *O Rio de Janeiro em prosa e verso*. Rio de Janeiro: J. Olympio, 1965.

Barbosa, Orestes. *Na prisão: chronicas*. 2d ed. Rio de Janeiro: Jacintho Ribeiro dos Santos, 1922.

——. *Bambambã!* 2d ed. Rio de Janeiro: Prefeitura da Cidade do Rio de Janeiro, 1993.

Barbosa, Rui. *A obra de Ruy Barbosa em criminologia e direito criminal (seleções e dicionário de pensamentos)*. Rio de Janeiro: Ed. Nacional de Direito, 1952.

——. *A questão social e política no Brasil: Conferência pronunciada no Teatro Lírico, do Rio de Janeiro, a 2–0 de março de 1919*. Evaristo de Morais Filho, ed. Rio de Janeiro: Fundação Rui Barbosa, 1983.

Barreto, Lima, *Marginália*. São Paulo: Editora Mérito, 1953.

——. *Feiras e mafuás: Artigos e crônicas*. São Paulo: Editora Brasiliense, 1956.

——. *Vidas urbanas: Artigos e crônicas*. 2d ed. São Paulo: Editora Brasiliense, 1961.

——. *Clara dos Anjos e outro contos*. 2d ed. São Paulo: Editora Brasiliense, 1961.

Barros, Hugo Laercio de. *O fabuloso império do jogo do bicho*. Rio de Janeiro: Editora Rosaly, 1957.

Bentham, Jeremy. *The Works of Jeremy Bentham, published under the Superintendence of his Exector, John Bowring*. Vol. 6. Edinburgh: William Tait, 1843.

Bilac, Olavo, and Manoel Bomfim. *Através do Brasil*. São Paulo: Companhia das Letras, 2000.

Carradore, Hugo Pedro. *Folclore do jogo do bicho*. São Paulo: Tribuna Piracicabana, 1979.

Cascudo, Luís da Câmara, *Dicionário do folklore brasileiro*. Rio de Janeiro: Livraria José Olímpio, 1954.

Castro, Luiz de. *Le Brésil Vivant*. Paris: Librairie Fischbacher, 1891.

Cavalcante, Eugênio Currivo. *Os bicheiros*. Rio de Janeiro: Editora A Noite, 1940.

Código de Política Municipal da Cidade do Rio de Janeiro, Posturas Municipais. September 1898.

Código Penal da República dos Estados Unidos do Brasil: Conversão das Penas, Fiança, Prescripção, systema penitenciária, cellulas, etc. por um magistrado Mineiro. Rio de Janeiro: Imprensa Nacional, 1892.

Código Penal e Legislação Complementar. Rio de Janeiro: Companhia Forense de Artes Gráficas, 1940.

Cooper, Clayton Sedgwick. *The Brazilians and Their Country*. New York: Frederick A. Stokes, 1917.

Costa, Emília de Sousa. *Como eu vi o Brazil*. Lisbon: Portugalia, 1925.

Cruz, Mario Ribeiro da, *Vale o escrito: casos de jogo do bicho*. Rio de Janeiro: Razão Cultural, 2000.

Dent, Hastings Charles. *A Year in Brazil, with Notes on the Abolition of Slavery, the Finances of the Empire, Religion, Meteorology, Natural History, etc.* London: Kegan Paul, Tranch, 1886.

Edmundo, Luis. *O Rio de Janeiro do meu tempo*. Rio de Janeiro: Imprensa Nacional, 1938.

Figueiredo, José Burle de. *A contravenção de vadiagem*. Rio de Janeiro: Typografia do Journal do Comercio, 1924.

Freyre, Gilberto. *Casa grande e senzala*. 43d ed. Rio de Janeiro: Editora Record, 2001 (1933).

———. *Sobrados e mucambos: Decadência do patriarchado rural no Brasil*. São Paulo: Companhia Editora Nacional, 1936.

Gerson, Brasil. *História das ruas do Rio*. 5th ed. rev. Rio de Janeiro: Lacerda Editora, 2000.

Hungria, Nelson. *Comentários ao Código Penal*. Rio de Janeiro: Editora Forense, 1982 (1950).

Kelsey, Vera. *Brazil in Capitals*. New York: Harper and Brothers, 1942.

Leal, Aurelino de Araujo. *A religião entre os condemnados da Bahia: estudo de psichologia criminal*. Bahia: 1898.

Leite, Fernando da França. *O Rio de Janeiro: Uma viagem no tempo*. Rio de Janeiro: Produtor Editorial Independente, 1953.

Leme, Ernesto. *Ruy e a questão social*. São Paulo: Martins, 1951.

Liszt, Franz von. *O Brasil na Legislação Comparada (Direito Criminal dos Estados Extra-Europeus)*. Rio de Janeiro: Imprensa Nacional, 1911.

Lombroso, Cesare. *Criminal Man*. Translated by Mary Gibson and Nicole Hahn Rafner. Durham: Duke University Press, 2006.

Lombroso, Cesare, and Guglieimo Ferrera. *Criminal Woman, the Prostitute, and the Normal Woman*. Translated by Nicole Hahn Raiter and Mary Gibson. Durham: Duke University Press, 2004.

Mathias, Herculano Gomes. *Viagem pitoresca ao velho e ao novo Rio*. Rio de Janeiro, 1965.

Matos, Claudia. *Acertei no milhar: samba e malandragem no tempo de Getúlio*. Rio de Janeiro: Paz e Terra, 1982.

Mendes, Cândido. *Código do Processo Penal: Anotado*. Rio de Janeiro: Imprensa Nacional, 1926.

Mendes, José. *Ensaios de philosophia do direito*. Vol. 1. São Paulo, 1905.

Ministério da Justiça. *Código Penal dos Estados Unidos do Brasil*. Rio de Janeiro: Imprensa Nacional, 1890.

Moraes, [Antonio] Evaristo de. *Reminiscências de um rábula criminalista*. Rio de Janeiro: Ed Briguiet, 1989.

Oakenfull, J. C. *Brazil in 1911*. Frome and London: Butler and Tanner, 1912.

——. *Brazil in 1912*. London: Robert Atkinson, 1913.

——. *Brazil (1913)*. Frome and London: Butler and Tanner, 1913.

Pacheco, Renato José Costa. *Antologia do jogo do bicho*. Rio de Janeiro: Organização Simões Editora, 1957.

Pinheiro, M. Fernandes. *Sentenças civeis e criminais: 14–2–1922 a 11–4–1927*. Rio de Janeiro: Terra de Sol, nd.

Piragibe, Vicente. *Consolidação das leis penais (aprovada e adotada pelo Dec. n. 22.213 de 14/12/1932)*. Rio de Janeiro: Typografia do Joural do Brasil, 1933.

Pompéia, Raul. *Crônicas do Rio*. Rio de Janeiro: Coleção Biblioteca Carioca, 1996.

Ramos, Joaquim Jose Pereira da Silva. *O Indicador Penal Contendo por ordem Alphabetica as desposições do Codigo Criminal do Império do Brasil e todas as leis penais posteriormente publicadas até o presente*. Rio de Janeiro: Eduardo e Henrique Laemmert, 1861.

Reis, Vicente. *Os ladrões no Rio*. Rio de Janeiro: Laemmert, 1903.

República dos Estados Unidos do Brasil. *Relatório do Ministro de Justiça e Negócios Interiores do Brasil*. Rio de Janeiro: Imprensa Nacional (1893–1948).

——. *Recenseamento do Rio de Janeiro (Districto Federal), Realisado em 20 de setembro de 1906*. Rio de Janeiro: Oficina de Estatistica, 1907.

Rio, João do. *As religiões no Rio*. Rio de Janeiro: Editora Nova Aguilar, 1976.

——. *A alma encantadora das ruas*. Rio de Janeiro: Coleção Biblioteca Carioca, 1995.

Rodrigues, Nina. *Os africanos no Brasil*. 6th ed. Brasília: Editora Universidade de Brasília, 1982.

Romeiro, João Marcondes de Moura. *Dicionário de direito penal*. Rio de Janeiro: Imprensa Nacional, 1905.

Romeiro, Sílvio. *Introdução a Doutrina contra doutrina*. Edited by Alberto Venacio Filho. São Paulo: Companhia das Letras, 2001 (1894).

Rosa, Francisco Ferreira de. *Rio de Janeiro, Edição Oficial da Prefeitura*. Rio de Janeiro: J. Schmidt, 1905.

Rougier, Georges. *Le Brésil em 1911*. Paris: Garnier Frères, Libraires-Éditeurs, 1911.

Saldanha, Gehisa. *O jogo do bicho: Como jogar e ganhar*. Rio de Janeiro: Ediouro, 1986.

Sampião, José Pereira de. *O Brazil mental*. Porto: Livraria Chardron, 1898.

Senna, Ernesto. *Através do Carcere*. Rio de Janeiro: Imprensa Nacional, 1907.

Silva, Evandro Lins e. *O salão dos passos perdidos: Depoimento ao CPDOC*. Rio de Janeiro: Editora Nova Frontiera/FGV, 1997.

Siqueira, Galdino. *Código penal, Rio de Janeiro*: Livraria Jacinto, 1941.

Sousândrade, Joaquim de. *Guesa errante*. São Luis, Maranhão: Edições Sioge, 1979 (1871).

Subiroff, Ivan. *A oligarquia paulista*. São Paulo: O Estado de São Paulo, 1919.

Sullivan, James W. *Markets for the People, The Consumer's Part*. New York: Macmillan, 1913.

Taunay, Visconde de. *O Encilhamento: Cenas contemporâneas da Bolsa do Rio de Janeiro em 1890, 1891, e 1892*. Belo Horizonte: Editora Itatiaia Limitada, 1971.

Tigre, Bastos. *Reminiscencias: a alegre roda da Colombo e algumas figuras do tempo de antigamente*. Brasília: Thesaurus, 1992.

Vidal, Armando. "A repressão do jogo do bicho. Relatório apresentado ao Dr. Aurelino Leal, Chefe de Polícia do Distrito Federal." Rio de Janeiro: Typografia dos "Annaes," 1918.

Viveiros de Castro, Antonio. *Jurisprudência criminal: Casos julgados, jurisprudência estrangeira, doutrina juridica*. Rio de Janeiro: H. Garnier, 1900.

Zweig, Stefan. *Brazil, Land of the Future*. Translated by Andrew St. James. New York: Viking Press, 1941.

SECONDARY SOURCES

Abreu, Martha. *O império do divino: Festas religiosas e cultura popular no Rio de Janeiro, 1830–1900*. Rio de Janeiro: Nova Fronteira, 2002.

Abreu, Mauricio de A. *Evolução urbana do Rio de Janeiro*. 2d ed. Rio de Janeiro: IPLANRIO/Jorge Zahar, 1988.

Abreu, Waldyr de. *O submundo do jogo de azar, Prostituição e vadiagem: Aspectos jurídicos, sociais e psicológicos*. 2nd ed. Rio de Janeiro: Livraria Freitas Bastos, 1968.

Adamo, Sam. "The Broken Promise: Race, Health, and Justice in Rio de Janeiro, 1890–1940." Ph.D. diss., University of New Mexico, 1985.

Addelson, Kathryn Pyne. *Moral Passages: Toward a Collectivist Moral Theory*. New York: Routledge, 1994.

Adelman, Jeremy. *Republic of Capital: Buenos Aires and the Legal Tranformation of the Atlantic World*. Stanford: Stanford University Press, 1999.

Agnew, Jean-Christophe. *Worlds Apart: The Market and the Theater in American Thought, 1550–1750*. New York: Cambridge University Press, 1986.

Aguirre, Carlos. "Speaking for the Subaltern? The Role of Legal Intermediaries in the Shaping of Legal and Political Cultures in Nineteenth- and Early Twentieth-Century Peru." MS, 2002.

——. *The Criminals of Lima and Their Worlds: The Prison Experience, 1850–1935*. Durham: Duke University Press, 2005.

Aguirre, Carlos, and Robert Buffington. *Reconstructing Criminality in Latin America*. Wilmington, Del.: Scholarly Resources, 2000,

Ahr, Johan. "Peddlers and Politics in the Second French Republic." Ph.D. diss., Yale University, 1999.

Algranti, Leila Mezan. *O feitor ausente: Estudos sobre a escravidão urbana no Rio de Janeiro, 1808–1822*. Petrópolis, R.J.: Vozes, 1988.

Alleau, René, ed. *Dicionario dos jogos*, Translated by Antonio Lopes Ribeiro. Porto: Editorial Inova, 1977.

Alonso, Iván, Fernando Iwasaki, and Enrique Ghersi, eds. *El comercio ambulatorio en Lima*. Lima: Instituto Libertad y Democracia, 1989.

Andrade, Manoel Correa de. *A revolução de 30: Da República Velha ao Estado Novo*. 2d ed. Porto Alegre: Mercado Aberto, 1988.

Araujo, Vicente de Paula. *A Bela Época do cinema carioca*. São Paulo: Editora Perspectiva, 1976.

Arrom, Silvia Marina. *Containing the Poor: The Mexico City Poorhouse, 1774–1871.* Durham: Duke University Press, 2000.

Atiyah, P. S. *Promises, Morals, and Law.* Oxford: Clarendon Press, 1981.

Baldessarini, Hugo. *Crônica de uma época (de 1850 ao atentado contra Carlos Lacerda): Getúlio Vargas e o crime de Toneleros.* São Paulo: Companhia Editora Nacional, 1957.

Bandeira, Maria. *A Igreja Católica na virada da questão social (1930–1964).* Rio de Janeiro: Edição Vozes, 2000.

Barata, Carlos Eduardo de Almeida, and Antônio Henrique de Cunha Bueno. *Dicionário de famílias brasileiras.* Vol. 1. São Paulo: Iberoamerica, 2000.

Barbosa, Irene Maria de F. "Escola e questão racial na história de Campinas (Final do Império)," *Simbologia, Tradição e mitos Afro-Brasileiros.* Annais do IV Congresso Afro-Brasileiro. Vol. 3. Recife: Fundação Joaquim Nabuco, May 1994.

Barbosa, Lívia. *O jeitinho brasileiro: A arte de ser mais igual que os outros.* Rio de Janeiro: Editora Campus, 1992.

Barman, Roderick J. *Citizen Emperor: Pedro II and the Making of Brazil, 1825–91.* Stanford: Stanford University Press, 1999.

Baronov, David. *The Abolition of Slavery in Brazil: The "Liberation" of Africans through the Emancipation of Capital.* Westport, Conn.: Greenwood Press, 2000.

Barros, Cristina and Marcos Buenrostro. *Las once y serenoooo! Tipos mexicanos siglo XIX.* Mexico, D.F.: Consejo Nacional para la Cultura y las Artes, 1994.

Beattie, Peter M. *The Tribute of Blood: Army, Honor, Race, and Nation in Brazil, 1864–1945.* Durham: Duke University Press, 2001.

Beezley, William H. *Judas at the Jockey Club, and Other Episodes of Porfirian Mexico.* 2nd ed. Lincoln, Neb.: Bison Books, 2004.

Beezley, William H., and Linda Curcio-Nagy, eds. *Latin American Popular Culture: An Introduction.* Wilmington, Del.: Scholarly Resources Books, 2000.

Benácchio, Rosilda. "Meninos vadios: Reeducação e maioridade penal aos nove anos de idade, Rio de Janeiro, 1900–1910." MS. Rio de Janeiro, 2001.

Benchimol, Jaime Larry. *Pereira Passos: Um Haussmann tropical: A renovação urbana da cidade do Rio de Janeiro no início do século XX.* Rio de Janeiro: Biblioteca Carioca, 1990.

Benton, Lauren. *Law and Colonial Cultures: Legal Regimes in World History, 1400–1900.* New York: Cambridge University Press, 2002.

Besse, Susan K. *Restructuring Patriarchy; The Modernization of Gender Inequality in Brazil, 1914–1940.* Chapel Hill: University of North Carolina Press, 1996.

Bethell, Leslie. *Brazil: Empire and Republic, 1822–1930.* New York: Cambridge University Press, 1989.

———, ed. *The Cambridge History of Latin America.* Vols. 5, 6. New York: Cambridge University Press, 1986.

Blackburn, Robin. *The Making of New World Slavery: From the Baroque to the Modern, 1492–1800.* New York: Verso, 1997.

Blok, Anton. *Honour and Violence.* New York: Polity Press, 2001.

Bluestone, Daniel M. " 'The Pushcart Evil': Peddlers, Merchants, and New York City's Streets, 1890–1940." *Journal of Urban History* 91:18 (1999), 68–93.

Boone, Christopher G. "Streetcars and Politics in Rio de Janeiro: Private Enterprise versus Municipal Government in the Provision of Mass Transit, 1903–1920." *Journal of Latin American Studies* 27:2 (May 1995), 343–65.

Borges, Dain. " 'Puffy, Ugly, Slothful and Inert': Degeneration in Brazilian Social Thought, 1880–1940." *Journal of Latin American Studies* 25:2 (May 1993), 235–50.

Brayner, Sônia. *Labirinto do espaço romanesco: Tradição e renovação da literatura brasileira, 1880–1920.* Rio de Janeiro: Civilação Brasileira, 1979.

Brenna, Giovanna Rosso Del. *O Rio de Janeiro do Pereira Passos: Uma cidade em questão II.* Rio de Janeiro: Index, 1985.

Bresciani, Stella, ed. *Imagens da cidade: séculos XIX e XX.* São Paulo: ANPUH, 1993.

Bretas, Marcos Luiz, ed. *Papeis avulsos.* Vol. 1, "Crime e castigo." Rio de Janeiro: Fundação Casa Rui Barbosa, 1986.

———. "O informal no formal: a justiça nas delegacias cariocas da Republica Velha." *Discursos sediciosos: Crime, direito, e sociedade,* 213–22. Rio de Janeiro: Instituto Carioca de Criminologia, 1996.

———. *Ordem na cidade: O exercício cotidiano da autoridade policial no Rio de Janeiro: 1907–1950.* Rio de Janeiro: Rocco, 1997.

———. *A guerra das ruas: Povo e polícia na cidade do Rio de Janeiro.* Rio de Janeiro: Arquivo Nacional, 1997.

———. "Daily Work in Rio de Janeiro Police Stations in the Early Twentieth Century." Paper presented at conference entitled "Crime and Punishment in Latin America," Yale University, 1997.

———. " 'The Sovereign's Vigilant Eye?': Daily Policing and Women in Rio de Janeiro, 1907–1930." *Crime, Histoire, et Société* 2:2 (1998), 55–71.

———. "Polícia e polícia política no Rio de Janeiro nos anos 1920." *Revista do Arquivo Público do Estado do Rio de Janeiro* (2000), 25–34.

Bronfman, Alejandra. *Measures of Equality: Social Science, Citizenship, and Race in Cuba, 1902–1940.* Chapel Hill: University of North Carolina Press, 2004.

Brown, Michael F. "On Resisting Resistance." *American Anthropologist* 98:4 (December 1996), 729–35.

Burke, Peter. *Varieties of Cultural History.* Ithaca: Cornell University Press, 1997.

Burns, E. Bradford. *A History of Brazil.* 3d ed. New York: Columbia University Press, 1993.

Caillois, Roger. *Quatre essays de sociologie contemporaine.* Paris: Olivier Perrin Éditeur, 1951.

———. *Man, Play, and Games.* Translated by Meyer Barash. New York: Free Press of Glencoe, 1961.

Caldeira, Teresa Pires do Rio. *City of Walls: Crime, Segregation, and Citizenship in São Paulo.* Berkeley: University of California Press, 2000.

Calhoun, Craig. "The Privatization of Risk." *Public Culture* 18:2 (2006), 257–64.

Callahan, John F. " 'American Culture Is of a Whole': From the Letters of Ralph Ellison." *New Republic* 220:9 (March 1, 1999), 34–49.

Calmon, Pedro. *História do Ministério da Justiça (1822–1972).* Vol. 1. Rio de Janeiro: Imprensa Nacional, 1972.

Campos, Alexandre. *Dicionário de curiosidades do Rio de Janeiro*. São Paulo: Comércio e Importação de Livros, 1965.

Cancelli, Elizabeth. *O mundo da violência: A Polícia na era do Vargas*. Brasília: Editora Universidade de Brasília, 1993.

Cândido, Antonio. "Dialética da Malandragem." *Revista do Instituto de Estudos Brasileiros* 8 (1970), 67–89.

Carone, Edgard. *Movimento operário no Brasil, 1877–1940*. São Paulo: Difel, 1979.

——. *Classes sociais e movimento operário*. São Paulo: Editora Atica, 1989.

Carvalho, José Murilo de. *Os bestializados: O Rio de Janeiro e a República que não foi*. São Paulo: Companhia das Letras, 1987.

——. *A formação das almas: o imaginário da República do Brasil*. São Paulo: Companhia das Letras, 1990.

——. *A construção da ordem: a elite politica imperial; Teatro de sombras: a política imperial*. 2d ed. rev. Rio de Janeiro: Editora UFRJ, Relume-Dumará, 1996.

——. *Cidadania no Brasil: O longo caminho*. 3d ed. Rio de Janeiro: Civilização Brasileira, 2001.

Carvalho, Lia de Aquino. *Contribuição ao estudo das habitações populares: Rio de Janeiro, 1886–1906*. Rio de Janeiro: Biblioteca Carioca, 1995.

Carvalho, Maria A. Rezende de. *Quatro vezes cidade*. Rio de Janeiro: Sette Letras, 1994.

Caulfield, Sueann. *In Defense of Honor: Sexual Morality, Modernity, and Nation in Early-Twentieth-Century Brazil*. Durham: Duke University Press, 2000.

Caulfield, Sueann, Sarah C. Chambers, and Lara Putnam, eds. *Honor, Status, and the Law in Modern Latin America*. Durham: Duke University Press, 2005.

Centeno, Miguel Angel, and Fernando López-Alves, eds. *The Other Mirror: Grand Theory through the Lens of Latin America*. Princeton: Princeton University Press, 2001.

Centro Cultural Banco do Brasil. *Dinheiro, diversão e arte*. Rio de Janeiro: Centro Cultural do Banco do Brasil, 1995.

Cerqueira Filho, Gilálio. *"Questão social" no Brasil: Crítica do discurso político*. Rio de Janeiro: Civilização Brasileira: 1992.

Chalhoub, Sidney. *Visões da liberdade: uma história das últimas décadas da escravidão na corte*. São Paulo: Companhia das Letras, 1990.

——. *Cidade febril: Cortiços e epidemias na Corte imperial*. São Paulo: Companhia das Letras, 1996.

——. *Trabalho, lar, e botequim: O cotidiano dos trabalhadores no Rio de Janeiro da Belle Époque*. 2d ed. Campinas, SP: Editora UNICAMP, 2001.

Chambers, Sarah C. "Crime and Citizenship: Judicial Practice in Arequipa, Peru, during the Transition from Colony to Republic." *Reconstructing Criminality in Latin America*, ed. Carlos A. Aguirre and Robert Buffington, 31–32. Wilmington, Del.: Scholarly Resources, 2000.

Chasteen, John Charles. "The Pre-History of Samba: Carnival Dancing in Rio de Janeiro, 1840–1917." *Journal of Latin American Studies* 28:1 (February 1996), 29–47.

Chaui, Marilena. *Conformismo e Resistência: Aspectos da cultura popular no Brasil*. São Paulo: Editora Brasiliense, 1986.

Chazkel, Amy. "The Crônica, the City, and the Invention of the Underworld: Rio de Janeiro, 1889–1922." *Estudios Interdisciplinarios de America Latina y el Caribe* 12:1 (January–June 2001), 79–105.

———. "Social Life and Civic Education in the Rio de Janeiro City Jail." *Journal of Social History* 42:3 (March 2009), 144–76.

Chinelli, Filippina, and Luiz Antonio Machado da Silva. "O vazio da ordem: relações políticas e organizacionais entre as escolas de samba e o jogo do bicho." Boletim do Laboratório de Pesquisa Social, DCS-IFCS-UFRJ, no. 2, June 1991.

Chvaicer, Maya Talmon. "'Embodying Difference': Multiculturalism and Performance in Brazil." MS, Tel Aviv University, June 2001.

Clapson, Mark. *A Bit of a Flutter: Popular Gambling and English Society, 1823–1961*. New York: Manchester University Press, 1992.

Clifford, James, and George E. Marcus. *Writing Culture: The Poetics and Politics of Ethnography*. Berkeley: University of California Press, 1986.

Coaracy, Vivaldo. *Memórias da cidade do Rio de Janeiro*. Vol. 3. Rio de Janeiro: Livraria Editora José Olympio, 1965.

Cohen, Esther. "Law, Folklore, and Animal Lore." *Past and Present*, no. 110 (February 1986), 6–37.

Cohen, Stanley, and Andrew Scull, eds. *Social Control and the State: Historical and Comparative Essays*. Oxford: Martin Robertson, 1983.

Cohen, Youssef. *The Manipulation of Consent: The State and Working-Class Consciousness in Brazil*. Pittsburgh: University of Pittsburgh Press, 1989.

Colloredo-Mansfeld, Rudi. "Money of Moderate Size: Playing Tricks on the Dollar in Ecuador." *Common-Place*; www.common-place.org 6:3 (April 2006).

Conniff, Michael. *Urban Politics in Brazil: The Rise of Populism, 1925–1945*. Pittsburgh: University of Pittsburgh Press, 1981.

Conniff, Michael J., and Frank D. McCann, eds. *Modern Brazil: Elites and Masses in Historical Perspective*. Lincoln: University of Nebraska Press, 1989.

Cope, R. Douglas. "Between Liberty and Constraint: Government Regulation of Petty Commerce in Mexico City, 1700–1780." MS, Latin American Studies Association, Washington, D.C., 2001.

Corrêa, Mariza. *Morte em família: representações jurídicas de papeis sexuais*. Rio de Janeiro: Graal, 1983.

———. *As ilusões da liberdade: A Escola Nina Rodrigues e a antropologia no Brasil*. Bragança Paulista, B.P.: EDUSF, 1998.

Crespo, Jorge. "Os jogos de fortuna ou azar em Lisboa em fins do Antigo Regime." *Revista de História Econômica e Social* 8 (July–December 1981), 77–95.

Cronon, William. *Nature's Metropolis: Chicago and the Great West*. New York: W. W. Norton, 1991.

Cross, Gary. "Crowds and Leisure: Thinking Comparatively Across the Twentieth Century." *Journal of Social History* 39:3 (spring 2006), 631–50.

——, ed. *Worktime and Industrialization: An International History*. Philadelphia: Temple University Press, 1988.

Cross, John C. *Informal Politics: Street Vendors and the State in Mexico City*. Stanford: Stanford University Press, 1998.

"The Culture of Risk and Pleasure." Special volume of *Eighteenth-Century Studies* 33:4 (summer 2000).

Cunha, Olívia Maria Gomes da. "Os domínios da experiência, da ciência e da lei: os manuais da polícia civil do Distrito Federal, 1930–1942." *Estudos Históricos* 12:22 (1998), 235–64.

——. "Intenção e gesto: Pessoa, cor e a produção cotidiana da (in)diferença no Rio de Janeiro, 1927–1942." Ph.D. diss. (1999).

——. *Intenção e gesto: pessoa, cor, e produção cotidiana da (in)diferença no Rio de Janeiro, 1927–1942*. Rio de Janeiro: Arquivo Nacional, 2002.

DaMatta, Roberto. *A casa e a rua: Espaço, cidadania, mulher, e morte no Brasil*. São Paulo: Editora Brasiliense, 1985.

——. *Carnivals, Rogues, and Heroes: An Interpretation of the Brazilian Dilemma*. Translated by John Drury. Notre Dame: Notre Dame University Press, 1991.

DaMatta, Roberto, and Elena Soárez. *Águias, burros e borboletas: um estudo antropológico do jogo do bicho*. Rio de Janeiro: Rocco, 1999.

Damazio, Sylvia F. *Um pouco da história do espiritismo no Rio de Janeiro*. Rio de Janeiro: Fundação Casa de Rui Barbosa, 1994.

Dávila, Jerry. "A 'mensagem' que os números da estatística brasileira querem enviar à nação." MS, 1999.

——. *Diploma of Whiteness:Race and Social Policy in Brazil, 1917–1945*. Durham: Duke University Press, 2003.

de Certeau, Michel. *The Practice of Everyday Life*. Translated by Steven Rendall. Berkeley: University of California Press, 1984.

Del Priore, Mary, ed. *Revisão do paraíso: Os brasileiros e o estado em 500 anos de história*. Rio de Janeiro: Editora Campus, 2000.

Departamento Editoral das Edições Melhoramentos. *Novo Dicionário de História do Brasil*. São Paulo: Melhoramentos, 1970.

de Soto, Hernando. *The Other Path: The Invisible Revolution in the Third World*. Translated by June Abbott. New York: Harper and Row, 1989.

Diacon, Todd A. *Stringing Together a Nation: Cândido Mariano da Silva Rondon and the Construction of Modern Brazil, 1906–1930*. Durham: Duke University Press, 2004.

Dias, Maria Odila da Silva. *Power and Everyday Life: The Lives of Working Women in Nineteenth-Century Brazil*. Translated by Ann Frost. Cambridge: Polity Press, 1995.

DiPiero, Thomas. "Buying into Fiction." *Diacritics* 18:2 (summer 1988), 2–14.

Douglas, Mary, and Baron Isherwood. *The World of Goods*. New York: Basic Books, 1979.

Eisenstadt, S. N., and Luis Roniger. *Patrons, Clients, and Friends: Interpersonal Relations and the Structure of Trust in Society*. New York: Cambridge University, 1984.

Engel, Magali. *Meretrizes e doutores: Saber médico e prostuição no Rio de Janeiro (1840–1890)*. São Paulo: Editora Brasiliense, 1988.

Evangelista, Helio de Araujo. *Rio de Janeiro: Violência, jogo do bicho e nacrotráfico segundo uma interpretação*. Rio de Janeiro: Revan, 2003.

Ewick, Patricia, Robert A. Kagan, and Austin Sarat, eds. *Social Science, Social Policy, and the Law*. New York: Russell Sage Foundation, 1999.

Fabian, Ann. *Card Sharks, Dream Books, and Bucket Shops: Gambling in Nineteenth-Century America*. Ithaca: Cornell University Press, 1990.

Faoro, Raymundo. *Os donos de poder: Formação do patronato político brasileiro*. 2d ed. rev. São Paulo: Editora Globo/Editora da Universidade de São Paulo, 1975.

Faria, Alberto de. *Mauá: Irenêu Evangelista de Souza, Barão e Visconde de Mauá, 1813–1889*. 2d ed. Rio de Janeiro: Biblioteca Pedogogica Brasileira, 1933.

Fausto, Boris. *Trabalho urbano e conflito social (1890–1920)*. Rio de Janeiro: DIFEL, 1976.

——. *Crime e cotidiano: A criminalidade em São Paulo (1880–1924)*. São Paulo: Editora Brasiliense, 1984.

——, ed. *História Geral da Civilização Brasileira*. Vol. 3, *O Brasil Republicano: Estrutura de poder e economia (1889–1903)*. São Paulo: DIFEL, 1975.

Feeley, Malcolm, and Deborah Little. "The Vanishing Female: The Decline of Women in the Criminal Process, 1687–1922." *Law and Society Review* 25:4 (1991), 719–58.

Fernandez, Sujatha. "Mambíses, Malandros, y Maleantes: Imaginárias Colectivas de Luchas e Supervivencia en el Rap Cubano e Venezolano." *Revista Iberoamericana* 72:217 (October–December 2006), 973–87.

Figueiredo, Carmem Lúcia Negreiros de. *Lima Barreto e o fim do sonho republicano*. Rio de Janeiro: Tempo Brasileiro, 1995.

Fischer, Brodwyn. "The Poverty of Law: Rio de Janeiro, 1930–1964." Ph.D. diss., Harvard University, 1999.

Foucault, Michel. *Discipline and Punish: the Birth of the Prison*. Translated by Alan Sheridan. 2d ed. New York: Vintage, 1995.

França, R. Limongi. *Enciclopedia Saraiva do Direito*. Rio de Janeiro: Edição Sariava, 1977.

Franco, Maria Sylvia de Carvalho. *Homens livres na ordem escravocrata*. 3d ed. São Paulo: Editora da UNESP, 1997 (1969).

Francois, Marie. "Cloth and Silver: Pawning and Material Life in Mexico City at the Turn of the Nineteenth Century." *The Americas* 60:3 (January 2004), 325–62.

Frank, Stephen P. "Narratives within Numbers: Women, Crime and Judicial Statistics in Imperial Russia, 1834–1913." *Russian Review* 55:4 (October 1996), 541–66.

Freire, Américo. *Uma capital para a república: Poder federal e forças políticas locais no Rio de Janeiro na virada para o século XX*. Rio de Janeiro: Editora Revan, 1998.

Freitas, Marcos Cezar de. *Historiografia brasileira em perspectiva*. São Paulo: Editora Contexto, 1998.

French, William E. *A Peaceful and Working People: Manners, Morals, and Class Formation in Northern Mexico*. Albuquerque: University of New Mexico Press, 1996.

Garland, David. *Punishment and Modern Society: A Study in Social Theory*. Chicago: University of Chicago Press, 1990.

Gaskill, Malcolm. *Crime and Mentalities in Early Modern England*. New York: Cambridge University Press, 2000.

Geertz, Clifford. "Deep Play: Notes on the Balinese Cockfight." *Rethinking Popular Culture: Contemporary Perspectives in Cultural Studies*, Chandra Mukerji and Michael Schudson, eds. 239–77. Berkeley: University of California Press, 1991.

Geertz, Clifford, Hildred Geertz, and Lawrence Rosen. *Meaning and Order in Moroccan Society: Three Essays on Cultural Analysis*. New York: Cambridge University Press, 1979.

Glassman, Jonathon. *Feasts and Riot: Revelry, Rebellion, and Popular Consciousness on the Swahili Coast, 1856–1888*. Portsmouth, N.H.: Heinemann, 1995.

Gomes, Angela de Castro. *A invenção do trabalhismo*. 2d ed. Rio de Janeiro: Relume Dumará, 1994.

——. *Essa gente do Rio: Modernismo e nacionalismo*. Rio de Janeiro: Editora Fundação Getúlio Vargas, 1999.

Gomes, Laura Graziela, Lívia Barbosa, and José Augusto Drummond, eds. *O Brasil não é para principiantes: Carnavais, malandros e heróis, 20 anos depois*. Rio de Janeiro: Editora Fundação Getúlio Vargas, 2000.

González Arce, José Damián. *Apariencia y poder: La legislación suntuaria castellana en los siglos XIII y XV*. Jaén: Universidad de Jaén, 1998.

González Echevarría, Roberto. *Myth and Archive: A Theory of Latin American Narrative*. Durham: Duke University Press, 1998.

Goodrich, Peter. "Signs Taken for Wonders: Community, Identity, and 'A History of Sumptuary Law.'" *Law and Social Inquiry* 23:3 (summer 1998), 707–28.

Gotkowitz, Laura. "Trading Insults: Honor, Violence, and the Gendered Culture of Commerce in Cochabamba, Bolivia, 1870s–1950s." *Hispanic American Historical Review* 83:1 (2003), 83–118.

Goux, Jean-Joseph. *The Coiners of Language*. trans. Jennifer Curtiss Gage. Norman: University of Oklahoma Press, 1994.

Graham, Richard. *Patronage and Politics in Nineteenth-Century Brazil*. Stanford: Stanford University Press, 1990.

Green, James N. *Beyond Carnival: Male Homosexuality in Twentieth-Century Brazil*. Chicago: University of Chicago Press, 1999.

Greenberg, David F., ed. *Crime and Capitalism: Readings in Marxist Criminology*. Philadelphia: Temple University Press, 1993.

Grinberg, Keila. "A Regulamentação das Relações de Trabalho no Código Civil Brasileiro." Paper presented at the XXII International Congress of the Latin American Studies Association, Miami, 2001.

——. *Código Civil e cidadania*. Rio de Janeiro: Jorge Zahar, 2001.

Guelfi, Maria Lúcia Fernandes. *Novíssima: Estética e ideologia na década de vinte*. São Paulo: Universidade de São Paulo Instituto de Estudos Brasileiros, 1987.

Gusfield, Joseph R. "Moral Passage: The Symbolic Process in Public Designations of Deviance." *Social Problems* 15:2 (1968), 175–88.

Gutting, Gary, ed. *The Cambridge Companion to Foucault*. New York: Cambridge University Press, 1994.

Guy, Donna J. "Parents Before the Tribunals: The Legal Construction of Patriarchy in Argentina," in *Hidden Histories of Gender and the State in Latin America*, Elizabeth Dore and Maxine Molyneaux, eds. Durham: Duke University Press, 2000, 172–93.

Hacking, Ian. *The Emergence of Probability: A Philosophical Study of Early Ideas about Probability, Induction, and Statistical Inference*. New York: Cambridge University Press, 1999 (1975).

Hagopian, Frances. *Traditional Politics and Regime Change in Brazil*. New York: Cambridge University Press, 1996.

Hahner, June E. *Poverty and Politics: The Urban Poor in Brazil, 1870–1920*. Albuquerque: University of New Mexico Press, 1986.

Halttunen, Karen. *Confidence Men and Painted Women: A Study of Middle-Class Culture in America, 1830–1870*. New Haven: Yale University Press, 1982.

Hannerz, Ulf. *Exploring the City: Inquiries Toward an Urban Anthropology*. New York: Columbia University Press, 1980.

Hardin, Garrett. "The Tragedy of the Commons." *Science* 162:3859 (1968), 1243–48.

Hardoy, Jorge E. *Urbanization in Latin America: Approaches and Issues*. Garden City: Anchor Press, 1975.

Harvey, David. *Consciousness and the Urban Experience: Studies and Theory of Capitalist Urbanization*. Baltimore: Johns Hopkins University Press, 1985.

——. *The Urbanization of Capital*. Oxford: Basil Blackwell, 1985.

Hay, Peter, Peter Linebaugh, John G. Rule, E. P. Thompson, and Cal Winslow. *Albion's Fatal Tree: Crime and Society in Eighteenth-Century England*. New York: Pantheon Books, 1975.

Henkin, David M. *City Reading: Written Words and Public Spaces in Antebellum New York*. New York: Columbia University Press, 1998.

Herschmann, Micael, and Kátia Lerner. *Lance de sorte: O futebol e o jogo do bicho na Belle Époque carioca*. Rio de Janeiro: Diadorim, 1993.

Heymann, Luciana Quillet. " 'Quem não tem padrinho morre pagão': Fragmentos de um discurso sobre o poder." *Estudos Históricos* 13:24 (1999), 232–349.

Hirschman, Albert O. *The Passions and the Interests: Political Arguments for Capitalism Before Its Triumph*. Princeton: Princeton University Press, 1977.

Hochman, Gilberto. *A era do saneamento: As bases da política de saúde pública no Brasil*. São Paulo: HUSITEC, 1998.

Holloway, Thomas H. *Policing Rio de Janeiro: Repression and Resistance in a 19th-Century City*. Stanford: Stanford University Press, 1993.

Holston, James, "The Misrule of Law: Land and Usurpation in Brazil," *Comparative Studies in Society and History* 33:4 (October 1991), 695–725.

Huggins, Martha Knisely. *From Slavery to Vagrancy in Brazil*. New Brunswick: Rutgers University Press, 1985.

Hughes, H. Stuart. *Consciousness and Society: The Reorientation of European Social Thought, 1890–1930*. Rev. ed. New York: Vintage Books, 1977.

Huizinga, Johan. *Homo Ludens: A Study of the Play Element in Culture*. Boston: Beacon Press, 1950.

Hunt, Alan. *Governance of the Consuming Passions: A History of Sumptuary Law*. New York: St. Martin's Press, 1996.

Hyde, Lewis. *Trickster Makes This World: Mischief, Myth, and Art*. New York: Farrar, Strauss, and Giroux, 1998.

Inellas, Gabriel Cesar Zaccaria de. *Dicionário de expressões criminais e linguagem policial*. São Paulo: Editor Juarez de Oliveira, 2000.

Jelin, Elizabeth. "Ciudadanía, Derechos e Identidad." *Latin American Research Review* 39:1 (2004), 197–201.

Johnson, Lyman L., ed. *The Problem of Order in Changing Societies: Essays on Crime and Policing in Argentina and Uruguay, 1750–1940*. Albuquerque: University of New Mexico Press, 1990.

Jones, David A. *History of Criminology: A Philosophical Perspective*. New York: Greenwood Press, 1986.

Kahn, Paul W. *The Cultural Study of Law: Reconstructing Legal Scholarship*. Chicago: University of Chicago Press, 1999.

Kalmanowiecki, Laura. "Soldados, ou missionarios domésticos: Ideologias e autoconcepções da polícia argentina." *Estudos Históricos* 12:22 (1998/2), 295–324.

Karasch, Mary C. "Slave Life in Rio de Janeiro, 1808–1850." Mimeo, 1972.

——. *Slave Life in Rio de Janeiro, 1808–1850*. Princeton: Princeton University Press, 1986.

Karst, Kenneth L., and Keith S. Rosen. *Law and Development in Latin America: A Case Book*. Berkeley: University of California Press, 1975.

Kavanagh, Thomas M. *Enlightenment and the Shadows of Chance: The Novel and the Culture of Gambling in Eighteenth-Century France*. Baltimore: Johns Hopkins University Press, 1995.

Kessel, Carlos. *O vitrine e o espelho: O Rio de Janeiro de Carlos Sampaio*. Rio de Janeiro: Secretaria das Culturas, Departamento Geral de Documentação e Informação Cultural, Arquivo Geral da Cidade do Rio de Janeiro, 2001.

Lambek, Michael. "The Value of Coins in a Sakalava Polity: Money, Death, and Historicity in Mahajanga, Madagascar." *Comparative Studies in Society and History* 43:4 (October 2001), 735–62.

Lamounier, Bolivar, Francisco C. Weffort, and Maria Victoria Benevides, eds. *Direito, cidadania e participação*. São Paulo: T. A. Queroz, 1981.

Langbein, John. "Albion's Fatal Flaws." *Past and Present* 98 (1980), 29–50.

Lara, Sílvia Hunold, ed. *Ordenações filipinas: Livro V*. São Paulo: Companhia das Letras, 1999.

Lauderdale Graham, Sandra. *House and Street: The Domestic World of Servants and Masters in Nineteenth-Century Rio de Janeiro*. New York: Cambridge University Press, 1988.

——. "Making the Public Private: A Brazilian Perspective." *Journal of Women's History* 15:1 (spring 2003), 28–42.

———. "Writing from the Margins: Brazilian Slaves and Written Culture." *Comparative Studies in Society and History* 49:3 (July 2007), 611–36.

Leal, Victor Nunes. *Coronelismo: The Municipality and Representative Government in Brazil.* Translated by June Henfry. New York: Cambridge University Press, 1977 (1949).

Lears, T. Jackson. "Playing with Money." *Wilson Quarterly* (August 1995), 7–41.

Lesser, Jeffrey. *Negotiating National Identity: Immigrants, Minorities, and the Struggle for Ethnic Identity in Brazil.* Durham: Duke University Press, 1999.

Levine, Lawrence. *Black Culture and Black Consciousness: Afro-American Folk Thought from Slavery to Freedom.* New York: Oxford Press, 1977.

———. *The Unpredictable Past: Explorations in American Cultural History.* New York: Oxford University Press, 1993.

Levy, Jonathan Ira. "Contemplating Delivery: Futures Trading and the Problem of Commodity Exchange in the United States, 1875–1905." *American Historical Review* 111:2 (April 2006), 307–35.

Levy, Maria Bárbara. *História da bolsa de valores do Rio de Janeiro.* Rio de Janeiro: IBMEC, 1977.

Lichtenstein, Alex. " 'That disposition to theft, with which they have been branded': Moral Economy, Slave Management, and the Law." *Journal of Social History* 21:3 (spring 1988), 414–35.

Lima, Evelyn Furquim Werneck. "Arquitetura do espetáculo: teatros e cinemas na formação do espaço público da Praças Tiradentes e Cinelândia, Rio de Janeiro, 1813–1950." Ph.D. diss., Universidade Federal do Rio de Janeiro, 1999.

Lima, Roberto Kant de. "Legal Theory and Judicial Practice: Paradoxes of Police Work in Rio de Janeiro City (Brazil)." Ph.D. diss., Harvard University, 1986.

Linhares, Maria Yedda, et al., eds. *História geral do Brasil.* 6th ed. rev. Rio de Janeiro: Editora Campus, 1990.

Lobo, Eulália Maria Laymeyer. *História do Rio de Janeiro: Do capital comercial ao capital industrial e financeiro.* Rio de Janeiro: IBMEC, 1978.

Lobo, Eulália, Lia A. Carvalho, and Myrian Stanley. *Questão habitacional e o movimento operário.* Rio de Janeiro: Editora UFRJ, 1989.

Lopes, Antonio Herculano, ed. *Entre Europa e África: A invenção do carioca.* Rio de Janeiro: Edições Casa de Rui Barbosa, 2000.

Lopes, Nei. *O negro no Rio de Janeiro e sua tradição: partido-alto, calango, chula e outras cantorias.* Rio de Janeiro: Pallas, 1992.

Lopes, Rodrigo, *A economia informal no Rio de Janeiro: Problema ou solução?* Rio de Janeiro: Mauad, 1996.

Lopez-Rey, Manuel. "Gambling in the Latin American Countries." *Annals of the American Academy of Political and Social Science* 269 (May 1950), 134–43.

Low, Setha. *On the Plaza: The Politics of Public Space and Culture.* Austin: University of Texas Press, 2000.

Low, Setha, and Neil Smith. *The Politics of Public Space.* New York: Routledge, 2006.

Lucas, Taís Campelo. "Cinearte: o cinema brasileira em revista, 1926–1942." M.A. thesis, Universidade Federal Fluminense, 2005.

Ludmer, Josefina. *The Corpus Delicti: A Manual of Argentine Fictions*. Translated by Glen S. Close. Pittsburgh: University of Pittsburgh Press, 2004.

Lustosa, Isabel. *As Trapaças da sorte: Pequeno relato das circunstâncias que resultaram na prisão do prefeito Pedro Ernesto, à luz das experiências de Maquiavel e de Toqueville*. Rio de Janeiro: Fundação Casa de Rui Barbosa, 1994.

Macry, Paolo. *Giocare la vita: Storia del lotto a Napoli tra Sette e Ottocento*. Rome: Donzelli Editore, 1997.

Magalhães, Felipe Santos. "Ganhou leva . . . Do vale o impresso ao vale o escrito: Uma história social do jogo do bicho no Rio de Janeiro (1890–1960)." Ph.D. diss., Universidade Federal do Rio de Janeiro, 2005.

Magalhães Tavares de Oliveira, Maria Paula, Dartiu Xavier da Silveira, and Maria Teresa Araujo Silva. "Pathological Gambling and Its Consequences for Public Health." *Revista de Saude Pública* 42:3 (June 2008), 1–7.

Maggie, Yvonne. *Medo do feitiço: Relações entre magia e poder no Brasil*. Rio de Janeiro: Arquivo Nacional, 1992.

Maram, Sheldon L. "Labor and the Left in Brazil, 1890–1921: A Movement Aborted." *Hispanic American Historical Review* 57:2 (May 1977), 254–72.

——. "Urban Labor and Social Change in the 1920s." *Luso-Brazilian Review* 16:2 (winter 1979), 215–23.

Marchant, Anyda. *Viscount Mauá and the Empire of Brazil: A Biography of Irineu Evangenista de Sousa (1813–1889)*. Berkeley: University of California Press, 1965.

Martinho, Lenira Menezes, and Riva Gorenstein. *Negociantes e caixeiros na sociedade da indepêndencia*. Rio de Janeiro: Biblioteca Carioca, 1992.

Martins, William de Souza Nunes. "Paschoal Segreto: 'Ministro das Diversões' do Rio de Janeiro: A trajetória de vida de um italiano que se tornou empresário dos divertimentos na capital federal—1886–1920." MS, Rio de Janeiro, 2001.

Mastrofski, Stephen D. "Community Policing as Reform: A Cautionary Tale." *Community Policing: Rhetoric or Reality?* ed. Jack R. Greene and Stephen D. Mastrofski, New York: Praeger, 1988, 47–72.

Mattos, Marcelo Badaró. "Vadios, jogadores, mendigos e bêbados na cidade do Rio de Janeiro do início do século." M.A. thesis, 1991.

Mattoso, Kátia. *To Be a Slave in Brazil*. Translated by Arthur Goldhammer. New Brunswick: Rutgers University Press, 1986.

Meade, Teresa A. *"Civilizing" Rio: Reform and Resistance in a Brazilian City, 1889–1930*. University Park: Pennsylvania State University Press, 1997.

Medeiros, Ethel Bauzer. *O Lazer no Planejamento Urbano*. Rio de Janeiro: Fundação Getúlio Vargas, 1975.

Meira, Selena de Mattos. "O papel da imprensa no jogo do bicho (1890–1920)." *Discursos Sediciosos: Crime, Direito, e Sociedade* 2:3 (1997), 205–12.

Mello, Marcelo Pereira de. "A história social dos jogos de azar no Rio de Janeiro, 1808–1946." M.A. thesis, Instituto Universitário de Pesquisas do Rio de Janeiro, 1989.

Mencarelli, Fernando Antonio. *Cena aberta: A absovição de um bilontra e o teatro de revista de Arthur Azevedo*. Campinas, Brazil: UNICAMP, 1999.

Merry, Sally Engle. "Legal Pluralism." *Law and Society Review* 22:5 (1988), 869–96.

Merryman, John Henry. *The Civil Law Tradition: An Introduction to the Legal Systems of Western Europe and Latin America.* 2d ed. Stanford: Stanford University Press, 1985 (1969).

Ministério da Educação e Cultura, Instituto Superior de Estudos Brasileiros. *Introdução aos problemas do Brasil.* Rio de Janeiro, 1956.

Moreira, Sílvia. *São Paulo na Primeira República.* São Paulo: Editora Brasiliense, 1988.

Morgan, Zachary Ross. "Legacy of the Lash: Blacks and Corporal Punishment in the Brazilian Navy, 1860–1910." Ph.D. diss., Brown University, 2001.

Morse, Richard M., and Jorge E. Hardoy, eds. *Rethinking the Latin American City.* Washington: Woodrow Wilson Center Press, 1988.

Moura, Roberto. *Tia Ciata e a Pequena África no Rio de Janeiro.* 2d ed. rev. Rio de Janeiro: Biblioteca Carioca, 1995.

Museu Histórico Nacional. *O Outro lado da moeda: Livro do seminário internacional.* Rio de Janeiro: Museu Histórico Nacional, 2002.

Nachman, Robert G. "Positivism, Modernization, and the Middle Class in Brazil." *Hispanic American Historical Review* 57:1 (February 1977), 1–23.

Nasaw, David. *Going Out: The Rise and Fall of Public Amusements.* New York: Basic Books, 1993.

Naufel, José. *Novo Dicionário Jurídico Brasileiro.* Vol. 2. Rio de Janeiro: COM-EXP, nd, 110.

Neder, Gizele, Nancy Naro, and José Luiz Werneck da Silva. *A polícia na Côrte e no Distrito Federal, 181–1930.* Rio de Janeiro: Pontifícia Universidade Católica do Rio de Janeiro, 1981.

Needell, Jeffrey. *A Tropical Belle Epoque.* New York: Cambridge University Press, 1985.

——. "The 'Revolta contra Vacina' of 1904: The Revolt against 'Modernization' in 'Belle-Epoque' Rio de Janeiro." *Hispanic American Historical Review* 67:2 (May 1987), 233–69.

Negro, Antonio Luigi. "Paternalismo, populismo e história social." *Cadernos Arquivo Edgard Leuenroth* 20/21 (2004), 9–37.

Nesvig, Martin. "The Lure of the Perverse: Moral Negotiation of Pederasty in Porfirian Mexico." *Mexican Studies/Estudios Mexicanos* 16:1 (winter 2000), 1–37.

Neuhaus, Paulo. *História monetária do Brasil, 1900–45.* Rio de Janeiro: IBMEC, 1975.

O'Brien, Jay, and William Roseberry, eds. *Golden Ages, Dark Ages: Imaging the Past in Anthropology and History.* Berkeley: University of California Press, 1991.

O'Malley, Michael. "Response to Nell Irvin Painter." *American Historical Review* 99:2 (April 1994), 405–8.

——. "Specie and Species: Race and the Money Question in Nineteenth-Century America." *American Historical Review* 99:2 (April 1994), 369–95.

Overmyer-Velázquez, Mark. *Visions of the Emerald City: Modernity, Tradition, and the Formation of Porfirian Oaxaca, Mexico.* Durham: Duke University Press, 2006.

Painter, Nell Irvin. "Thinking About the Languages of Money and Race: A Response to Michael O'Malley, 'Specie and Species.' " *American Historical Review* 99:2 (April 1994), 396–403.

Palmié, Stephan. *Wizards and Scientists: Explorations in Afro-Cuban Modernity and Tradition*. Durham: Duke University Press, 2002.

Parker, David S. "Law, Honor and Impunity in Spanish America: The Debate over Dueling, 1870–1920." *Law and History Review* 19:2 (summer 2001), 331–41.

Peard, Julyan. *Race, Place, and Medicine: The Idea of the Tropics in Nineteenth-Century Brazilian Medicine*. Durham: Duke University Press, 1999.

Pechman, Robert Moses. *Cidades estreitamente vigiadas: O detetive e o urbanista*. Rio de Janeiro: Casa da Palavra, 2002.

Peiss, Kathy. *Cheap Amusements: Working Women and Leisure in Turn-of-the-Century New York*. Philadelphia: Temple University Press, 1986.

Peixoto, Antonio Carlos, et al., eds. *O liberalismo no Brasil imperial: Origens, conceitos e prática*. Rio de Janeiro: Revan, UERJ, 2001.

Pencak, William, Matthew Dennis, and Simon P. Newman, eds. *Riot and Revelry in Early America*. University Park: Pennsylvania State University Press, 2002.

Pereira, Anthony W. *Policial (In)justice: Authoritarianism and the Rule of Law in Brazil, Chile, and Argentina*. Pittsburgh: University of Pittsburgh Press, 2005.

Perlman, Janice E. *Myth of Marginality: Urban Poverty and Politics in Rio de Janeiro*. Berkeley: University of California Press, 1976.

Piccato, Pablo. *City of Suspects: Crime in Mexico City, 1900–1931*. Durham: Duke University Press, 2001.

Pina-Cabral, João de. *Between China and Europe: Person, Culture, and Emotion in Macao*. Oxford: Berg, 2002.

Pitkin, Hanna Fenichel. *Fortune Is a Woman: Gender and Politics in the Thought of Niccolò Machiavelli*. Chicago: University of Chicago Press, 1999.

Poggi, Gianfranco. *Money and the Modern Mind: Georg Simmel's Philosophy of Money*. Berkeley: University of California Press, 1993.

Polayni, Karl. *The Great Transformation: The Political and Economic Origins of Our Time*. Boston: Beacon Press, 2001 [1944].

Portes, Alejandro, Manuel Castells, and Lauren A. Benton. *The Informal Economy: Studies in Advanced and Less Developed Countries*. Baltimore: Johns Hopkins University Press, 1989.

Queiroz, Suely Robles Reis de. *Os radicais da República: Jacobinismo: ideologia e ação, 1893–1897*. São Paulo: Brasiliense, 1986.

Raat, William D. "Leopoldo Zea and Mexican Positivism: A Reappraisal." *Hispanic American Historical Review* 48:1 (February 1968), 1–18.

Rago, Margareth, *Do cabaré ao lar: A utopia da cidade disciplinar, Brasil 1890–1930*. São Paulo: Paz e Terra, 1985.

———. *Os prazeres da noite: Prostituição e códigos da sexualidade feminina em São Paulo (1890–1930)*. São Paulo: Paz e Terra, 1991.

Ramos, Julio. *Divergent Modernities: Culture and Politics in Nineteenth-Century Latin America*. Translated by John D. Blanco. Durham: Duke University Press, 2001.

Randall, Andrian, and Andrew Charlesworth, eds. *Moral Economy and Popular Protest: Crowds, Conflict and Authority.* London: Macmillan, 2000.

Rangel, Inácio. *Dualidade básica da economia brasileira.* Rio de Janeiro: Textos Brasileiros de Economia, 1957.

Rebelo, Marques, and Antonio Bulhões. *O Rio de Janeiro da Bota-Abaixo: Fotografias de Augusto Malta.* Rio de Janeiro: Salamandra, 1997.

Reis, João José. *Rebelião escrava no Brasil: A história do levante dos Malês em 1835.* Rev. ed. São Paulo: Companhia das Letras, 2003.

Reith, Gerda. *The Age of Chance: Gambling in Western Culture.* New York: Routledge, 1999.

Ribeiro, Carlos Antonio Costa. *Cor e criminalidade: Estudo e analise da justiça no Rio de Janeiro (1900–1930).* Rio de Janeiro: Editora UFRJ, 1995.

Ribeiro, Renato Janine. *A sociedade contra a social: O alto custo da vida pública no Brasil.* São Paulo: Companhia das Letras, 2000.

Rocha, Oswaldo Porto. *A era das demolições: Cidade do Rio de Janeiro, 1870–1920.* Rio de Janeiro: Biblioteca Carioca, 1995.

Rodrigues, Julia. "The Idea of Responsibility in Argentine Code Law, 1887–1921." MS, 2001.

Roniger, Luis. *Hierarchy and Trust in Modern Mexico and Brazil.* New York: Praeger, 1990.

Rose, R. S. *One of the Forgotten Things: Getúlio Vargas and Brazilian Social Control 1930–1945.* Westport, Conn.: Greenwood Press, 2000.

Rosen, Lawrence. *Bargaining for Reality: The Construction of Social Relations in a Muslim Community.* Chicago: University of Chicago Press, 1984.

Rosenfeld, Anatol. *Negro, macumba, e futbol.* São Paulo: Perspectiva, Editora da Universidade de SP, 1993.

Rosenn, Keith S. "Brazil's Legal Culture: The Jeito Revisited." *Florida International Law Journal* 1:1 (fall 1984), 2–43.

Ruggiero, Kristin. *Modernity in the Flesh: Medicine, Law, and Society in Turn-of-the-Century Argentina.* Stanford: Stanford University Press, 2004.

Salem, Marcos David. *História da polícia no Rio de Janeiro: Uma instituição a serviço das classes dominantes.* Rio de Janeiro: Editora Lumen Juris, 2007.

Salvatore, Ricardo D. "State Legal Order and Subaltern Rights: The Modernization of the Justice System in Argentina (1870–1930)." MS, nd.

———. *Wandering Paysanos: State Order and Subaltern Experience in Buenos Aires during the Rosas Era.* Durham: Duke University Press, 2003.

Salvatore, Ricardo D., and Carlos Aguirre, eds. *The Birth of the Penitentiary in Latin America: Essays on Criminology, Prison Reform and Social Control, 1830–1940.* Austin: University of Texas Press, 1996.

Salvatore, Ricardo D., Carlos Aguirre, and Gilbert M. Joseph, eds. *Crime and Punishment in Latin America: Law and Society since Late Colonial Times.* Durham: Duke University Press, 2001.

Sandroni, Carlos. *Feitiço Decente: Transformações do samba no Rio de Janeiro (1917–1933).* Rio de Janeiro: Jorge Zahar, 2001.

Santiago, Silviano. "Worldly Appeal: Local and Global Politics in the Shaping of Modern Brazilian Culture." Paper presented at Yale University Department of Spanish and Portuguese, 1995.

Santos, Boaventura de Sousa. "The Law of the Oppressed: The Construction and Reproduction of Legality in Pasargada." *Law and Society Review* 12:1 (autumn 1977), 5–126.

Santos, Myrian Sepúlveda dos. "A prisão dos ébrios, capoeiras e vagabundos no início da Era Republicana." *Topoi* 5:8 (June 2004), 138–69.

Santos, Noronha. *As freguesias do Rio antigo.* Rio de Janeiro, Edições o Cruzeiro, 1965.

Sarat, Austin. "Legal Effectiveness and Social Studies of Law: On the Unfortunate Persistence of a Research Tradition." *Legal Studies Forum* 9:1 (1985), 23–31.

Schwarcz, Lília Moritz. *O espetáculo das raças: Cientistas, instituições e questão racial no Brasil, 1870–1930.* São Paulo: Companhia das Letras, 1993.

Scott, James C. *Seeing Like a State: How Certain Schemes to Improve the Human Condition Have Failed.* New Haven: Yale University Press, 1998.

Secretaria de Estado de Justiça. DOPS: *A lógica da desconfiança.* 2d ed. Rio de Janeiro: Arquivo Público do Estado, 1996.

Sevcenko, Nicolau. *Literatura como missão: Tensões sociais e criação cultural no Primeira República.* São Paulo: Editora Brasiliense, 1983.

——. *Orfeu extático na metrópole: São Paulo soceidade e cultura nos frementes anos 20.* São Paulo: Companhia das Letras, 1992.

——, ed. *História da vida privada no Brasil: República: da Belle Époque à Era do Rádio.* Vol. 3. São Paulo: Compania das Letras, 1998.

Shell, Marc. *Money, Language, and Thought: Literary and Philosophic Economies from the Medieval to the Modern Era.* Baltimore: Johns Hopkins University Press, 1993.

Sherman, Rachel. *Class Acts: Service and Inequality in Luxury Hotels.* Berkeley: University of California Press, 2007.

Silva, Eduardo. *Prince of the People: The Life and Times of a Brazilian Free Man of Color.* Translated by Moyra Ashford. New York: Verso, 1993.

——. *As queixas do povo.* Rio de Janeiro: Paz e Terra, 1988.

Silva, Fernando Teixeira da. *Operários sem patrões: Os trabalhadores da cidade de Santos no entreguerras.* Campinas, S.P.: Editora Unicamp, 2003.

Silva, Iara Ilgenfritz da. *Direito ou Punição? Representação da Sexualidade Feminina no Direito Penal.* Porto Alegre: Editora Movimento, 1985.

Silva, Marilene Rosa Nogueira da. *Negro na Rua: A nova face da escravidão.* São Paulo: Editora HUCITEC, 1988.

Skidmore, Thomas E. *Black into White: Race and Nationality in Brazilian Thought.* Durham: Duke University Press, 1993.

Slater, Candace. *Stories on a String: The Brazilian Literatura de Cordel.* Berkeley: University of California Press, 1983.

Smith, Gavin. "Towards an Ethnography of Idiosyncratic Forms of Livelihood." *International Journal of Urban and Regional Research* 18:1 (1994), 71–87.

Smith, M. Estellie, ed. *Perspectives on the Informal Economy: Monographs in Economic Anthropology,* No. 8. Lanham, Md.: University Press of America, 1990.

Spivak, Gayatri Chakravorty. "Scattered Speculations on the Question of Value."
   Diacritics 15:4 (winter 1985), 73–93.
Soares, Carlos Eugênio Líbano. *A negrada instuição: Os capoeiras na Corte Imperial,*
   1850–1890. Rio de Janeiro: Editora Acces, 1999.
———. *A capoeira escrava e outras tradições rebeldes no Rio de Janeiro (1808–1850).*
   Campinas, S.P.: Editora UNICAMP, 2001.
Soares, Luiz Carlos. *Rameiras, Ilhoas, Polacas: A prostuição no Rio de Janeiro no século*
   XIX. São Paulo: Editora Ática, 1992.
Soares, Mariza de Carvalho. *Devotos da cor: Identidade étnica, relisiosidade, e*
   escravidão no Rio de Janeiro, século XVIII. Rio de Janeiro: Civilização Brasileira,
   2000.
Soares, Simone Simões Ferreira. *O Jogo do Bicho: A Saga de um Fato Social Brasileiro.*
   Rio de Janeiro: Bertrand Brasil, 1993.
Socolow, Susan. "Women and Crime: Buenos Aires, 1757–97." *Journal of Latin*
   American Studies 12:1 (May 1980), 39–54.
Soihet, Rachel. *Condição feminina e formas de violência: Mulhers pobres e ordem*
   urbana, 1890–1920. Rio de Janeiro: Forense Universitaria, 1989.
Sommer, Doris, ed. *Places of History: Regionalism Revisited in Latin America.* Durham:
   Duke University Press, 1999.
Souza, Mériti de. *A experiência da lei e a lei da experiência: ensaios sobre práticas sociais*
   e subjetividades no Brasil. São Paulo: FAPESP, 1999.
Stallybrass, Peter, and Allon White. *The Politics and Poetics of Transgression.* Ithaca:
   Cornell University Press, 1986.
Stein, Stanley J. *Vassouras: A Brazilian Coffee County, 1850–1890.* New York:
   Atheneum, 1976.
Stepan, Nancy Leys. *"The Hour of Eugenics": Race, Gender, and Nation in Latin*
   America. Ithaca: Cornell University Press, 1991.
Straccia, Carlos, Cláudia Fatigatti, Luiz Antonio Ferreira, Márcia Lígia Guidin, and
   Oscar D'Ambrosio. *O espetáculo das massas na literatura brasileira: edição*
   comentada do romance O cortiço, de Aluísio Azevedo. São Paulo: Selinunte, 1992.
Susman, Warren. *Culture as History.* New York: Pantheon, 1985.
Süssekind, Flora. *As Revistas do Ano e a Invenção do Rio de Janeiro.* Rio de Janeiro:
   Nova Fronteira, 1986.
———. *Cinematógrafo de Letras: Literatura, técnica e modernização no Brasil.* São Paulo:
   Companhia das Letras, 1987.
Tannuri, Luiz Antônio. *O Encilhamento.* São Paulo: HUCITEC-FUNCAMP, 1981.
Thompson, E. P. *Whigs and Hunters: The Origin of the Black Act.* New York:
   Pantheon, 1975.
———. "Folklore, Anthopology, and Social History." *Indian Historical Review* 3 (1977),
   247–66.
———. *Customs in Common: Studies in Traditional Popular Culture.* New York: New
   Press, 1993.
Topik, Steven. "The Evolution of the Economic Role of the Brazilian State, 1889–
   1930." *Journal of Latin American Studies* 11:2 (1979), 325–42.

———. *The Political Economy of the Brazilian State, 1889–1930.* Austin: University of Texas Press, 1987.

Tórtima, Pedro. "Polícia e Justiça de Mãos Dadas: A Conferência Judiciária Policial de 1917 (Uma contribuição aos estudos sobre o enfrentamento da 'Questão Operária' pelas classes dominantes e pelo Estado—Rio de Janeiro—1900–1925)." M.A. thesis, Universidade Federal Fluminense, 1989.

———. *Crime e castigo para além do equador.* Belo Horizonte: Inédita, 2002.

Urrutia, Mayra Rosario, " 'La tentación de la suerte': Criminalización y castigo por el juego de la bolita, 1948–1958." Paper presented at the Latin American Studies Association International Congress, September 2001.

Velloso, Mônica Pimenta. "As tias baianas tomam conta do pedaço: Espaço e identidade cultural no Rio de Janeiro." *Estudos Históricos* 3:6 (1990), 207–28.

———. *Modernismo no Rio de Janeiro.* Rio de Janeiro: Fundação Getúlio Vargas, 1996.

Vianna, Humberto. *The Mystery of Samba: Popular Music and National Identity in Brazil.* Translated by John Charles Chasteen. Chapel Hill: University of North Carolina Press, 1999.

Vieira, Dorival Teixeira. *Evolução do sistema monetário brasileiro.* São Paulo: Instituto de Pesquisas Econômicas, 1981.

Villela, André. "The Quest for Gold: Monetary Debates in Nineteenth-Century Brazil." *Brazilian Journal of Political Economy* 21:4 (84) (2001), 79–92.

Viotti da Costa, Emilia. *The Brazilian Empire: Myths and Histories.* Rev. ed. Chapel Hill: University of North Carolina Press, 2000.

Viqueira Albán, Juan Pedro. *Propriety and Permissiveness in Bourbon Mexico.* Translated by Sonya Lipsett-Rivera and Sergio Rivera Ayala. New York: SR Books, 1999.

Ward, Peter M. "Introduction and Overview: Marginality Then and Now." *Latin American Research Review* 39:1 (2004), 183–87.

Warner, Michael. "Publics and Counterpublics." *Public Culture* 14:1 (2002), 49–90.

Weber, Max. *Economy and Society: An Outline of Intepretive Sociology.* New York: Bedminster Press, 1968.

Weinstein, Barbara. *For Social Peace in Brazil: Industrialists and the Remaking of the Working Class in São Paulo, 1920–1964.* Durham: Duke University Press, 1996.

White, Luise. "Telling More: Lies, Secrets, and History." *History and Theory* 39 (2000), 11–22.

Williams, Daryle. *Culture Wars in Brazil: The First Vargas Regime, 1930–1945.* Durham: Duke University Press, 2001.

Williams, Raymond. *What I Came to Say.* London: Hutchinson Radius, 1989.

———. *Resources of Hope.* London: Verso, 1989.

Wilson, H. T. "Rationality and Capitalism in Max Weber's Analysis of Western Modernity." *Journal of Classical Sociology* 2:1 (2002), 93–106.

Wilson, Tamar Diana, ed. "The Urban Informal Sector." Special issue of *Latin American Perspectives* 25:2 (March 1998).

Wolcott, Victoria W. "The Culture of the Informal Economy: Numbers Runners in Inter-War Black Detroit." *Radical History Review* 69:1 (fall 1997), 46–75.

Woodard, James P. "Coronelismo in Theory and Practice: Evidence, Analysis, and Argument from São Paulo." *Luso-Brazilian Review* 42:1 (2005), 99–117.

Zaluar, Alba. *A máquina e a revolta: as organizações populares e o significado da pobreza.* São Paulo: Brasiliense, 1985.

Zea, Leopoldo. *Positivism in Mexico.* Translated by Josephine H. Schulte. Austin: University of Texas, 1974.

Zelizer, Viviana A. *The Social Meaning of Money.* New York: Basic Books, 1994.

INDEX

dictatorship, 254, 256, 261

disease and public health, 20, 21, 76–77

divorce, 73

Dois Rios Correctional Colony. *See* penal colonies

domestic sphere, 167, 195. *See also* private domain

Dom Pedro II (Emperor), 52, 270 n. 22

dreams, 41, 163, 188; dream books and, 189; jogo do bicho and interpretation of, 43, 190, 193

drug traffic, 243, 261–62

Drummond, Baron João Batista Vianna, 27, 29–39, 47, 50–52, 63, 65–66, 200, 227, 253, 274 n. 22

drunkenness, 86, 122, 226

Dutra, Eurico Gaspar, 258

ecclesiastical law, 83

economic conditions (Brazil), 52, 144–45, 149–53. *See also* money; speculation

Edwiges, Manoel, 231–32

Ellison, Ralph, 300 n. 73

emancipation. *See* slavery in Brazil

Empire (Brazil), 7, 52, 77, 83–85, 105–6, 110, 121, 149–51, 159, 208; fall of, 18, 31, 58, 84, 178

Encilhamento, 142–47, 163

Encilhamento, O (Taunay), 143

enclosure of commons, 8–11; as urban phenomenon, 28, 50, 121, 166–67, 194, 221, 256, 262–63, 268

England, 9, 10, 70, 265–66

Enlightenment, 84

entertainment: commercialization of, 10, 33–34, 51–53, 59–60, 77, 126, 167–68, 193–202, 221; in Europe, 38; popular urban, 34, 38, 40, 154, 165, 168, 194–201, 203, 306 n. 67; of urban elite, 51–52, 165, 194–95, 197. *See also* cinema; theater

Ernesto, Pedro, 225, 250, 256

Escola da Polícia do Rio de Janeiro, 91

escravos de ganho. See negros de ganho

estado de sítio. See state of emergency

Estado Novo, 208, 256

eugenics, 225

Europe, 6–7, 72, 76, 79–80, 99, 122, 145, 217–19, 249

Evaristo de Morais, Antonio, 98, 143

evidence, rules of. *See* criminal procedure

factories, 30, 41, 97, 110, 118, 138, 169, 198, 257, 292–93 n. 18, 293 n. 21, 294 n. 50

family, 184–85, 187, 196

favelas, 13, 220, 235, 249

fear of popular classes, 17, 19, 28, 45, 55–56, 65, 74, 81, 106–7, 124, 182, 185. *See also* repression; social control

Federal District. *See* Brasília; Rio de Janeiro

feiras livres (public markets), 109–10, 112, 117

Ferri, Enrico, 79

festa junina. See June festivals

First Republic (Brazil), 18–20, 31, 56, 58, 83–84, 107, 121, 145, 150–54, 159, 178, 184–85, 219–20; urbanism in 21–23

folhetins (pamphlets), 2, 178–79, 189

folklore, 170–72, 174–77, 181–83, 202–3, 249–50. *See also* jogo do bicho: in literature

Fonseca, General Deodora da, 151

fortaleza, 259–60

Freud, Sigmund, 300 n. 73

Freyre, Gilberto, 4, 173–74, 303 n. 14

Frontin, Paulo de, 51

frontões, 34, 40, 278 n. 103

Frossard, Denise, 262

Galvez, Luiz, 35

gambling, 54, 77, 221, 255–57; houses of, 46, 96–97; modernity and, 3–4, 49, 195–96; moralism and, 172–74, 178–81, 185, 195; prohibitions of, 39–40, 54, 56–65, 76, 86–88, 94, 106, 153–54, 212,

Labanca, Guiseppe, 199, 260

Lacerda, Maurício de, 304–5 n. 38

Latin America, 74, 241; criminology in, 225; legal history of, 75, 79; post-colonial liberalism in, 16, 73, 184; social protest in, 219

laudo de exame, 237–38

law, 70–78; Ibero-American legal culture and, 245; inequality and, 16, 166; juris-prudence and, 83, 98–99; jurisdic-tional issues and, 61, 241; legal plural-ism and, 13; popular understandings of, 168, 206, 208, 242–48, 250–51, 265–66; schools of, 79, 225; social reform and, 81, 249

law and society scholarship, 17, 71–72

Law of the Free Womb (1871), 273 n. 8

lawyers, 52, 85, 229–30, 235, 237, 241, 259

Leal, Aurelino de Araujo, 211, 214–15, 218, 228

legal medicine, 81, 225–26. *See also* criminology

legislature (federal), 64, 84, 87, 215–17, 303 n. 18

legislature (municipal), 58–60, 61, 65, 215–17

Lei Bancária (1888), 151

Lei da Boa Razão, 74

leisure. *See* entertainment

LIESA (Independent League of Samba Schools), 263

Lima Barreto, Alfonso Henriques de, 9, 107–8, 136, 154–56, 178, 266–67

literacy, 45, 92, 115, 245–46; writing and, 206, 244–45

livestock, 8, 104, 154–56

Lombroso, Cesare, 79

lotteries, 24, 37, 40, 45–49, 57, 77–78, 87, 171, 194–95, 204–7, 213, 215–17, 240–41; as means of buying goods, 147, 153–55, 163

luck, 3, 78, 87, 168, 170–72, 182, 187, 191, 193

Machado de Assis, Joaquim Maria, 145–46, 177–78, 193, 205

malandro, 181, 250

marginality, 13, 268

martial law. *See* state of emergency

masculinity, 182–83, 185–87

Mauá, Baron de (Irineu Evangelista de Sousa), 29, 50–52

May Day, 219, 258

media. *See* newspapers

Mello Moraes Filho, Alexandre José, 171

Memórias de um Sargento de Milícias (Almeida), 182–83

merchants, 52–53, 145, 150, 260

Mexican Revolution, 219

Mexico, 18, 79, 92, 120, 219; Porfiriato, 16

middle classes, 79, 125, 147–48, 167–68, 175, 184–85, 194–95

migrants, 78, 117, 156, 189, 195, 219–20, 249, 267, 289 n. 66

military coups and revolts, 19, 20, 63, 152, 219, 261

military rule, 254, 311 n. 18

Minas Gerais, 29, 220

minor (age). *See* children

misdemeanor. See *contravenção*

Modern Art Week, 220

monarchy. *See* Empire (Brazil)

money, 141–43, 147–48, 150–51, 195, 265; counterfeit, 23, 113, 138, 149, 152, 159–63, 246; currency units, xix, 259, 273 n. 12, 286 n. 6; economic conditions in Brazil and, 52, 144–45; monetary pol-icy and, 113; popular cash economy and, 9, 104–5, 265

monopolies, 9, 49–50, 53–55, 68, 111–12, 215

moral economy, 266, 268

morality, 57–58, 77, 120–22, 139, 167, 172–74, 177–80, 185, 195, 203, 215, 221, 241–43, 256

moral passage, 66

"moral sanitation," 155, 221, 231, 256

musical revues, 107, 181, 196, 197

Public Archive of the State of Rio de
Janeiro, 253
public domain, 76–78, 82, 98, 166–67,
185
public finance. *See* taxation
public health, 20, 21, 76–77
public servants. *See* civil servants
public space, 8–11, 28, 111–13, 119–20,
125–26, 166–68, 187–88, 194–96, 207,
253, 259–66, 270 n. 24
public virtue. *See* morality
public works, 47, 53

race, 16, 18, 65, 74, 77, 225, 283 n. 60
raffles. *See* lotteries
Rangel, Ignácio, 12–13
"Raul Capitão," 262
recordkeeping, 127–28, 207, 224–26.
See also jogo do bicho: in historical
record; writing
religious festivals, 41, 107–8, 143, 163,
171–72, 196. *See also* June festivals
repression, 8, 16–18, 25, 28, 210, 212, 214,
218, 226–27, 233, 249, 251, 261, 268; of
popular culture, 17, 45, 167, 174, 194,
202–4, 221, 223, 250, 263, 306 n. 67.
See also social control
resistance, 264–66, 268
Revolution of 1930, 249
Ribeiro, Cândido Barata, 225
Rio de Janeiro, 20–23, 30, 107–12, 115,
121–24, 197, 220, 226–28; during
Empire, 29, 50–53, 78, 110, 117, 154,
196, 286 n. 15; as federal capital, 19,
145–46, 261; historic center of, 125–
26, 155, 165–66, 194; housing for lower
classes in, 78, 196; population of, 19,
220–21, 287 n. 32; public order in, 19,
34, 137, 139, 214, 216–17, 250; rural
zone and hinterland of, 8, 29, 51, 150,
267; South Zone (Zona Sul) of, 258;
suburban zones of, 9, 10, 154, 160;
urbanization of, 8–9, 29, 31, 50, 104
risk. *See* gambling; hedging; speculation

resistance, 70, 72
Rodrigues Alves, Francisco de, 21
Romero, Sylvio, 159
rua do Ouvidor (Rio de Janeiro), 22–23,
35, 114, 119, 125–26, 165, 196–97
rule of law, 20, 73, 75, 95, 207–8, 214, 223,
239, 265
rumors, 95
rural oligarchy, 14, 150, 209, 249, 265
Russian Revolution, 218–19

salaries. *See* wages
Salvador da Bahia, 20, 211
samba, 250, 262–63. *See also* Carnival
Santos, 217–18
São Paulo, 211, 217–20, 249, 261, 305 n. 53
satire. *See* humor
schools, 53
Segreto, Paschoal, 197–200, 260
Semana da Arte Moderna, 220
Service for the Repression of Prohibited
Games, 258
sexuality, 225
shantytowns. See *favelas*
Silva, Luiz Inácio Lula da, 312 n. 25
slavery in Brazil, 7, 13, 18–20, 29, 51, 73,
79, 86, 102–3, 115, 138, 145, 150–51, 156,
245, 273 n. 8
social clubs, 148, 221, 223, 228
social control, 8, 17–18, 21, 80, 92, 208,
226
social darwinism, 22
social question, 16, 210, 249–51
social reform, 81, 210, 249–50
social welfare, 92, 216–17, 249–50, 262–
63
sorcery, 72, 171–72
Spanish America, 73
speculation, 14, 29, 51, 142–46, 152.
See also Encilhamento
staple goods, 54, 104, 109–10
stare decisis, 83
state formation: in Brazil, 208–9; in
Latin America, 74

state of emergency, 20, 217–18, 220
state of siege. *See* state of emergency
Stevenson, Robert Louis, 202
stock market, 29, 143–47, 152
street vendors, 11–12, 53–55, 101–6, 110–
    11, 114–21, 126, 134–37, 209, 227;
    women as, 115, 117–18
strikes, 219. *See also* working-class
    organizing
suffrage, 18, 184
sumptuary law (Europe), 6–7

Taunay, Visconde de (Alfredo D'Escrag-
    nolle Taunay), 143–44
Távora, Belisário, 231
taxation, 5, 21, 25, 31, 59–60, 97, 109, 114,
    178, 214, 215, 256
tenements, 21, 78, 110, 196. *See also*
    Rio de Janeiro: housing for lower
    classes in
tenentista revolts, 220, 226
Termo de Bem Viver, 86
theater, 6, 167, 181, 183, 195, 197–98, 221
Thompson, Edward P., 10, 17, 70, 265
Tia Ciata (Hilária Batista de Almeida),
    289 n. 66
tinterillos, 241
tramway. *See* transportation
transportation: public, in cities, 10, 21,
    29, 34, 50–51, 67, 111, 160–61, 220;
    regional railway system, 23, 50, 160
trickster. *See malandro*
trust, 206–8, 215, 241–48

underground economy. *See* informal
    economy
urban modernization, 16, 29, 49, 50, 53,
    104, 107–8, 111, 220, 267. *See also* Rio
    de Janeiro: urbanization of
urban planning, 29, 224

urban poverty, 13, 50, 58, 78, 147, 152, 154,
    165–66, 201, 216, 249, 267–68. See also
    favelas
usury, 120
utilities. *See* urban modernization

vagrancy, 16–17, 82, 86, 88–90, 98–99,
    105, 127, 130, 132–33, 211, 222, 226, 258
vales. See coupons
Vargas, Getúlio, 208, 220, 224, 245, 247,
    249–50, 256–57
vice. See *contravenção*
vida pregressa, 311 n. 10
Vidal, Armando (Leite Ribeiro), 25, 155,
    211–14, 221, 229, 240
Vila Isabel (Rio de Janeiro), 23, 29, 31–
    34, 47, 50–51, 65, 129
violence, 260–62; use of, by police, 207,
    231–33, 242
Viveiros de Castro, Francisco José, 75–
    76, 81

wages, 14–15, 34, 43, 118, 149, 151, 153, 167,
    195, 202, 219, 226
Warwick School. *See* Thompson,
    Edward P.
Washington Luis (Pereira de Sousa),
    248–49
Weber, Max, 270 n. 29, 280 n. 20
wheel, in games of chance, 47–48, 136,
    154, 188, 191
women, 115, 117–18
working-class organizing, 24, 185, 196,
    205, 210, 212, 217–20, 222, 226, 231, 249
writing, 206, 244–45. *See also* literacy

Zevada, Manoel Ismael, 35, 125
zoo (Rio de Janeiro), 1, 31–39, 47–50,
    58–62, 65–66, 196, 254

Amy Chazkel is an associate professor in the Department of
History at Queens College, City University of New York.

Library of Congress Cataloging-in-Publication Data
Chazkel, Amy.
Laws of chance : Brazil's clandestine lottery and the making of
urban public life / Amy Chazkel.
p. cm. — (Radical perspectives)
Includes bibliographical references and index.
ISBN 978-0-8223-4973-0 (cloth : alk. paper)
ISBN 978-0-8223-4988-4 (pbk. : alk. paper)
1. Gambling—Brazil—Rio de Janeiro—History—20th
century. 2. Gambling and crime—Brazil—Rio de Janeiro—
History—20th century. 3. Gambling—Law and legislation—
Brazil—Rio de Janeiro—History—20th century. 4. Rio de
Janeiro (Brazil)—Social life and customs—20th century.
I. Title. II. Series: Radical perspectives.
HV6722.B82C439 2011
795.3′80981—dc22   2010049646